This book ma~ ~ ~ ~~t

MAGAZINES

UNIVERSITY OF ILLINOIS PRESS, URBANA, 1964

MAGAZINES IN THE TWENTIETH CENTURY

in the Twentieth Century

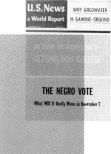

by Theodore Peterson

Second Edition, Second Printing

© 1964 by the Board of Trustees of the University of Illinois. Manufactured in the United States of America. Library of Congress Catalog Card No. 64-18668.

10-29-66 Baker & Taylor $7.50.

To Helen

Preface

Almost as soon as the first edition of this book appeared in December, 1956, magazine publishers inconsiderately set about making it out of date. Indeed, changes probably came more rapidly in the half-dozen or so years after 1956 than in any similar span since the modern magazine was born in the late nineteenth century. The end of the Crowell-Collier magazines, the troubles of Curtis and the company's struggles to solve them, the race for multimillion circulations at any cost, the spread of regional editions, the virtual disappearance of the digest magazines (except for that prosperous grandfather, *Reader's Digest*), the boom among special interest magazines, the dwindling profits and diversification, the swift climb of *Playboy* to affluence and a circulation of a million, the rise and decline of *Confidential*, the birth of *Together* and the death of *Coronet*—those and other things all have happened since 1956. Even the emergence of television as an almost universal medium and a prime competitor of magazines had not been completed by the mid-fifties.

In this second edition, I have tried to cover such developments to bring the story of the modern magazine down to 1964. Curiously, there has been no single volume that has traced the history of the American magazine after 1900, the period of its greatest development and greatest importance.

Histories of the magazine do exist, of course. Frank Luther Mott has written an excellent four-volume account of the American magazine from 1741 through 1905. Other scholars have carefully hoed this same earlier ground, but apart from Mott's books, which carry the stories of some individual publications down to the present, their works do not greatly enlighten the person curious about the contemporary magazine. James Playsted Wood has written a one-volume history of the magazine from 1741 onward. In both his original edition and his 1956 revision, however, Wood devotes roughly half of his space to the period before 1900 and hence is silent about many of the developments in the industry since the turn of the century.

This book, which grew out of a doctoral dissertation at the University of Illinois, is an attempt to remedy the deficiency. My aim has been to tell the story of the popular magazine since its origins in the late nineteenth century. I have tried to explore the major tendencies in the magazine industry and the social and economic forces that helped to shape them. For this edition, I have added accounts of some publications that seemed slighted in the first edition or that did not exist when it came out; in addition, I have rather extensively reworked some of the original material.

However, I have found no reason to change my major theme, which if anything seems substantiated by recent developments in the industry. Although I have not used a strictly chronological approach, this book does have a narrative, and the reader can best follow it if he reads it in summary before he approaches the documentary detail.

The low-priced popular magazine of national circulation was born in the late nineteenth century as America made the transition from an agrarian to an industrial economy. It emerged as changes in the distribution of consumer goods brought about a growing volume of advertising. By joining the magazine with the system of marketing, national advertising affected many aspects of the magazine industry. As the volume of advertising increased, magazines grew in numbers and in circulation.

Also important to the development of the magazine was an expanding market both for magazines and for the goods advertised in their pages. The magazine audience was widened by a rise in population and by such fruits of democracy and industrialization as an increase in leisure time, an increase in the general level of education, and a redistribution of income. Magazines of mammoth circulation became commonplace after World War I as a result of the expanding market, technological advances, and improvements in the logistics of magazine publishing.

Although a few magazines of large circulation carried the bulk of advertising, they were by no means invulnerable to competition. The magazine industry was relatively hospitable to those with talent and fresh ideas, and the new publisher often could experiment with less financial risk than the publisher of an established magazine. As new publishers introduced new magazines reflecting the changes in American life, many of the magazines which had once led in circulation and prestige were driven out of business. They were replaced by new leaders which achieved huge circulations in fairly short periods, especially after World War I. Since some of these new leaders were based on original approaches to publishing, and since other publishers imitated the successful innovations, whole new classes of magazines emerged. Those are some of the points which the book will try to document.

In general, I have limited my scope to commercial magazines edited for the lay public. Therefore, this book does not cover several categories of magazines. It does not cover trade, technical, scientific, and professional journals. Nor does it treat in any detail the farm magazines, which have been essentially trade journals for the farmer. Those important types of magazines demand full-length studies of their own to do them justice. Also excluded are house organs, which are supported by big and little businesses to tell their stories to employees or to the public at large, and fraternal and organizational magazines, which draw all or part of their support from the organizations publishing them.

In the first edition, I allowed myself the luxury of inconsistency by giving attention to the journals of opinion, which have been spectacularly unsuccessful as commercial ventures but which have been too important a part of the American cultural scene to be ignored. This edition compounds the inconsistency by giving somewhat greater attention than the first edition did to religious magazines and to the so-called little magazines of literature and criticism. My treatment of those last two types is still perfunctory, however, since many religious magazines have church affiliations and since most of the little magazines have not been published with commercial intent.

Missing from this edition is a rather extensive bibliography that appeared in the first edition. For a number of reasons, I concluded that it was of limited value; certainly for the great majority of readers it represented excess baggage for which they should not have to pay extra fare. I have drawn on a variety of sources—on the magazines themselves; on annual reports of publishing companies and the statements that have appeared in Standard and Poor; on industry reports; on reminiscences and observations of publishers, editors, writers, and others; on the advertising trade press. Throughout the forties, *Tide* was a good chronicler of developments in magazine publishing. Especially from the early fifties onward, *Advertising Age* has given better coverage to the magazine field than perhaps any other one publication. Throughout the text, I have tried to leave a trail of sources in footnotes.

Probably every author of a book such as this has wondered how free he should be with footnotes. I have tried to hold them to a minimum. I have used them to indicate sources of direct quotations, sources which some readers may wish to consult for additional information, and sources which might carry some bias. Since none of the footnotes amplifies textual matter, the reader not interested in sources can skip them all without loss.

A few words of explanation are necessary for an understanding of some of the revenue data. Most of the figures for gross advertising revenue were compiled by the Publishers Information Bureau and released by the Magazine Advertising Bureau, the clearinghouse for such information. Such figures are calculations which do not take into account advertising agency discounts and cash discounts; moreover, they are based on rates for single insertions. Consequently, the gross actually received by the magazine in each instance was slightly more than 80 per cent of the figure given.

Scores of persons in the magazine industry have left me in their debt by supplying me with raw material and answering my questions, sometimes as impertinent as pertinent. To name them all would be impractical. Some, however, do deserve special mention. John Herbert and Robert E. Kenyon, Jr., of the Magazine Publishers Association were always prompt and patient in answering my questions about the industry as a whole. W. H. Mullen, when he was associated with the Magazine Advertising Bureau, generously supplied me with much material that was not readily available elsewhere. Time Inc. allowed me to spend a month studying its operations and freely interviewing some seventy of its personnel, who gave me insights into publishing that extended far beyond the company's own magazines. Several publishing companies supplied the photographs from which the illustrations in this book were selected.

I also wish to record my debt to several others who helped to steer the manuscript toward the press. Fred Siebert, now dean of the College of Communications Arts at Michigan State University, gave me encouragement and sound advice when I was writing the manuscript for the first edition. Miss Norma Carr of the University of Illinois, my wife Helen Peterson, and Jean Cain and Bruce Mc-Daniel of the Press staff gave me a great deal of help with both the original edition and this one. Miss Eleanor Blum, journalism and communciations librarian at the University of Illinois, tracked down elusive books, periodicals, and just plain facts. The University Research Board made funds available for having the manuscript of this edition typed.

To all of them I am grateful, although they obviously should not be held responsible for the accuracy of my facts and interpretations.

THEODORE PETERSON

Urbana, Illinois
February, 1964

Contents

The Birth of
the Modern Magazine

1

Sometime in the last decades of the nineteenth century, the modern national magazine was born. One may arbitrarily assign various dates to its birth: 1879, when Congress stimulated the growth of periodicals by providing low-cost mailing privileges; 1893, when S. S. McClure, John Brisben Walker, and Frank Munsey tapped a whole new reader audience by bringing the price of magazines within reach of the mass of the population; 1897, when Cyrus H. K. Curtis bought the feeble *Saturday Evening Post* for a thousand dollars and began reviving it; 1899, when George Horace Lorimer slid into the editor's chair of the *Saturday Evening Post* and set about attuning it to popular tastes. In fact, however, the modern national magazine was born in no one year but in a period stretching across more than a decade.

There had been magazines in America for some 150 years before the modern national magazine was born. One February day in 1741, Andrew Bradford brought out the first magazine in America, his *American Magazine, or a Monthly View of the Political State of the British Colonies.* It was born of competition, as magazines have been ever since, for it anticipated by three days the *General Magazine,* which Benjamin Franklin had projected as the first magazine in America. Neither magazine lasted long. Bradford's died in three months, Franklin's in six.

In the following century and a half, most American magazines were shaky ventures, low in income, low in advertising, low in circulation, short in life span. Few magazines circulated far from their places of publication; no general magazine reached a truly national audience before 1850. The two decades after the Civil War brought what one contemporary called "a mania of magazine-starting," a boom no doubt encouraged by the general spirit of expansion, by the availability of capital, by technological advances in the printing trades, and, in the eighties, by the favorable mailing rates for periodicals resulting from the Postal Act of March 3, 1879. In those two decades the number of periodicals increased more than fourfold, from 700 in 1865 to 3,300 in 1885.[1] By 1900 there were no fewer than fifty national magazines, some of them with circulations of more than 100,000, some of them launched amid a quiet revolution in the magazine industry in the closing years of the century.

When the last decade of the nineteenth century opened, Americans could buy periodicals representing a wide range of specialized interests. There were such magazines of science as *Popular Science Monthly* and *Scientific American;* such magazines of travel and exploration as *National Geographic;* such magazines of fashions and homemaking as *Glass of Fashion, Home Arts,* and *Ladies' World;* and even a magazine on infant care, *Babyhood.* There were such forerunners of the modern picture magazines and news magazines as *Harper's Weekly* and *Leslie's* with their many topical illustrations. There were magazines devoted to phrenology, voice culture, the single-tax movement, and gardening. There were humor magazines, business and trade magazines, literary magazines, sports magazines, magazines of many types.

Yet the average citizen was not a magazine reader. Available to him at one end of the scale were the quality monthly magazines—so called because they addressed an audience well above average in income and intellectual curiosity—magazines like *Harper's* and *Scribner's,* priced beyond his means and edited beyond his scope of interests. At the other end of the scale were the cheap weeklies, the sentimental story papers, the miscellanies. Between there were few magazines of popular price and general appeal.

---

[1] Frank Luther Mott, *A History of American Magazines 1865-1885* (Cambridge, 1938), p. 5.

In 1890, educated readers of substance, readers who could easily afford magazines, had a place on their library tables for perhaps only *Century, Harper's,* and *Scribner's.* In artistic and literary quality, in volume of respected advertising, in sales, these three magazines were the leading general monthly periodicals. Their editors edited not for the great mass of the population, which Munsey and others would later appeal to, but for gentlefolk of means. Yet their circulations, low by later standards, were respectable enough for the time; *Harper's,* for example, apparently had between 100,000 and 200,000 readers in 1891, and few other magazines had more than that.

Concerned as they were with editorial fare for the genteel, the magazines in retrospect seem curiously remote from the dramatic changes then taking place in American life. Literature, art, manners, travel, and history got their attention, and their editors often seemed to have had their eyes more closely on Europe than on America. Thus the reader of *Harper's,* skimming his copies for 1890, could settle down to subjects as remote from the contemporary American scene as Edwin Lord Weeks's "Street Scenes of India," "The Social Side of Yachting," Prof. F. B. Goodrich's "The Young Whist Player's Novitiate," and "Agricultural Chile." But even such topics held their perils: when *Scribner's* illustrated an article about French art with reproductions of nudes, an upstate New York banker wrote the editors in protest that a "young female of his household," on encountering the article, "uttered a low cry and fled from the room." [2]

Such content did not entirely represent an unawareness of reality. As Frederick Lewis Allen has remarked, it represented a valid ideal —"the ideal of the educated man, the philosopher, who is at home not merely in his own land and his own age, but in all lands and all ages; from whose point of perspective the Babylonian sealworkers are as interesting as the Pittsburgh steelworkers; who lives not merely in the world of food and drink and shelter and business and politics and everyday commonplace, but in the timeless world of ideas." [3] Nor should one undervalue the quality of their content. They printed the best and most popular authors of their times, and their illustrations were outstanding.

---

[2] Frederick Lewis Allen, "Fifty Years of Scribner's Magazine," *Scribner's,* 101 (Jan., 1937) 20-21.
[3] Allen, p. 21.

Yet beneath this high stratum of genteel readers was a tremendously large and ever growing audience for low cost magazines suited to less esoteric tastes. Frank Munsey, S. S. McClure, John Brisben Walker, George Horace Lorimer, and others realized that this large untapped audience existed, and they edited their magazines for it. As they did so, they laid down the patterns for the modern national magazine.

The times favored them, for as America shifted from an agrarian to an industrial economy, conditions were propitious for magazines of large, national circulations. Factories, growing in size and number, had begun to produce for a national or regional rather than for a largely local market. Railroads, pushing their lines across the country, had helped to make a national market possible. So had changing techniques in retailing. The local media, the signs and handbills and newspapers which had sufficed when marketing was largely local, were no longer adequate. The need was for a medium which could take the advertiser's message simultaneously to large groups of consumers over a widespread area.

Consider the situation. The average manufacturing plant, in the sixty years from 1850 to 1910, increased its capital more than thirty-nine times, its number of wage earners nearly seven times, and the value of its output more than nineteen times. The consolidations and combinations which resulted in the Sherman Anti-trust Act of 1890 continued to increase after 1896. And as manufacturing grew, so did the channels for taking mass-produced goods to the consumer. During the 1800's, railroads laid some 70,000 miles of track; and although the panic of 1893 briefly retarded expansion, mileage continued to mount by about 5,000 miles a year as the century turned. Communication with the farmer was facilitated by the growth in the number of rural free delivery routes—from forty-four in 1897 to 4,000 in 1900 to 25,000 in 1903.

Moreover, changes in retailing assisted in the distribution of mass-produced goods. The department store, which made shopping convenient for the customer, had a continuous growth between 1876 and 1900 and an accelerated growth in the new century. Chain stores began dotting the nation with retail outlets after 1900. Up to 1900, the Great Atlantic and Pacific Tea Company, for instance, had fewer than 200 stores; by 1914, it had 1,000 and by 1928 about 17,000. Founded in 1879, the F. W. Woolworth Company had fewer than 600 stores grossing about $4,000,000 a year in 1900; by 1914, it had 737 stores grossing $69,000,000 a year. In the new century, other chains began: United Cigar Stores in 1901, J. C. Penney in 1902, Piggly Wiggly before World War I, and so on. Then, too, both manufacturers and retailers were beginning to favor packaged merchandise. Before 1900, there were few packaged goods; druggists still sold perfume from large bottles on their shelves, and grocers still literally dipped into the cracker barrel. The shift from bulk to packaged merchandise led manufacturers to use brand names and trademarks to identify their products for consumers and thus to advertising campaigns to make their brand names known. Significantly, perhaps, the number of trademarks registered with the U.S. Patent Office jumped from 1,721 in 1900 to 10,282 in 1920.

By the last ten years of the nineteenth century, advances in the printing trades were making possible magazines of large circulations and were introducing to magazine publishing such mass-production methods as timed production scheduling, conveyor systems, and assembly lines. The slow flatbed press began giving way to the swifter rotary press. In 1886, R. Hoe and Company built a rotary press for *Century Magazine* which could do ten times the work of a similarly sized flatbed press; and in 1890, C. B. Cottrell and Sons Company turned out a rotary web perfecting press which was used by *Youth's Companion, Harper's, Lupton's, McCall's,* and other magazines. An enlarged, improved version of the Cottrell press was built for *Munsey's Magazine* in 1898.

Magazines no longer had to depend for their art work on reproductions of sketches, laboriously and expensively engraved by hand on copper or wood—and even colored by hand, as when *Godey's Lady's Book* hired 150 women to tint its illustrations. A Hoe rotary art press built for *Century* in 1890 printed the finest halftone illustrations from curved plates, and three years later Hoe built the first multicolor rotary press. The Curtis Publishing Company installed the first Cottrell multicolor rotary press in 1908.

The technological advances in printing favored the publisher who was enterprising enough to try for the large circulation that developments in marketing and expansion in transportation had made possible. They enabled him to compete on fairly equal terms with the established publisher with large working capital. No longer did the established publisher have an advantage in magazine production because he could afford expensive engravings from drawings and sketches, engravings which alone cost the *Century Magazine* $5,000 a month. Photoengravings from photographs were comparatively inexpensive. Furthermore, setting copy into type and getting the printing forms ready for printing represented fixed costs, the same regardless of circulation. Presses were efficient enough to turn out attractive magazines at a low unit cost; and the public, accustomed to price reductions on other commodities, was in a mood to welcome price cuts in its reading fare.

In such a setting, the low-priced, mass-circulation magazine was born. Assisting at its birth, each in his own fashion, were S. S. McClure, John Brisben Walker, Frank A. Munsey, Cyrus H. K. Curtis, George Horace Lorimer, and Edward W. Bok.

Born in Ireland, S. S. McClure came to the United States in 1866 as a boy of nine; in his early life poverty was never far away. At seventeen, with fifteen cents in his pocket and with one suit of homemade clothes, he enrolled at Knox College in Galesburg, Illinois, to start what turned out to be a protracted struggle for an education. He drifted into journalism. Within two months of leaving college in 1882, he became the first editor of *The Wheelman*, a magazine published in Boston by Colonel Albert A. Pope, a manufacturer who held basic patents on the bicycle. He left to become proofreader at the De Vinne Press, a printing house in New York, and later joined the Century Company.

The idea for a newspaper syndicate came to McClure while he was working for the Century Company. He had often hungered for something inexpensive to read when he was a boy, and browsing through files of *St. Nicholas,* which the Century Company published, he felt that he had missed a great deal. He thought that it would be a good idea to syndicate old stories from *St. Nicholas* to weekly newspapers throughout the country. With little more than hard work and faith in his idea, despite what at first seemed failure, he established a successful newspaper syndicate; in doing so, he aimed at a reading public which publishers had largely ignored, a public he was soon to reach as a magazine publisher.

McClure had not read magazines when he was a college student because they were too expensive. He was convinced that an inexpensive popular magazine could succeed. For one thing, he was impressed by the success in England of such inexpensive publications as *Strand* and *Country Life* and in the United States of *Ladies' Home Journal,* which by 1893 had rolled up a circulation of 700,000 at ten cents a copy. For another thing, he believed that the development of photoengraving had made it financially possible for newcomers such as he to compete with established publishers in bringing out well-illustrated magazines. *Century,* for instance, had paid up to $300 for a page-size woodcut; now a publisher could buy a halftone for under $20.

Early in 1892, with $7,300 capital (of which he committed $5,000 as the annual salary of his advertising manager), he began to plan a fifteen-cent monthly for readers who could not afford to spend twenty-five or thirty-five cents, the usual price of magazines. The first issue of *McClure's Magazine* was on the press when the panic of 1893 made additional capital hard to raise.

And McClure met unexpected competition from *Cosmopolitan,* edited by John Brisben Walker. Walker, who had made and lost a fortune manufacturing iron, bought the dying *Cosmopolitan* in 1889 and increased its circulation from 16,000 to 400,000 in five years. McClure had thought that it would be a year or two after *McClure's* first appeared before another inexpensive magazine would enter the field. But Walker left him no such lead; he cut the price of *Cosmopolitan,* long a twenty-five-cent magazine, 12½ cents, 2½ cents under the price of *McClure's.* That price cut produced a minor uprising.

The big revolution in the magazine industry came almost at once, in October, 1893. The New York *Sun* proclaimed it on a Monday morning in a black-faced advertisement which announced that *Munsey's Magazine* had cut its price from twenty-five to ten cents, its yearly subscriptions from $3 to $1. "We can do it," the advertisement said, "because we deal direct with news dealers and save two profits you pay on other magazines. No middlemen; no monopoly." [4]

The revolutionist was Frank A. Munsey, who vividly demonstrated a basic economic principle of twentieth-century magazine publishing—a principle which McClure, Walker, Curtis, and others were discovering in the late nineteenth century. It was simply this: one could achieve a large circulation by selling his magazine for much less than its cost of production and could take his profits from the high volume of advertising that a large circulation attracted. For not only did Munsey, like McClure and the others,

---

[4] Advertisement from New York *Sun,* Oct. 2, 1893, reproduced by George Britt, *Forty Years—Forty Millions: The Career of Frank A. Munsey* (New York, 1935), facing p. 39.

make his appeal to a large mass of hitherto ignored readers; he also made his appeal to a large and untapped class of advertisers, advertisers as eager for inexpensive space rates as readers were for inexpensive magazines. Not long after his announcement in the *Sun*, advertisers knew him for his famous rate of $1 a page for each thousand of circulation.

Unlike McClure and Edward W. Bok, who sincerely wanted to carry inexpensive reading matter to the masses, Munsey wanted only profits from his magazines; his unprincipled quest for them earned him few admirers. One rival said that he was not a magazine publisher but a magazine manufacturer. When he died in 1925, William Allen White wrote of him: "Frank Munsey contributed to the journalism of his day the talent of a meat packer, the morals of a money changer and the manner of an undertaker. He and his kind have about succeeded in transforming a once-noble profession into an 8 per cent security. May he rest in trust." And one congressman made the superbly equivocal comment, "His death is as great a loss to the country as to his profession." [5]

After he had acquired wealth and power, Munsey had genealogists search out his family line so that, as he said, he could know his own history as he would know the pedigree of a horse he was going to bet on. He was born near Mercer, Maine, on August 21, 1854, the son of a moneyless farmer-carpenter. When he was twenty-three, he became manager of the office of the Western Union Telegraph Company in Augusta, Maine, and there he saw at first hand the money to be made from carlot publishing. Augusta was then the home of two inexpensive mail-order magazines of wide distribution, both of them filled with trashy editorial matter and even trashier advertisements, but both highly profitable to their publishers. One was Peleg O. Vickery's *Vickery's Fireside Visitor;* the other was Edward Charles Allen's *People's Literary Companion*, which in 1894 merged with *Comfort*, which in turn flourished well into the thirties with a circulation of a million or more. As a result of talks about publishing with Allen in Augusta House, Munsey gradually decided that his fortune lay in publishing.

Munsey started his first magazine, *Golden Argosy*, "Freighted with Treasures for Boys and Girls," in New York in December, 1882. For five years he was often broke, often in debt, and when

---

[5] Britt, p. 17.

he could not afford to buy manuscripts he wrote them himself. He dabbled in other publishing ventures which were uniformly unsuccessful. *Argosy* prospered for a while in 1887; but when the panic of 1893 struck, Munsey found himself with two failing magazines and with $100,000 in debts. He was desperate.

In his desperation, Frank Munsey revolutionized magazine publishing and made his fortune. One of his failing magazines was *Munsey's,* which he had switched from weekly to monthly publication in October, 1891. In 1893 he slashed the price of *Munsey's* from twenty-five cents to ten cents and took space in the New York *Sun* to announce his decision. The September issue of his magazine also announced the cut in price:

> At ten cents per copy and at a dollar a year for subscriptions in advance, *Munsey's* will have reached that point, a point below which no good magazine will ever go, but to which all magazines of large circulation in America must eventually come. The present low price of paper and the perfecting of printing machinery make it possible to sell at a profit a magazine at these figures—as good a magazine as has ever been issued, provided it is not too heavily freighted with advertisements.[6]

Munsey's reasoning was correct; like McClure, he realized that most readers had little middle choice between the inexpensive trash of the *People's Literary Companion* and the expensive elegance of the *Century-Harper's-Scribner's* triumvirate. But getting his magazines into the hands of his readers was quite another matter, for between Munsey and his public stood the American News Company, which distributed the bulk of American magazines. The company had branches throughout the United States and in Canada for wholesaling magazines to dealers, and it owned the Union News Company, one of the largest retailers of magazines. Its virtual monopoly of magazine distribution allowed it to dictate even the price of magazines. American News saw little commission for itself in a ten-cent magazine. When Munsey offered his magazine to the company at 6½ cents a copy, company officials told him that they would pay him 4½ cents a copy as a favor. Munsey indignantly decided to go directly to the news dealers themselves. He wrote them letters and sent out broadsides by the thousand. His battle with American News was short and successful.

He won the contest because *Munsey's* itself was successful from the start. When readers heard of the ten-cent magazine, they asked

---

[6] Quoted in Britt, p. 81.

dealers for copies; and as orders piled up, dealers who had remained unimpressed by letters and handbills asked Munsey for
copies. Even the mighty American News Company yielded, but
Munsey refused to come to terms, for he was getting so many
orders from dealers that he had a hard time filling them. He
stopped production of the first ten-cent issue to start work on the
next. Circulation mounted: 40,000 copies of the first ten-cent issue
in October, 1893; 60,000 in November, 1893; 200,000 in February,
1894; 275,000 at the end of the first year; and 500,000 by April,
1895. In March, 1898, Munsey boasted that his magazine had the
largest circulation of any magazine in the world; in 1901, he claimed
for it a circulation double the combined circulations of *Century*,
Harper's, and *Scribner's*.

Munsey was not alone in his success. After a period of losses,
debts, and scurrying to raise additional working capital, McClure
established his magazine as a circulation leader and money-maker.
He cut its price from fifteen cents to ten cents and served up article
after article that caught on with the public—Ida M. Tarbell's "Life
of Napoleon" in 1894, for example, and her "Life of Lincoln."
More and more readers bought copies. The first issue in 1893 sold
but 8,000 of the 20,000 copies which McClure optimistically had
had printed. At the end of 1894, however, circulation was 40,000
and a few months later 80,000. Before long, it was booming: 120,000
in August, 1895; 175,000 in November, 1895; 250,000 in December,
1895. Two and a half years after the first issue, *McClure's* far
exceeded *Century*, *Harper's*, or *Scribner's* in circulation, and not
long after that its circulation topped that of the three old leaders
combined.

At first, however, *McClure's* was a financial flop. During its first
summer, losses ran about a thousand dollars a month; as its circulation increased, losses mounted, and throughout 1895 the magazine
was costing its publisher about $4,000 a month. As early as 1895,
McClure was demonstrating what the Curtis Publishing Company
was to learn in the first years of the twentieth century with its
Saturday Evening Post and what Time Inc. was to learn in 1936
with its *Life:* success itself may threaten to kill a magazine. If
circulation far outruns adjustments in advertising rates, as it did
with *McClure's* and *Life*, the costs of meeting the public demand
for his magazine may ruin a publisher. *McClure's* low advertising
rates and its rapidly climbing circulation cost its publisher thou-

sands of dollars, as a similar situation was later to cost Time Inc. $5,000,000 in a year and a half. But S. S. McClure, like Curtis and Time Inc., brought his rates in line with his circulation, and in 1896 his magazine was clearing $5,000 a month and had established its prosperity and standing.

It was a happy time for magazines, that last decade of the nineteenth century, and fortunes were in the making as publishers reached persons who had seldom if ever before bought magazines. Cyrus H. K. Curtis, who had a genius for choosing brilliant editors and giving them a free hand, was building up three magazines which in the 1920's would take in a third or more of all money spent on national advertising in magazines. One cannot trace the emergence of the modern popular magazine without some mention of at least two Curtis publications. Curtis was alert to the new markets opening up for periodicals, and perhaps no publisher of his time had as profound a faith in advertising, the foundation on which the big national magazines were built.

In 1883 Cyrus Curtis, after indifferent success with a few publications operated on a shoestring, was partner in a four-year-old weekly, the *Tribune and Farmer*. Its women's department, taken over by Mrs. Curtis when she became exasperated with her husband's selections for it, had become so popular that Curtis decided to issue it as a separate publication. So in December, 1883, with Mrs. Curtis as editor, the *Ladies' Home Journal* first appeared. In a split over policy, Curtis gave his partner the *Tribune and Farmer*, which soon failed; he himself retained *Ladies' Home Journal*, which transformed the field of women's magazines and was one of the first magazines ever to reach a circulation of a million.

When Edward W. Bok took over the editorship from Mrs. Curtis in October, 1889, the *Ladies' Home Journal* was well established with readers and advertisers and had a comfortable circulation of 440,000. Bok continued to build on Mrs. Curtis' success. Under the pseudonym "Ruth Ashmore," he originated a department, "Side Talks with Girls," which he turned over to Isabel A. Mallon because the letters it evoked were too intimate for his eyes and which in sixteen years brought in some 158,000 letters from readers and kept three stenographers busy with replies. He advised women on how to raise babies, how to play the piano, how to understand and appreciate the Bible, how to improve the interiors of their homes. He campaigned against French fashions, killing birds to adorn women's hats, public drinking cups, venereal disease. He published the best and best-known authors he could attract. And in doing so, he broke with the sentimentality, the moralizing and piety which had long characterized the women's magazine; he helped to make the women's magazine an organ of service to its readers, a publication keyed to their tastes and practical problems.

Of more general interest than the *Ladies' Home Journal* was the *Saturday Evening Post,* which Curtis originally intended as a men's magazine but which, because men carried it home where their wives could read it, became in time symbolic of the reading fare of middle-class America. In 1897 when Curtis bought the magazine for $1,000, with a down payment of $100, the *Post* was dying; and Curtis' chances of resuscitating it seemed so slight that the advertising trade paper *Printers' Ink* remarked that he seemed bent on "blowing in all the profits" of the *Ladies' Home Journal* on "an impossible venture." For a time, Curtis did sink the profits of the *Journal* into the *Post.* To the dismay of the company treasurer, the new weekly showed a loss of a million and a quarter dollars before the public demand for it became so great that the presses could scarcely turn out copies fast enough. But once the *Post* caught on, both circulation and advertising revenue bounded:

Year	Average Circulation	Advertising Revenue
1897	2,231	$ 6,933
1902	314,671	360,125
1907	726,681	1,266,931
1912	1,920,550	7,114,581
1917	1,833,070	16,076,562
1922	2,187,024	28,278,755

Curtis himself could take a good deal of credit for the *Post's* popularity. As the Curtis Publishing Company was to do in the mid-1940's with *Holiday,* he was willing to suffer huge financial losses to keep alive a magazine in which he had faith; and he managed its business affairs well. Moreover, once he found a successful editor he gave him a free hand.

The editor was George Horace Lorimer, a Boston minister's son, who at twenty-two had quit a job with the Armour packing company paying $5,000 a year, to prepare himself for journalism by taking a two-year course in general literature at Colby College. Curtis hired him for the *Post* at a thousand dollars a year, a salary which would increase one-hundredfold before he retired. Lorimer did so well that Curtis gave up his idea of luring Arthur Sherburne Hardy, a former editor of *Cosmopolitan,* to the *Post* as editor. Instead, in 1899, he made Lorimer editor.

Curtis founded the revived *Saturday Evening Post* on the proposition that a man's chief interest in life is the fight for livelihood —business. On the stage, in fiction, in articles, he thought, the business world was being misrepresented; and he reasoned that businessmen would welcome a magazine carrying authoritative articles and stories about business. Lorimer, translating Curtis' proposition into words and type, demonstrated that men—and women—did welcome such a magazine. Ex-presidents, premiers, senators, the best-known authors wrote for the *Post,* and when Lorimer could not buy what he wanted, he wrote it himself; advertisers paid thousands of dollars to get their messages alongside the *Post's* fiction and its articles about romantic business and successful businessmen. From slim beginnings, the *Post* waxed fat and conservative, and at the end of World War I it had achieved the then fantastic circulation of 2,000,000.

As the century turned, then, the characteristics of the twentieth-century popular magazine were clearly discernible. What were they? First, magazines had become low in price. Their low price, ten cents and even five cents, put them within reach of an increased proportion of the American people. Frank Munsey, an astute observer, estimated that between 1893 and 1899 the ten-cent magazine increased the magazine-buying public from 250,000 to 750,000 persons. Second, as a result of their low price, as a result of mass production and of mass distribution over the entire nation, magazines had achieved undreamed-of circulations. Before the last decade of the nineteenth century, publishers had been extremely proud of circulations between 100,000 and 200,000; but by 1900, Bok's *Ladies' Home Journal* was moving rapidly toward a circulation of 1,000,000. Third, advertising, attracted by large circulations as manufacturers quested for a national market, had become virtually essential for the success of a low-priced magazine. To attract many readers, the publisher needed a low price; to maintain his low price, he needed advertising volume. And, finally, magazine content had become "popular" as publishers and editors reached new audiences. This is not to suggest that magazines then were or now are edited for "the masses." Then, as now, magazines were edited for little publics within the population as a whole; but they were discovering new publics to which to appeal.

The change in content was important to the success of the new magazines which emerged in the late nineteenth century. Editorial matter became geared to the problems, perplexities, and interests of readers as never before; neither highbrow nor lowbrow, it rode the large middle ground of public taste. The change is apparent to one who thumbs through the files of *Century* and *Munsey's*, of *Harper's* and *McClure's*, of *Scribner's* and the *Saturday Evening Post*.

The old leaders still looked across the sea and to the past. The newcomers looked at America and to the present—or future. In 1893 readers of *Harper's* could read such pieces as "An Artist's Summer Vacation" and "A French Town in Summer." But in 1894, when railroads were burgeoning, when coal miners were busily feeding the furnaces of industry, *McClure's* took its readers for a ride in the engine of "the swiftest train in the world" on its journey from New York to Chicago and into the depths of a coal mine with Stephen Crane. *Harper's* could run articles about "The Riders of Egypt"; *McClure's* wrote of circuses and the cattle brands of the West. The magazines had an "extraordinarily vital and stimulating quality," to borrow a description from a Scottish critic who remarked of them early in the new century: "There is nothing quite like them in the literature of the world—no periodicals which combine such width of popular appeal with such seriousness of aim and thoroughness of workmanship."

In an even more obvious fashion, magazines became a part of their readers' lives. Self-improvement had already become an American characteristic by the 1890's. Facilities for formal education were increasing faster than the population, public libraries were rapidly springing up, and the Chautauqua was drawing crowds. Magazines, whose success reflected this interest in education, made direct contributions. Edward Bok offered an expense-paid education at leading conservatories to young women who obtained the requisite number of subscriptions to *Ladies' Home Journal*, and later he extended the plan to include regular college scholarships. John Brisben Walker, somewhat impulsively, founded a correspondence university sponsored by *Cosmopolitan* and by May, 1898, had 20,000 men and women on its rolls. In still other ways magazines sought to help their readers improve themselves and their ways of living. Bok commissioned architects to prepare building plans which would improve the small-house architecture of the country, and sold the plans by the thousand. He printed portfolios of art reproductions to improve the quality of pictures hanging on the walls of American homes.

Magazine illustration was being revolutionized. Both McClure and Munsey, especially the latter, used photographs lavishly. From the first issue, *McClure's* had a success in its "Human Document" series, photographs from the lives of famous men. Frank Munsey discovered the nude female and took her into the American home. Like publishers since, he used subterfuge: he used her to illustrate such articles as his series, "Artists and Their Work."

In fiction, publishers were discovering that the story itself was more important that the literary skill with which it was told. Who told it was important, as Lorimer recognized, and some magazines sought showcase bylines; but, at bottom, the tale itself was the thing. Frank Munsey, an expert at tuning in on the public taste, outlined his prescription for the short story in 1895: "We want stories. That is what we mean—stories, not dialect sketches, not washed out studies of effete human nature, not weak tales of sickly sentimentality, not 'pretty' writing. . . . We do want fiction in which there is a story, a force, a tale that means something—in short a story. Good writing is as common as clam shells, while good stories are as rare as statesmanship." [7]

It was this gearing of content to the contemporary American scene, to the readers' interests and problems, that produced the era of muckraking which began in late 1902 and lasted, with ups and downs, for a decade. The biggest story in America at the time was Business. In the half-dozen years after 1896, industrial consolidation was one of the outstanding features of American economic life, a movement encouraged by industrial and agricultural prosperity. In this period of somewhat chaotic industrial expansion, politics at various levels and in various degrees became the handmaiden of business. Magazine editors knew it, and they tackled their big story in different ways. With a conservatism which was to guide him until his retirement, Lorimer steered his *Saturday Evening Post* on a steady course of romantic business, successful

---

[7] Britt, p. 98.

business, a course which left the magazine respected and prosperous when several of its muckraking contemporaries later were in their graves. As early as January, 1900, *Munsey's*, whose own publisher, in the spirit of the times, was bent on consolidating a publishing empire, ran two articles which reflected the public interest in trusts, although the magazine never became a muckraker. Other magazines, too, wrote of trusts and corruption in government.

Meanwhile, S. S. McClure sensed the big story of his day. It called for handling, for McClure believed that besides being an inexpensive source of good reading, a popular magazine should be an authoritative reporter of modern civilization. He encouraged Ida M. Tarbell in her *History of the Standard Oil Company,* a study which was to take her five years, and put Lincoln Steffens to work investigating municipal government. By coincidence, *McClure's* for January, 1903, carried three articles similar in theme and handling—Tarbell's third article on Standard Oil, Steffens' "The Shame of Minneapolis," and Ray Stannard Baker's "The Right to Work"—and the era of muckrakers officially opened. McClure later recalled: "It came from no formulated plan to attack existing institutions, but was the result of merely taking up in the magazine some of the problems that were beginning to interest people a little before newspapers and other magazines took them up." [8]

Most of the muckrakers were journalists, not reformers. For the most part, they reported unhappy conditions without advancing a program for correcting them. Robert Cantwell has argued that the successful popular appeal of muckraking was literary rather than political, for the movement was the journalistic equivalent of the literary realism that was beginning to captivate readers.

Whatever the reason, people were interested in the muckraking articles; as Ray Stannard Baker recalled in his autobiography, "everybody seemed to be reading them." And people had a multitude of articles to choose among, for magazine after magazine engaged in muckraking: *Arena, Collier's, Cosmopolitan, Everybody's, Hampton's.* In 1906, several staff members of *McClure's,* including Baker, Steffens, and Tarbell, quit to buy the *American Magazine,* which they converted into a muckraking organ for a brief period.

Militant from 1903 through 1905, the muckraking movement was

---

[8] S. S. McClure, *My Autobiography* (New York, 1914), p. 246.

an important force by 1906. Although it ebbed in 1908, it reached another high point in 1911, but by 1912 had spent itself. Why did it die? One historian of the movement, C. C. Regier, gives this explanation: "Because muckraking was to some extent merely a fad—of which the public grew tired, because of the pressure of financial interests, because some of the evils exposed had been remedied, and because of the inherent weakness of the movement itself, muckraking came to an end. Even liberalism, of which muckraking was but a part, received a stunning blow when the United States entered the World War." [9]

In his balance sheet, Regier credits the movement with a part in many reforms, among them a federal pure-food law, child labor laws, a tariff commission, and workmen's compensation, as well as a part in the introduction of Congressional investigations and the development of sociological surveys. For the articles in *McClure's* and the other leading magazines were really exercises in popular sociology. They probed but did not advocate, and such an extraordinary amount of research went into them that McClure put the cost of Ida M. Tarbell's articles about Standard Oil at $4,000 each and of Steffens' articles at $2,000 each. Not all of the magazines that joined the muckraking crew were as thorough, and some were frankly sensational. Yet Regier has concluded that the general reliability of the muckraking magazines was high.

By the time that the muckrakers laid down their pens, the new journalism, with its pressure for huge circulations, its pitching of content to mass audiences, its scramble for the advertising dollar, was well on its way. Editors of national periodicals of broad appeal had found their market and had learned to give readers what they wanted. Advertising had appeared in sufficient quantity to give publishers a taste of the rewards for those who best won the reading public's approval and, as much as any one thing, had begun to shape the twentieth-century magazine and the industry which produced it.

---

[9] C. C. Regier, *The Era of the Muckrakers* (Chapel Hill, N.C., 1932), p. 214.

Advertising:
Its Growth and Effects

2

After 1900, magazine publishing was profoundly affected by changes in the American economy, particularly those in the distribution of consumer goods which led to the growth of advertising. As advertising grew it made the magazine a part of the system of marketing in the United States. This development had manifold effects on the magazine industry. It transformed the publisher from dealer in editorial wares to dealer in consumer groups as well. It helped to expand the sale of magazines, and it significantly altered the publisher's attitude toward circulation. It stimulated the publisher to research, especially in the characteristics of the market he served and in the effectiveness of his publication in reaching that market. It affected the format of magazines and their presentation of editorial copy. It raised the threat of influence by advertisers on editorial policy. In short, it affected virtually all aspects of the magazine industry.

The expanding volume of advertising as the century turned was a reflection of the shift of the United States from an agricultural nation to an industrial one. Until 1850 most manufacturing had been done in shop and household, and until the eighties agriculture was the chief source of wealth. But by 1890 manufacturing had pushed ahead, and by 1900 the value of manufactured products was more than double that of agriculture.

As new inventions brought new industries into existence, as old industries stepped up their production and large factories turned out standardized goods in profusion, as an expanding system of roads and railways linked producer and consumer, there were important changes in methods of distribution. The small shops and households had produced for local or regional markets, and their methods of distribution were makeshift. But with the industrial revolution, which was one of the outstanding features of American economic life after the Civil War, the market became national, and by 1914 the conception of the domestic market had changed from specific places to widely scattered consumers.

More than that, manufacturers had come to recognize the financial value of the brand name. In a sense, the brand name enabled a producer to achieve a monopoly even in a highly competitive field. No one else could use his brand name and trademark if he properly protected them. Therefore, his aim was to convince consumers that his product met their needs and desires better than any competing one. If he succeeded, he had some assurance of repeat orders; he also could charge his customers a higher price for his product because of the real or psychic satisfaction they got from it.

The emergence of new industries and the expansion of old ones helped to swell the volume of magazine advertising in the last years of the nineteenth century and the first years of the twentieth. So did the drive to exploit trademarks and brand names. American industry, which had spent $360 million on advertising of all types in 1890, spent $542 million in 1900 and $821 million in 1904. Reflecting on the growth of advertising in the previous two decades, *Printers' Ink* commented in 1905: "Suddenly the manufacturing world has developed an intense, anxious interest in both advertising and consumers. It is glad to talk plans of advertising and discuss trade-marks with solicitors, where a year ago the latter would have got no hearing."

Manufacturers found magazines an efficient means of spreading their sales messages over a wide area, and an advertiser could get results from an annual advertising expenditure of $25,000 when the new century opened. Through advertising, the makers of established products such as Royal Baking Powder, Ivory Soap, and Baker's Chocolate reached new consumers; and manufacturers of new products such as the Eastman Kodak and the Gillette safety razor gained acceptance for their wares earlier than they could have without the magazine. The bicycle industry was the first to demonstrate the effectiveness of national advertising. In the eighties and nineties, rival manufacturers used magazines as well as other media not only to advertise their products but also to sell the bicycle as a form of transportation. Their success paved the way for advertising by the automotive industry, which was just coming into existence.

An important increase in magazine revenues during World War I and after came from advertisers new to magazines, advertisers selling their goods and services on a national scale for the first time. As the economy expanded, the number of national advertisers grew, and new ones replaced the ones who disappeared as their companies merged or went out of business. Even at midcentury, the increase in the number of national advertisers was impressive. Between 1939 and 1956, the number of national advertisers went from 936 to 2,742, and the number of brands of merchandise which they sold through advertising jumped from 1,659 to perhaps 6,000. The number of national advertisers using magazines increased from 660 to 2,278 in that period. Newcomers since the start of World War II accounted for about one-third of all of the dollars spent on national advertising in magazines in 1952. Moreover, as the century wore on, advertisers could no longer conduct a national campaign on a budget of a few thousand dollars, as they could when the century opened. Of the hundred leading national advertisers in 1961, seventy-eight spent at least a million dollars on magazine advertising. The General Motors Corporation alone spent $32,309,761 on general magazine advertising in 1961, and American Telephone and Telegraph spent $13,003,818.

Magazine advertising had existed in America, of course, long before the low-priced national magazine emerged in the last years of the nineteenth century. Almost as long as there have been magazines in America, there has been magazine advertising. In its issue of May 10, 1741, the *General Magazine and Historical Chronicle* carried a four-line reading notice, inserted at the cost of a few shillings. That seems to have been the first magazine advertisement in America.

But not until after the Civil War did advertising begin to appear in magazines in any volume. By then the advertising agency had appeared, if in somewhat crude form, and some of the agencies concentrated on developing magazine advertising. One of the first, founded in 1864, was the Carlton and Smith agency, which specialized in promoting advertising first for the religious weeklies, the major periodical medium in the third quarter of the century, and later for general magazines. J. Walter Thompson, who took over the agency in 1878, is often credited with being the one man who, more than anyone else, promoted the magazine as an advertising medium.

Well into the latter half of the nineteenth century, however, magazine publishers were almost exclusively purveyors of editorial matter, and many of them believed that advertising lowered the standing of their publications. Some publishers refused it altogether; others suffered it in limited quantities. Their attitude toward advertisers and advertising men was often cavalier. George P. Rowell, a pioneer advertising agent, watched wide-eyed as Fletcher Harper turned down $18,000 offered by Elias Howe's son-in-law for the last page of *Harper's* for a year to advertise the Howe Sewing Machine. Harper wanted the space to advertise Harper books. Another day the same George Rowell strode into the offices of *Harper's Weekly*, then in demand as an advertising medium, to coax the publishers into revealing its circulation. The publishers plainly regarded him as a prying busybody. One of them quietly remarked to his colleagues, "It seems to me that if Mr. Rowell talks that way we don't want to do business with him." Nor did they. They rejected the next advertisements that the Rowell agency submitted.[1]

Gradually, timidly, some of the magazines which had declined advertising opened their pages to it. For a time, they made small effort to solicit advertising, however, and some of them rationed the space they allowed for it. One of the first magazines of high standing that actively sought advertising was *Century*. A dignified magazine edited for a dignified reader group, it imparted a certain decorum to advertising. Its devotion to advertising in the seventies and eighties has been credited with overcoming the reluctance of general and literary magazines to run ads.

By the turn of the century, general magazines had begun to seek and encourage advertising. The *Youth's Companion* and the *Century* had been doing so since the seventies, but now they were

---

[1] George P. Rowell, *Forty Years an Advertising Agent* (New York, 1906), pp. 23, 410-11.

joined by others: the *Ladies' Home Journal, Cosmopolitan, Collier's, Delineator, McCall's, McClure's,* and *Munsey's,* to name a few. And as the general weeklies and monthlies cultivated advertising, the religious weeklies, for half a century a favorite advertising medium, lost ground. Sensing the change, some religious magazines, among them *Outlook* and *Independent,* converted themselves into secular magazines. To the delight of advertisers, to the dismay of some readers, advertisements began moving forward from the last pages of magazines to rest between divisions of editorial matter.

Changes also were taking place in the advertising business. Advertising agencies were expanding their services. Until about 1890, advertising agencies were generally space brokers which bargained with publishers for large blocks of space and sold it, in smaller units, to their clients. Their prices were not standardized, and the agencies offered their clients no such services as copywriting and layout. By 1890, however, advertising agencies were numerous, and they had begun to give their clients a hand with choosing media, writing copy, and even some rudimentary market analysis. Moreover, there was some standardization in advertising rates. Magazine publishers had begun to base their charges for space on circulation. To get their money's worth, some advertisers tried to improve the effectiveness of their advertisements. They heard talks on the use of psychology in advertising, and they began to test the drawing power of their advertisements by key numbers and checking systems. More and more, they began to recognize the value of continuity in advertising. A few books on advertising began to trickle from the presses. In 1900 Professor Harlow Gale published his pamphlet on the psychology of advertising, and in 1903 Professor Walter Dill Scott brought out his *Theory of Advertising.*

As the century turned, magazines seemed full of advertisements, although they carried nowhere near the volume that they later would. But to the readers of the time the increase seemed phenomenal. A statistician devised a table to show that in just one year— 1900—*Harper's,* long an advertisers' favorite, carried a greater volume of advertising than in the entire preceding twenty-two years combined.

A discerning subscriber, especially if he subscribed to the right magazines at the right times, could have seen for himself the growth of magazine advertising in the twentieth century. When a reader of 1908 picked up a copy of a monthly magazine favored by advertisers, he encountered an average of 137 pages of advertisements, about 54 per cent of the total pages. When he picked up a similar monthly in 1947, he found 208 pages of advertisements, about 65 per cent of the total space. But the reader would have detected the greatest growth in the weeklies. In 1908 the leading weeklies carried an average of nineteen pages of advertising an issue; in 1947 their average was 159 pages.[2]

Throughout the twenties, the weekly in which the reader could have best seen the expanding volume was the *Saturday Evening Post*, which grew so fat on advertising that enterprising merchants reportedly bought up current copies for five cents as an inexpensive means of getting scrap paper. A monument of sorts was the issue of the *Post* for December 7, 1929. Weighing nearly two pounds, the 272-page magazine contained enough reading matter to keep the average reader occupied for twenty hours and twenty minutes. From the 214 national advertisers appearing in it, Curtis took in revenues estimated at $1,512,000.

That same year *Sales Management* concluded that radio had not seriously cut into magazine revenues, although it may have caused some industries to reduce their expenditures on the print media. "For the most part, however, there is fairly clear proof in the figures that advertising in the air is used as a feeder of or supplement to other forms of advertising," the magazine said in its issue of March 16, 1929. Therefore, it added, many publishers welcomed rather than feared the new medium, as they felt anything that helped advertising worked to their own long-term advantage.

Magazine advertising certainly did continue to climb, even when radio was in its prime. In the early twenties, a publisher regarded himself as successful if his magazine grossed $2,000,000 a year in advertising. After World War II, some magazines carried that much in a single issue. For instance, the *Ladies' Home Journal* boasted that its 246-page issue of October, 1946, brought in $2,146,746 worth of advertising from 334 advertisers; an issue two years later carried $2,677,260 worth. A single issue of *Life* in October, 1960, carried $5,000,000 worth; another in November, 1961, had revenues of $5,202,000. Indeed, *Life*'s advertising receipts in

[2] *Printers' Ink*, 225 (Oct. 29, 1948) 108.

1963 were substantially more than the combined total for the thirty magazines leading in advertising in 1925.

No competitor ever gave publishers as many fretful hours as television, which grew rapidly in the postwar boom. Expenditures on television advertising—network, spot, and local—climbed from virtually nothing in the late 1940's to more than $1.7 billion in 1963.

When magazine profits declined in the late 1950's and early 1960's, many observers were quick to blame the trouble on television. Some pointed out that magazines were losing their share of total expenditures on national advertising. In an article that was based on his doctoral dissertation and that appeared in *Advertising Age*, October 15, 1962, Charles Yang, a C.B.S. economist, reported magazines had experienced a relative decline in advertising during the postwar period. He attributed some of their loss to television. The Television Bureau of Advertising used data from the *Printers' Ink* marketing yearbooks to show that magazines' share of expenditures on national advertising dropped from 16.6 per cent in 1949, when television began to emerge as a serious competitor, to 12.8 per cent in 1960. Some observers pointed out that magazines had lost favor with the biggest spenders on advertising. *Tide,* the advertising trade paper, in 1958 analyzed the records of 379 corporations and associations spending a million dollars or more a year on advertising. Their total expenditures on advertising rose from $773 million in 1950 to $1.4 billion in 1957, and network television accounted for about two-thirds of the increase. In that same period, according to the study, network television's share of money spent by million-dollar advertisers rose from 5 per cent to 35 per cent.

On the other hand, some observers were not persuaded that television had really cut into magazine revenues. James B. Kobak of J. K. Lasser and Company, accountants and auditors to the magazine industry, said in September, 1961, he could not find that television had really harmed magazines. "It's hard to say that circulation has been hurt when circulation has increased between 1950 and 1960 by 21 per cent," he remarked. "It's hard to say that television has hurt advertising revenue when that's increased some 86 per cent in that ten year period."

There were some indications that Mr. Kobak was right. For instance, the ratio of dollars spent on magazine advertising to consumer spending seems to have been fairly constant over the years;

it appears to have been about the same in 1935, 1950, and 1961, some indication that magazines held their share of the market. Early in 1960 the commercial research department of the Minnesota and Ontario Paper Company made a long-range forecast of paper requirements of the magazine industry. Although the volume of magazine advertising had risen and fallen since 1915, the report noted, on the whole it had shown a consistent upward trend. Magazines had always overcome such hindrances to their growth as the advent of radio, the Depression of the 1930's, and the emergence of television. They had shown the same growth pattern in the previous ten years as they had since 1915, according to the report, and their future linage could be expected to grow at least as well as in the past. The forecast predicted that magazine receipts from advertising would reach $1.5 billion by 1975.

In the early years of television, at least, much of the money that advertisers allocated to it seems to have come from new appropriations. No one can tell for sure how much money advertisers would have spent on magazines if television had never come along, of course. Yet there is little convincing evidence that television seriously diverted revenues from magazines generally, although individual publications may have suffered from its competition.

From early in the century onward, magazine advertising revenues showed a relatively consistent increase. Reliable information on amounts for the last years of the nineteenth century and the first years of the twentieth is not available. However, Table 1 shows the approximate sums spent on national advertising in magazines from 1915 through 1963. The figures are totals for the publications covered by the Publishers Information Bureau, and they take account of the bulk of commercial magazines. Especially after World War II, a good part of the revenue increases were accounted for by higher advertising rates as a result of increased circulations. Page volume of advertising grew far more slowly than dollar volume.

Advertising in large measure made possible the low-priced magazine of large circulation which emerged during the last years of the nineteenth century. Frank Munsey, S. S. McClure, and, above all, Cyrus H. K. Curtis with his *Saturday Evening Post*, effectively demonstrated what soon became a basic principle of publishing: that a publisher could lose millions of dollars on circulation by selling his magazine at less than production cost and yet could reap millions of dollars in profit from advertising. It was with this prin-

Table 1. Gross National Advertising in General and Farm Magazines, 1915-63

Year	General Magazines	Farm Magazines	Total	Year	General Magazines	Farm Magazines	Total
1915	$ 25,294,000	$ 2,839,000	$ 28,133,000	1940	156,276,000	9,368,000	165,644,000
1916	33,405,000	3,455,000	36,860,000	1941	168,809,000	9,699,000	178,508,000
1917	41,449,000	3,775,000	45,224,000	1942	164,171,000	9,422,000	173,593,000
1918	54,652,000	3,780,000	58,432,000	1943	214,334,000	12,931,000	227,265,000
1919	87,378,000	7,001,000	94,379,000	1944	254,048,000	14,896,000	268,944,000
1920	119,875,000	9,591,000	129,466,000	1945	286,371,000	16,446,000	302,817,000
1921	87,711,000	6,224,000	93,936,000	1946	361,189,000	18,248,000	379,437,000
1922	91,735,000	6,031,000	97,766,000	1947	415,802,000	24,269,000	440,071,000
1923	110,160,000	7,477,000	117,637,000	1948	429,993,000	28,684,000	458,677,000
1924	123,911,000	7,858,000	131,769,000	1949	412,501,000	28,380,000	440,881,000
1925	143,166,000	8,002,000	151,168,000	1950	428,419,000	30,032,000	458,451,000
1926	155,694,000	9,348,000	165,041,000	1951	482,742,000	31,109,000	513,851,000
1927	171,116,000	9,984,000	181,100,000	1952	520,825,000	32,990,000	553,815,000
1928	171,046,000	9,953,000	180,999,000	1953	570,039,000	33,075,000	603,114,000
1929	185,723,000	10,544,000	196,266,000	1954	565,347,000	31,795,000	597,142,000
1930	182,484,000	9,634,000	192,118,000	1955	630,371,000	26,962,000	657,333,000
1931	150,303,000	6,948,000	157,251,000	1956	661,457,000	30,271,322	691,728,000
1932	104,907,000	5,667,000	110,574,000	1957	710,004,000	28,635,000	738,640,000
1933	92,577,000	4,780,000	97,357,000	1958	668,193,000	24,899,000	693,092,000
1934	111,254,000	6,405,000	117,659,000	1959	757,708,000	26,059,000	783,767,000
1935	115,907,000	7,001,000	122,908,000	1960	830,092,000	23,073,000	853,165,000
1936	133,015,000	8,633,000	141,648,000	1961	809,290,000	21,968,000	831,258,000
1937	150,380,000	9,646,000	160,026,000	1962	852,483,000	23,283,000	875,766,000
1938	132,736,000	8,428,000	141,164,000	1963	906,780,000	24,500,000	931,280,000
1939	141,648,000	9,190,000	150,838,000				

Source: Magazine Advertising Bureau. The calculations are based on the records of the Publishers Information Bureau. Sunday supplements are excluded.

ciple in mind that one publisher of the 1890's remarked: "If I can get a circulation of 400,000 I can afford to give my magazine away to anyone who will pay the postage." [3] As publisher after publisher applied the principle, magazine publishing became a mass-production enterprise.

As magazines came to depend on advertising for economic support, the role of the typical publisher underwent a major change. No longer was he interested in the reader as just a reader; he became interested in the reader as a consumer of the advertiser's goods and services. No longer was he a producer of just a convenience good; he became also the seller of a service, that of carrying the advertiser's message to a group of consumers—as magazines became more and more specialized in editorial appeal, to a carefully screened, homogeneous group of consumers. As a specialist in groups of consumers, the magazine publisher became a part of the whole system of marketing in the United States, as a later chapter will show in some detail.

As advertisers began paying for space on the basis of circulation, as advertising agencies began extending their services to clients, advertising men began to take a keen interest in magazine circulation; passing was the day when a publisher could regard circulation as a business secret. In the scramble for circulation that the low-priced magazine unleashed, some publishers padded their circulation figures. Understandably, advertisers sought some sound basis for evaluating circulation claims.

In 1899 the Association of American Advertisers made the first attempt to verify circulations of magazines and newspapers on the basis of uniform standards. But because publishers were hesitant to allow examination of their records, because of their lack of standardization in methods of bookkeeping and accounting, because of a shortage of funds, the attempt ended unsuccessfully in 1913 with the association heavily in debt to some of its sponsors. In 1913, however, the Association of National Advertisers set about establishing a new group to audit circulations. Meanwhile, the Association of American Advertisers, in conjunction with the Western Advertising Agents' Association, started a new audit association to replace the one which had failed. Out of these two new auditing

---

[3] Frank Presbrey, *The History and Development of Advertising* (Garden City, N.Y., 1929), p. 471.

groups, which merged in 1914, came the Audit Bureau of Circulations.

At first, publishers resented the advertisers' attempts to verify their circulation claims. Cyrus Curtis, when asked to join the Audit Bureau, remarked, "No one doubts the circulation statements of my company." He joined after A.B.C. representatives convinced him that by staying out he would be helping the cause of the circulation padders. The list of A.B.C. publications lengthened over the years so that eventually most of the large-circulation consumer magazines were members. The number of consumer magazines with membership in A.B.C. was twenty-six in 1914, 161 in 1924, 173 in 1934, 212 in 1944, 281 in 1954, and 292 in 1963.

Thus advertisers, through A.B.C., were a major force in changing the attitude of magazine publishers toward circulation. Far from being a trade secret, as in the days of *Harper's Weekly*, or something to be taken on faith, as when Curtis balked at joining A.B.C., circulation became a subject of close scrutiny. Advertisers wanted to know more than just how many copies a magazine sold; they wanted to know something about the quality of circulation as well. The A.B.C. reports told them how the circulation was obtained, how many subcribers actually paid for the magazine and under what arrangements, and a good deal of similar information that helped them to assess quality. For the publisher, of course, membership in A.B.C. became an asset; it was a reasonably convincing guarantee.

The A.B.C. was given power to suspend members guilty of padding their circulation figures. Rarely did any large publisher do so. When a new management took over Macfadden Publications, Inc., in 1941, however, it discovered that during the previous year *True Story* had falsified its sales by an average of 76,697 copies, *Liberty* by 21,185. The new management, which was not involved in the falsifications and which did not know about them until reexamination of the company's books, paid rebates to advertisers. Although A.B.C. sustained a charge of "fraudulent practices" against the company, it did not suspend the company from membership because the new management was not involved in the padding, because it cooperated fully with A.B.C. in the reaudit, and because it made full and voluntary refunds.[4]

---

[4] *Tide*, 15 (June 15, 1941) 57-58; 15 (July 15, 1941) 14.

Besides making publishers take a new attitude toward circulation, advertising to a large extent stimulated magazines to research, especially research to uncover data about the readers they served and their effectiveness in reaching those readers, research that had value in promoting their publications among advertisers.

Before 1920, advertisers and advertising agencies themselves, for the most part, accepted the efficacy of advertising largely on faith. They had seen the success of companies that spent large sums on advertising, and they concluded that advertising must be effective. Although even before 1920 some men wanted more conclusive evidence than that of advertising effectiveness, their suggestions were not generally accepted.

The decade from 1920 to 1930 was one of advances in merchandising generally. Marketing men learned a lesson from the plight of the Model T Ford. In early years, because it was cheap and durable, it sold well without much advertising. But after motorists began attaching importance to beauty, convenience, and comfort as well as to the prestige of owning an expensive car, the Model T sold poorly even with advertising. A conclusion was that advertising alone was not enough; the product itself was important. Market research became an important basis of product improvement; national advertising, in turn, became important as a means of capitalizing on product improvement. Then, too, after the crash of 1929, when advertising budgets were slashed, advertising men turned to research to document the effectiveness of advertising and to get the most for their clients' appropriations. Market research became an important part of the national advertising campaign.

As space came to be bought less on faith than on fact, magazine publishers, through their own staffs or through commercial agencies, undertook research of interest to the advertiser. Competition from other media and from other magazine publishers probably forced them to. By the late twenties, radio was rapidly becoming an important competitor for advertising appropriations; the gross advertising carried by networks jumped from $4,000,000 in 1927 to $10,000,000 in 1928 to $19,000,000 in 1929. Some magazines recognized the threat; the *Saturday Evening Post* ran many articles about stage and screen but paid the scantiest of editorial attention to radio. To convince advertisers that magazines were still important as a medium, publishers compiled evidence based on research.

Magazine research really dates from these efforts of magazines in the late twenties to sell themselves as a medium, according to W. H. Mullen, former director of the Magazine Advertising Bureau. Later, in the thirties when publishers saw that radio was not eating into their share of total advertising appropriations, magazine research became competitive. Each individual magazine strove to convince advertisers that it was the best medium for reaching their markets, and to do so the publisher had to learn a great deal about his reader group and its buying and reading habits. The development of sampling and polling techniques by Dr. George Gallup and others, and especially the success of those methods in predicting results of the 1936 Presidential election, no doubt gave a boost to magazine research.

Although magazines generally turned to research only in the late twenties and early thirties, a few individual publishers had set up research staffs earlier than that. The first marketing research organization of any kind in the United States was established by the Curtis Publishing Company in 1911, when the company created a division of commercial research as a part of its advertising department and installed Charles C. Parlin as head. Cyrus Curtis had been among the first magazine publishers to recognize the potentialities of national advertising, and the company's interest in research seemed an outgrowth of this recognition. The Curtis Publishing Company itself has described the origin of its research in this way: "It began because the Company sensed the need for an understanding of markets. Curtis realized the need for obtaining information about its own publications and about the industries of the advertisers and potential advertisers in its publications. It needed to know about its own products and about the products produced by these advertisers, about the market for these products and about the people who bought and consumed them." [5]

When Parlin went to work, Curtis had just recently bought *Country Gentleman,* and no one in the company knew much about agriculture; so Parlin as his first project made a six-month study of the agricultural implement industry. After he had finished a 460-page report about it, he conducted other surveys—one of department stores, which involved 37,000 miles of travel and 1,121 interviews; a census of distribution; a year-long study of the automotive industry. So many other studies followed it, studies

---

[5] Curtis Publishing Company, Research Department, "Research Department of Curtis Publishing Company" (Philadelphia, n.d.), p. 1.

of industries, buying habits, reading habits, and a host of kindred matters, that four volumes were needed to condense the findings of the Curtis research staff from 1911 through 1949. Reorganized from time to time, the research division in 1943 was given full departmental status equivalent to that of advertising, circulation, manufacturing, editorial, procurement, public relations, and the business office, and made directly responsible to the president.

What sort of research did magazines do? Some, a comparatively small amount, was conducted to guide their editorial staffs in turning out publications with reader appeal. Such research is discussed in a later chapter. The bulk of the research was conducted with the advertiser in mind.

Some research dealt with the readership of advertisements. Annually in the early 1960's *Advertising Age* was listing some fifty or so magazines that planned advertising readership studies during the year. Much of it dealt with the market for advertisers' goods and services. For example, *Popular Gardening* reported on the quantities of fertilizer, insecticides, weed killers, seeds, and gardening equipment that its readers had purchased the previous year and how much they planned to buy during the coming year. *Natural History* issued information on the special interests, possessions, and purchasing activity of its audience. *Boys' Life* showed the extent to which its readers were a market for bicycles, camping gear, candy, soft drinks, and radio equipment.

To convince advertisers that their publications reached the market that the advertisers wanted to reach, magazines gathered extensive data about their readers' geographical distribution; their standard of living; their age, sex, and marital status; their possessions; and so on. *Business Week*, in its "executive profile," for instance, detailed the corporate responsibility of its readers, their board memberships, their income and investments, and their influence on purchasing. *Better Homes and Gardens* offered information about its readers' "economic venturesomeness," their willingness to try new products, and about the extent to which they referred to clippings and back issues. *Life* reported in detail on its audience penetration as compared with that of the *Saturday Evening Post, Look,* and leading radio and television programs. *Reader's Digest* issued voluminous reports comparing its audience with that of six other publications in size, characteristics, reading habits, purchasing intentions, and so on.

Magazines also examined the readership of their own and competitors' publications; and while such studies might be termed editorial research, they seem to have been undertaken primarily to impress advertisers with the acceptance of a publication by its readers. In 1955, for instance, *McCall's* had been studying the magazine reading habits of American women for about twenty years. In a survey in 1946 it tried to learn which of twenty-two magazines women preferred and what sort of content in those publications most interested them. Its study in 1953 sought to learn just who read *McCall's* and just what part the magazine played in their daily lives. *Good Housekeeping* in 1954 sponsored a study to learn the attitudes of women toward eight magazines and their responses to advertising in those magazines.

Research became a weapon not only in the battles that magazines waged among themselves but also in their warfare with rival media. Studies were used to show advertisers that Magazine A reached a more select group of consumers than Magazines B or C, that its readers studied its pages with deep and abiding interest but just casually flipped the pages of other publications. Studies also were used to show the superiority of magazines over other media, as when *McCall's* in 1962 produced figures to show that it reached a larger audience of women than television programs.

As research grew in volume, advertising men became increasingly skeptical of findings intended to show the strengths of a given medium or of an individual publication or broadcast station. Much of such research, critics said, was conflicting, misleading, and self-seeking. In 1950 *Tide* questioned some 200 leaders in advertising, marketing, public relations, and allied fields on the objectivity of media research. More than 75 per cent of those replying agreed that criticism of media research was largely justified; 85 per cent believed that an impartial group should be set up to evaluate such research. One of the men who replied pretty well summed up objections to media research: "Too many surveys start out with intent to prove a specific point rather than to discover the truth about the point in question. Too many surveys use shoddy techniques or misuse known and reliable techniques. Too many media studies are conducted by the media themselves rather than have the work done by reputable and objective independent research organizations." [6]

---

[6] *Tide*, 24 (July 28, 1950) 20.

Yet if research were the promotional weapon of the publisher, it was the tool of the advertiser. What he wanted was not less research but less self-seeking research. What he wanted was research that helped him solve his own problems—how best to address potential consumers with a minimum of waste, for instance, and some estimate of the effectiveness of a proposed advertising campaign.

In 1957 the Advertising Research Foundation sought to raise $800,000 among publishers, advertisers, and agencies for a comprehensive study of magazine audiences. Alfred Politz Research was chosen to handle the project, which would cover thirty-four leading magazines and would involve 30,000 interviews. Publishers, however, felt that they were being pressured into the project by advertisers and their agencies. The large publishers, especially, objected that they had already made studies of their own, yet would have to bear about 75 per cent of the total cost; five of the major ones declined to participate. The Magazine Publishers Association announced that it could not support the project because of sharp differences of opinion over its value not only among publishers but also among advertising personnel, and because it posed legal problems for the association. The Advertising Research Foundation abandoned the whole plan in late March, 1958, "in view of the desirability of avoiding divisiveness within the industry."

Commercial research firms tried to give advertisers some of the information they were looking for. By 1963 at least six of them were offering advertisers comparable data on the various media.

To provide some check on research techniques, the Advertising Research Foundation began offering publishers a consulting service. Before undertaking studies, they could get confidential advice from the foundation and could learn if their proposed objectives, research design, procedures, and so on met the foundation's criteria.

In format and in layout, magazines also were influenced by advertising, which can take a good deal of credit for their improved appearance and legibility in the twentieth century. The development of advertising affected makeup and format in at least four ways: (1) it caused standardization of page sizes; (2) it caused editorial matter and advertising to be run side by side; (3) it stimulated the attractive presentation of editorial features; and (4) it increased the use of color in magazines.

When respected magazines first allowed advertisers to buy space, the publications confined advertising to a special section in the rear of the book. As the volume of advertising grew, at the turn of the century, the individual advertiser suffered, for his message, surrounded by other advertising, had an increasingly difficult time attracting the reader's attention. Consequently, many advertisers took their business to magazines with large pages, such as the *Saturday Evening Post* and some of the women's magazines. The large pages gave them room to experiment with arrangements of art and copy for the best display of their message and could easily accommodate editorial matter alongside the advertising. When Time Inc. was planning *Life* for its debut in 1936, Daniel Longwell insisted on a large page size not only to give pictures good display but because he knew that *Life* would be competing with large-paged *Collier's* and the *Saturday Evening Post*. Most magazines seeking advertising, however, increased their pages to about nine by twelve inches, a size adequate for display and for handling editorial matter alongside advertising.

Some standardization of page size held down the advertiser's costs, for once he had an advertisement prepared, he could use duplicate plates to run the same ad in several magazines. If a publisher expected to get advertising, he virtually had to adopt a standard page size. In 1929, when *World's Work, Golden Book, Review of Reviews,* and *Forum* simultaneously increased their page sizes, they did so in part to give the advertiser ample display space but also to permit him to use one set of plates in his advertising campaigns. Likewise in 1962 twenty-five state and local farm magazines adopted a uniform page size to encourage advertisers to buy space in all of them as a unit. By midcentury magazines had so settled on a few standard sizes for their pages that the printer of *Harper's,* believing that few modern presses could handle its outdated page size, raised his price 27 per cent. Instead of paying the increase, *Harper's* changed printers and page size.

If a publisher brought out an off-sized magazine, he could not expect to sell any great amount of space in it. Advertisers hestitated to use magazines of unusual size because of the expense of pre-paring special advertisements and plates. Gardner Cowles began *Quick* in 1949 as a vestpocket-sized magazine, and in a short time it had a circulation of more than a million. Rising production costs made it necessary for the magazine to seek advertising, but it found little. Some advertisers said that preparing special advertisements would be worthwhile if the circulation exceeded 2,000,000. Cowles decided that the future of the magazine as an advertising medium was too uncertain to risk the large cost of building up his circulation, so he disposed of the publication in 1953.

Pocket magazines did not conform to the standard size, but with rare exceptions they were not major advertising vehicles. When *Reader's Digest* opened its pages to advertising in 1955, it was able to offer advertisers a circulation large enough to justify the expense of preparing special advertisements and plates.

The page sizes that magazines settled on were large enough to accommodate editorial copy alongside advertising. At first, the aim of the advertiser seems to have been to get his message out of the special advertising section in the rear of the magazine, where it was lost among others. On a page along with or adjacent to editorial copy, the advertisement would be more likely to catch the reader's eye. In time, advertisers decided that some positions were more certain of reader attention than others: pages 1, 3, 5; the page facing the first page of editorial copy; the first page following the body of editorial matter; and so on. The Campbell Soup Company for so many years bought the first right-hand page after the body of editorial matter that the page became known in magazine and advertising offices as "the Campbell Soup position."

The national magazine was still in its infancy when publishers freed advertising from its segregated sections. Edward W. Bok has taken credit for opening the gate. In 1896, he recalled in his autobiography, he began carrying parts of *Ladies' Home Journal* fiction into the advertising pages to give them increased readership. Before long, most magazines were running at least some editorial matter alongside advertisements. From then on, editors and publishers experimented with techniques to build reader traffic throughout the entire magazine—running cartoons in the rear pages, for instance, or displaying major articles throughout the book—so that advertisers in all positions would benefit. It was to increase reader exposure to advertising that Otis Weise, editor and publisher, completely redesigned the makeup of *McCall's* in 1950. He compared his plan for increasing the amount of timely copy alongside advertising to traffic planning by cities to give stories in every neighborhood a fair chance in attracting customers. That basic idea was behind the redesign of numerous other magazines later in the decade and in the early 1960's. *McCall's* itself underwent a thorough overhaul after Herbert Mayes succeeded Weise as editor in 1958. Mayes gave a free hand to his art director, Otto Storch, and a dramatic emphasis on design made *McCall's* for a time the most talked-about magazine in advertising circles.

Two things forced the editor to pay increasing attention to the attractive presentation of editorial material—the larger page sizes magazines settled on, and the advances of advertisers in displaying their sales messages. There was a limit to the size of page that the reader would accept with little or no typographical adornment; because many magazines adopted standard pages of about nine by twelve inches, editors had to use such devices as hand-lettered titles, white space, drawings and photographs, and so on to break up the gray monotony of their pages. Moreover, editorial copy had to compete with advertising copy for the reader's attention; and as advertisers made increasingly skillful use of art work, typography, and white space, editors were encouraged to dress up their own pages. In time they came to realize that design could contribute as much to the personality of their magazines as the editorial content they ran. Magazines improved considerably in visual appeal during the twentieth century, especially after World War II, and by the early 1960's editorial display had so adopted the tone and methods of advertising display that the two at times were in conflict.

As advertisers sought maximum effectiveness for their advertisements, they began using color to attract attention, to contribute toward realism in photographs of their products, to identify their products or trademarks, to suggest qualities associated with their products, such as warmth or coolness, and so on. In the 1880's, color in magazines was a rarity; by the 1930's, it had become commonplace, but its big growth was after World War II. The share of pages in two or more colors rose from 29.8 per cent of total advertising space in 1939 to 49.3 per cent twenty years later, the number of color pages from 5,746 to 14,860.

A reader who compared copies of magazines of the mid-1930's with those of the late 1950's could see for himself how the use of four-color advertising had grown. Take, for instance, *McCall's*. In 1936, it carried 256 four-color pages, which made up 36 per cent of its total advertising space. In 1946, it ran 552 pages or 54 per cent, and in 1959 it carried 633 pages, 63 per cent. Or consider the

New Yorker. It carried 296 four-color pages in 1936, 746 in 1946, and 1,240 in 1959. The story was the same for magazine after magazine.

To gain a competitive advantage, *McCall's* in 1962 began charging no more for advertising space in color than for black and white. New presses, the company said, made a single rate possible. *Editor & Publisher,* the newspaper trade weekly, responded by taking space in the New York *Times* and *Herald Tribune* to deride the move. All previous users of color in *McCall's* should ask for a rebate, the advertisement said, and current users of black and white "should ask for a discount because they know it costs less to produce their ad than it does one in color." After *McCall's* protested that the *Editor & Publisher* advertisement was "irresponsible" and "presumptuous," both newspapers publicly acknowledged that they should not have run it. With its issue of October, 1963, *McCall's* dropped its one-rate plan. It lowered its rates for black and white advertising because, it said, of "competitive circumstances."

Color was one of the advantages that magazines retained over their competitor television. The networks were broadcasting some programs in color in the early 1960's, but receivers were still too costly to interest most viewers and production costs were too high to interest most advertisers. Even so, the widespread use of color on television seemed an ultimate certainty—some experts looked for it by the end of the decade—and some leaders in the magazine industry were taking a special interest in color as a tool of effective printed communication. Newspapers made rapidly growing use of color in the 1950's and early 1960's. Magazine publishers, however, seemed to fear their competition less than that of television.

Another influence of advertising after 1900 was on the editorial content of magazines. The amount and nature of advertising pressure on editorial policies, and the amount of resistance to it, can scarcely be estimated with any accuracy. One can collect instances of suppression to please the advertiser, as George Seldes and Upton Sinclair have done for newspapers; but one often cannot clearly distinguish between what was "suppression" and what was rejection for sound editorial reasons. And how to gauge indirect editorial pressure? Independent as an editor may have been consciously, to what extent may he have been subconsciously influenced by the mere existence of advertising support? Certainly some publishers yielded to pressure, direct or indirect; certainly others resisted it. A safe generalization perhaps is that direct advertising pressure—especially successful pressure—was much less than the average reader may guess; that most advertising pressure was subtle and just a part of a greater pressure, the economic struggle for survival, a point developed at length in a later chapter.

This is not to say that advertisers did not try to influence editorial policies and sometimes succeeded. Although historians seem to agree that the muckraking movement died from a number of causes, they also seem to agree that financial retaliation against publishers was partly responsible for its end. Advertising pressure in 1937 kept *Ken* from becoming the liberal magazine that some of its founders intended, according to George Seldes, for a time one of its editors.[7] *Ken* was published by David Smart of Esquire, Inc., who originally saw it as a cross between the *Nation* and *Life*, a lively liberal magazine telling "the truth behind the news" and tapping a mass circulation among American liberals. But, Seldes charged, Smart kept watering down its content, kept scrapping its best features, as advertisers threatened not only *Ken* but also Smart's prosperous *Esquire*.

Esquire itself, in April, 1941, publicly apologized to its advertisers after running an article, "Go Get a Guitar," a plea for group singing in which the author said a guitar was better accompaniment than a piano. Six months after the article appeared, *Esquire* ran a full-page editorial which said: "We lost all our piano ads, like so many clay pigeons. . . . We can and do beg the pardon of the piano makers, severally and collectively, but we have no kick coming as we kiss the ads goodbye. We earned the rap we're taking. . . ."[8]

Certainly it was advertising pressure, direct or indirect, that in 1948 and 1949 inspired several magazines to campaign against the tax of 20 per cent on cosmetics. The cosmetics industry was a large advertiser; in 1949, advertisements for toiletries and toilet goods accounted for $37,434,000 of the $413 million spent on national advertising in magazines. The women's magazines, of course, got a large share of it; and among movie magazines, cosmetics advertising was the single largest source of advertising income.

---

[7] George Seldes, " 'Ken'—The Inside Story," *Nation*, 146 (April 30, 1938) 497-500.
[8] "Torch Song, Pianissimo, to the Piano Makers," *Esquire*, 15 (April, 1941) 6.

In 1948 and 1949, *Tide* reported a campaign conducted by several magazines for repeal of the 20 per cent tax on cosmetics. One of the first moves was by William Cotton, president of the Ideal Publishing Company, which published *Movie Stars, Movie Life, Personal Romances,* and *Intimate Romances.* In an editorial in all four of those magazines and in newspaper advertisements in five cities, Mr. Cotton urged women to combat the "man-made tax on feminine necessities." [9] His magazines played such themes as "protest the tax on your attractiveness" and "is it a luxury to be attractive?" The promotion manager of Ideal Publishing Company prepared kits of antitax materials for 40,000 women's clubs. Other magazines joined in the campaign. The beauty editor of *Screenland* and *Silver Screen* asked readers to protest the tax to their Congressmen. Fawcett Publications in its *Today's Woman* ran an article in which "an angry housewife sounds off on luxury taxes." [10]

A former editor, writing under a pseudonym in *Harper's* for October, 1962, charged that the dividing line on fashion magazines was no longer between editors and advertising departments but between editors whose pages brought in revenue and editors who merely edited—between the fashion and beauty departments, which could be used to coax advertising, and the fiction and features, which could not. The change was a development of the previous ten years, as she saw it, and she attributed it to the increasing difficulties of fashion magazines to attract advertising, to their loss of editorial authority, and to the plethora of publications, all much alike, serving the same basic market. As a result, she said, the editors had succumbed to a series of advertising, promotional, and even managerial pressures, the first two characterized by the word "must": "A must is a garment (with appropriate fabric credit), a travel location, a car, even furniture and sterling silver —anything to which 'editorial support' has been pledged."

Addressing the Television Bureau of Advertising in November, 1962, Paul S. Willis, president of the Grocery Manufacturers Association, said that his industry got a better editorial break from newspapers and magazines than from television, despite its heavy advertising expenditures on television. In the previous year, grocery manufacturers had invited sixteen major magazines to consider publishing articles favorable to the food industry, he said: "We suggested to the publishers that the day was here when their

---

[9] *Tide,* 22 (Sept. 24, 1948) 44.
[10] *Tide,* 23 (Jan. 28, 1949) 49.

editorial department and business department might better understand their interdependent relationships as they contribute to the operating results of the company and as their operations affect the advertiser—their bread and butter." As evidence of the resulting cooperation, Willis cited a number of favorable articles published in nearly a dozen magazines.[11]

On the other hand, a number of editors and publishers treated advertisers in a manner ranging from indifference to downright belligerence. They recognized, of course, that a minority of advertisers might withdraw their support when editorial content seemed inconsistent with their interests. The Knights of Columbus, for instance, withdrew its advertising from *Harper's* in 1960 after its supreme knight had attacked one of the magazine's contributors as unfit to write for decent persons and had criticized the placement of his organization's advertisements. The general manager of the American Dairy Association in March, 1961, charged that magazines had published many premature and irresponsible articles about nutrition and diets. One of the magazines that disturbed the association was the *Reader's Digest*, which had carried articles about pricing of milk and the dangers of eating animal fats. The association contended that the magazine should have notified it of the articles in advance so that it could have refuted them or withdrawn its advertisements from the issues in which they appeared. Although the dairy association would not try to influence magazine policies, its spokesmen said, it would advertise only "in magazines which have respect for editorial integrity."

From the founding of the *New Yorker*, its editor, Harold Ross, insisted on an editorial department free from any domination by the business office; and he was fortunate in having as a major financial backer Raoul Fleischmann, who believed in a separation of the editorial and business functions. "Great advertising mediums are operated for the reader first, for profits afterwards," the magazine observed in its code of publishing practice in 1933, and that attitude was reflected in an intraoffice memorandum by the advertising director more than thirty years later: "We must all bear in mind always that our first obligation is to our readers and our second obligation is to our present and past advertisers." Ross insisted on the right to veto all advertising copy; after his death, the editorial and advertising staffs cooperated in turning down

[11] *Advertising Age,* 33 (Nov. 19, 1962) 1.

thousands of dollars worth of advertising each year. Reasons for rejection varied. Among them were that the product or the advertisement itself was in poor taste, that the product would not appeal to readers of the magazine, that copy and layout were below its standards of quality, and that space was not available. The editorial staff complained that the magazine carried too much advertising; it could not, it said, obtain enough editorial content of quality to balance the advertising. For that reason, the magazine in 1960 limited its number of advertising pages. The *New Yorker's* treatment of advertisers struck some as cavalier; one correspondent complained in the letters column of *Advertising Age* in 1960: "Their salesmen do not see you, they grant you an audience; their advertising departments do not sell advertising, they accept it."

Editorial staff members of Time Inc., from its first lean years onward, are said to have viewed advertisers with what amounted almost to hostility. Briton Hadden himself, one of the founders of *Time*, seemed to delight in running stories that advertisers would object to; and in 1925, after his advertising manager had just landed the Fisher Body account, Hadden so antagonized Fisher Body and Packard with a story that they at once canceled fifty-two pages of advertising.[12] Other advertisers, among them Chrysler and Boeing, withdrew their business because of stories they objected to; but like Packard and Fisher, they later returned. An official of Union Carbide and Carbon, which spent about $100,000 a year in *Time*, once remarked: "The last time they ran a big chemical story I didn't know about it in time to get one of our ads into the issue." [13] Even so disenchanted a former employee of Time Inc. as Dwight Macdonald, who was on the staff of *Fortune* from 1929 to 1936, said that in the early thirties the *Fortune* management stood firmly against attempts at advertising pressure. For calling the Matson liner *Malolo* by its nickname among travelers, "Malolo the Roller," he said, *Fortune* lost Time Inc. some $50,000 in advertising. Macdonald's complaint was that Henry Luce and his editors, defiant to crude forms of pressure, were susceptible to subtle forms of influence, such as a discreet word from a banker or businessman.[14]

Editorial independence at the Curtis Publishing Company was

[12] Noel F. Busch, *Briton Hadden: A Biography of the Co-Founder of Time* (New York, 1949), pp. 190-91.
[13] "Life with Time" *Forbes*, 72 (Aug. 15, 1953) 12-13.
[14] Dwight Macdonald, " 'Fortune' Magazine," *Nation*, 144 (May 8, 1937) 527.

established under Cyrus H. K. Curtis, Edward Bok, and George Horace Lorimer, and thereafter was taken for granted, according to Ben Hibbs, who edited the *Saturday Evening Post* for two decades after 1942.[15] Most national advertisers, he thought, were sold on it as a matter of sound business.

And indeed both editorial and business staff members of various magazines have justified editorial independence on a business basis, apart from responsibilities to their readers, which they also acknowledge. In the long run, they have held, editorial purity is profitable to publisher and advertiser alike. Their arguments have gone something like this: "The advertiser's money is wasted if his ads aren't believed. To be believed, his ads must be in a publication that readers trust. And if advertisers start having a say-so about editorial content, then it's not going to be long before readers find out and lose respect for the magazine." An advertising executive on one large magazine once explained to the author why he had been pleased with a sharp division between its editorial and business functions: "We do business with a lot of advertisers, and if I start to use a little influence on the editorial staff for one advertiser, I'm in a spot where every advertiser can ask me to do him a favor. This way is easier. They know now that I don't have any influence, and I can treat them all alike."

What bothered some observers, especially after television had emerged as a competitor for revenues, was not so much direct advertising pressure as the pervasiveness of the sales pitch in magazines. Critic Marya Mannes in 1962 found two major ways in which advertising impinged on and affected editorial material: "at the one extreme it is difficult at first glance to tell what is a feature and what is an ad; at the other, incongruous advertising is jarringly juxtaposed with editorial matter." [16] Four years earlier William Nichols, editor and publisher of *This Week*, had publicly decried the growth of magazine advertisements that tried to fool the reader into thinking they were editorial features. Louis Lyons, curator of the Nieman Fellowships at Harvard, complained to magazine publishers in 1963 that they had structured their publications so the reader could not miss the advertisements even though he might have a hard time finding and completing an article

---

[15] Ben Hibbs "You Can't Edit a Magazine by Arithmetic," *Journalism Quarterly,* 27 (Fall, 1950) 370.
[16] Marya Mannes, "The Intruders," *Reporter,* 27 (Aug. 16, 1962) 51.

he wanted to read. And an English professor gave *New Republic* readers a detailed, caustic account of an incongruous juxtaposition he had found in a recent issue of the *New Yorker:* a moving essay by Negro novelist James Baldwin nestled amidst advertisements for expensive furs, diamond clips, pearls, and other luxuries.[17]

To test charges of that sort, the staff of the *Columbia Journalism Review* examined current issues of the eight magazines leading in advertising revenues. In varying degrees, it found advertisements to look like editorial features, editorial space chewed up to permit eccentric placement of advertising, semiadvertising or promotional matter in editorial columns, and clashes of editorial pages in color with advertising. Only rarely did it find a "jarring juxtaposition" of advertisements and editorial matter—partly, it ruefully noted, because some magazines did not carry material of sufficient editorial weight opposite advertisements to cause any disturbance.[18]

In sum, what happened, then, was that advertising came to magazines in the third quarter of the nineteenth century as a timid guest, shut off in its own room, tolerated rather than welcomed. In the 1890's, publishers discovered that the guest, far from just paying its own bills, could foot the bills of the entire establishment. The guest became an important member of the household—in time one with a voice in just how the household should be managed.

---

[17] John Seelye, "Black on White," *New Republic*, 147 (Dec. 29, 1962) 21-23.
[18] "Advertising Meets Editorial," *Columbia Journalism Review*, 1 (Fall, 1962) 14-22.

3

The Expanding Magazine Market

Four times in the first half of the twentieth century, gloomy observers shook their heads and speculated over a drop in the extent of magazine reading. The first time was after World War I when the automobile became a pleasure and business vehicle for all classes of people instead of a novelty for the well-to-do. "The automobile will take people out of their homes," observers said, "and they won't have time for magazine reading." The second time was in the mid-twenties when radio aerials sprouted from housetops across the country and stations scrambled to affiliate with national networks. The third time was in 1927 when the movies found their voice. The fourth time was after World War II when television boomed as radio had a quarter of a century earlier.

Despite pessimistic forecasts from time to time, however, magazines had a tremendous growth after 1900. The number of magazine readers increased remarkably. When Frank Munsey brought out his *Munsey's Magazine* in 1893, he later estimated, there were about 250,000 magazine purchasers in the United States. By 1899, the ten-cent magazine, he further estimated, had increased the number to 750,000. In 1947, in its nationwide audience study, the Magazine Advertising Bureau found 32,300,000 magazine reading families—those in which members could identify specific items from recent issues.[1] In 1959 a study for the Magazine Advertising Bureau and the Magazine Publishers Association conservatively estimated that 41,492,000 households —80.8 per cent of the U.S. total—comprised the magazine market.[2] The number of individual magazines also increased; there were probably well over a thousand more magazines in the United States in 1963 than in 1900. The aggregate circulation of all magazines in the nation mounted steadily, and the sales of individual publications soared from thousands to millions. In 1900 probably just one magazine, *Comfort,* had a circulation of a million copies an issue; in 1963, at least fifty general and farm magazines had circulations of 1,000,000 or more, and one of them had sales of more than 14,500,000 for its domestic edition alone. Before examining the expansion of the magazine industry in detail, let us look at some reasons for its growth.

The burgeoning of the magazine industry was the result of an expanding market in a twofold sense: a growing demand for advertisers' goods and services, and a growing demand for the publishers' own products, magazines. The magazine industry shared in the expansion of the American economy as a whole in the twentieth century, just as did manufacturers of automobiles, refrigerators, and dentifrices, and such other communications media as newspapers and broadcasting.

Under a system of advertising support, in which the publisher performed a marketing function, the fortunes of the magazine industry came to depend closely upon the health of the economy in general. When the national magazine emerged in the late nineteenth century, the magazine publisher became a dealer in consumer groups as well as a dealer in editorial matter. He decided upon a group of consumers which advertisers wanted to reach, and he attracted the consumers to his magazine with a carefully planned editorial formula. Just as often, perhaps, he issued his publication and let it find its audience. Then he sold advertisers space in his magazine to tell their sales stories to the readers he collected. Selling his magazine for less than production cost, he took his profits from advertising.

[1] Magazine Advertising Bureau, *Nationwide Magazine Audience Survey: Report 2—Individuals, Report 4—Families* (New York, 1948).
[2] Magazine Advertising Bureau, *"The Profitable Difference": A Study of the Magazine Market* (New York, 1960).

Counting on national advertising for his revenue, the magazine publisher came to depend upon the demand for advertisers' goods and services. Economists have shown that over the years magazine revenues from national advertising have matched consumer spending. In fact, Richard G. Gettell, chief economist for Time Inc., once suggested that consumer spending is an important forecasting tool, for if one can obtain reasonable predictions about the economy as a whole, he can pretty closely guess how many dollars magazines will get from national advertising.[3]

From 1935 to 1950, Gettell noted, changes in the amounts that consumers spent for goods were matched by almost exactly proportional changes in amounts spent on national advertising in all principal media. Consumer spending and national advertising paralleled one another through depression and recession in the thirties, through mobilization and war in the early forties, through reconversion in the late forties. The media did not share alike in national advertising throughout the whole period. But the share that magazines received was the most stable of that of any medium in relation to both consumer spending and total advertising expenditures. Year after year, except for a dip in World War II, magazines took in from $3.50 to $3.75 for every $1,000 that consumers spent for goods; year after year their percentage of total advertising revenues fluctuated the least. What Gettell was saying in substance, then, was that the revenues which magazines derived from advertising were exceedingly sensitive to changes in the overall level of consumer spending. As consumer spending rose or fell, so did magazine income from advertising, hence the usefulness of consumer spending as a predictive tool. Others have commented on the same point. Economists of the Federal Communications Commission concluded in 1947: "Of the three media, broadcast appears to be the least sensitive to changes in disposable personal income, magazines most sensitive."[4]

As Americans spent increasing sums to raise their material standard of living, magazines benefited from the expanding market for advertisers' goods and services. But the publisher, besides selling his service to advertisers, had his own product to market in com-

---

[3] Richard Glenn Gettell, "What Will Advertising Be Like in a Mobilized Economy?" (talk at thirty-third annual meeting, American Association of Advertising Agencies, Hotel Greenbrier, White Sulphur Springs, W.Va., April 20, 1951).
[4] Federal Communications Commission, *An Economic Study of Standard Broadcasting* (Washington, 1947), p. 60.

petition with claims on readers' time by other media and activities. Helping him to sell his magazines despite this competition were a number of changes in American life in the twentieth century, among them a great increase in leisure time and advances in education and literacy.

Marketing men are fond of saying that "the market is a diamond." People comprising the horizontal band across the middle of the diamond—those in what is loosely termed "the middle class"—buy the great bulk of consumer goods and the great bulk of magazines. During the twentieth century, as the population increased and as purchasing power became more and more equitably distributed, the diamond grew in size and changed in shape: the top and bottom of it drew together and flattened out the center. Let us see what happened.

The market, in raw numbers, expanded enormously as a result of population increases. When Munsey brought out his low-priced magazine in 1893, the estimated population was 66,970,000; in 1960 it was 178,464,000, excluding Alaska and Hawaii. For every two persons in the United States in Munsey's day, there were five in 1960.

But of greater importance, there were more people with more money to buy things. True, even in the 1960's, there were stubborn pockets of poverty and of actual want, and there was still some disparity of income, but certainly not on the grand scale of 1900 when Andrew Carnegie's personal tax-free income of $20,000,000 was at least 20,000 times that of the average workingman's. The graduated income tax, increasing productivity, the powerful bargaining position of the labor unions after 1932—those and other things narrowed the extremes in purchasing power and widened the American middle class. About 7,000,000 American families had incomes of more than $10,000 in 1963, nearly three times the total of just a decade previously, according to the National Industrial Conference Board. Those families had come to spend their money on an increasingly wide range of luxuries and comforts, proportionately less on food, clothing, and necessities. What all of this meant was that more and more persons could afford magazines, no longer the expensive luxury they had been in the nineteenth century, and more and more persons were a market for the advertisers who bought space in magazines.

The spread of popular education was also important to the

magazine industry and its advertisers, for studies show that education and magazine reading tend to go hand-in-hand. In 1890, just about the time that the national magazine was born, only seven out of every hundred boys and girls aged fourteen through seventeen attended high school; in the early sixties, the figure was close to ninety. The school term lengthened, and the number of pupils who dropped out declined. The 1,838,000 pupils who got their high school diplomas in 1960 represented about twenty times the number of graduates in 1900. College enrollments, too, increased tremendously. Rising slowly from 1900 to 1920, they spurted between 1920 and 1940, dropped during World War II, and shot up after 1946. For every student on college campuses in 1900, there were about fifteen in 1960. Magazines benefited—not only from the growing audience with interests they could serve but also from the expanding range of interests.

Certainly another factor in the growth of the magazine market was an increase in the amount of leisure time resulting from a shorter work week in business and industry, from a lightening of household tasks by electrical appliances, from improvements in transportation, and so on. The spread of inexpensive electricity, which meant convenient home lighting, probably induced many persons to spend more time reading. In the nineties, magazines circulated primarily among the upper and middle classes. One reason, no doubt, was that they had the most time to read them, for they could best afford the cheap domestic help to perform many of the jobs done by electricity in the average home of the sixties.

The typical homemaker in the sixties surely had more free time than her counterpart of 1900. The family she cared for was smaller. Her household tasks had become less burdensome, if no less monotonous, over the years, as appliances did many of the jobs she had once done by hand. Her problems of cooking and storing food had become lightened by gas, then electric ranges, by electric refrigerators and food freezers. Many of the tasks she once performed in the home had been taken over by manufacturers and service establishments—by commercial bakeries (which even sliced bread for her), by food processors, by laundries and dry cleaners, by manufacturers of baby food, and so forth. Her husband, too, had more free time than his counterpart of 1900. In both factory and office, the work week had become shortened over the intervening years, and the paid vacation of two or three weeks had become a standard benefit.

This increase in leisure was accompanied by an increased competition for the typical American's time and attention. Consider, for instance, the competition that the magazine received from just the other mass media of communication.

In the fifties and early sixties, the medium that gave publishers their largest share of worries was television. Actually, television had existed experimentally since the twenties. A regular schedule of broadcasts, begun in 1939, was halted by the war. Television started to become a major medium in the immediate postwar period, but its development was retarded for almost four years by the Federal Communications Commission, which froze all new frequency assignments in 1948 while it considered problems of channel allocation and color television. Once the freeze was lifted, television grew with astonishing rapidity. Before the end of the fifties, Americans were devoting more time to it than to any activity, except sleeping, and were spending more on sets than on any possessions except homes and automobiles. In just ten years, television penetrated into more homes than the telephone had in eighty years. The 577 commercial and 68 noncommercial stations on the air in 1962 were broadcasting their programs into 91 per cent of all American homes, and the average receiver was tuned in for slightly more than five hours a day. By then, advertisers were spending more than $1.6 billion a year on the new medium. By then, too, television had become so powerful and pervasive a medium that, directly or indirectly, it had affected all of the other media.

From their beginnings, of course, magazines had faced competition. Their chief rivals in 1900 were the newspaper and the book, the newspaper perhaps more than the book, but the competition multiplied with a rush in the years that followed. When the century was young, movies were still used to round out vaudeville bills or to entice coins from the curious in nickelodeons. By the twenties, however, they had emerged as an important form of popular entertainment with marble palaces of their own. They provided many Americans with one of their chief pastimes until midcentury, when television gave each family its own private theater. In 1948, just before television began its swift expansion,

the nation had some 20,000 movie theaters with a weekly attendance estimated at about 90,000,000. A decade later the number of
movie houses had dropped by almost half, but an industry survey
showed that theaters were still selling 54,200,000 tickets a week.
The movies may have come upon hard times, but they had by no
means vanished.

In the twenties, radio spread across the nation with a speed
unmatched until television came along. The number of broadcasting stations climbed swiftly: 30 in 1922, 608 a decade later, 923 in
1942. So did the number of homes with sets: 60,000 in 1922,
16,800,000 in 1932, 30,800,000 in 1942. About 95 per cent of all
U.S. adults were daily radio listeners when television began its
ascent. Although television drained advertising revenues, changed
the nature of radio broadcasting, and altered listening patterns, it
did not drive radio into extinction. Each year manufacturers continued to turn out at least as many sets as before television appeared, and the 94 per cent of U.S. homes with receivers in 1962
were served by 3,794 A.M. and 1,062 F.M. stations.

As the century grew older, printing presses ground out an increasing volume of newspapers and books, with which magazines
had to compete for the reader's leisure. Although the number of
newspapers declined from its peak in 1909, total daily circulation
rose from 15,102,000 in 1900 to 59,848,688 in 1962. The marketing
of books was revolutionized in 1926 when the Book-of-the-Month
Club sent out 4,500 copies of Sylvia Townsend Warner's *Lolly
Willowes* to its subscribers. By the end of the fifties, the club had
distributed so many books that the shelves of all of the libraries in
the United States could not hold them. Other book clubs sprang
up; directories in 1963 listed more than seventy-five of them—
clubs for antique collectors, gardeners, executives, amateur historians, drama and art lovers, science fans, yachtsmen, racial and
religious minorities, clubs for a long list of tastes and interests.

Perhaps as revolutionary as the book club was the modern
revival of inexpensive paperback books. Just before World War II,
publishers began loading them onto racks in depots, bus stations,
drugstores, and bookstores. One of the pioneers, Pocket Books,
Inc., in just eight years sold more than 200 million copies of 475
titles. The paperback and the magazine had much in common in
distribution and in potential reader market. Perhaps for that reason
a number of magazine companies, among them Curtis, Dell, Faw-

cett, Macfadden-Bartell, and Popular, began to publish them. At first paperbacks were reprints of hard-cover books and sold for a quarter. Eventually, however, some were original works. Eventually, too, the low-priced, mass-marketed paperbacks were joined by the so-called quality paperbounds, which sold for one, two, or more dollars. Although some companies had been selling dollar paperbacks for years, the big boom of scholarly and literary books in paper covers came during the mid-fifties. Anchor Books had sold a million copies of its line by 1955, and other publishers began scanning their backlists for possible titles. Paperbacks accounted for more than 30 per cent of all book titles published in 1962, when publishers issued 7,056 of them, 1,866 aimed at the mass market.

Especially during and after World War II, magazines got some competition for their readers' time from house organs—newspapers or magazines published by industries and businesses for their employees and customers. There were a few house organs as the century turned, and a rash of them appeared during World War I but died with the peace. A number of forces during the twenties and thirties encouraged the growth of the house publication. The gains of labor unions and a widening audience for the labor press; trends in government, which some segments of management saw as a threat to the free enterprise system; a sharpening sense of public relations in the business world; the growing complexity of industry, with its widely dispersed plants and its system of subcontracting, all of which made it hard for the worker to see how he contributed to the finished product—all of those things helped to explain the emergence of the house organ as an important means of industrial communication. There were perhaps 2,400 house organs in the United States in 1940. During World War II, they multiplied at a fantastic rate, a rate accelerated by tax policies and by the need to train new workers in defense industries. In 1963 there were perhaps somewhat between 6,500 and 10,000 of them, some as slickly elegant as commercial magazines, a few with circulations of more than a million.

More and more, as the century advanced, the mass media filled the American's eyes and ears with sights and sounds, and a spate of other activities—mahjong, contract bridge, and canasta; miniature golf, full-scale golf, and bowling; candid camera photography, model airplaning, and hot-rod racing—rushed in to fill any gaps in his leisure time.

Why was the magazine industry able to grow in the face of such competition? One good guess, and there is some documentation to support it, is that each new medium has stimulated rather than diminished use of the existing media. Book publishers learned that a Hollywood dramatization of a book spurred rather than harmed the sale of copies. Newspapers feared infant radio so much that some of them would not run program listings (one reason of course was that broadcasting stations competed for advertising as well as audience); yet as a larger number of persons listened to radio newscasts and to broadcasts of current events, newspaper circulations increased at a rate faster than the population. When television began to turn its cameras on news events, many publishers no longer feared the new medium as a threat to circulation; television, they thought, sharpened their readers' appetites for printed news.

A clue to understanding this phenomenon may lie in the communications behavior of Americans. To think of the audience of magazines as an entity distinct from the audiences of the other media is as misleading as to think of all members of the magazine audience as cut from the same pattern. Individuals varied tremendously in how many magazines they read (if indeed they read any at all), in the amount of time they spent with them as compared with the other media, and in the uses they made of them. One general principle emerging from many audience studies was what Paul Lazarsfeld and Patricia Kendall called the "all or none tendency," the tendency of a person above average in exposure to one medium to be above average in exposure to all. For example, in the forties they found that the great majority of book readers were also magazine readers, that radio fans were likely to be both movie fans and regular magazine readers as well.[5] They thought that two possibilities, interest and opportunity, accounted for that tendency. If a person were interested in a particular type of content, he could better satisfy his interests by using all of the media than by using just one or two. If a person were too busy to spend much time with any medium, he probably made little use of all of them.

The "all or none" tendency seemed to apply not just to the

[5] Paul Lazarsfeld and Patricia Kendall, "The Communications Behavior of the Average American," in Wilbur Schramm, editor, *Mass Communications* (Urbana, Ill., 1960), pp. 425-37.

use of all of the media but also to the use of magazines alone; a person who regularly read magazines at all was likely to read not just one but several. Lazarsfeld and Wyant commented on this tendency in their study of overlapping magazine audiences, published in 1937.[6] A decade later, there was evidence of it in the national magazine audience survey conducted by the Magazine Advertising Bureau, which reported that approximately half of all magazine readers read four or more magazines, that about 32 per cent read two or three, that about 18 per cent read only one. According to the study of the M.A.B. in 1959, 44 per cent of all households qualified as heavy or medium heavy in magazine exposure; one or both heads of the family had looked at six or more issues during the week of the interviews.

But as Lazarsfeld cautioned, the all or none tendency had many exceptions. For instance, studies showed some sharp differences between heavy magazine readers who were light in television viewing and heavy television viewers who were light users of magazines. Cornelius DuBois, director of research for a New York advertising agency, reported some of the differences he found in a study of the communications patterns of women:

Two-thirds of the readers but only one-third of the viewers are in the $5,000-and-over income bracket.

Over half of the readers but only one-fifth of the viewers have white-collar husbands, the remainder in each case being primarily in blue-collar jobs, but including some families where the husband is retired, or a student, or where there is no husband in the family.

Five-sixths of the readers compared with one-half of the viewers have at least some high school education.

And there is just as wide a gap between the two groups in general activity, if going out can be taken as an index of activity.[7]

W. R. Simmons and Associates also found significant differences between readers and viewers: "Proportionately more people in the former group are younger, have high social position, more education, higher household income, and better occupations." [8]

Once television had losts its novelty, it apparently did little to cut down the amount of reading; what it seemed to affect was the kinds of reading people did. In one of the most thorough studies

---

[6] Paul F. Lazarsfeld and Rowena Wyant, "Magazines in 90 Cities—Who Reads What?" *Public Opinion Quarterly*, 1 (Oct., 1937) 35-36.

[7] Cornelius DuBois, "What Is the Difference Between a Reader and a Viewer?" *Mediascope*, 3 (Oct., 1959) 47.

[8] *Advertising Age*, 34 (Aug. 5, 1963) 1, 103.

of the impact of television on children, Wilbur Schramm and two of his associates found that it performed what could be called a displacement function.[9] The chief part that television played in the lives of children was in stimulating fantasy seeking and fantasy behavior. By displacing escape activity, it cut into their comic reading, movie attendance, play time. But it was far less important as a source of information useful in daily living. Therefore, it had little effect on their reading of general magazines, books, and newspapers. In a study of library circulations in Illinois, Edwin Parker found further evidence that television displaced escapist fare rather than sources of serious information. It had cut down library circulations by slightly more than one book per capita a year, a drop accounted for by a decline in the circulation of fiction. It evidently had brought about no change in the circulation of nonfiction, which however had grown for other reasons. Perhaps consistent with that displacement function was the growth of magazines of serious information and ideas. Between 1947 and 1963, the news magazines more than doubled their aggregate circulation, for instance, and *Atlantic, Harper's, New Yorker,* and *Saturday Review* came close to doing so.

Perhaps one other reason that magazines were able to grow despite competition from other media was that magazines over the years appealed to an expanding range of tastes and interests, as later chapters will show in some detail. Magazines, as we have seen, generally were published for homogeneous groups of readers. The number of magazines, then, was probably somewhat related to the number of interest groups or little "publics" within the public as a whole. If a publisher found a sufficient number of persons with interests in common, especially persons whom advertisers would pay to reach, he felt justified in bringing out a magazine for them.

Publishers were quick to sense new interests of the public and also quick to establish new magazines catering to them. For example, when moviegoers grew curious for glimpses into the private lives of film stars, *Photoplay* appeared to satisfy their curiosity; from a skimpy booklet, the magazine developed into one of the leading publications for movie fans. In 1923, when intellectuals protested the Babbitry they saw abounding in American life, H. L.

---

[9] Wilbur Schramm, Jack Lyle, and Edwin Parker, *Television in the Lives of Our Children* (Stanford, Calif., 1961), *passim.*

Mencken and George Jean Nathan started the *American Mercury,* a little green-covered organ of dissent which delighted the iconoclasts and outraged the conventional with its attacks on provincialism, prohibition, the Bible Belt, and boobs. In 1934, when model railroad fans were still numbered in the hundreds, A. C. Kalmbach was so sure that their hobby would become widespread that he gambled on a magazine for them, *Model Railroader;* his fortunes grew with the hobby, which by 1950 had attracted more than a hundred thousand men and women. In 1944, when the wartime boom created an acute manpower shortage on the West Coast, Harold Dreyfus founded *Jobs,* a ten-cent magazine to help workers find jobs and employers to find workers. In 1951, when the aqualung put the ocean depths within limits of skillful swimmers, Jim Auxier started *Skin Diver,* which under new ownership was selling about 46,000 copies a month in 1963. Examples of that sort could be cited by the score.

Whole new categories of magazines sprang up as imitative publishers copied the most successful ideas of their competitors—the confession and digest magazines, for instance, and others covered in detail in later chapters. In the early sixties one could scarcely name a specialized subject, from game breeding to geriatrics, that some magazine did not attempt to cover. On many subjects, magazines were the main source of current information; and partly for that reason, perhaps, the industry was able to compete successfully with the other communications industries. The rise of television and the magazines of multimillion circulation in the fifties probably helped rather than hurt specialized periodicals, for playing to mammoth audiences, they could not afford to treat minority concerns with any great frequency or detail.

But probably the market for magazines grew primarily as a result of the factors already mentioned: the increase in population, the redistribution of purchasing power, the advances in education, the increase in leisure time. It is possible to show a relationship between some of those factors and increases in circulation.

A growing population provided a growing market for magazines, and by midcentury the majority of adult Americans were magazine readers. Estimates of the actual proportion of magazine readers in the population ranged from about two-thirds to more than 85 per cent, partly because different studies used different research techniques and different definitions of the term "magazine reader."

Most attempts to measure the size of the magazine reading public have been conducted or sponsored by magazines, alone or jointly. Although sponsored by interested parties, such studies give the best available estimates of the number of magazine readers.

In 1946, after reviewing what it called the "scanty data" on magazine readership, the Magazine Advertising Bureau concluded that from 70 to 80 per cent of all persons aged fifteen or older read one or more of the thirty-five or forty leading magazines with "a fair degree of regularity." A year later, the M.A.B. sponsored a nationwide readership survey that gave more precise information about the size of the audience. Nearly seven out of every ten Americans aged fifteen or older, 68.9 per cent, were magazine readers, it reported, and the average reader read an average of 4.6 separate magazines. In actual numbers, there were 71,500,000 readers, 32,-300,000 nonreaders. There were more women than men readers, 73.5 per cent against 63.6 per cent. There was no huge difference between the percentage of readers living in urban areas and those living on farms. Of the urban population, 70.6 per cent were magazine readers as compared with 65.9 per cent of the rural nonfarm and 66.7 per cent of the farm populations.

Although the increase in population may have improved the health of the magazine industry, that by itself was certainly not enough, for magazine readers were not evenly distributed throughout the population. Income and magazine readership tended to go hand in hand. Therefore, the redistribution of purchasing power was perhaps of major importance to the growth of magazines.

On several occasions, spokesmen for the magazine industry have shown a relationship between buying power of readers and circulations of leading magazines. They also have correlated increases in circulation with increases in retail sales to suggest the relationship between buying power and magazine sales. Audience studies also indicated that purchasing power and circulation were related, for magazine readership was correlated with income. The audience survey made by the Magazine Advertising Bureau in 1947, for instance, showed that 98.2 per cent of families with total annual incomes of $5,000 or more were reader families but only 1.8 per cent were nonreader families. On the other hand, 41.5 per cent of families with annual incomes of $500 to $1,000 were nonreader families and 58.5 per cent were readers. Moreover, the number of magazines read by each hundred reader families rose sharply with ascending economic status. It moved up gradually from 500 copies for each hundred reader families in the lowest income group to 900 in the highest. The M.A.B. study made in 1959 also showed a relationship between magazine reading and income. For instance, in 42 per cent of all households with incomes of $10,000 or more the head of the household was heavily exposed to magazines.

There also seemed to be a relationship between education and magazine readership. As the level of formal education rose, so did magazine readership, according to Lazarsfeld and Kendall in their study of communications behavior, which was cited earlier. They found that 86 per cent of all college educated respondents regularly read magazines, as did 68 per cent of those with high school educations, but only 41 per cent with grade school educations were regular readers. The national survey by the Magazine Advertising Bureau in 1947 showed that the median educational level of magazine readers was three years of high school, that the median of nonreaders was less than six years of grade school. The average number of magazines read by each hundred persons, readers and nonreaders, rose swiftly with education; 155.2 magazines for each hundred persons with eighth grade education or less, 451.4 for each hundred with high school education, and 528.8 for each hundred with four or more years of college. The 1959 study made much the same general point.

With changes in population, purchasing power, education, and leisure, then, the market for magazines expanded, and the expanding market was able to support a larger number of magazines, and magazines of larger circulation than in 1900. Individual publishers, who at the turn of the century numbered their readers in thousands, began to talk in terms of millions of readers. Indeed, as early as 1950 *Life* could boast that it reached one in five Americans; eleven years later it reached 25 per cent of all U.S. adults, according to A. C. Nielsen Company, *Reader's Digest*, 27 per cent, *Look*, 21 per cent, and *Saturday Evening Post*, 18 per cent.

From the turn of the century onward, the number of magazines fluctuated as some died and others were born, but it is fairly certain that there were approximately a thousand more magazines in the United States in the early sixties than in 1900. Just how many magazines existed in 1900, no one knows. One estimate, perhaps not far off, put the number at 3,500. Of those, at least fifty were national magazines. The number of periodicals had grown to 4,610 in 1947, according to the census, and to 4,455 in 1958.

Because of difficulties in definition and the lack of reliable data, it is practically impossible to chart the growth of magazine numbers over the years. The U.S. census is of small help for the early years of the century, as it lumped magazines under the general heading "periodicals," a term which embraced newspapers as well as magazines. However, making necessary adjustments in U.S. census figures, one can estimate the number of periodicals as 3,085 in 1923, 3,635 in 1925, 3,860 in 1927, and considerably more than 4,500 in 1929. The census itself gives the number of periodicals as 4,887 in 1931, 3,459 in 1933, 4,019 in 1935, 4,202 in 1937, 4,985 in 1939, 4,610 in 1947, and 4,455 in 1958.

Those seem conservative figures. The Ayer's *Directory of Newspapers and Periodicals* gives larger numbers. In Ayer's, too, magazines are tabulated under the broad heading of "periodicals," which covers other publications as well. Excluding periodicals appearing more often than once a week since they probably are not magazines, one gets the following approximate numbers of magazines: 5,485 in 1936, 6,260 in 1940, 5,705 in 1944, 6,660 in 1948, 6,920 in 1952, 7,600 in 1956, and more than 8,500 in 1962.

The number of monthly periodicals is perhaps a good barometer of trends in the number of magazines. According to Ayer's, there were 2,369 monthly periodicals in 1900, 2,977 in 1910, 3,415 in 1920, 4,110 in 1930, 3,501 in 1940, 3,655 in 1950, 3,904 in 1956, and 4,166 in 1962. Conflicting as the various data are, all figures seem to point to a significant growth in the number of magazines in the twentieth century.

It is in circulation, not in numbers, however, that magazines had their most remarkable growth. Four sorts of estimates help to show that growth: aggregate circulations of all magazines published in the United States, aggregate circulations of all magazines for which reliable figures are available, circulations of individual magazines leading in sales, and the number of magazines with circulations of a million or more.

Estimating the aggregate circulations of magazines in the United States over the years is a highly speculative pastime. Yet even crude estimates can point up the large climb in magazine circulations. In 1900, according to one estimate, the combined circulation of all 3,500 magazines was 65,000,000 an issue. In 1963, just the eight leading consumer magazines surpassed that total. According to various census data, the aggregate per-issue circulation of all magazines in the United States was as follows:

Year	Circulation	Year	Circulation
1900	65,000,000	1933	174,759,000
1923	128,621,000	1935	178,621,000
1925	153,375,000	1937	224,275,000
1927	165,702,000	1939	239,693,000
1929	202,022,000	1947	384,628,000
1931	183,527,000	1958	391,936,000

Since the founding of the Audit Bureau of Circulations in 1914, reliable records are available for a limited number of magazines, including most of those leading in circulation. The magazine industry has often charted the aggregate circulation of A.B.C. members to dramatize the growth of magazine sales. Such charts and tables must be regarded warily; their figures are inflated because they are not adjusted to allow for the lengthening roster of A.B.C. members. The same caveat applies to Table 2. Based on a compilation by the Magazine Advertising Bureau, it traces the circulation growth of A.B.C. members and of nonmembers listed in Standard Rate and Data Service that either made a sworn statement of distribution or gave a circulation guarantee. That study, too, covered a growing number of publications. Nevertheless, the average circulation of each magazine increased by about 47 per cent between 1929 and 1962.

Table 2. GROWTH OF MAGAZINE CIRCULATION BY SELECTED YEARS, 1929-62

Year	No. of Magazines	Average Circulation Per Issue (in thousands)	Copies Sold Annually (in thousands)
1929	365	94,836	1,804,796
1933	365	86,610	1,620,221
1938	492	119,053	2,200,342
1945	472	192,021	2,980,166
1950	567	223,581	3,461,916
1955	616	243,759	3,856,051
1960	650	250,034	4,286,962
1962	706	268,241	4,518,568

The circulation records of individual publications also show how magazine sales have grown since the birth of the national magazine in the eighties and nineties. Circulation figures for the nineties are neither plentiful nor reliable; but one signpost is that *Harper's*, among the leaders in sales, was distributing between 100,000 and

200,000 copies in 1891. In the mid-nineties, Munsey, McClure, and Curtis turned loose the low-priced magazine, and the scramble for circulation was on. In 1900 and the years immediately following, circulations began to soar toward undreamed-of figures. In 1900, the circulation of *Munsey's*, which had begun with initial sales of 60,000 seven years earlier, was 700,000, of *Delineator*, 500,000, of *McClure's*, 360,000, and of *Cosmopolitan*, 300,000. *Pearson's*, which started in 1899 with a distribution of 100,000, was selling nearly 300,000 in 1906. In just a year or two, *Everybody's* ran its circulation from 197,000 to 735,000 in 1904 and 1905. The circulation of *Hampton's* zoomed from 13,000 in 1907 to 444,000 four years later. The sale of *Collier's* rose from 500,000 in 1909 to more than 1,000,-000 in 1912. To appreciate how the circulation of one leading publication grew with the century, one needs only to look at the record of *McCall's*, which outlived most of its nineteenth-century contemporaries:

Year	Circulation	Year	Circulation
1900	201,200	1935	2,400,500
1905	682,200	1940	3,116,700
1910	1,060,300	1945	3,400,600
1915	1,262,600	1950	3,807,100
1920	1,350,100	1955	4,522,500
1925	2,115,200	1960	6,560,500
1930	2,505,100	1963	8,220,800

Circulations that were heady on the eve of World War I were commonplace in the fifties and sixties. Few things underline that point as well as the increase in the number of magazines with circulations of a million or more. Just one magazine, *Comfort*, possibly had sales of a million in 1900. The *Ladies' Home Journal* also passed that mark in 1904, but up until World War I it had been joined by only a handful of other publications, *Collier's*, *Cosmopolitan*, *McCall's*, and the *Saturday Evening Post* among them. In 1963 there were fifty general and farm magazines with circulations of at least a million and almost half had circulations of at least twice that. Some had sales of several times a million. The *Reader's Digest* sold more than 14,500,000 copies of its domestic edition alone. *Everywoman's*, *Family Circle*, *Life*, *Look*, and *TV Guide* all had distributions of more than 7,000,000; *Better Homes and Gardens*, *Ladies' Home Journal*, *Saturday Evening Post*, and *Woman's Day* were above 6,000,000.

Drawing on a number of records, the author has been able to chart the growth of magazines with circulations of a million or more after 1925. His findings are summarized in Table 3. In the first eleven years, 1926 through 1936, the number wavered around twenty-five. It dipped as low as twenty-three in 1933 and twice went as high as twenty-seven, once in 1931 when *Ballyhoo*, a humor magazine which consisted largely of cartoons and parodies of advertisements, flashed momentarily as a sales leader, and once again in 1935.

Mammoth circulations, the figures suggest, were not warborn, as some industry spokesmen have intimated. They seem to have begun in 1937 when the *Saturday Evening Post* first topped 3,000,-000, as did *Pictorial Review* as the result of a merger with *Delineator*, and when *Life* started its climb toward the top-circulation bracket. Despite paper shortages, the circulation giants grew larger during the war years, 1942 through 1945. But the greatest expansion, both in the number of magazines with circulations exceeding a million and in circulations of individual magazines, came after the end of the war.

Part of the circulation growth in the fifties and early sixties arose from the determination of some publishers to compete with television on its own ground. If television could reach millions, so could they, and their single-minded drive for mass audiences made the term "numbers game" a part of the publishing vocabulary. Four circulation leaders—*Reader's Digest, Saturday Evening Post, Life,* and *Look*—boasted in 1960 that a single advertisement placed in them would reach every other person in the United States 2.3 times, and two years later *McCall's* bought space in the trade press to compare its reach with that of television. In the dozen years after 1950, *Look* and *McCall's* more than doubled their circulations.

As single-copy sales accounted for a declining share of their circulation, magazines conducted massive direct-mail campaigns to lure readers with reduced prices. Bargain rates accounted for a substantial proportion of subscriptions and renewals for some publications. When the *Reader's Digest* lowered its subscription price in the early sixties, it was selling more than 99 per cent in that fashion. *Life* sold 79 per cent of its subscriptions at reduced rates in 1962, *Atlantic,* 89 percent, *Time,* 73 per cent, *Newsweek,* 65 per cent, *McCall's,* 57 per cent.

Actually, bargain rates were not an innovation of the big push

Table 3. Number of Magazines With Circulations of 1,000,000 or More, 1926-63

Year	Total	Number of Magazines with Circulations of:ᵃ									
		1–1.99 Million	2–2.99 Million	3–3.99 Million	4–4.99 Million	5–5.99 Million	6–6.99 Million	7–7.99 Million	8–8.99 Million	9–9.99 Million	10 or More Million
1926	25	19	6								
1928	26	19	7								
1930	25	15	10								
1932	25	16	9								
1934	25	17	8								
1936	27	17	10								
1938	30	20	6	4							
1940	26	12	9	5							
1942	28	12	10	4	1	1					
1943	30	13	11	4	1	1					
1944	30	14	10	3	2			1			
1945	32	16	10	4	2						
1946	31	14	11	3	2				1		
1947	40	20	12	5	1	1			1		
1948	42	22	10	7	2						1
1949	44	24	8	8	2	1			1		
1950	42	22	8	7	3	1				1	
1951	46	24	11	7	2	1				1	
1952	47	27	8	7	3	1					1
1953	47	23	10	8	3	2					1
1954	46	23	10	6	5	1					1
1955	46	22	11	4	7	1					1
1956	48	23	9	6	5	2	2				1
1957	44	22	8	3	2	5	3				1
1958	44	24	8	3	2	4	2				1
1959	47	27	6	3	3	4	3				1
1960	50	28	7	4	3	3	3	1			1
1961	50	29	6	4	1	3	5	1			1
1962	52	33	5	3		3	2	3	2		1
1963	50	30	6	3		1	4	3	1	1	1

ᵃ Excludes magazine groups, comic books, Sunday supplements, and house organs.

for numbers in the fifties and sixties. They had long been an entice-
ment that publishers justified as a way of getting potential readers
to sample their magazines. Indeed, for some circulation leaders—
for instance, *Life* and *Look*—they were responsible for a lower
percentage of subscriptions than they had been before the war.
However, in sheer numbers they generated tremendously more
orders than ever before.

Some advertisers, some publishers, and an occasional Congressman had harsh words for the numbers game. By aping television,
magazines sacrificed their traditional strength of selectivity of
market, advertising men warned; more than that, the subscribers
magazines worked hardest to get were of least value to advertisers,
who nevertheless had to bear the cost of attracting them and
reaching them. Some publishers complained that the race for circulation was a race to the poorhouse and that only the large
magazines could halt its hazardous course. A few Congressmen
remarked that it was strange that publishers could afford the costly
drive for circulation at bargain rates but could not, as they said,
afford higher postal rates. Several publishers at the close of 1963
said that the numbers game was over or denied that it had ever
existed. At least one, pointing to his mammoth circulation and his
costs of getting it, argued that the effort had been remarkably
profitable.

What kinds of magazines achieved circulations of a million or
more? There was a fairly consistent pattern of types of magazines
on the list. From 1926 until 1941, the list each year included three
general-interest weeklies, *Collier's*, *Liberty*, and the *Saturday Evening Post*, and a varying number of general-interest monthly publications, such as *American*, *Cosmopolitan*, *Good Housekeeping*,
and *Reader's Digest*. Nearly every year there was one travel magazine, *National Geographic*, and about half the time a current events
magazine, *Literary Digest*. Almost every year from 1926 to 1941,
there were two home service magazines, *Household* and *Better
Homes and Gardens*, joined by *American Home* in 1937. A confession magazine, *True Story*, was on the list each year. More
women's magazines than any other type amassed circulations exceeding a million, and they were among the top leaders in circulation. Four or five farm magazines regularly appeared on the list.
After the birth of the picture magazines in 1936, *Life* and *Look*
were consistently present. That pattern scarcely altered during the

war and in the postwar boom, but a few other types of magazines then regularly appeared on the list: a news magazine; men's magazines, which before the war had rarely hit circulations of a million; one or two science magazines; and a spate of movie and confession magazines.

Significantly, several magazines with circulations of more than a million died or were merged with other publications. *Literary Digest, Liberty, Delineator, Farm and Fireside, Pictorial Review, American, Collier's, Woman's Home Companion, Town Journal, Better Living, Household, Coronet*—they all vanished. Their passing, in a period when circulations were growing steadily, indicated that the quest for the advertiser's dollar and the reader's time and attention was highly competitive. In the next chapter, let us see just how competitive the magazine industry was.

The Economic Structure
of the Industry

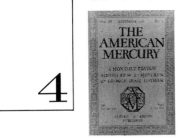

Tidily cutting his lamb chop at luncheon in Hotel Pierre one autumn day in the early sixties, a New York publisher who had been in the magazine business since the mid-twenties complained that it had become harder and costlier to start a new magazine. His elderly companion across the table nodded in agreement; he had lost more than a million dollars on a magazine venture in the previous eighteen months. Both had prospered from magazine publishing, but they agreed that the business was a gamble, as indeed it was.

In the fall of 1963 a Chicago publishing firm tried out its idea of a magazine for business and professional women with 125,000 copies of *Realm*. After the second issue was printed but before it was through the bindery, the magazine died. The publishers had already lost $300,000, according to trade reports, and the advertising they had hoped for had not come in.

Despite many such unhappy and expensive false starts, the magazine industry was by no means closed to the outsider. In 1942, for example, John H. Johnson, who was employed by an insurance company in Chicago, founded the world's largest publishing company for Negroes on a borrowed $500. His idea was the simple one of giving Negroes their own magazines with formulas that had proved successful with other audiences. He collected an assortment of articles into a small magazine that he called *Negro Digest* and found a printer willing to print the first issue on credit. During the first years, his associate Ben Burns single-handedly edited the magazine at home after his day's work with the Chicago *Defender*. The digest did so well that Johnson was encouraged to start several other publications. His next, in 1945, was *Ebony*, a picture magazine for Negroes that Burns put out with the help of freelance contributions until he recruited the first staff for Johnson Publications in 1946. More than any other magazine, *Ebony* demonstrated to advertisers the importance of Negroes as consumers, and perhaps as a result its own advertising revenues of $3,631,000 in 1962 were more than triple what they had been a decade earlier. In 1950 Johnson started *Tan*, a service magazine for Negro women, and the next year *Jet*, one of the few vestpocket news magazines to survive into the sixties. Although Johnson killed off *Negro Digest* in 1951 when *Ebony* caught on, he later revived it because of reader demand. Altogether, his magazines were selling more than a million copies an issue in 1963.

The point is not just that Johnson found rapid success in publishing but also that he was new to the industry. On into the fifties and sixties, a fortunate few newcomers found riches in magazine publishing; Hugh Hefner did in 1953 when with a few hundred dollars he started *Playboy*, the foundation of enterprises that he valued at $20,000,000 less than a decade later. In some ways, magazine publishing represented the freest of free enterprise. It was a bitterly competitive industry in which magazines fought with one another for the small pool of talent on which they drew, for their share of the advertiser's dollar, for the reader's time and attention, for display space on the newsstands. It was an industry so lacking in homogeneity that although it provided trade magazines for coin machine operators and store window dressers, it was rarely able to support a business paper of its own. It was an industry of such swiftly changing fortunes that an aggressive outsider with few more assets than a headful of ideas could hope to found a publishing empire. It was an industry filled with broken dreams and quick failures, with shining promise and fantastic successes.

The industry always had room for the venturesome newcomer. He could hope to succeed as a result of the growing volume of advertising, the expanding market for magazines, the new interests which the public was forever discovering, and the nature of the industry itself. The number of publishers rose and fell, but there was no evidence that it was diminishing. New publishers continued to enter the field. Many of them failed. Yet many others flourished and jockeyed for position with the established leaders, some of which lagged, some of which toppled.

True, the small publisher could see that a handful of mammoth publishers took in the bulk of the money spent on national advertising and issued a large share of the total copies of magazines. But the giants did not cast their shadows over his own operations as, say, the General Motors Corporation did over those of the small manufacturer of automobiles. There were various levels and arenas of competition. At the top, the big leaders fought among themselves to hold or to improve their positions. Beneath them, smaller magazines scrambled for existence and tried to pull themselves upward. In one sense, then, the huge publishers were not competitors of the small publisher at all. Moreover, there were many battlefields, not just one. Each publisher produced a unique product, one designed for a very special group of readers. His struggle was chiefly for his share of the advertising and reader market which he had chosen to serve. His competition was with publishers whose magazines were roughly similar to his own and who threatened to take away his advertising and readership.

Thus the publisher of *Sports Afield*, for example, probably was little affected by much of the warfare in the magazine industry over the years. He may have noticed that George Horace Lorimer of the *Saturday Evening Post* and Ray Long of *Cosmopolitan* were trying to outbid one another in the late twenties for the most famous authors. He may have noticed that the *Saturday Evening Post* and *Life* changed their on-sale dates to gain a competitive advantage in the big-weekly field. He may have noticed that *Newsweek, Time,* and *U.S. News* each was trying to convince advertisers in the fifties that it reached the largest audience of influential business executives. Yet it is hard to imagine that he worried when *Life* picked up another hundred thousand readers or when the *Post* gained another million dollars in advertising. Probably much more important to the conduct of his business were considerations which had no effect on the policies of the big general magazines: that *Field and Stream* had become strong enough in 1930 to buy out the oldest of the outdoor magazines, *Forest and Stream;* that *Hunting and Fishing* was able to increase its circulation guarantee by 450,000 in 1950 after merging with *Outdoorsman;* that his own magazine was purchased by the Henry Holt book firm in 1951; that *Outdoor Sportsman* suspended publication in 1955; and so forth.

If the giants had little effect on the day-to-day operations of the smaller publisher, neither did their presence keep new publishing companies from starting in business nor prevent small firms from moving into higher levels of competition. Despite the growth of a few magazine empires, there is no evidence that the number of magazine-publishing companies showed a downward trend during the twentieth century, although any such generality must be based on scanty information. Figures in the census of manufacturers, which seems to be about the only source, suggest that the number of periodical establishments fluctuated with the state of the economy from 1925 onward. It varied from a high of 2,925 in 1929 to a low of 2,002 in 1933, and was 2,323 in 1958.

The really significant characteristic of the magazine industry in the twentieth century was its fluidity. The significant characteristic was that magazines with circulations of more than a million could vanish with scarcely a trace, as did the *Literary Digest, Pictorial Review, American, Woman's Home Companion, Collier's, Coronet,* and others; that on a capital of $86,000 young men like Briton Hadden and Henry Luce could establish a publishing company which twenty-five years later achieved the largest gross income of any magazine-publishing firm up until that time; that on a borrowed $5,000, DeWitt Wallace could launch his *Reader's Digest,* which in a few years was pouring millions of dollars into the bank accounts of its two owners and was blanketing the world with copies.

What counted most was the Big Idea. If one had a fresh idea for a magazine, there were often persons willing to help him finance it; and if he had the faith and funds to sustain himself while he sought acceptance of his magazine by readers and advertisers, there was always some chance that he could achieve a modest success and a remote chance that he could wind up in company with the giants.

To understand the freedom of opportunity that the magazine industry offered the inventive entrepreneur, one must understand the role of the publisher, which goes a long way toward explaining many of the developments in magazine publishing since the nineties. Although there were other explanations as well, the role of the publisher helps to clarify such points as the diversity of magazines, the fewness of certain kinds of magazines, and the sameness of editorial content in a given magazine.

The role of the publisher underwent a crucial change when he began to count on the advertiser for support, for then magazines became inextricably linked with the marketing system. Advertising converted the magazine publisher from a dealer in reading matter into a dealer in consumer groups as well. Before the low-priced magazine came along, the publisher was essentially a dealer in editorial copy. His eye on his budget, he got together stories and articles which he thought would interest his subscribers. Before the days of international copyright agreements, he took much of his material from British periodicals, and he paid his domestic contributors as little as possible; in the 1870's, quality magazines paid contributors only about $10 a page. Art work was more expensive. But if he were lucky, the publisher held down his costs so that his sales to the reader brought him a profit. Some magazines in the nineteenth century were adjuncts of book-publishing firms, and one of their functions was to stimulate interest in the publisher's books.

A number of publishers, notably those of pulps, digests, annuals, comic books, and a few other types of periodicals, remained essentially dealers in reading matter even after advertisers were spending large sums on magazines. They derived their income from a small unit profit on a high turnover of copies instead of from advertising, but rising production costs eventually drove the pulps and most of the digests out of business. A few hardbound periodicals like *American Heritage* and *Horizon* got along by charging a high price for their subscriptions. Still other magazines relied on a trade association, a fraternal organization, or a professional group to make up any deficit.

But with the rise of national advertising, by far the greatest percentage of magazines came to count on advertising for their income. As they did so, the publisher became closely affiliated with the marketing system. He continued to sell the reader an editorial product, but he also sold the advertiser a service—that of carrying the advertiser's message to the special audience of consumers he had collected. Sometimes it was merely a large audience; sometimes it was a highly screened, homogeneous one.

In essence, magazine publishing came to consist of the publisher's deciding on a consumer group which advertisers wish to reach, devising an editorial formula to attract and hold it, and then selling advertisers access to it. Sometimes, of course, the publisher first designed his magazine and then let it seek its audience. Some publishers chose relatively small audiences high in purchasing power, a market for high-priced necessities and luxuries; others chose large audiences of middle income, a market for mass-produced necessities and minor luxuries; yet others picked an audience sharing some common leisure-time activity or specialized interest. But in any event, the publisher became a dealer in consumer groups. Condé Nast, who achieved success as a magazine publisher, made that point in 1931:

> Before embarking on the publishing business I had thought of periodical publishing as something very grand—even very mysterious. But a little clear thinking led to the conclusion that such a publisher is only a name-gatherer; that the publishing business, analyzed to its basic elements, resolved itself into nothing more nor less than a Name-Brokerage Business.
> The publisher fills a certain number of pages with reading matter, drawings and photographs. He, so to speak, baits his pages with such editorial matter as he believes will attract either a great number of readers, or a specific class of readers. Then he offers these pages to the reading public at a price considerably lower than his cost of gathering and manufacturing them.
> At this stage . . . he has a very considerable loss; but he then turns to the advertisers and merchants of the country, in the manner of a Name-Broker, and says:
> "I have gathered together a list of names. Access to these names will enable you to promote your business. I will let you have such access to them. When I am sending my editorial message to these names, I will permit you, for a consideration, to include a page in which you may deliver to them your own message about your merchandise." [1]

In a talk after World War II, Willard Chevalier, then executive vice-president of McGraw-Hill Publishing Company, succinctly outlined what he regarded as the "essence of publishing." To succeed, he said, a magazine needed three common denominators of interest: a common denominator of reader interest, that is, the editorial fare had to appeal to most of the chosen reading public; a common denominator of buying interest, that is, the readers had to be interested in buying the same things; a common denominator of market interest, that is, the publisher had to attract a sufficiently large group of readers who bought enough of a wide variety of

---

[1] Quoted in John Bakeless, *Magazine Making* (New York, 1931), p. 5.

things, to attract a volume of advertising which would support his publication.

That is the essence of publishing: to establish an editorial formula that will enable [the publisher] to develop a reader group, then to assemble an advertiser group who wants to address that audience. . . .

.   .   .   .   .

Suppose, for instance, that somebody wants a publication that is only going to secretaries with red hair and blue eyes. The advertiser says "That is our market. That is the kind of readers we want—red haired secretaries with blue eyes."

All right, you say, "We will get out a paper for them." That's . . . a chore, because you have to get editorial matter that is only going to appeal to secretaries with red hair and blue eyes. Don't ask me what it is. . . . You have to find it. You have a highly selective circulation effort that is going to cost a lot of money. The result is that when you have figured up your cost of rendering your particular service to that group of advertisers, it is very high per thousand readers. But if those readers are what he wants and you deliver them, he will pay you the price, presumably in the form of an advertising rate that justifies the effort you put in to get them.

A homogeneous reader group simplified editing and gave the magazine its value as an advertising medium. By addressing like-minded individuals, the editor was able to capitalize on the tastes and interests of a large share of his audience. Indeed, those tastes and interests helped to establish a magazine's *raison d'être*. Readers turned to *Gourmet* for its articles on good food, good wine, and culinary esoterica; to *Antiques* for the newest ideas and information on the oldest of furnishings and bibelots. Advertisers benefited because magazines screened out potential buyers of their goods and services. The screening process simplified the task of the advertising copywriter; he could use the advertising appeals most likely to prove effective with a given audience. Although some dealers of mass-produced goods wished to reach as many consumers as possible and there were magazines for them, the industry as a whole was characterized by its selectivity of audience.

Thus virtually every magazine came to be designed for some homogeneous public within the total population. The publisher would try to saturate his chosen market, but ordinarily he could not expect to extend his circulation beyond it without altering the editorial pattern which attracted its original readers. For example, *Seventeen* was begun in 1944 as a magazine for girls under twenty.

To attract them, the magazine gave a distinctive approach to the features about fashions, beauty, careers, sports, cultural activities, and other subjects that made up its editorial pattern. If the publisher had decided to enlarge his audience to include women of, say, thirty-five, he would have had to change the editorial pattern of the magazine. One result, apart from a weakening of the selectivity of the publication as an advertising medium, no doubt would have been the loss of a large number of young readers.

In choosing the audience he would serve, the magazine publisher was not limited by geography, as were broadcasters and newspaper publishers. Individual members of his reader group were usually scattered across the nation. True, he may have found it profitable to restrict his circulation to a circumscribed area. *Successful Farming*, for example, was aimed primarily at farmers in the Midwestern states so that it could attract advertisers on the basis of its concentrated circulation in the most prosperous agricultural region of the United States. *Sunset* magazine borrowed editorial techniques from nationally circulated *Better Homes and Gardens* to reach an audience on just the West Coast. But such geographical restrictions were from choice, not from necessity.

This role of the publisher in appealing to little publics within the entire population helps to explain why the gates to the industry were open to the new entrepreneur. The important thing was that a publisher have an idea for a magazine which would capitalize on the latent or burgeoning interest of a public which other publishers were not serving at all or were serving inadequately. In effect, the number of magazines was limited by only two considerations: first, by the number of special interests with enough potential buyers of advertisers' goods and services and, second, by the number of advertisers willing to pay an adequate sum for reaching the consumers whom the publisher had chosen.

Publishers astute enough to recognize the profound changes taking place in American life in the twentieth century were sometimes able to build up valuable properties from small initial investments. The speeded-up tempo of life after World War I, for example, probably accounted in part for the rapid acceptance of the digest magazines, the news magazines, and the picture magazines. The emancipation of American women, who began holding down positions which had once been the prerogative of men, opened up a market for magazines aimed at the career girl—

magazines such as *Charm* and *Glamour*. The increasing number of young persons was served in the fifties by a flock of magazines catering to teen-age interests. Publishers also were able to build up at least short-term successes by capitalizing on passing fads and fancies. For example, magazines arose to profit from the self-improvement boom in the thirties, from the "do-it-yourself" boom after World War II, and from the craze for diving underwater with aqualungs in the early fifties.

The principle of audience selection, then, helps to explain the diversity of American magazines after 1900. The number of publics in the nation was reflected in its periodicals. Just a short listing of random titles published at various times since 1900 illustrates the wide range of interests which magazines appealed to: *Catholic Boy, Modern Youth, Stage, National Recovery Survey, Economic Forum, Garden Gossip, American Rifleman, Saddle and Bridle, American Swedish Monthly, Home Craftsman, Wedding Bells, Dog World, Cats, National Motorist, Natural History, American Photography, Dance, Eastern Skier, Evangelist*, and *Independent Woman*.

Just as it helps to explain the diversity of magazines, the principle of audience selection also makes understandable the absence or relative fewness of certain kinds of magazines. The publisher's aim was to deliver to the advertiser a screened group of good potential buyers. Therefore, publishers often found it unprofitable to pioneer among low-income groups, and even assembling an audience of desirable consumers was often too costly to justify the effort.

Once a publisher had struck upon an editorial balance which drew the readers he wanted, his profitable policy was to continue that same formula month after month, year after year. Consequently, there was a certain sameness to the editorial content of a given magazine. For example, in each issue of *Collier's* in the thirties, a reader could expect to find an article each about politics or economics, sports, a personality in the entertainment world, and some topic of interest chiefly to women; three short stories, one of them filling less than a single page; two serials, usually dealing with mystery or romance; a column of miscellany; an editorial; and a scattering of cartoons. For years, *Good Housekeeping* used a formula based on a mixture of such ingredients as food and nutrition, beauty and toiletries, apparel and accessories, home furnishings and management, home building and modernization, and children, all laced with a strong gob of light fiction. The good editor was one who could sense when a formula was weakening and could shift to an equally good balance of material without losing his readers.

Several characteristics of the industry facilitated access to it. A magazine could be begun as a small business. The publisher needed to make no large capital investment in equipment, and often he could find printers and suppliers who were willing to stake him in his venture.

Apart from the few giants in advertising and circulation which battled among themselves on the heights far above the rest of the industry, magazine publishing firms in the twentieth century were relatively small businesses. In 1958 about half of the 2,323 periodical establishments recorded by the census had fewer than five employees each, and 95 per cent had fewer than a hundred; only five companies had a thousand or more employees.

There was no good reason that a magazine publishing firm had to be large. If the publisher did not wish to have his staff write all of the editorial copy, he could buy his articles and stories from freelance writers; advertising agencies, retained by his advertisers, prepared the advertisements that he ran. He could distribute his copies by mail at preferential postal rates or contract with a distributor to place them on the newsstands. Indeed, he could even arrange for a subscription agency to build up his list of subscribers.

Unlike the newspaper publisher and the broadcaster, the magazine publisher did not have to invest in equipment for production. The large majority of publishers did not own printing facilities. The best available source of information, the census of manufacturers, reported that in 1925 there were 616 periodical establishments with printing facilities, 2,032 without; in 1939 there were 600 with, 1,958 without; and in 1958 there were 157 with and 2,166 without. Even some of the largest publishers, including Time Inc. and the Reader's Digest Association, let out their printing on contract instead of maintaining their own presses. To get the best available facilities, some publishers financed the purchase of presses and other equipment by their printers and amortized the costs over relatively long periods. Some publishers owning printing plants kept their presses busy turning out magazines for other publishers. For instance, Condé Nast Publications, Inc., did a large volume of printing for other publishers. At its plant in Dayton, Ohio, the McCall Corporation for several decades printed dozens of magazines for other publishers, among them *Reader's Digest, Newsweek,* and *U.S. News.* It printed many more at two other plants acquired in the early sixties. Printing, in fact, was responsible for 54 per cent of the company's revenues in 1960. Printing magazines also accounted for the bulk of the business of such large printing firms as Cuneo Press, Inc., R. R. Donnelley and Sons Company, and the Kable Brothers Printing Company.

What the publisher did need, however, was an idea for a magazine and sufficient capital to finance the publication until it was accepted by advertisers and readers. The largest share of that capital went for production costs; and because it did, publishers often turned to printers and suppliers for financial aid in launching a new publication or in keeping an ailing one alive. Printers were frequently willing to gamble on a magazine to keep their presses busy, and paper manufacturers were sometimes willing to extend credit to a publisher with a promising idea. To tide himself over when he was building up his company, for example, Cyrus Curtis got $100,000 credit from Crocker, Burbank and Company of Fitchburg, Massachusetts, a paper firm. In 1932 the West Virginia Pulp and Paper Company gave William H. Eaton financial aid so he could lease *American Home* from Doubleday, Doran and revitalize the magazine. In 1939 Norman H. Anthony found a printer and paper dealer who would speculate on three issues of a magazine he had in mind, *Hellzapoppin.* So it was on into the sixties.

Not uncommonly printers and suppliers found themselves owners of a magazine to which they had overextended credit; and in the hope of recovering their losses and keeping the magazine's business, they sometimes staked a new publisher, even to the extent of plowing new capital into the magazine. John Cuneo, the printer, and the International Paper Company in 1932 became owners of Screenland Magazine, Inc., as a result of overdue debts. They installed Paul Hunter, an experienced magazine man, as publisher, and transferred stock to him each year until he was majority owner of the publishing house. Unpaid bills gave the Kable Brothers Printing Company control of *Judge* in 1936, and for at least a year, the company sought a new publisher to whom it could sell the humor magazine. In 1941 when Bernarr Macfadden withdrew from Macfadden Publications, four printing and paper supply houses— Cuneo Press, W. F. Hall Printing Company, Kimberly-Clark Paper Company, and West Virginia Pulp and Paper Company—advanced the money so that a group of management employees could buy the property. The four companies were represented on the board of directors. *Liberty*, for a time a Macfadden publication, was kept alive for several years by financial injections from its suppliers. John Cuneo and Kimberly-Clark in 1942 reportedly were so anxious to retain the business of the moribund weekly that they put up a million dollars to keep it going. In 1944 they turned their holdings in the magazine over to Paul Hunter, who had rescued *Screenland* for Cuneo in 1932.

Although access to the magazine industry was relatively easy, survival was quite another matter. The characteristics which made it easy for one publisher to enter the industry made it easy for competitors to enter. Furthermore, a publisher had to count on operating at a loss at least until he learned just what the response to his new magazine was. Books and movies were reviewed soon after their issue, but not so magazines; there was little immediate feedback from reader to publisher. A publisher sent his magazines into the world and waited for them to succeed or fail. If readers did not share his enthusiasm for a new publication, he often had a hard time learning just why his idea had gone wrong. Advertisers were cautious about buying space in an untried publication, although they sometimes gave false encouragement to publishers of projected new magazines with talk of future orders. Even if the magazine soon won a reader following, advertisers often were slow to find a place for it in their allocations.

If the publisher did devise a brilliantly successful magazine, he could not entirely hide the pattern for its success, since he was forced by the nature of publishing to exhibit his best ideas in public; and a successful magazine invariably bred imitators. Then, too, readers were fickle. Their tastes and interests changed, and it required a brand of editorial genius to anticipate those changes before they were reflected in a declining circulation. Over all else hung the threat to the balance sheet which arose from the economics of publishing. A publisher, in consequence, was tagged by the threat of failure—failure to hold his readers, failure to hold his advertisers, failure to hold the position of his magazine, failure to maintain its very existence.

This threat was reflected in the day to day operations of magazines. They fired a steady barrage of research and sales talk to convince the advertiser that they best served the market which he wished to reach. They assailed him with trade paper advertising that denounced competitors by name and that proved their own supremacy with incontrovertible statistics—or, perhaps more correctly, with controvertible statistics, since each of two rivals often could find proof in the same set of figures. They fought for the best display positions on newsstands and on rare occasions engaged in open warfare. They studied the rises and dips in circulation of their own and competitors' magazines as closely as ever a physician watched a patient's temperature, and a few used readership studies to measure the response to editorial features. On many a magazine, the tenure of top personnel was short. When circulation or advertising fell ominously, the reaction of many publishers was to fire key staff members and to bring in fresh minds. Such staff upheavals, to an outsider, seemed a frantic game of musical chairs, for magazines drew their ablest personnel from a small reservoir of talent, and when staff members were crowded out of one magazine they dashed for seats on others. At least one major publisher, to forestall stagnation, frequently transferred staff members from one position to another within the organization as a matter of company policy.

Intensifying the struggle for existence was the economics of publishing and its eternal paradox: a publisher needed a large circulation to make a profit, yet this same circulation could conceivably ruin him financially. The paradox was inherent in the system of magazine support. Nearly all publishers depended on advertising for most of their income. They sold their magazine to the reader for less than the cost of production and took their profits from the advertising which their circulation attracted. As a carrier of advertising, the magazine was sensitive to changes in business conditions. Yet when advertising volume dropped suddenly, when production costs rose suddenly, the publisher had to continue publishing a magazine of essentially the same size and quality as ever, if only in the hope of regaining the advertising linage he had lost. A publisher could rarely trim operating costs rapidly enough to compensate for losses in advertising. In fact, his production costs sometimes rose when advertising declined, for then he had to pay for editorial material to fill the space formerly occupied by advertising.

Just getting his copies printed was a major expense. In the early thirties, *Fortune* estimated that printing, paper, and postage accounted for about half the cost of publishing a monthly magazine similar to Ray Long's *Cosmopolitan*.[2] In the early sixties, the paper that spun through the presses at thirty miles an hour alone cost $1 out of every $4 that a publisher took in, and for some magazines it was double that figure, according to Truman Bradley, production manager of the McCall Corporation. On the average, all costs in 1962 broke down in this fashion for the eighty-seven consumer magazines surveyed by Bernard Gallagher: mechanical and distribution, 47 per cent; editorial, 15 per cent; circulation, 9 per cent; advertising, 14 per cent; and overhead, 10 per cent. Average profit before taxes was 5 per cent.[3]

As their fixed costs shot rapidly upward in the years right after World War II and on through the fifties, publishers saw their profits decline or vanish altogether. During the decade of the fifties, the overall expenses of magazine publishing increased by somewhere between 40 and 50 per cent, according to James B. Kobak of J. K. Lasser and Company. The cost of printing rose by 44 per cent, paper by 31 per cent, salaries by 41 per cent, postage by 89 per cent, and those items took about $9 out of every $10 a publisher spent. Meanwhile, profits for thirty-five of the largest publishers slumped from 4.3 per cent after taxes in 1950 to 1.7 per cent in 1960. Four out of every ten magazines reporting to the Lasser firm lost money in 1960, and the figure was about the same two years later.

Partly because they sought economic stability, partly because expansion was an outward sign of success, many companies published not just one magazine but several. Time and again a company began with one publication, nursed it along to modest or spectacular financial success, and then originated or bought other publications, just as Frank Munsey increased his holdings after the success of *Munsey's*. It was natural for a publisher to exploit a market to the fullest once he had learned what it liked in a magazine. Therefore, a publisher frequently aimed a variety of publications at a reader group with which he had had some experience. John H. Johnson did so with *Ebony*, *Tan*, and *Jet*; other publishers did so by bringing out both confession and movie fan magazines, both of which were read by the same sort of women. On the other hand, a number of companies each produced several publications for widely dissimilar audiences.

---

[2] "The Cosmopolitan of Ray Long," *Fortune*, 3 (March, 1931) 51.
[3] *The Gallagher Report*, 11 (Feb. 18, 1963), sec. 2, p. 2.

Like Munsey, some publishers endured over the years by killing off titles that slipped in public favor and replacing them with new ones. Street & Smith, a leading publisher of pulp magazines after the nineties, was ever quick to drop titles when readers began to lose interest in them, just as quick to replace them with new ones. In 1949 the company in one blow wiped out its last four pulp magazines and five comic books to concentrate on its more profitable slick magazines, *Charm*, *Mademoiselle*, and *Living for Young Homemakers*.

In general, the lower the profit margin on each copy sold, the more titles a publisher had in his stable. During the thirties, for instance, the publishers of pulp fiction magazines walked a thin line between profit and loss. The net on an issue of 100,000 copies often amounted only to somewhere between $460 and $730. To have even a modest income, the publisher had to own a number of magazines. In the forties, fifties, and early sixties, the owners of the longest lists of titles were publishers of pulps, comics, detective magazines, movie fan magazines, and confession magazines, most of which were lean on advertising and depended on sales for much of their revenue.

In the struggle to hold their shares of the market, many publishers and many magazines failed. The mortality rate of magazines has always been high. "The expectation of failure is connected with the very name Magazine," Noah Webster wrote in 1788; and Herbert Hungerford, drawing on his many years' experience in the magazine industry, observed in the 1930's: "With the exception of theatrical ventures, I doubt if there is, in any other field of endeavor, such a large proportion of failures among all the new projects that are started." [4]

Just what proportion of the new ventures ended in failure, it is impossible to say. There is no central clearinghouse reporting on all the magazines established; even if there were, it would probably overlook the many publications which reached trial dummy issues but died before their first public appearance. A writer working for the publisher of directories of periodicals once estimated that only one magazine in every 300 attempted ever attained commercial success. Hungerford, writing in the thirties, concurred in that estimate. But in 1953 a veteran in the magazine industry who wished to remain anonymous estimated a much lower proportion of fail-

---

[4] Herbert Hungerford, *How Publishers Win* (Washington, 1931), pp. 22-23.

ures. "You have to distinguish between the outright gambles and the magazines carefully planned and adequately financed," he said. "I'd guess that perhaps no more than half of the magazines of serious intent fail."

Certainly the mortality rate for magazines was high, even if it were considerably lower than Hungerford's estimate. Hundreds upon hundreds of magazines were begun, only to be killed off, sometimes after a single issue, sometimes after several years' publication. The fact that a magazine survived for a number of years was no evidence of its financial success. *Success* magazine, which consistently failed to live up to its name, stayed alive for years only because at least seven different backers, one of whom sank more than a million dollars into it, were willing to take chances on it. *Liberty,* too, seems to have spent much of its lifetime of more than a quarter-century in the red. *Liberty* was begun in 1924 by Colonel Robert McCormick of the Chicago *Tribune* and Joseph M. Patterson of the New York *Daily News,* who reportedly lost some $12,-000,000 on it in their seven years of ownership. In 1931 Bernarr Macfadden took it over and operated it, sometimes in the red, sometimes in the black, until he withdrew from Macfadden Publications. Throughout the forties, several new owners, each apparently more optimistic than the last, tried to make a go of *Liberty;* but in 1951, after having been taken over by a publisher of cheesecake magazines, it finally died.

On the other hand, some publishers had little patience with magazines that needed nursing along, and their practices helped to account for the large turnover in magazine titles. They launched new publications largely on a sink-or-swim basis; they allocated comparatively small sums to keep the magazine afloat until it acquired acceptance by readers and advertisers. If the magazine caught on, it was retained until it slipped; if it did not catch on at once or at least show promise, it was promptly abandoned. The Dell Publishing Company and Fawcett Publications, both of which concentrated on publications depending on newsstand sales rather than on subscriptions, rapidly disposed of magazines which did not operate in the black. They were continually starting new magazines and killing off old ones; Dell designed many of its new publications as one-shots.

There were a number of reasons for the high mortality rate of magazines. No two magazines ever died for exactly the same reasons; but the magazines that failed had certain common weaknesses, according to Harlan Logan, a former publishers' consultant and former editor of *Scribner's*. [5] Examining a long list of failures, he noted that several of the following weaknesses were always present:

1. Lack of editorial reason for existence.
2. Lack of clearly defined editorial pattern.
3. Lack of advertising reason for existence.
4. Lack of realistic budget projections.
5. Lack of realistic schedule of time required to gain either reader or advertising acceptance.
6. Lack of knowledge of the magazine field in general and of the specific competition.
7. Lack of accurate information about the personnel which is hired to produce the new magazine.
8. Lack of an objective and independent (nonstaff) audit of the potentialities of the new magazine and of the publishing program that has been set up.

Logan also estimated the costs and risks of starting a new magazine in 1949. Although his calculations were out of date in the sixties, they are presented in Table 4 in the absence of later data. In the early sixties, the overall costs of publishing were perhaps 40 to 50 per cent higher than when Logan made his estimates, and the odds against success were certainly higher. Logan's figures, intended only as general estimates, were based on the capital necessary to sustain a publication for four years, the time he thought necessary for it to achieve acceptance by readers and advertisers.

If the death rate of new magazines was high, so was the death rate of those which had established themselves. In just the decade bracketed by 1950 and 1960, for instance, one out of every eight magazines belonging to the Audit Bureau of Circulations died or was merged out of existence. The industry was one of continuous entrances and exits, and success was never permanent. Newcomers in the twentieth century challenged and often unseated their longer-lived contemporaries, just as *Munsey's* and *McClure's* had surpassed many of the leaders of their time. There seemed to be an ebb and flow in the lives of magazines and a point at which they were vulnerable to attack. Edmund Wilson, the literary critic and

---

[5] Harlan Logan, "Tomorrow's New Magazines," *Magazine Industry*, 1 (Summer, 1949) 19.

Table 4. INVESTMENT REQUIRED TO FINANCE A MAGAZINE ADEQUATELY
FOR FOUR YEARS (MONEY FIGURES IN MILLIONS)

Magazine Group	For estab. publisher	For new publisher	Odds Against Success Even with This Investment:	
			For estab. publisher	For new publisher
General Weekly: Competition for *Life*, *Satevepost*, etc.	$5 to $10	$7.5 to $15	2 to 1	3 to 1
General Monthly: Competition for *American*, *Cosmopolitan*, etc.	$2.5 to $5	$4 to $7	7 to 1	10 to 1
Women's Service: Competition for *Good Hskp.*, *L.H.J.*	$3.5 to $7.5	$5 to $10	2 to 1	3 to 1
Pocket Size: Competition for *Reader's Digest*, *Pageant*, etc. (No adv.)	$1 to $2	$2 to $3	3 to 2	2 to 1
News Weekly: Competition for *Time*, *Newsweek*	$2.5 to $5	$5 to $10	2 to 1	3 to 1
Specialty Service: Competition for *Harper's Bazaar*, *Mademoiselle*, etc.	$2 to $3	$2.5 to $5	Even	2 to 1
Miscellaneous Monthly: Scientific, travel, youth, the arts, etc.	$1 to $4	$2 to $5	Even	2 to 1

Source: Harlan Logan, "Tomorrow's New Magazines," *Magazine Industry*, 1 (Summer, 1949) 17.

himself a magazine writer, noticed in 1935 that magazines, like
other living organisms, have a youth, a maturity, and an old age:
"In its earliest years, a magazine may seem spontaneous, novel and
daring; but by the time it has reached its maturity it has, as the
French say, 'taken its fold,' and it succumbs to the force of inertia
against which the youngest and freshest editor is as powerless as
the oldest and stalest. Thereafter, it grows old, declines and dies." [6]
There is some documentation of that point in later chapters that

[6] Edmund Wilson, "The Literary Worker's Polonius," in *The Shores of Light*
(New York, 1952), p. 593.

give short histories of some of the magazines which toppled and of some of the new publications which replaced them. But here let us illustrate that remark in a general way; let us consider the changing positions among the leaders in advertising and circulation. After 1900 a small number of magazines took in the great share of national advertising and sold a high percentage of total copies. But many of the magazines which were at the top in the early years of the century had vanished by the forties and fifties. The magazine industry was so competitive and fluid that even new periodicals started with little financial backing could work their way up into the small circle of leaders.

One can easily show that a few publishers and a few magazines collected a large share of the money which national advertisers spent in magazines from 1918 onward. It is much harder to show that advertising revenue was concentrated in few hands between 1900 and 1918, as data are sketchy and unreliable. However, since the advertising revenues of the Curtis Publishing Company began a sharp increase in about 1908 and since its publications had emerged as the leading advertising media in the United States by 1918, one can conjecture that by the early years of the century a handful of publishers was receiving a very high proportion of the money spent on national advertising.

By 1918 the concentration of advertising revenues was clearly apparent. In that year, about 43 per cent of all dollars spent on national advertising in general and farm magazines went to the three publications of the Curtis Publishing Company, *Saturday Evening Post, Ladies' Home Journal,* and *Country Gentleman,* which together took in $25,288,000 of the $58,432,000 total. Each year from then until 1930, the Curtis publications accounted for from 38 to 43 per cent of the money which national advertisers spent in general and farm magazines. The weekly *Saturday Evening Post* alone took in from 27 to 31 per cent of such funds each year from 1918 through 1929.

Although the Curtis Publishing Company led by far in advertising income in the twenties, other publishers also accounted for good-sized shares of national advertising revenues. For instance, the Crowell Publishing Company in 1920 grossed $15,449,000, or 12 per cent of the total, and in 1925, its *American, Collier's, Farm and Fireside,* and *Woman's Home Companion* took in $16,754,000, or 11 per cent.

The concentration of advertising in that period is underlined by a few additional figures. Just Curtis and Crowell shared 51 per cent of the dollar volume of national advertising in general and national farm magazines in 1920, and 54 per cent in 1925. The top five leaders in advertising revenue in 1920—*Saturday Evening Post, Literary Digest, Ladies' Home Journal, Pictorial Review,* and *Woman's Home Companion*—grossed $71,922,000, or 56 per cent of the total, and the top ten accounted for 70 per cent. In 1925, the top five accounted for 55 per cent, the top ten for 70 per cent.

The bulk of national advertising continued to gravitate to the columns of just a handful of magazines throughout the thirties, forties, fifties, and into the sixties. During the thirties, Curtis magazines carried from one-fifth to one-third of the dollar volume of all national advertising in magazines. In 1947, about 47 per cent of all money spent on national advertising in magazines went to just five magazines of three publishers and about 83 per cent of it to the ten magazines leading in advertising revenues. In 1955 the gross revenues of just three publishers—Crowell-Collier, Curtis, and Time Inc.—amounted to almost half of the total sum spent on national advertising in consumer magazines. Just the top five magazines in 1963 accounted for more than 40 per cent of the total.

However, despite that concentration of advertising, the life blood of the great majority of commercial magazines, new publishers launched publications that were able to achieve mammoth circulations and large volumes of advertising. One of those publishers was Time Inc. In 1923, the year that Time Inc. was established, Curtis Publishing Company was taking in 43 per cent of the total dollar volume of national advertising. Twenty years later Time Inc. had surpassed Curtis, and in 1963 its gross advertising take outstripped that of Curtis more than two to one.

The position of an advertising leader was never secure. Of the top twenty magazines leading in advertising revenues in 1927, exactly half were gone twenty years later and another one of them vanished within the next five years. They had died or been merged out of existence. On the other hand, of the twenty top carriers of advertising in 1962, fifteen were not in existence before 1920. A few of them were published by companies that existed before then, but most were not.

In circulation as in advertising revenue, a few magazines accounted for a great share of the total. The twenty-five circulation leaders in 1927 sold about 24 per cent of all copies distributed, and the situation was much the same six years later when the twenty-three magazines with circulations of a million or more accounted for about 23 per cent of total magazine distribution. The concentration persisted through the forties and fifties; in the early sixties the top dozen circulation leaders were responsible for about 27 per cent of total magazine circulation. Those figures are highly approximate, coming as they do from sources not strictly comparable, but the general conclusion seems valid.

One indication that a few publications had the bulk of total circulation appeared in the report of a Senate committee during hearings on postal rates. In one three-month period in 1949, according to the report, 43.6 per cent of the weight and 43.2 per cent of the revenue in second-class mail, the class giving preferential rates to periodicals, was derived from the eighteen largest magazines and two of the largest newspapers. Ten corporations published those twenty publications, the nine largest of which were controlled by three corporations.[7]

But in circulation as in advertising, magazines fell from the top and new ones took their places. In 1930 twenty-five general and farm magazines had circulations of at least a million. Fifteen of them were dead thirty years later. Indeed, of the forty-two general and farm magazines with sales of more than a million in 1950, one in every six had vanished by the early 1960's. Conversely, there were fifty general and farm magazines with circulations of a million or more in 1963. Exactly half of them were launched in 1920 or after. Ten of the general and four of the farm publications were started in the first decade of the century, six in the second, nine in the 1920's, ten in the 1930's, four in the 1940's, and two in the 1950's.

The speed with which some of the new publishers and new magazines grew into circulation giants was remarkable. It took the *Literary Digest* some thirty years to achieve a circulation of 2,000,-000. Bernarr Macfadden's *True Story*, which first appeared in 1919, cornered almost 2,000,000 readers in about seven years. It took the *Ladies' Home Journal* approximately twenty years to reach a circulation of a million. *Better Living* guaranteed advertisers a million circulation from its first issue in 1951.

Although the magazine industry was freely competitive and publishers rose and descended rapidly, there were some surface

---

[7] *Tide*, 24 (March 17, 1950) 38.

indications of concentration of resources and market. Individual companies tended to publish several magazines. There was some cross-media ownership. Such ownership of a sort existed in the eighteenth century when some of the early magazines were off-shoots of newspapers and printing activities and in the nineteenth when some grew out of book-publishing houses.

In the twentieth century, magazine publishers ran paper mills, printing and engraving plants, periodical subscription and distribution agencies, and research organizations; they owned such related communications enterprises as newspapers, newspaper syndicates, newsletters, radio and television stations, motion picture studios, text and trade-book–publishing houses, and book clubs.

But especially in the late fifties and early sixties, when profits for some magazines were low or nonexistent, diversification took many forms: record clubs; night clubs; outdoor lighting equipment; data processing; maps, globes, and atlases; an iron mill, a toy store.

However, one gets the impression that over the years, magazine publishers were interested primarily in their magazines. With few exceptions even those who owned other communications media seemed to give their magazines their special attention and their special love. When they began to diversify in the late fifties, they apparently did so to protect the existence of their magazines by finding new sources of income.

Perhaps significantly, the two publishers who built up vast communications empires, Frank Munsey and William Randolph Hearst, both hit their stride in publishing at a time when consolidations, trusts, and concentrations of economic power were an outstanding characteristic of American economic life. The times encouraged dreams like Munsey's of a single large corporation operating hundreds of newspapers and magazines on a mass-production basis from a central headquarters. Starting as a magazine publisher, Munsey chased his dream of a long chain of periodicals by buying up newspaper after newspaper, magazine after magazine. And, with an eye on his ledger, he killed off or combined the ones that weakened. In time, magazines and newspapers were but part of his extensive holdings, which included banks, hotels, and stores.

William Randolph Hearst entered journalism in 1887 as publisher of the San Francisco *Examiner*, a newspaper belonging to his father. After almost a decade of experimenting with techniques to attract a mass audience, he invaded New York in 1895 with the purchase of the *Journal*. He broke into the magazine field in 1903 when he founded *Motor.* Thereafter, he began or bought, combined or killed off, a number of magazines. At his peak in 1935, he owned twenty-six dailies in nineteen cities, their combined circulation amounting to 13.6 per cent of total daily circulation in the country; thirteen magazines; eight radio stations; two motion picture companies; the Sunday supplement *American Weekly;* International News Service, Universal Service, and International News Photos; and the King Feature Syndicate.[8] Although the empire had contracted by 1963, the Hearst Corporation and its subsidiaries still owned eleven magazines in the United States and six in other countries, ten daily newspapers, six broadcasting stations, a paperback-book—publishing firm, a feature syndicate, a movie newsreel, and numerous other properties at home and abroad.

By comparison, the holdings of most other publishers were modest. Some newspaper publishers, like Hearst, moved in to the magazine field, and some magazine publishers, like Munsey, moved into the newspaper field, although on a more modest scale. Cyrus Curtis, Arthur Capper, the New York Times Company, Marshall Field III, John and Gardner Cowles, the Washington Post Company, S. I. Newhouse, John Hay Whitney, and others owned newspapers and magazines at one time or another, and some also owned broadcasting stations.

In 1913 Cyrus Curtis branched from magazine publishing into newspaper publishing by buying the Philadelphia *Public Ledger* for $2,000,000. Evidently to keep the *Ledger* alive, he bought and killed three other Philadelphia newspapers, the *Evening Telegraph,* the *Press,* and the *North American.* He acquired the New York *Evening Post* in 1923 and the Philadelphia *Inquirer* in 1930. In 1926 Cyrus Curtis told an interviewer: "I've really just started to become a newspaper publisher. As I've said before, I don't want to become owner of a chain of newspapers. . . . I want to make what I have the very best in the daily field. . . . I've realized my ambitions as a magazine publisher. Now I'm tackling the daily field. I want to make a go of it." [9] But he was never as fortunate with his newspapers as with his magazines. When he died in 1933, his newspapers were valued at more than $50,000,000, but they were a drain on his finances instead of money-makers. In 1933 J. David Stern bought the New York *Post,* and three years later Moses L. Annen-

---

[8] Edwin Emery, "William Randolph Hearst: A Tentative Appraisal," *Journalism Quarterly,* 28 (Fall, 1951) 431.
[9] *Editor & Publisher,* 59 (July 10, 1926) 11.

berg bought the Philadelphia *Inquirer*. By the time the *Ledger* died in 1942, the last of the Curtis newspapers, Cyrus Curtis and his heirs had spent a reported $42,000,000 on their excursion into newspaper publishing.

In 1893, about the time that Cyrus Curtis was getting his publishing company well under way, a young Kansan named Arthur Capper returned to Topeka from Washington, where he had been correspondent for the Topeka *Capital*. In 1957 Capper Publications, Inc., and its subsidiaries published magazines and newspapers reaching about 5,000,000 subscribers and operated one radio station and one television station. Its periodicals included *Household*, a monthly home-service magazine; *Capper's Farmer*, a farm magazine circulating mainly throughout the Midwest; *Kansas Farmer* and *Missouri Ruralist*, semimonthly magazines with statewide circulations; and *Capper's Weekly*, a weekly feature publication. Its newspapers were the Topeka *Daily Capital*, a morning and Sunday paper. A subsidiary, Capper-Harman-Slocum, Inc., published three semimonthly farm magazines, *Michigan Farmer*, *Ohio Farmer*, and *Pennsylvania Farmer*. Another subsidiary operated radio station WIBW and WIBW-TV in Topeka. Bit by bit after 1957 Capper Publications disposed of its magazines. It folded *Household* in 1958, *Capper's Farmer* two years later. In 1961 it sold *Kansas Farmer* and *Missouri Ruralist* and its interest in Home State Farm Publications, Inc., formerly Capper-Harman-Slocum.

Gardner and John Cowles, members of a family in the newspaper business since 1903, turned to magazine publishing in 1937 when they brought out *Look*. The holdings of Cowles Magazines and Broadcasting, Inc., in 1963 included two newspapers in Florida and one in Puerto Rico, two magazines and a newsletter, radio, and television stations in Des Moines and Memphis, subscription agencies, and a book and encyclopedia division. S. I. Newhouse, who at the time owned ten newspapers and had interests in seven broadcasting stations, branched into magazine publishing when he bought Condé Nast Publications and Street & Smith in 1959. The publisher of the Washington *Post* acquired *Newsweek* in 1961; the company also owned *Art News* magazine, a radio and television station in Washington, and a television station in Jacksonville, Florida. The Whitney Communications Corporation of John Hay Whitney, which in the early sixties published the magazines *Environment* and *Interior Design*, held a controlling interest in the New York *Herald Tribune* and a Paris edition of it; *Parade*, a Sunday newspaper supplement; and five television and two radio stations. Whitney also held a majority interest in Vip Radio, Inc., which through four subsidiaries owned four radio stations in the metropolitan New York area.

A number of magazine publishers became book publishers and vice versa at various times during the twentieth century, as when Alfred Knopf published the *American Mercury* in the twenties, Doubleday published *American Home* and *Country Life* in the twenties, and Ziff-Davis Publishing Company in 1942 created a book division for itself by buying the Alliance Book Corporation. The McGraw-Hill Publishing Company was a major publisher of both books and magazines, chiefly trade periodicals and scientific journals. Its trade-book division published and distributed fiction and nonfiction for the general reader, and other divisions published texts for secondary schools, business institutes, and colleges.

Until the early sixties, however, magazine publishers who produced books generally concentrated on cookbooks and other service publications, which arose as by-products of their magazines, or inexpensive paperbacks, which could be distributed much as their magazines were. Among the publishers of paperback books were Curtis, Dell, Fawcett, and Macfadden-Bartell. When income from magazines generally began to dip, several companies engaged in other types of book publishing. Time Inc. in 1961 set up a special division to publish informational books for adults; founded the Time Reading Program, a book club; and in 1962 bought Silver Burdett Company, a venerable textbook house. In the early sixties, Meredith Publishing Company, which had been publishing cookbooks since 1930 and other service publications since the forties, acquired Lyons and Carnahan, publisher of elementary and high school texts; Appleton-Century-Crofts, publisher of college texts, reference works, and trade books; and Duell, Sloan, and Pearce, publisher of trade books. It also started the Family Book Service, a club offering members monthly selections of Meredith and other books. Its other activities in 1963 included printing magazines and catalogs; designing, manufacturing, and distributing a line of geographical globes; and operating radio and television stations in Kansas City, Omaha, Phoenix, and Syracuse.

A few magazine publishers besides Hearst tried their hands at producing movies. Time Inc. in 1934 formed its cinema unit, the March of Time, which produced film documentaries released through Twentieth Century-Fox and which prepared special films on assignment for such clients as the State of New York, the New York Stock Exchange, and the Standard Oil Company of Indiana. Its first documentary, "Speak-easy," was shown in 417 theaters; eventually its releases were shown every four weeks by more than 9,000 theaters around the world to an audience estimated at 30,000,000. In the early fifties, when its business with theaters had fallen off, the March of Time turned to producing movies for television. It closed its production offices entirely in the spring of 1954. The National Broadcasting Company took over its collection of films, McGraw-Hill its collection of theatrical shorts, and Twentieth Century-Fox the television rights to its productions.

As a personal venture, David Smart of Esquire, Inc., in 1940 formed a company to film color-sound instructional movies for schools. During the war, the company produced training films for the Navy. In the fall of 1944, Smart reorganized his private project as Coronet Instructional Films, a division of Esquire, Inc., which invested $1,000,000 in it. In 1949 Esquire, Inc., acquired control of Ideal Pictures Corporation and its affiliates, rental distributors of 16-mm. nontheatrical films of all types, with twenty-nine branches in the United States and Hawaii. *Look* magazine, in cooperation with a Manhattan firm, in October, 1943, began producing "*Look's* World Spotlight," a ten-minute feature which appeared monthly for about two years and which was shown in about fifty theaters.

There seems to have been almost no vertical integration in the magazine industry. As we have seen, most publishers owned neither printing facilities nor means of distributing their copies to newsstands. Indeed, some publishers regarded integration as a handicap rather than as a blessing. Some publishers, however, did move slightly toward self-containment. In a program to build up paper supplies and printing capacity after World War II, Time Inc. branched out by acquiring several paper mills. Although it did not buy printing plants, it did assist its contract printers in enlarging their establishments; and it set up a wholly owned subsidiary to develop and market technical improvements in the printing and allied trades. One of the few self-contained magazine publishers in the United States, probably the only one, was Curtis Publishing Company. As the company expanded after 1900, it added to its holdings so that it eventually owned forests for making paper, pulp and paper mills, printing plants and binderies, and agencies for soliciting subscriptions and distributing copies to the newsstands.

Unlike Curtis, most magazine publishers did not handle their own distribution of copies to retailers. From the nineteenth century onward, such distribution was controlled by a few organizations. A publisher had no trouble getting his copies to regular subscribers; the Post Office Department delivered them at preferential rates. But getting copies to dealers throughout the United States and Canada, shifting copies from places where they sold slowly to places where the demand exceeded the supply, and recalling copies that dealers were unable to sell—those tasks were too big for most publishers. The few who did undertake them usually found it good business to handle the publications of other publishers as well.

The American News Company dominated the distribution of magazines to retail outlets from the 1880's, when publishers became aware of the importance of single-copy sales, until the mid-1950's, when it was servicing some 95,000 dealers from more than 350 branch offices. But beginning in 1955, its role as distributor was affected by terms of a consent decree arising from an antitrust action, changes in policies that came with changes in management, and the loss of several major accounts. The company withdrew completely as a national distributor in August, 1957.

American News was founded in 1864 to distribute periodicals to retailers, but it soon branched into wholesaling stationery, books, toys, and eventually hundreds of other items. In 1872 its subsidiary, Railroad News Company, bought the Union News Company, also established in 1864 to sell reading matter and merchandise to passengers on Commodore Vanderbilt's New York and Harlem Railroad. In time, American News expanded its network of branches across the United States and into Canada.

In 1955 its activities were manifold. Directly or through its subsidiaries, it not only imported and exported, wholesaled, and retailed newspapers, magazines, and books; it also operated newsstands, restaurants, lunchrooms, cafeterias, soda fountains, bakeries, coffee shops, tobacco shops, book shops, toy shops, drugstores, barber shops, parcel checking facilities, weighing and vending machines, ice and roller skating rinks.[10]

American News sold more than half of the total number and dollar value of magazines distributed throughout the United States by national independent distributors. It was the largest wholesaler of books in the world; through its book department it accounted

---

[10] Standard and Poor, *Standard Corporation Descriptions*, 16, no. 10. sec. 2 (April 7, 1955) 3438-39.

for from 25 per cent to 35 per cent of the total sale of a popular best seller. Its foreign department handled wholesale distribution of periodicals in Central and South America, the West Indies, Newfoundland, Iceland, Spain, Portugal, Africa, Australia, New Zealand, the Asiatic countries, and the U.S. possessions.

The largest wholly owned subsidiary of American News was the Union News Company, which operated concessions in hotels, transportation terminals, office buildings, public parks, and golf courses in thirty-two states and the District of Columbia. Its system of newsstands made it the largest retailer of magazines in the world; its gross sales volume of magazines in 1950 was about $7,500,000. It had about 170 contracts giving it the exclusive concession to sell magazines in certain department stores, hotels, and transportation systems. Early in 1949, it acquired all of the restaurant business of the Savarins Company, which operated a chain of restaurants in New York City.

Another subsidiary of American News was the International News Company, which by the thirties was the world's largest importer and exporter of reading matter. One of its functions was to stimulate interest abroad in American books and periodicals. It also distributed foreign magazines, newspapers, and books in the United States; before World War II, it handled the retail distribution in the United States of more than 900 foreign publications from all over the world. Still another wholly owned subsidiary was American Lending Library, Inc., which operated a system of lending libraries.

In June, 1952, the Department of Justice, filing suit under the Sherman Anti-trust Law, charged American News and Union News with monopolizing the distribution of magazines from publishers to news dealers through independent distributors. American News, according to the complaint, used its relations with Union News to obtain exclusive national distribution rights. Union News refused to sell magazines not handled by American unless the parent company consented, the government charged; it gave preferential display to periodicals for which American held exclusive national distribution rights. The action ended with a consent decree three years later. Under the consent decree, Union News would buy, display, and sell magazines solely on the basis of its own interest as a dealer in periodicals. American News would not claim that it could obtain preferential treatment in the sales of magazines by Union News.

When Henry Garfinkle became president of American News in June, 1955, two months before the consent decree, he made a fundamental change in company policy. Garfinkle, who had quit school at thirteen to help support his family, had risen from newsboy to one of the largest newsstand concessionaires in New York City. Early in 1955 he and some 200 business associates began quietly buying up American News stock. By summer they had emerged with working control of the company and its subsidiary, Union News. Immediately on assuming the presidency, Garfinkle announced that American News was abandoning its traditional policy of handling magazines only if it had exclusive rights to national distribution. In the future, he said, the company would also distribute magazines locally or regionally without insisting on national distribution rights. In effect, then, the company sought to serve other distributing agencies in communities and areas in which they wished wholesale representation.

As a result of this policy change, such distributors as the Curtis Circulation Company, International Circulation Distributors, and others used the best of the American News branches selectively. Publishers whose magazines were distributed by American News were able to withdraw their publications from handling by its least efficient branches. By early 1957, after *Collier's* and *Woman's Home Companion* had died, American News had lost the last of its big mass-circulation clients, and by May several remaining ones were leaving for other distributors. The company entirely pulled out of the national distribution business in August.

When the national magazine was born, American News had a virtual monopoly distribution to local retailers. Frank Munsey in 1893 demonstrated that a publisher could bypass American News in getting his copies on the newsstand, and Cyrus Curtis in the late nineties shipped his *Saturday Evening Post* directly to news dealers. But publishers did not achieve national distribution of consequence through independent wholesalers until the first years of the twentieth century. The Curtis Publishing Company began distributing all of its magazines in that fashion in 1911, the Hearst organization in 1913. The Popular Science Monthly Company and the McCall Company, after breaking relations with American News, formed the S-M News Company in 1919. Its operation was typical of the new distributing companies that were arising. At first it handled only the publications of its founders, but later it took on those of other publishers. It developed its own contacts with whole-salers, and in small towns, with retailers; helped to gauge the market for a publication at hundreds of newsstands throughout the country; sought good newsstand display for its magazines; and transferred copies of an issue from outlets with too many to those with too few. The original two founders owned the company until 1947. Thereafter they sold interests to several other major pub-lishers, among them the Reader's Digest Association and Time Inc., and changed the company name to Select Magazines, Inc.

Magazines in the early sixties were distributed largely through a few companies like Select Magazines, Curtis Circulation Com-pany, and Publishers Distributing Corporation that worked with some 800 independent wholesalers throughout the United States and Canada. Publishers sometimes complained that instead of being at the mercy of a national monopoly such as American News enjoyed in the late nineteenth century they were at the mercy of many local monopolies. Most of the wholesalers had no competition in the areas they served, and they largely determined the effective-ness of sales at the retail level. For their part, the wholesalers complained that they suffered from high costs and from inadequate commissions.

After a lengthy investigation in the early sixties, the Federal Trade Commission obtained consent agreements from more than twoscore publishers and distributing companies to end payment of allowances to favored newsstands in order to obtain preferential display for their magazines.[11]

Despite concentrations of power, magazine publishing remained a highly fluid industry in the early sixties. Magazines, large and small alike, were still appearing and disappearing, and today's success could still be tomorrow's failure. The odds in starting a new magazine perhaps favored the established publisher, and a newcomer could not expect to challenge the leaders on a shoe-string budget. Yet new companies continued to enter the industry, and publishers of long standing continued to prepare new publi-cations. Some of both, as ever, would probably be phenomenally successful.

---

[11] *Advertising Age,* 31 (Feb. 23, 1959) 1; 32 (Sept. 18, 1961) 32; 31 (July 18, 1960) 3, 10; 33 (July 16, 1962) 81; 33 (Aug. 20, 1962) 72.

The Logistics
of Magazine Publishing

A railroad employee, paid off with a complimentary subscription, shot off his report to Time Inc. one day in the late fifties: "Delivery of *Life* is one day late in Dayton, Ohio." He was one of 550 "subscription reporters," chosen for their permanence in key locations, who for more than a decade had been keeping Time Inc. informed of distribution snarls around the world. The company tabulated the reports, investigated delays, and changed delivery schedules for its magazines.

Although the railroad man was remote in place and in function from the editorial centers of New York, he nevertheless had a part to play in magazine logistics. Producing a million or more copies of a magazine each week or month was a highly complex operation which demanded the close coordination of a multiplicity of activities. Before magazines of mammoth circulation could become commonplace, the industry had to develop systematic methods of obtaining subscriptions and of keeping rosters of subscribers up to date. A system of rapid and orderly distribution had to be organized; copies had to be delivered simultaneously across the nation both to subscribers and to a hundred thousand news dealers without too many or too few copies to each. There had to be presses capable of printing millions of copies in a matter of hours and paper to feed the presses. Strongly responsible for the success of

Life was what Roy Larsen, its publisher, in 1939 called a "two-year revolution in the paper, printing, and distribution business." "The magazine *Life*, as we know it today, printed on its kind of paper, with its grade of printing, and in a four-day span," Larsen said, "would have cost a minimum of fifty cents and possibly even a dollar a copy in 1913. Today's current issue costs well *under* the ten cents we charge for it."[1] The editorial techniques of popular magazines, under the pressures of speed and competition, also acquired some of the features of mass production, and the role of the editor was altered in consequence.

An important aspect of logistics was getting one's magazine into the hands of readers. In the sixties magazines were sold principally by subscription or by the single copy at retail outlets. In the nineties the chief means of distribution was through newsstands in railway terminals and in bookstores, but systematic methods of gathering subscribers were also beginning to emerge.

Catalog agencies, which had existed in the United States since the 1850's, represented perhaps the first attempt at organized subscription solicitation. They were a major source of subscriptions in the nineties. They came about when some individuals—housewives, school teachers, postmasters—began selling magazine subscriptions to friends and neighbors in their spare time. At first these agents arranged with individual publishers to buy subscriptions at a discount, but eventually clearinghouses arose to coordinate orders from many agents and for many magazines. In the early sixties, there were eleven major agencies of that sort, the oldest including American News, Hanson-Bennett, and Moore-Cottrell, and each one annually issued a catalog listing details about hundreds of publications.

After World War I, when publishers scrambled for large circulations in order to get their share of the mounting volume of advertising, there was a blossoming of field-selling agencies which sent crews of aggressive young door-to-door salesmen throughout the country. Some publishers set up their own agencies, which usually sold other magazines as well. The magazine salesman who was working his way through college became a part of American folklore and contributed in large measure to the huge circulations of the twenties and thirties. The crews could penetrate areas beyond

---

[1] *Editor & Publisher,* 72 (May 13, 1939), sec. 2, p. 10.

the reach of newsstands, and their salesmen were so persuasive and the market so fertile that a fresh crew could often set a sales record in a territory which had just been worked over. About 20,000 field salesmen of independent agencies journeyed about the United States before World War II. During the war, door-to-door solicitation languished because of shortages of gasoline, manpower, and magazine paper, but it was revived after the war. In the early sixties about twenty major publisher-owned and independent agencies were selling subscriptions door-to-door, at department stores, and by telephone.

Many field salesmen used high pressure, sob stories, and trickery to get subscriptions, and their tactics reflected unfavorably on the magazines they sold and on the industry as a whole. In 1940 magazine publishers created the Central Registry of Magazine Subscription Solicitors to enforce a code of sales practices acceptable to Chambers of Commerce and Better Business Bureaus. Penalties for violations of the code included reprimands, damages of up to $500 for each offense and up to $2,000 for certain repeated offenses, and expulsion from the organization. Central Registry was maintained cooperatively by the Magazine Publishers Association, independent field agencies, and the subscription agencies of individual publishers.

Circulation men developed other ways of getting subscriptions. A few agencies worked out campaigns with newspapers, and carriers solicited subscriptions to magazines along with subscriptions to the papers they delivered. Direct mail, seldom used in the nineties because of the difficulty of finding good lists of prospects, was used by some publishers in the twenties and by a good many after World War II. In the fifties and sixties, when competition from television and from within the industry itself set magazines to racing for enormous circulations, mass mailings of bargain offers were a chief means of getting new readers. The Publishers Clearing House and Catholic Digest's Better Magazine Club specialized in direct-mail campaigns to get subscriptions for a variety of publishers.

As circulations grew, it became more and more burdensome to keep records of subscribers up to date and to get copies addressed for mailing. After World War II, such chores, once done largely by hand, became increasingly mechanized. For instance, subscription fulfillment at Time Inc. in 1945 was a completely manual operation involving metal stencils and galleys. Progressively mechanized, it was done in the sixties by electronic-tape computers that stored information about subscribers and turned out 131,000 address labels an hour. Esquire, Inc., at its mechanized fulfillment center at Boulder, Colorado, was servicing the subscriptions of twenty-one other publications in 1963.

Magazines to subscribers could be mailed under special low postal rates authorized by Congress in March, 1879, to encourage the dissemination of knowledge. Postmasters General repeatedly complained that this second-class mail was being carried at a loss to the government. Publishers challenged such statements so vigorously that from 1906 onward there were numerous attempts to determine the costs of the various postal services. From time to time after 1910, Congress proposed making the second-class service pay for itself by postal rate increases, which publishers strenuously opposed. Many publishers said that they were willing to pay their fair share of costs but contended that the accounting methods used by the postal service did not reveal what they were. Then, too, many publishers argued, increases in postal rates would force many magazines out of business. In the forties, when the Curtis Publishing Company had a postal bill of about $3,000,000 a year, they pointed out that a doubling of rates would wipe out its profit of about $1,000,000. In 1962 they used much the same argument to fight a proposed rate increase; the raises would cost the *Atlantic* an additional $91,000, more than seven times its before-taxes profit, they said, and would work similar hardships on other magazines. Although Congress did gradually raise the rates over the years, publishers were successful in holding down the increases.

News dealers were responsible for a steadily increasing proportion of sales of A.B.C. magazines from 1925 through 1945. Single-copy sales accounted for 32.3 per cent of the total circulation of such magazines in 1925, for 44.2 per cent in 1940, and for 62.3 per cent in the last half of 1945, according to a study made by the Magazine Advertising Bureau. Put another way, single-copy sales in that period increased 365.6 per cent while subscriptions increased 34.4 per cent. After World War II, however, the ratio of subscriptions to newsstand sales began to increase, and in the sixties, subscriptions accounted for the great bulk of sales for most magazines.

There were several reasons for the shift from subscriptions to newsstand sales after 1925. Most publishers found single-copy sales more profitable than subscriptions. Many advertisers were more impressed by newsstand sales, which they regarded as an indication that the reader bought the magazine because he really wanted it, not because he had been inveigled by high-pressure sales talks, premium offers, or bargain rates. Some editors—Ben Hibbs of the *Saturday Evening Post* was one—used single-copy sales as an informal measure of the popularity of their magazines. Then, too, the mobility of the population during World War II caused many readers to buy their copies on newsstands instead of by subscription. Indeed, many publishers discouraged subscriptions during the war, when paper was rationed.

After the war, however, changed habits, changed patterns of living, and other forces all helped to bring about a drop in the share of magazines sold by the single copy. Consider, for instance, the shifts in the circulation patterns of just a few magazines. In 1940 *Life* and *Look* sold roughly 60 per cent of their copies on the newsstand; in 1962 they sold about 9 per cent. In 1940 *Esquire* sold 41 per cent of its circulation by the single copy; in 1962 it sold 17 per cent. For the *Saturday Evening Post,* the drop was from 31 per cent to 12 per cent, for *Time* from 22 per cent to 10 per cent. Although the change was not that great for all magazines, the subscription nevertheless had come to account for the majority of sales. Even so, there was some variety in the ways in which individual publications sold their copies. Each magazine was aimed at a special audience, and it had unique problems; the methods that served it best were not always the best for other publications.

Newsstands, of course, remained a major outlet for single-copy sales. Yet no newsstand could possibly handle more than a small fraction of American magazines, and display space for even them was limited. Venders sometimes complained that distributors refused to supply them with best-selling magazines unless they accepted certain publications they did not want. Circulation men complained that newsstands were so laden with magazines that good display was impossible. Prominent display was important to circulation, and publishers' agents sometimes went from stand to stand pushing their own magazines to the forefront, their competitors' magazines to the background. Venders ordinarily paid little attention to such tactics, as they customarily made as much profit from one magazine as from another of the same price.

Tactics of that sort were perhaps most common among publishers who depended largely on single-copy sales for their circulation. Warfare broke out periodically in the thirties between two such publishers, Fawcett and Macfadden. In 1938 Fawcett bought space in newspapers of six large cities to urge its readers to report instances in which they had been prevented from buying copies of *True Confessions* for February. Meanwhile the company attempted to prove that some of the 265 organizers of salesboys for Macfadden had covered up copies of *True Confessions* on the stands and had thrown copies into dealers' return bins. After a meeting of circulation directors of the two companies, S. O. Shapiro of Macfadden explained, "With such a flock of new magazines on the stands, it has become almost impossible to get good display for any magazine. All publishers are constantly engaged in a struggle to maintain their places, and this is just a fight for display, such as goes on regularly." [2] The two companies skirmished again in 1941. A promotion man for Macfadden then allegedly planted a secret microphone in a Louisville hotel to eavesdrop on a meeting at which Fawcett representatives were planning their sales campaign for the next year.[3]

Whether sold by newsstand or by subscription, magazines were a highly perishable product which had to be distributed simultaneously across the entire nation. Costs, competition, and the necessity of speedy distribution directly and indirectly influenced the dispersal of operations in magazine publishing. They encouraged publishers to select New York as headquarters for their editorial and advertising operations, some outlying city as their printing and distribution point.

New York had replaced Boston and Philadelphia as the center of magazine publishing long before 1900. Editorial and artistic talent clustered there, and the largest part of the nation's advertising came from there. Consequently, even magazine publishers who began elsewhere, like the Fawcetts of Minneapolis, David A. Smart of Chicago, and Gardner Cowles, Jr., of Des Moines, moved their editorial and advertising offices to New York.

But publishers moved their printing and distribution operations out of New York. Costs, which were important in so competitive a business as magazine publishing, were one factor. By choosing a centrally located production point, a magazine could reduce its postage bill; and labor, at least when the exodus from New York

---

[2] *Editor & Publisher,* 71 (Jan. 29, 1938), sec. 1, p. 24; *Time,* 31 (Jan. 31, 1938) 27-28.
[3] *Time,* 38 (Dec. 15, 1941) 55.

began, was thought to be less costly in outlying areas. An official of the Condé Nast company, which printed some magazines for other publishers, said in 1963 that plants in the Midwest had offered to print its magazines for $800,000 less a year than it cost to print them in its own plant in Connecticut.[4] Distributing from the Midwest also cut the time necessary for getting copies into the hands of readers.

The move from New York seems to have begun in the early twenties when Hearst and several other magazine publishers transferred their printing operations to the Midwest. The McCall Company closed down its printing shop in the East and opened its large plant in Dayton, Ohio, in 1923. Crowell-Collier, which for many years had done its printing in New York, moved its printing plant to Springfield, Ohio, in 1924. Time Inc., then a struggling little company, moved its entire operation to Cleveland in 1925, partly because it wanted the economies of Midwest printing and distribution but could not afford the telegraph tolls involved in a split operation. However, the company could afford to work from a distance with a Chicago printer in 1927 when it moved its editorial office back to New York. As Time Inc. grew larger, it carried its dispersal of printing even further. In 1940 it had its copies for Eastern distribution printed in Philadelphia. In 1943 it became one of the first publishers of a leading national magazine to print west of Chicago by using facilities in Los Angeles for printing its copies distributed on the West Coast. Not surprisingly, some of the largest printers of magazines arose in the Midwest: Cuneo Press, R. R. Donnelley and Sons, and W. F. Hall Printing Company, all of Chicago, and Kable Brothers of Mount Morris, Illinois.

By printing in centrally located plants and by utilizing advances in technology, magazines narrowed the gap between deadline and publication date. *Time,* for example, had a four-day spread between its deadline and on-sale date before it began printing in Philadelphia and Los Angeles; afterwards, it went on sale the third morning after forms had closed. Time Inc. took great pride in the speed with which it could get editorial copy and advertisements to the reader on special occasions. Copies of *Sports Illustrated* with three pages of color photographs of the 1960 Kentucky Derby were on the presses thirty-nine hours after the race. For a 10 per cent premium, *Life* in 1958 offered advertisers a special service that cut

---

[4] *Advertising Age,* 34 (April 15, 1963) 34.

the closing time for black-and-white and two-color to seven days. Several other publishers said at the time that they were operating with similar speed. As early as the mid-thirties, *Farm Journal* boasted that it reached readers four days after its editorial deadline. Other magazines also reduced the time necessary for production and distribution. Editors, driven by competition to keep their contents fresh, and advertisers, wishing for flexibility in planning their campaigns, both benefited from increases in timeliness. Even so, however, advertisers sometimes complained in the fifties that magazines generally had done little in the previous twenty years to shorten the period between the closing of advertising forms and the distribution date. In 1955 Frank Braucher, then president of the Magazine Advertising Bureau, explained why magazines seemed to have progressed so little. For one thing, no other industry had so complicated a problem of distribution, he said. For another, the circulation of the average magazine had more than doubled in the previous decade; therefore, if publishers had not adopted every technical advance, magazine closing dates in 1955 would have to have been at least twice as far in advance as ten years earlier.[5]

The life of a magazine on the newsstands was short. Therefore, publishers were guided by the habits of the reading public and by the tactics of competitors in setting their on-sale dates. The *Saturday Evening Post* for years went on sale on Thursday because in the nineties most retail shopping was done on the weekend. In 1931 it gained two days' display on the stands and an advantage over its competitors by appearing on Tuesday, although it later shifted to Wednesday. The five-day work week and the increased importance of grocery stores as outlets for magazines were partly responsible for a change in the on-sale dates of several leading magazines in 1954. Grocers were so busy at the end of the week that they often did not have time to unbundle magazines and put them on the racks. To gain an extra weekday on the stands, the *Post* went on sale on Tuesday instead of Wednesday; *Newsweek* and *Time* on Wednesday instead of Thursday; and *American, Collier's, Life, Woman's Home Companion* on Thursday instead of Friday.[6]

Publishers thought that sales of a magazine would be negligible

[5] *M. A. Briefs* (Jan., 1955) 4-5.
[6] *Tide,* 28 (Feb. 27, 1954) 51; 28 (Aug. 14, 1954) 49.

after the date of issue on its cover. As early as the 1870's, their practice was to put magazines on sale far in advance of the official publication date, and the custom persisted into the twentieth century. In the thirties, the general weeklies *Collier's* and *Liberty* appeared more than a week before their cover dates; and in 1955 *Collier's*, then a biweekly, went on sale fifteen days in advance of its date of issue. It was not unusual for the Christmas issue of a monthly magazine to reach readers before Thanksgiving, the Easter issue before the new year had begun.

The tactic of bringing out issues weeks or months before the cover date resulted in manifold troubles for advertisers and editors. Advertisers, trying to merchandise their goods according to seasonal buying habits, found that the practice seriously complicated their schedules. Editors were often embarrassed by articles which had seemed a good idea at deadline time but which were outdated or in bad taste by publication day.

Most such embarrassment arose from the delay inevitable in printing and distributing thousands of copies of a magazine, of course, and some came about from coincidence; but the custom of advanced dating was certainly an aggravating factor. The editor of almost every major magazine had at least one such incident that he would have preferred to forget. When William Jennings Bryan died in 1925, *Life* scrapped 20,000 copies of an issue making sport of him in jokes and cartoons. The *Saturday Evening Post* in March, 1925, carried a photograph of a prominent manufacturer who had died several weeks earlier. *Vanity Fair* in 1928 published a vicious burlesque of a novel by Frances Newman, whose death was in the news just as the issue went out to readers. Huey Long's death in 1935 coincided with an issue of *Life* which contained a number of unfavorable remarks about him, including the news that he had led all candidates in a "public nuisance" poll. Two days after the surrender of the Japanese in World War II, *Collier's* came out with Quentin Reynolds' "authoritative picture" of how difficult the invasion of Japan would be. Editors of a number of magazines, forgetting their usual prudence, guessed wrong on the 1948 Presidential elections in which Harry S. Truman won an unexpected victory over Thomas Dewey; *U.S. News*, for instance, went to press ahead of the elections with an interpretation of Dewey's victory. Three days after William Faulkner died in 1962, the *New Leader* appeared with a review that called him one of the worst prose stylists who ever lived and charged him with failing to publish anything first-rate in twenty years. After President Kennedy was assassinated in 1963, *Look* carried an article suggesting he could be defeated in the next election. High-speed printing and rapid distribution reduced the chances of such embarrassments, but they remained an occupational hazard so long as magazines had a long lag between deadline and distribution.

As publishers competed for readers and as the demand for magazines grew, there was a large increase in the number and types of retail outlets at which Americans could buy periodicals. In 1915 an estimated 50,000 to 55,000 retail outlets sold magazines as a part of their stock. After 1930, many drugstores, department stores, and grocery stores began to carry magazines for the first time, and the number of outlets grew to about 80,000 by the mid-thirties. In the fifties and sixties, it seemed to be stationary at about 100,000 since a large supermarket carrying magazines could put out of business a half-dozen smaller outlets in its neighborhood.

The supermarket was the most important new outlet that circulation men discovered. Practically no grocery stores stocked magazines before 1930. Then in the thirties several grocery chains began to sell or give magazines of their own to customers. The success of those magazines, the great growth of supermarkets, and the development of shopping centers around supermarkets all led to the emergence of the grocery store as a major retail outlet for magazines, especially after World War II. Although the grocery chains at first handled only their own publications, they eventually set up racks for other magazines, and in the early sixties they accounted for almost a fourth of single-copy distribution. Circulation men promoted the installation of racks by reminding grocers that the markup of 23 per cent on magazines was greater than that on most comestibles. However, in 1963 the stores had started to limit the number of magazines they would carry because they had begun to handle soft goods and housewares, which had higher profit margins.

Merchandising commercial magazines through grocery stores was a natural outgrowth of a type of publishing which began to flourish in the thirties. From 1930 onward, several publishers produced magazines for exclusive distribution by variety and grocery chains and by department stores. One of the pioneers was Catherine McNelis, an advertising woman, who persuaded the F. W. Woolworth Company in 1929 to be sole distributor of a string of publications which would advertise products sold by the chain. She formed Tower Magazines, Inc., to publish the periodicals, which included screen, detective, love story, and children's magazines. Although the venture seemed astonishingly successful on the surface, the company filed a bankruptcy petition in 1935. High production costs and the large percentage of unsold copies, the company reported, had forced it to insolvency. The government charged that Miss McNelis and associates had defrauded advertisers of $1,000,000 by falsifying circulation figures of their various periodicals. They were convicted in 1939 of using the mails to defraud.[7] The Woolworth Company, in no way implicated in the illegal transactions, nevertheless refused to handle any magazines for several years. In the forties, however, it began to sell comic books and similar publications of Dell, Fawcett, and Macfadden.

Impressed by the apparent success of Tower in its early years, other publishers arranged to produce magazines exclusively for competing chains. The Dell Publishing Company in 1930 agreed to publish *Modern Romances* and *Modern Screen* for sole distribution by the S. S. Kresge and S. H. Kress variety chains in towns where they had stores and for newsstand sale elsewhere. Futura Publications, Inc., was formed in 1931 to publish movie and romance magazines for a number of smaller chains with a total of 1,345 stores.

Apparently among the first to recognize the potentialities of the grocery store as a dealer in magazines were officials of the Kroger Grocery and Baking Company, which operated several thousand stores in the Midwest. In 1930 they argued that the typical chain grocery was handier to the home than the typical drugstore and invited publishers to supply them with magazines. Curtis marketed the *Saturday Evening Post* and *Ladies' Home Journal* in Kroger stores for a time, but the plan was eventually dropped. Each magazine was in a wrapper bearing the Kroger name and saying that most of the advertised foods could be bought at the store. Curtis sold through only a few stores when it inaugurated the plan in February, 1930, but it increased the number to about 1,800 by the end of the year.[8]

---

[7] *Editor & Publisher,* 71 (July 23, 1938) 10; 73 (Jan. 6, 1940) 46; 73 (Jan. 20, 1940) 37.

[8] *Time,* 16 (Nov. 3, 1930) 30.

The big boom in store-distributed magazines was started by Harry Evans, a former managing editor of *Life*, who in 1932 brought out *Family Circle*, a gravure-printed tabloid of twenty-four pages with features for the homemaker. Five years later the Great Atlantic and Pacific Tea Company formed a subsidiary to publish its own magazine, *Woman's Day*. *Western Family*, started in 1941, confined its circulation to the West Coast. *American Family*, distributed by the Independent Grocers Alliance, died soon after its first issue in 1942, reappeared in 1948, but was suspended again in 1954. Perhaps a hundred such publications were attempted in the twenty years after *Family Circle* first appeared, but only a few survived. The fifties were a time of warfare and consolidation. In 1951 the McCall Corporation backed *Better Living;* that same year John Cuneo of the Cuneo Press and several associates brought out *Everywoman's,* and for the next several years the two magazines battled with one another for a share of the market. *Better Living* died altogether in 1956, and *Everywoman's* was merged into *Family Circle,* which with *Woman's Day* dominated the field in 1964.

The expansion of the market for magazines as a result of international publishing after World War II, however, had far greater implications than the opening up of new avenues of distribution, for it promised to extend the influence of the American press over large areas of the world. By promoting the sales of their titles abroad, some publishers uncovered a whole new market for magazines in the forties, just as Munsey had done in the nineteenth century.

Only a few American companies published abroad before World War II, and their activities were limited. *Harper's* had maintained a British edition for a time as early as the eighties. Condé Nast, Hearst, and Macfadden all issued foreign editions of some of their magazines in the twenties and thirties. The *Reader's Digest* started to publish editions abroad in 1938, and Time Inc. began its overseas operations on a modest scale in 1941.

But most of the American magazines which reached foreign readers before World War II were back numbers. In the twenties and thirties a man could earn a comfortable living by buying up old magazines which dealers had been unable to sell and marketing them in foreign countries. Irving Manheimer, who became a major stockholder in Macfadden Publications in 1951, started to sell back-number magazines abroad in 1927. His Publishers Surplus Corporation was soon shipping 5,000,000 copies of magazines a month to London and thousands of others to Australia, Egypt, New Zealand, South Africa, and Palestine. His company was the leading exporter of old magazines until World War II ended the traffic in them.

American troops acquainted the peoples of many nations with American periodicals and intensified their curiosity about American life. Under an arrangement with the Army, twenty-seven magazines supplied overseas editions for servicemen in 1944. Some magazines, *Time* and *Newsweek* among them, produced six-by-nine-inch adless "pony" editions which were sped to military installations. The *New Yorker* and *Saturday Evening Post* culled the best material from four weekly issues and brought it together in an adless monthly edition. Still other magazines like *Coronet* and *Reader's Digest* furnished their regular editions.

American magazines were also introduced to people of the world by the government, which published several periodicals edited by professional magazine men as a part of its information program. One of the best known of its magazines was *Victory*, a bimonthly published by the Office of War Information under a nonprofit arrangement with Crowell-Collier. The magazine carried a limited amount of advertising to keep it from looking like a propaganda organ, and it was sold instead of given away. Published in six languages, *Victory* circulated 875,000 copies in forty-six countries in 1944. Response to it abroad was enthusiastic. In Lisbon readers bought all available copies in forty-eight hours, and potential purchasers were so numerous when one issue appeared that dealers required police protection. In Italy black-market operators bought copies from the stands, rented them until they were dog-eared, then sold them. There were several other such government periodicals: *Amerika, Choix, Kijk, Photo Review, U. S. A.,* and *Voir*. In addition, scores of American magazines granted the Office of War Information permission to syndicate their contents among foreign periodicals and radio stations. After the war, the United States Information Agency published more than fifty magazines abroad as a part of its program, and it distributed unsold copies of U.S. magazines published outside of this country. One of its magazines was *America Illustrated*, which sought to give the Russian people a continuing portrait of life in America. On its fifth anniversary in 1960, the publication had a circulation of 52,000 copies a month inside the Soviet Union.

When World War II ended, scores of publishers looked for new markets abroad. As peoples throughout the world aspired to the standard of living that industrialization had brought to the people of America, they exploited their resources and built plants of their own, often with help from the United States; the book value of direct investments abroad by Americans almost quadrupled in the fifteen years after 1945. As more and more American companies did business in the international market place, they contributed to the growing dollar volume of goods shipped out of the United States. Advertising agencies opened offices in London, Paris, Rome, and Tokyo, and international advertisers kept raising their expenditures in international magazines, until the leading hundred were spending $17,800,000 annually in the early sixties.

Some publishers looked upon foreign editions as an additional source of profit or potential, some as a source of prestige. Nevertheless, American publishers were bringing out more than a hundred international publications by 1961.

Publishers spoke to their audiences outside of the United States in a number of ways. Some just let publishers abroad reprint their articles, and some simply exported copies of their domestic edition. Others edited magazines in the United States for distribution abroad, either in English or in the languages of the countries in which they circulated, or set up foreign subsidiaries. Still others franchised foreign publishers to use their names and supplied them with editorial content and other assistance.

The largest international publishers in the early sixties were the *Reader's Digest* and Time Inc. The *Reader's Digest* went abroad in 1938 when it started an edition for the British Isles. Twenty-five years later it had major offices in twenty-five countries outside the United States, and its twenty-nine basic international editions, published in thirteen languages, circulated in all of the noncommunist countries of the world. Four of them had circulations of more than a million, and in some countries the *Digest* was the largest-selling magazine. Altogether, the international editions had a circulation of 10,415,000. Time Inc. in the early sixties published five basic international editions of *Time* each week, one of *Life* each fortnight, and one of *Life en Español* each fortnight. They were administered by Time-Life International, formed in 1945 to handle the company's news coverage and distribution abroad. In addition, the company entered into arrangements with foreign nationals to copublish such magazines as *Panorama* in Italy and *President* in Japan.

The publisher who looked outside the borders of the United States for all or some of his readers ran into a number of difficulties. They varied with time and place, with whether he simply shipped copies of his magazine abroad or printed them there. They included import restrictions, confusing terms of sale, currency problems, and lack of facilities for printing and distribution.

Censorship, official and unofficial, was also a continuing threat. Governments dealt with offending magazines in a number of ways; they banned magazines or issues entirely, confiscated or destroyed copies, clipped or deleted material, delayed deliveries. Sometimes they proscribed a single issue; sometimes they kept a publication from entering a country for extended periods. Sometimes they banned just a single magazine; sometimes they kept out all United States publications. Time Inc. alone reported 857 instances of censorship involving its international editions from July, 1940, through July, 1963.

In the British Isles, an unofficial censorship was imposed on occasion by magazine distributors, the largest of which was W. H. Smith and Son. In 1936 distributors refused to handle American periodicals mentioning the romance between King Edward and Mrs. Wallis Warfield Simpson. The issue of *Time* for August 31, 1936, appeared on British stands minus a page containing references to Mrs. Simpson; it apparently had been deleted by distributors. The Wholesale News Agents Federation announced in 1939 that it would no longer distribute *Time*, which lost about 1,500 circulation as a result, although 750 copies still reached the stands by other routes.

Canada, from time to time, kept out United States magazines carrying material that it thought libelous or salacious. Its parliament in 1949 outlawed all crime comic books, including those published in Canada from mats and plates shipped in from the United States.

Magazines from the United States had long circulated in Canada, which publishers regarded more as an extension of their domestic market than as a foreign one. As early as 1906, P. T. McGrath reported the consequences in the *Review of Reviews:* Canadians read more periodicals published in the United States than published in the Dominion, and publications from south of the border could flood Canada because their enormous sale at home enabled them to keep costs below those of their Canadian counterparts.[9] Deputations of Canadian publishers and printers periodically went to Ottawa to protest such unfair competition and to petition for restrictions upon it.

Canadian publishers in the mid-twenties, for instance, asked for curbs on unfair advantages which enabled eight copies of United States magazines to circulate in Canada for every copy of a Canadian magazine. The Canadian publisher, they protested, was obliged to pay duties on paper, ink, and engravings which he imported from the United States; but the United States publisher could send those things into Canada duty-free in the form of finished magazines. Moreover, advertising entering Canada for inclusion in Canadian-produced booklets and catalogs was taxed, they said, but was untaxed when it appeared in magazines from the United States.[10] A decade later the printing trades union claimed that the free entry of magazines from the United States had thrown many Canadian printers out of work.[11] And in 1947 Canadian publishers again asked for tariff protection because United States publishers enjoyed the advantages of longer press runs, better machinery, and better paper; because aid to Canadian magazines would benefit the entire graphic arts industry in Canada; and because restrictions on United States magazines would increasingly cause advertisers to use Canadian media.[12]

In the fifties and sixties, Canadian publishers continued to press for measures that would enable them to compete with magazines from the United States. Since they prized a free trade in ideas, they did not wish to keep out foreign magazines, they said; but they did want to preserve an independent and indigenous voice that could speak to Canadians about their own affairs and to its neighbor to the south in friendly criticism when it thought it should. In the forty years after 1920, they pointed out, more than 200 Canadian consumer magazines were discontinued or absorbed; in 1963 *Mac-*

[9] P. T. McGrath, "What the People Read in Canada," *Review of Reviews*, 33 (June, 1906) 720-22.
[10] *Editor & Publisher*, 58 (March 27, 1926) 12; 58 (April 3, 1926) 38.
[11] *Editor & Publisher*, 69 (March 21, 1936) 24.
[12] *Tide*, 21 (Feb. 28, 1947) 28-31.

lean's and *Chatelaine* were virtually the only survivors. What they were asking for, they said, were measures that would enable them to compete on a reasonably equitable basis with the United States magazines entering their country.

Over the years, the Canadian government took various steps to help them. For a few years in the thirties, it imposed a tariff on U.S. magazines. In 1957 it levied a 20 per cent excise tax on gross advertising revenues of special Canadian editions of foreign magazines. In practice, the tax affected only Time Inc. and *Reader's Digest*, and it was repealed after eighteen months. The government in 1960 appointed a three-man royal commission headed by Grattan O'Leary, president and editor of the Ottawa *Journal*, to "enquire into and make recommendations concerning the position of and prospects for Canadian magazines and periodicals." Its report, delivered in May, 1961, recommended, among other things, that income tax deductibility for advertising, the tariff schedule, and postal rates all be used to strengthen the position of Canadian periodicals. By the end of 1963, the government had raised postal rates for U.S. magazines but had not acted on the other proposals, although there were indications that it ultimately would.

Objections much like those of the Canadian publishers were heard from other parts of the world when American magazines vigorously sought foreign markets at the close of World War II. Some publishers and members of the intelligentsia feared that the superior technical resources of American magazines and their wealth in a war-impoverished world could lead only to American cultural imperialism, and there were cries against "Coca-Colonization" and the spread of "a *Reader's Digest* culture." Even at home there were instances of protest, as when Senator Joseph Guffey of Pennsylvania called the *Reader's Digest* a "world cartel" and spoke of an antitrust suit, which, however, did not come about. The majority of foreign readers seemed to share little of his concern, for circulations of American magazines abroad continued to rise.

After World War II, publishers not only brought out special editions for foreign audiences; they also introduced regional editions for various parts of the United States. Indeed, the rapid growth of regional editions, aimed at narrower and narrower geographical areas, was one of the major developments in magazine publishing during the late fifties.

Regional magazines once had been common, of course, but they had given way to the national magazine as advances in communication, mass production, and mass distribution erased regional differences and enabled the manufacturer to market his product across the land instead of in his own locality. After World War II, however, the expanding population and the high-level economy made some sections of the country as important as markets as the entire nation once had been. Moreover, as circulations grew, several magazines distributed as many copies in some states as they had once sold nationally.

The regional edition and the split run enabled the advertiser to buy just part of the total circulation of a magazine and to address consumers in selected markets. By helping to overcome one of its traditional shortcomings, tying in national advertising with the local retailer, they put the magazine into competition at national, regional, and local levels with television, with the Sunday supplements, and with newspapers. Because of their flexibility, they opened up new sources of income for magazines. The regional edition was suited to the national advertiser who wished to concentrate his sales efforts in specific localities, to capitalize on seasonal influences, to test-market his products, or to match his advertising with the market-by-market distribution and growth of his new products. It was an accommodation to the national advertiser who sold his products under different brand names in different parts of the country, and it permitted the advertiser who did business in just a limited locality to capitalize on the prestige of a national medium without paying for waste circulation.

Although a few magazines had brought out different editions for various sections of the country as early as the twenties, the big growth of regional publishing came in the fifties, especially at the end of the decade. In 1959 *Look* became one of the first large-circulation magazines to come out in regional editions; under its original Magazone plan, advertisers had their choice of seven, matched to standard marketing areas. A few months later the *Saturday Evening Post* introduced its Select-a-Market plan in seven basic versions. From then on, magazine after magazine broke down its circulation for the benefit of advertisers. More than 150 magazines had regional or split-run editions in 1963, and individual publications kept splintering them into smaller and smaller units. In 1961, for instance, *Life* gave advertisers a choice of seven editions; the following year, it divided up its circulation to cover twenty-six marketing areas in the United States and three in Canada. *TV Guide* had seventy editions in 1963; *Better Homes and Gardens* had ten and offered to custom-make editions to suit the needs of the advertiser. *Good Housekeeping, Time,* and *Reader's Digest* each had nine; *Esquire* and *Sports Illustrated* five; and *Sunset,* a regional magazine to begin with, four. Some of the largest magazines had special editions for Los Angeles and New York; *Life* even accepted classified advertising for its New York edition.

The circulations of a few of those regional editions were as great as the entire national distribution of a good many magazines. Just the metropolitan New York edition of the *Reader's Digest* had sales of 1,200,000 in 1963. The Mid-Atlantic edition of *Good Housekeeping* had a circulation of 1,154,000, the East Central edition of *Better Homes and Gardens,* 1,185,000.

For the most part, magazines used regional publishing as a marketing device; they usually ran the same editorial copy in all editions. Nevertheless, advertising men at first were divided over the value of the development. Some agency heads speculated that the editions would diminish the prestige of magazines as a national medium and that their costs of production would not generate enough new business for them to be profitable. A greater number, however, thought that their flexibility enhanced the value of magazines as a medium.

At least some competitors worried about the development. The newsletter of Broadcast Advertising Reports in 1959 warned that regional editions were making inroads on the money spent for spot announcements on television and cited instances in which advertisers defected from television to magazines. The Television Bureau of Advertising asked salesmen to report advertisers who had been lured away from television so it could determine the extent of the loss by personal interviews.[13] The executive vice-president of a Sunday supplement called them "one of the most competitive forces working against Sunday magazines and the newspapers themselves."[14] On the West Coast, where the regionals were heavy, newspaper publishers met to map out a strategy for competing with them.

The regional editions did, in fact, account for a larger and larger share of advertising income. For general magazines, revenues from

---

[13] *Broadcasting,* 59 (Oct. 17, 1960) 38, 40, 42.
[14] *Editor & Publisher,* 93 (Jan. 30, 1960) 18.

them jumped from $65,615,000 in 1960 to $109,411,000 two years later. *Life* alone took in $25,233,000 from them in 1962. An advertiser buying only a part of the circulation of a magazine paid a higher rate for each thousand readers than if he bought the total distribution. He paid a premium of 51 per cent to use the Los Angeles edition of the *Reader's Digest* in 1963, for instance, and one of 34 per cent to use the Southwest edition of *Good Housekeeping*.

Despite their expense, sectional editions seemed a permanent part of magazine logistics by 1963, when publishers sought ways to hold down their production costs, to produce them efficiently on equipment not designed for them, and to prevent their proliferation into smaller and smaller units. At the same time some publishers speculated that magazines would be soon using computers to sort out their subscribers according to income, occupation, and other characteristics of interest to the advertiser. C. R. Devine of the *Reader's Digest* predicted that the day was not far distant when an advertiser could place his message in copies going only to automobile owners, families with children, or households with incomes of more than $5,000.[15] For a period in 1963, *Time* in fact carried special inserts from a pharmaceutical company in copies going to 60,000 physicians, chosen from its subscription rolls by computer.

As magazines competed for ever larger audiences and as they were turned out with increasing speed, their staffs, perhaps inevitably, adopted a basic principle of mass production—standardization. Magazine content became increasingly reduced to formula. At work, too, was the magazine's selectivity of audience, for a magazine adopted the tone and the editorial features which would win and hold the readers it wanted.

A magazine, to draw and hold its audience, had to give its readers what they wanted. Once the editor had struck a combination of features which readers liked, his profitable policy was to continue it. What emerged was an editorial formula, a balance of different types of material, which the editor adhered to issue after issue. The reader of the *New Yorker* for most of its life, for instance, could expect a typical issue to contain "The Talk of the Town," a column of comment and anecdotes; a "Profile" or "Reporter at Large" feature; reviews of books, plays, records, and movies; two

---

[15] *Advertising Age,* 34 (Oct. 7, 1963) 142.

or three short stories; an assortment of cartoons; and so on. Virtually all magazines, even those denying that they had a formula, had some such pattern to their content.

This editorial formula, along with the tone of the writing, the approach to the subject matter, and the overall graphic design, gave a magazine the "personality" which distinguished it from other magazines and maintained continuity from issue to issue. As standardization invariably does, it also simplified the task of choosing material.

Research became an aid of some editors in working out their editorial formulas after the mid-thirties when the success of Dr. George Gallup in predicting the 1936 elections stimulated the use of his polling technique. Although the large bulk of magazine research was done primarily in the interests of advertisers, some magazines used it to learn the reading habits of subscribers and to find out their readers' preferences in art work, layout, and editorial content.

Crowell-Collier in 1935 set up the *Woman's Home Companion* Opinion Poll, a monthly survey of a panel of 2,000 readers, who were questioned on a wide variety of subjects. Although the panel at first was intended chiefly to publicize the magazine, it gave the editors an idea of what women were thinking, and a number of articles resulted from it. In 1940 the company began a three-year study of the editorial policies of the *American*. As a result of the findings, the *American* dropped its serial fiction, eliminated crossword puzzles and similar features, began to emphasize informative articles by nationally known authorities as distinguished from professional writers, increased its number of women authors to attract women readers, and redesigned its title for newsstand appeal.

Two of the largest publishers in the United States held contrary views on the value of research for editorial guidance. The Curtis Publishing Company used research extensively after 1940 to learn reader likes and dislikes and to test the editorial appeal of a new magazine. Time Inc., although it conducted a great deal of research of interest to advertisers, apparently had small use for studies of readership and reader preferences.

Many changes in the *Saturday Evening Post* in the forties and fifties were based on editorial research. Twice monthly, investigators interviewed a sample of readers to get answers to such questions as these:

Do readers find a Western adventure story more entertaining than a tale of romantic love? Is there a variation between men and women in their response to historical fiction, or to humor, or to poetry? Will more or fewer readers be attracted by a discussion of domestic politics than by a serious study of the international situation? How many people read and enjoy a "who dunnit" run in weekly installments? Can the editors expect a large percentage of their audience to be pleased with the treatment one writer has accorded his factual story of activities centered in one geographical region? [16]

When Curtis found a high reader interest in science, the *Post* hired a science editor and began paying greater attention to scientific developments; when it found an interest in "people and places," the magazine introduced a long series about the cities of America.

Research also helped the *Post* make the transition to peace after World War II. Ben Hibbs, its editor, said that anyone could edit a magazine in wartime when customers needed little coaxing to buy copies and advertisers begged for space. When the war ended, Hibbs turned to research for help in adjusting the weekly to postwar competition. Guided by reader likes and dislikes, he changed the typography, added a column of letters to the editor and a short feature about the current cover, and ran novelettes and long features complete in a single issue. Studies indicating that interest in the war lingered on well into the peace weighed heavily in his decision to buy General Eisenhower's diaries and Admiral Halsey's story. One research worker, drawing on the accumulated information about readers' editorial preferences, even devised a "Predictograph," which had considerable success in predicting before publication the percentage of readers who would read a given article.[17]

As *Holiday* moved from blueprint to newsstand, research studies helped to guide its way. Once Curtis had decided to publish a magazine dealing with recreation, the research staff collected a large amount of information on the size of the recreation market, on magazine readers' plans for travel and their interests in a travel magazine, and on readers' reactions in the past to various kinds of art and editorial appeals. After the editorial staff had prepared its first prepublication dummy, the research department analyzed it, item by item, in the light of previous editorial research. In Novem-

[16] Donald M. Hobart, editor, *Marketing Research Practice* (New York, 1950), pp. 285-86.
[17] Herbert C. Ludeke, "The Role of Research in the Editorial Reconversion Problems of a Magazine," *Journalism Quarterly*, 25 (Sept., 1948) 214-17.

ber, 1945, three months before the first issue appeared, the research department used a second dummy to learn consumer reactions to the magazine. Copies of the dummy were left in homes of representative magazine readers in selected cities across the United States, and interviewers questioned the families on their reactions. Even after *Holiday* first appeared on the newsstands in February, 1946, it was still subjected to close research scrutiny.

On the other hand, some staff members at Time Inc. thought such studies a threat to the experimentation that was essential if a magazine were to have vitality. Their protest was a familiar one: that the reader is incapable of imagining what he would like and therefore must vote for "what is." One staff member, in a conversation with the author, put the objection this way: "If anyone had asked the average person of a century ago what sort of home lighting he wanted, he probably would have said that he wanted a lamp that would be cleaner and that would burn less fuel and things like that. It never would have occurred to him to say that he wanted electric lights that he could click on with a switch. The same sort of thing holds true in the magazine field. It just never occurs to the average person that he might like some kinds of features or magazines until an editor with imagination tries them out on him."

Not even editors using editorial research claimed it to be a substitute for editorial judgment. Commenting on the trend toward editing by mathematical formula, Ben Hibbs of the much researched *Saturday Evening Post* said in 1950: "Despite all the help we get from readership surveys, I think the greatest folly an editor could commit would be to follow such indices too slavishly. . . . There are times—and these times come almost every week—when the editor must fly in the face of known popular appeal if he is to maintain the character and responsibility of his publication." [18]

Although some editors found research useful in starting new magazines or in keeping old ones in tune with readers' interests, perhaps the great majority found little use for it. In general, editors as a whole probably made far less use of research than other departments, especially the advertising department. The editor knew who his readers were and worked out an editorial pattern that he thought would appeal to them, but he preferred empathy with his

---

[18] Ben Hibbs, "You Can't Edit a Magazine by Arithmetic," *Journalism Quarterly*, 27 (Fall, 1950) 371.

readers to statistical analyses of their likes and dislikes. Herbert Mayes of *McCall's* expressed a common sentiment when he remarked, "I'll gamble a hunch against a statistic anytime." [19]

The good editor had faith in his experience and in his editorial judgment. Robert Jones of *Everywoman's Family Circle*, for instance, could predict with some assurance when reader interest would be highest in features about child care, foods, and fashions, and the times were not always the ones a layman would guess.

Because the editor had to make his magazine greater than the sum of its parts, because he had to impart some of his own personality to it, he invariably insisted on having a free hand and accepting responsibility for the consequences. The good editor was, perhaps had to be, somewhat authoritarian. Ken Purdy once summed up his philosophy of editing in these words:

> This, I think, is the sovereign secret of successful editing: the arbitrary attitude. No boards, no committees, no surveys, no IBM machines can replace it. The successful editor of course knows the magazine very well before he takes it over; he has formed in his subconscious a definite ideal for it; when the authority is given him, he simply seeks material that will adorn his ideal and he rejects that which will harm it. This is not at all the same thing as the conscious erection of a synthetic policy, which has been done with notable success by some men. This process might produce commercially sound magazines which will show a pattern of continued growth. Inevitably, you will find, they lack all the evidence of greatness: fanatic readership, wide quotation, publication of stories that are long-remembered. Instinctive editorship, and instinctive editorship alone, produces those things.[20]

The intensified use of the editorial formula, whether it was derived from research or from empathy, affected both editor and writer. The formula, one can hypothesize, reduced the editor from a chef who created original masterpieces to a cook who simply gave his competent individual touch to standard recipes. As it did so, it shortened the tenure of editorships. At the same time, the formula diminished opportunities for the freelance writer by increasing the proportion of magazine material planned by the staff. All of this is generality, of course, but it seems essentially true nevertheless.

In the late nineteenth century and early twentieth, successful editors strongly impressed their personalities on their magazines.

---

[19] *Advertising Age*, 32 (April 3, 1961) 116.
[20] Letter to author, July 22, 1957.

They were often associated in the public mind with the magazines they edited—Bok of the *Ladies' Home Journal*, for instance, and Lorimer of the *Saturday Evening Post*. A magazine derived its uniqueness from the personality of its editor and its continuity from his long tenure. The leading magazines were characterized by editors with long periods in their service: Henry Mills Alden of *Harper's*, fifty years; Dr. Albert Shaw, Sr., of *Review of Reviews*, forty-six years; George Horace Lorimer of the *Post*, forty years; Edward Bok of the *Ladies' Home Journal*, thirty years; William Seaver Woods of the *Literary Digest* and Richard Watson Gilder of the *Century*, twenty-eight years; and E. L. Burlingame of *Scribner's*, twenty-seven years. True, in the early sixties there still remained editors like DeWitt Wallace and Henry Luce, whose personalities dominated their magazines, but they seemed a decreasing minority.

As magazines became increasingly edited to formula, as competition made editors increasingly concerned with giving the reader what he wanted, the situation was reversed. The formula, not the editor, gave a magazine its character and continuity. The editor became an anonymous technician, skilled but highly expendable, whose task was to achieve maximum results with the formula. Editors could come and go, but the essential personality of the magazine could remain virtually unchanged; and if the original personality of the magazine paled, a new editor could be called in to give it a new one. Frequent changes in key personnel came to be the custom. Thus *Pageant* had three editors in the five years between its birth and 1950; the *Ladies' Home Journal*, after the Goulds had edited it for twenty-seven years, had three editors in about eighteen months. Indeed, most publishers and advertisers in late 1963 probably could not even name the editor of the *Journal*. An editor skilled in the art of winning readers moved from magazine to magazine, as Ken Purdy transferred from the Annenberg publications to *Victory* to Crowell-Collier's proposed international magazine to *Parade* to *True* to *Argosy*, all in little more than a decade.

The changed role of the magazine editor had its counterpart in other media. Much earlier, newspapers had been transformed from personal organs of editors like Horace Greeley into corporate organs of anonymous voice. The mention of a newspaper in the twentieth century rarely called to mind its editor, as it had in the days of Henry W. Grady or Joseph Pulitzer. Motion pictures underwent a similar change as their stars eclipsed their directors, who had stamped films with their personalities in the days of D. W. Griffith, King Vidor, and Mack Sennett, although some foreign directors took on a renewed prominence in the fifties.

In a business as competitive as magazine publishing, the editor with a talent for winning readers could command a substantial salary. At his peak in the late twenties, Ray Long of *Cosmopolitan* earned $100,000 a year and had his pick of jobs. Lorimer, as top editor at Curtis, drew a similar salary. Both of them were at the top, of course, and they did more than edit a single publication. In the early sixties, when taxes took a large cut but when compensation usually included pension benefits and stock options, the editorial director of one major publishing house drew an annual salary of $92,300; the editor of a large women's magazine, $70,800; the editor of a fashion magazine, $40,350; and the editor of a general monthly, $35,000. A survey at the time showed the range of editors' salaries to be $24,000 to $40,000.

Considering the size of the investment that hung on their ability and the insecurity of their jobs, editors do not seem to have been overpaid. The ability of an editor was measured pretty much by circulation and reader interest. When they fell, so did the editor. Not all publishers were capricious in hiring and firing their editors, but at least a few were. One major publisher in the forties and fifties periodically fired his editors, along with other executives, because he thought that such unexpected changes "toned up the staff." For their part, editors could be quick to leave a magazine if they thought their authority or editorial integrity challenged. Some editors felt in the early sixties that publishers were treating them with a respect greater than at any time since before World War II. Editors played an increasingly influential part in the affairs of the Magazine Publishers Association, and in 1963 they formed their own organization under its auspices, the American Society of Magazine Editors, which set the championing of editorial independence as one of its main objectives. On occasion, editors could be more effective spokesmen for the industry than publishers. "Take the postal fight," said Ted Patrick of *Holiday*, first chairman of the editors' society. "A couple of editors appeared before the Congressional postal committee. This put the magazine industry's approach on a different level from, 'Damn it, you're not letting us make any more money,' to a philosophical level of 'You might destroy the communications business, which is needed very badly.' " [21]

The practice of editing by formula was accompanied by a system under which staff members planned the bulk of the magazine and either wrote the articles themselves or assigned them to reliable freelance writers. The typical editor of a leading magazine in the latter half of the nineteenth century was an aloof individual who plucked what interested him from among the manuscripts that authors had hopefully submitted. It was beneath his dignity to solicit contributions; authors had to seek him out. One of the first editors to break with that practice was Walter Hines Page. A capable editor could not withdraw from the company of men, Page believed, nor could he wait for articles to come to him. While he was editor of the *Forum* from 1887 until 1895, Page shocked his colleagues by jotting down his table of contents in advance of publication and then asking qualified authors to write the articles.

The Page method made good sense. Amidst the competition and specialization which characterized twentieth-century publishing, an editor could not count on freelance authors to furnish the kinds of articles he wanted when he needed them or even to capture the peculiar tone and slant which gave his magazine its personality. The sensible thing was to plan articles that fitted into his balance of content, then to assign them to staff writers or to freelance authors who had demonstrated their ability to produce the sort of copy the editor wanted. "We must make up twelve balanced issues a year, being a monthly," the editor of *American Legion Magazine* said in 1950. "They must be planned—for no magazine can be successful if it depends for its editorial balance and quality on what just comes in over the transom." [22]

By creative editing, editors assured themselves of features and fiction which would win readers by their variety and timeliness. Far more features than fiction were written to order, but even stories were composed to specification, as when the editors of the *Saturday Evening Post* decided against an article on professionalism in athletics and assigned a writer to cover the subject in a serial instead. The percentage of articles originating with the staff

---

[21] *Advertising Age*, 34 (Sept. 30, 1963) 80.
[22] Kenneth Marne Baker, "Editorial Requirements for Higher-Paying Magazines" (unpublished Master's thesis, University of Illinois, Urbana, 1951), p. 41.

varied from magazine to magazine. Many magazines of small circulation and small budget depended largely on contributions for their material. But the leaders in circulation and in advertising planned by far the greatest proportion of their nonfiction. In the middle thirties, for instance, *McCall's* and *Pictorial Review* originated all of their nonfiction and the *American Mercury*, virtually all; *Collier's* and *Nation's Business*, 90 per cent; *Better Homes and Gardens*, 50 per cent; *Scribner's*, 40 per cent; and *Field and Stream* and *Theatre Arts Monthly*, 25 per cent.[23] In 1950 magazines planned similarly large amounts of their nonfiction: *Holiday*, 99 per cent; *House Beautiful*, 98 per cent; *Seventeen*, 95 per cent; *American Legion, American Home, American, Charm, Collier's*, and *Look*, all 90 per cent; and *Photoplay*, 80 per cent.[24] Percentages in the sixties were no doubt similar.

Staff planning meant that magazines bought only miniscule percentages of the articles and stories with which freelance contributors filled their mails. Editors relied largely on professional freelances with whom they maintained close liaison. The percentages of unsolicited contributions which earned checks instead of rejection slips in the mid-thirties should have discouraged any but the most optimistic of writers. *McCall's* and *Pictorial Review*, for instance, bought no unsolicited articles whatsoever; the *American Mercury* bought .001 per cent; *Ladies' Home Journal*, .01 per cent; *Collier's* and *Scribner's*, 1 per cent; and *Better Homes and Gardens* and *Good Housekeeping*, 5 per cent. The author who sent off a story or article in 1950 could have been equally certain that the mailman would bring it back. Typical magazines and the percentages of nonfiction they rejected included the *American*, 99 per cent; *Argosy*, more than 99 per cent; *House Beautiful*, 98 per cent; *Nation's Business*, 99 per cent; *Sports Afield*, 90 per cent; and *True Confessions*, 90 per cent. Figures for fiction were no more encouraging, since the *American* rejected 98 per cent of all unsolicited stories; *Astounding Science Fiction*, 95 per cent; *Nation's Business*, 99 per cent; and *True Confessions*, 95 per cent. This is not to say that unknown writers did not sell a part of what they wrote. They did. But the number of freelance authors who could earn a living entirely by writing for magazines was exceedingly limited.

[23] Mitchell V. Charnley and Blair Converse, *Magazine Writing and Editing* (New York, 1938), p. 144.
[24] Baker, pp. 60-61.

But then the freelance writer seems to have been much more myth than reality throughout the entire history of American magazines. It is extremely unlikely that any significant number of authors ever managed to earn a living from magazines unless they held staff positions. The myth of the freelance writer persisted tenaciously; it was encouraged by teachers of writing, by the books on magazine writing which rolled from publishers' presses from the thirties on, by the roseate journals for amateur authors, by the correspondence schools which promised to make anyone a writer in ninety days, and by the editors themselves.

In the nineteenth century the magazine writer was denied a living by the copyright situation and by the customarily low rates of payment. So long as publishers were able to reprint British material which was not protected by copyright in America, they hesitated to buy from native writers. Even after copyright agreements prevented publishers from helping themselves to British writing, magazines were impecunious from want of advertising and their rates to contributors were perforce low. "If the average magazine writer could readily place all that he can conscientiously write," Charles Astor Bristead said in 1870, and his complaint was a familiar one, "then with three hundred working days in the year he could make a fair clerk's wages. . . ." [25]

In the twentieth century competition forced the leading magazines to pay good rates for contributions, and advertising made those rates possible. No longer could major magazines take months to reject or accept a contribution, as they had in the nineteenth century when Frank Parker Stockbridge was paid in 1895 for a story he had sold four years earlier. George Horace Lorimer of the *Post* began the practice of giving the author a decision in no more than a week and of paying for material on acceptance.

At least from the early twenties onward, the big magazines competed fiercely for authors whose names had showcase appeal and for authors who could deliver the kind of copy which editors wanted. Ray Long nagged and bid for an article by Calvin Coolidge from the day the President announced, "I do not choose to run." When he got the article for his issue of April, 1929, he took elaborate precautions to keep the scoop from competitors until *Cosmopolitan* appeared on the stands. At the printing plant, only

[25] Frank Luther Mott, *A History of American Magazines 1865-1885* (Cambridge, 1938), p. 15.

John Cuneo and his chief assistant knew what the article was; printers set incomprehensible fragments of the article into type, and a private detective stood on guard while the pieces were assembled and plates made. In late 1939, after months of negotiation, *Collier's* got Franklin Roosevelt to agree to write a weekly or fortnightly piece for an annual salary of $75,000 once he had left the White House, although he did not live to fulfill the contract. *Life* and the New York *Times* jointly paid Winston Churchill more than $1,000,000 in 1947 for his then unwritten memoirs, and *Life* alone in 1953 paid more than half that sum to Harry S. Truman for his memoirs.

In the twenties and thirties, when magazines were heavy with fiction, much of the battle was for the relatively small circle of storytellers whose bylines were magnets which drew readers to magazines. For the fiction it wanted, *Cosmopolitan* in the early thirties paid authors up to $5,000 for a short story, and up to $40,000 for a serial, although reasonable averages were perhaps $2,500 and $25,000 respectively. Fiction comprised an increasingly smaller part of magazine content during the war and after it; and in the fifties, when about three-fourths of magazine copy was non-fiction, the battle was for the top professional freelance reporters. The rewards were high for reporters who could produce what editors were looking for. The *Reader's Digest* paid an average of $2,000 an article and often sent bonuses to favored authors. *Collier's* paid about $1,500 an article, sometimes more; and the *Post* paid authors $750 for their first article and raised them in steps of $250 to as high as $3,000. Editors used lures other than money. Some painstakingly coached and encouraged promising professionals. The *Post* built up goodwill by trying to give a decision on an article or idea thirty hours after getting it.

But contributions were a raw material on which magazines spent only a few cents of every dollar they took in. Jerome Ellison, former managing editor of *Collier's*, estimated in 1946 that popular magazines spent from 2 to at most 10 per cent of their profits on contributions. "One magazine clears $200,000 an issue and pays $10,000 an issue for material," he said. "Another, generally considered fantastically generous, clears $900,000 an issue and pays its contributors $45,000." [26] His remedy was a magazine named 47, which was owned on a profit sharing basis by 363 writers, artists, and pho-

---

[26] *Newsweek, 27* (Jan. 21, 1946) 84.

tographers; but it filed a bankruptcy petition a little more than a year after its first issue appeared in March, 1947, and it ceased publication in July, 1948.

Ellison's calculations do not appear to have been far off. In the early thirties a typical monthly magazine spent probably 8.3 per cent of its total budget on features, short stories, and serials; more than 45 per cent went for paper and printing. In 1949 J. K. Lasser estimated that a typical consumer magazine spent four cents of each dollar of revenue on stories, articles, and pictures, while the paper dealer got thirty-four cents, the printer got thirty-nine.[27] A decade later, magazines with circulations of a million or more paid about forty-six cents of each dollar of income to the printer and paper supplier and spent about eight cents on editorial expenses, which included salaries, art work, photographs, and engravings, according to a report the Lasser firm filed with the Magazine Publishers Association. Furthermore, for every magazine which paid $1,000 for articles, there were hundreds which paid $100 or less. Only the large-circulation magazines paid big money, and a handful of authors competed for it as keenly as the magazines competed for authors.

A more substantial effort to raise the economic and professional status of the magazine writer than 47 was the formation of the Society of Magazine Writers in 1948. Members of the society were serious professionals, not the amateurs who belonged to the hundreds of other writers' organizations throughout the country. The sixty-five members of the society in 1951 had a total income of more than $750,000. In 1952 the society adopted a code of ethics which it hoped would improve the precarious financial position of the professional freelance and would standardize relationships between writers and editors.

The money magazines spent on contributions could support only a few freelance authors. Magazines bid thousands of dollars for the memoirs of generals, admirals, former Presidents, and abdicated kings, but those persons did not depend on their pens for their livelihoods. The magazine industry could provide a living for only a thousand freelance writers at $3,000 a year apiece, Jonathan Norton Leonard calculated in 1935; but since payments to authors were unequally distributed, he thought that the industry could

[27] J. K. Lasser, "How Good Publishing Management Works Today," *Magazine Industry*, 1 (Winter, 1950) 19-20.

support only about fifty-four professionals.[28] The situation had not greatly altered by 1950. The editors of *See* estimated that about a hundred writers supplied 90 per cent of the material to American magazines, the editors of *Better Homes and Gardens*, that 250 wrote 50 per cent of what magazines published.

A safe guess is that no more than 300 authors wrote virtually all of the fiction and nonfiction which magazines published in the fifties and early sixties and that fewer than half of them were able to support themselves by their writing. The others held jobs as newspaper reporters, college teachers, businessmen.

Even the successful freelance lived in uncertainty. From time to time, he was obsessed by the idea that editors did not appreciate him. He sometimes submitted four article ideas for every one that editors liked. He often earned but $3.50 an hour while writing articles for major magazines, and the money had to support him when editors were not buying his output. He frequently got no more than expense money when commissioned articles did not turn out as editors had expected. He knew that the editors who favored him today might be jobless tomorrow and then he would have to rebuild his contacts in editorial offices. "Since the decline of the oldtime prospector, few people have worked with less companionship, few have had to rely more on their own resources," said Morton Sontheimer, past president of the Society of Magazine Writers, in summing up the discouraging side of freelancing:

> You have to be provident enough, or have good enough credit, to live for months sometimes without income. You have to endure seeing all your capital assets—your ideas and your manuscripts—tied up interminably by indecisive editors. You have to take a philosophical view of payment checks long overdue from rich magazines. You have to preserve your sanity through barren periods when there's no work and through busy periods filled with nothing but cursed revisions. You have to develop a six-inch armor-plate insensibility to what editors may do, or make you yourself do, to those words you all but bled for.[29]

If they could adjust to the insecurity, successful freelances led comfortable if arduous lives, and few of them would have traded their jobs for anything else. After nine years as a *Life* writer, Ernest Havemann turned to freelancing in 1956; seven years later, he was

---

[28] Jonathan Norton Leonard, "Learning How to Write," in Norman Cousins, editor, *Writing for Love or Money* (New York, 1949), pp. 14-18.
[29] Clive Howard, editor, *The Society of Magazine Writers: A Guide to Successful Magazine Writing* (New York, 1954), pp. 8-9.

earning more than $50,000 annually, although some of it came from books and other assignments. Frank J. Taylor, in semiretirement in 1955, still sold ten or twelve articles a year to major magazines, and in his prime wrote thirty-five or forty. Frederick S. Faust, who was killed in 1944 while serving as a war correspondent in Italy, was the king of the pulps in the twenties and thirties. For years he lived with his wife and family in an Italian villa staffed with servants, and he once calculated that he needed at least $70,000 a year to maintain his standard of living. He maintained it, at his peak, by writing some 2,000,000 words a year for the pulps at the top rate of four cents a word. His pseudonyms included Max Brand, Evan Evans, George Owen Baxter, Nicholas Silver, Frank Austin, Hugh Owen, Walter C. Butler, George Challis, John Frederick, Lee Bolt, Dennis Lawton, Henry Uriel, Peter Henry Moreland, and David Manning.

Only a tiny band of authors reached the top, and the climb was difficult and treacherous. Yet the *Saturday Evening Post* in the fifties received between 60,000 and 100,000 unsolicited manuscripts a year from hopeful authors, and in the sixties the mails brought contributions by the thousands to other magazines. The myth of the freelance author refused to die.

6

The Old Leaders That Died

At 10:30 P.M. on December 14, 1956, after a long meeting, the directors of the Crowell-Collier Publishing Company announced their decision. They were killing off the company's two remaining magazines, *Collier's* and *Woman's Home Companion,* with the issues then on the presses.

The deaths were not entirely unexpected. Both magazines had been in financial trouble for several years, and the company had killed off the *American* the previous summer. Yet their ends came with brutal swiftness. With eight shopping days remaining before Christmas, some 440 editorial, advertising, and business employees learned by telegram that they had received their last paychecks; a little later, word that they were jobless went out to 2,300 printing plant employees. Only a few weeks earlier, Crowell-Collier had given a reception at the Waldorf-Astoria for grocery manufacturers, a potential source of advertising for *Woman's Home Companion;* and even as newspapers were running obituaries of the magazines, the *American News Trade Journal* carried a cheerful Crowell-Collier advertisement wishing news dealers a merry Christmas and happy new year and reminding them that magazines were one of their most salable items during the holiday season.

They were the largest magazines to die, *Collier's* and *Woman's Home Companion.* Each had a circulation of more than 4,000,000 and together they had brought in advertising revenues of $26,189,000 in their final year. Their passing made publishers, advertisers, and indeed the general public uncomfortably aware of magazine mortality. Like old men reading the obituary pages, publishers wondered which would be the next to go. They learned on December 27, when its publisher announced that he was closing down *Town Journal,* which could trace its lineage back more than sixty years and which had a circulation of more than 2,000,000 on its deathbed. *Etude,* a magazine for musicians, survived that winter but died in the spring after seventy-four years of publication.

Tragic and dramatic as those deaths were, they should have surprised no one familiar with magazine history. By World War II most of the magazines that had led in prestige and circulation when *Munsey's* and *McClure's* first appeared had long since vanished. The magazine world was a little like life itself. At midcentury *Harper's* was still around and so was the *Atlantic,* like wise old men who had outlived their contemporaries. Yet many old and once eminent magazines had died and had been succeeded by the young and active; the young themselves had aged, and many of them, too, had died. Over the years the trade press carried the obituaries of leaders among all classes of magazines—the respected quality magazines, current affairs magazines, general interest magazines, humor magazines, women's magazines, children's magazines —and one recalls their names with nostalgia: *Scribner's* and *Century,* for instance, and *Literary Digest, Delineator, Judge,* and *St. Nicholas.*

Until illness overtook them, many of them, like *Collier's* and the *American,* seemed a permanent part of the American scene. But the magazine industry represented the freest of free enterprise, and publishers were forever gambling on magazines which they hoped would be so excitingly new, so responsive to latent public interest that readers and advertisers would come flocking. Some publishers created such new magazines, and their periodicals helped to push a number of recognized leaders into the background or into their graves. For old and young alike, survival was made difficult by the rapidly increasing costs of doing business, especially after World War II.

When the Crowell-Collier magazines died, observers began speculating on the causes. Bernard Gallagher, in his industry newsletter for January, 1957, blamed a near-sighted management, which for twenty years, he said, had drained off profits without plowing money back into the company for growth and expansion. Ben Hibbs, editor of the *Saturday Evening Post*, acknowledged various causes but thought that lack of editorial independence was the basic one: "During the last ten years of their existence, as financial troubles deepened, the editors were given less and less freedom of action. Someone from the business office was always looking over their shoulders. Things often were done editorially solely to attract advertising—always a vain procedure and in the end usually a fatal mistake." [1] The media director of a large advertising agency thought that *Collier's*, at least, had lost its distinctive personality: "A magazine now has to create a personality for itself in people's minds, it has to have a character, and it has to have force. *Collier's* could prove to us that it could reach millions of people more cheaply than its competitors, but it couldn't prove that it was effective." [2] Hollis Alpert—no doubt correctly—found not one cause but many: "Rising costs, changing tastes, intangible rumors, unsuccessful financial decisions, editorial vacillation—each of these was a separate knife stuck into the struggling magazines." [3]

The Crowell-Collier magazines that died in 1956 had existed before the turn of the century, but the company itself was built up after 1900 by Joseph Palmer Knapp, certainly the least known of all major publishers. When he died in early 1951 at the age of eighty-six, he was not listed in *Who's Who*, and the New York *Times* gave him but a few short paragraphs of obituary. Yet he controlled a publishing empire that included the Crowell-Collier Publishing Company with its three mass-circulation magazines and its book-publishing activities; the United Newspaper Magazine Corporation, which published *This Week*, the magazine supplement for Sunday newspapers; and Alco-Gravure, the world's largest rotogravure printer. For years he also had been a director of the Metropolitan Life Insurance Company, which his father had helped to found. His fortune was estimated to be as much as $100 million.

Born in Brooklyn, Joseph Palmer Knapp was the son of Caroline Knapp, a composer of hymns for the Methodist church, and Joseph Fairchild Knapp, a printer who became the second president of

[1] *Advertising Age*, 30 (Feb. 16, 1959) 8.
[2] "Magazine Paradox: Are They Thriving or Dying?" *Business Week*, no. 1429 (Jan. 19, 1957) 90.
[3] Hollis Alpert, "What Killed *Collier's?*" *Saturday Review*, 40 (May 11, 1957) 11-42.

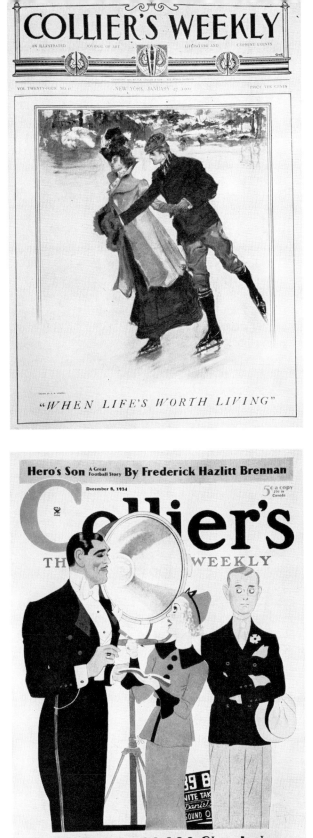

the Metropolitan Life Insurance Company and its largest stock-holder when it was still a stock company. Young Knapp left Columbia College after his freshman year to work for his father's printing firm at the wages of an apprentice—$5 a week, of which $3 went to the Methodist church, according to one account.[4]

Noticing that salesmen made the best living, Knapp asked his father if he could sell printing on commission. His father agreed only on the condition that the young man continue his job as apprentice printer, so Knapp did his selling during his lunch hours and after work. One noon he called on James B. Duke, who was later to become one of the chief founders of the American Tobacco Company. Duke was so pleased to find someone else who worked during the lunch hour that he became one of Knapp's best customers and closest friends.

As a salesman Knapp prospered—so much so that his father worried over his large income. To keep his son's cash income from growing too large, the elder Knapp began paying him off in stock in the company as well as in cash. The father, as self-protection, had the option of buying back his son's stock; the agreement provided that in the unlikely event that the son did not wish to sell, he could instead buy his father's stock. After a quarrel, during which his father sought to enforce their agreement, young Knapp did something for which his father never forgave him: he borrowed enough money on his own stock to buy out his father's printing business.

Over the years, Knapp expanded his printing business. He founded the American Lithographic Company, which, except for the Alco-Gravure division, he sold in 1929. He also helped to develop improvements in color printing. As a printer, he gave Edward Bok his start as editor. Bok, a boy at the time, got the idea of printing biographies on the backs of illustrated cards given away with cigarettes. One lunch hour he called on Knapp, who was then doing the printing for the tobacco company, and explained his idea. Knapp offered him $10 each for hundred-word biographies of a hundred famous Americans. When the first series was done, Knapp ordered a second and a third; and Bok, unable to supply copy fast enough by himself, hired friends to write the sketches for $5 and edited their work.

[4] *Tide*, 25 (Feb. 9, 1951) 48.

From printing, Knapp branched into publishing. For a time, with his friend James B. Duke, he published a daily newspaper in New York City. In 1903 he started one of the first of the magazine supplements for Sunday newspapers; and eleven years later, when competing supplements began appearing, he converted it into a three-cent weekly magazine, *Every Week*, which died from acute paper shortage during World War I.

As Knapp's printing concern grew into a mammoth factory, he looked around for printing orders to keep his presses busy. In 1906, for $750,000, he bought control of two promising magazines from their founder, John Crowell of Springfield, Ohio, who had decided that they were growing too large for his tastes. One of them was *Farm and Fireside*, the other *Woman's Home Companion*.

A printer, an inventor, and then publisher of a house organ for a farm implement manufacturer in Louisville, Kentucky, John Crowell was twenty-seven years old when he went to Springfield, Ohio, in 1877, to produce *Farm and Fireside* as a house organ for Phineas P. Mast and Company, farm implement makers. The house organ became so popular that Crowell, Mast, and Mast's nephew, Thomas Kirkpatrick, set up an independent company to publish it and began selling subscriptions to it. In 1885 the company added a second magazine, the *Ladies' Home Companion*, renamed the *Woman's Home Companion* in 1897, which grew out of the great interest in the women's page of *Farm and Fireside*, just as Cyrus Curtis' *Ladies' Home Journal* grew out of the women's page of his *Tribune and Farmer*. Both magazines were prospering when Crowell, no longer able to manage them comfortably, sold out his interest to Knapp and Knapp's friends, Samuel Untermeyer and Thomas W. Lamont, later president of J. P. Morgan and Company. Knapp became the majority stockholder, and he set the policies.

In 1911, under Knapp, the Crowell Publishing Company added the *American Magazine*, a descendant of the *Popular Monthly* that Frank Leslie started in 1876. A group of muckrakers who had become disenchanted with the policies of S. S. McClure, among them Ray Stannard Baker, Lincoln Steffens, and Ida Tarbell, had taken over the *American* in 1906, when McClure's partner John S. Phillips organized the Phillips Publishing Company, bought the magazine, and began almost a decade as its editor. In 1911 Knapp bought the *American,* reportedly for $40,000 in cash and $334,000 in preferred stock in the Crowell Publishing Company. Phillips stayed on as editor until his resignation in 1915.

Next, in 1919, Knapp's Crowell Publishing Company bought *Collier's,* which had had its day as a crusading journal but which had fallen on hard times. *Collier's* was founded in 1888 as *Once a Week* by Peter Fenelon Collier, an Irish immigrant who had prospered in America selling bargain-rate books. The weekly was offered as a premium to bookbuyers, and by the early 1890's it had picked up a circulation of 250,000. The founder rechristened it *Collier's* in 1896 and two years later turned its management over to his son, Robert J. Collier.

Young Collier himself edited the magazine for four years. Then in 1902 he hired Norman Hapgood as editor but retained overall direction of the publication. Under their leadership, *Collier's* achieved a certain editorial distinction. It gave good coverage to current affairs, Finley Peter Dunne wrote editorials and his "Mr. Dooley" essays for it, Mark Sullivan joined its staff, and its artists under contract included Maxfield Parrish, Frederic Remington, and Charles Dana Gibson, whom it is said to have paid $104,000 for fifty-two double-page spreads. Its circulation climbed from 170,000 in 1900 to 642,000 in 1914.

Robert J. Collier was poorly equipped, in temperament and training, to manage the affairs of the large company, which he took over after his father's death in 1909. For the first time in the history of the company, he borrowed money, and bankers and auditors began checking on the business to protect the loan. Hapgood, worried that the invasion by business interests would mean the end of editorial independence, left the editorship in 1912 after a disagreement with Robert Collier over policy. Collier himself edited the magazine until 1914; then Mark Sullivan edited it until 1917; and Finley Peter Dunne carried on until 1919. But the magazine's affairs were confused and its health weak.

The company was in a chaotic state when Robert J. Collier died in 1918. Then Joseph Palmer Knapp moved in. He did so at the urging of Thomas H. Beck, a onetime soap salesman who had been sales manager of *Collier's* before he joined the Crowell Publishing Company and in a short time worked up to a vice-presidency. For settling its debts, at a cost of about $1,750,000, Knapp got control of the Collier business. His publishing house continued as the

Crowell Publishing Company, for a time. In June, 1934, P. F. Collier and Son Company was merged with Crowell, and from 1939 on the firm was known as Crowell-Collier Publishing Company.

By 1919, then, Knapp's company had acquired the magazines that for many years put it among the major publishers—*American*, *Collier's*, *Woman's Home Companion*, and *Farm and Fireside*, the last of which was renamed *Country Home* in 1929 and suspended in 1939. For a decade the company published still another magazine, the *Mentor*, which it never tried to commercialize. The *Mentor* was founded before World War I by William A. Moffat, a former publishing executive, to give readers authoritative information from specialists. Each issue was devoted to a single topic, and the specialists included Luther Burbank, Dan Beard, Roger Babson, and Fritz Kreisler. Crowell-Collier bought the magazine in 1920. Its circulation climbed to 100,000, but it was scarcely a commercial success when compared with the company's other publications. In 1929, after Moffatt retired, Hugh A. Leamy, a former associate editor of *Collier's*, took over the editorship, spruced up the pages of the magazine, and abandoned its policy of a separate theme for each issue. But Crowell-Collier had become a mass producer of magazines, and its executives thought that the *Mentor* would fare better under a smaller publisher. In April, 1930, the company sold the *Mentor* to George R. Martin of the World Traveler Magazine Corporation, who took it over with the June issue.

The second magazine that Crowell-Collier disposed of was *Country Home*, born out of the *Farm and Fireside* which Knapp acquired with *Woman's Home Companion*. *Farm and Fireside* had grown steadily. Its circulation climbed from 600,000 in 1915 to 1,237,000 in 1927, when its advertising income was $990,000. But in 1929, although there had been no serious drop in advertising, production costs were eating up profits. The publishers weighed the possibilities of killing off the magazine, of selling it, or of revamping it. Deciding to revamp it, they gave it a new editor and a new name, *Country Home*. They brightened it up with coated paper and a four-color cover. They converted it from a strictly farm magazine into a "magazine of home, garden, and farm."

By 1937, with a gross advertising revenue of $1,313,000, *Country Home* was the only large farm magazine that had surpassed its peak revenues of 1928 and 1929. Yet it had a hard time breaking even. In late 1939, the company suspended publication of *Country Home*, then third in circulation and sixth in advertising revenue among farm publications, for the same reason that Curtis got rid of *Country Gentleman* sixteen years later: to concentrate in more profitable and promising fields.

Not only was Crowell-Collier a major publisher of magazines; it also was a major publisher and distributor of books, and it had an affiliation with a major Sunday newspaper supplement. *This Week*, the magazine supplement for newspapers, was not a Crowell-Collier publication, but it was closely related to Crowell-Collier through Publications Corporation, the company through which Joseph Palmer Knapp operated his publishing and printing empire.

Under Knapp, the Crowell-Collier Publishing Company was unique among major publishers in that it was built entirely on magazines that had been founded by others; in forty-five years, it never launched a new magazine of its own. Each of the magazines it took over was born again at least once in its offices, however, and the infants sometimes needed a good deal of pampering.

The publications did not always hold fast to a profitable course once they were put on it. They were in serious difficulties two years after the deaths of Knapp and Beck. In 1953 all of the Crowell-Collier magazines were losing money, and the company ended the year with a deficit of $4,349,000 as contrasted with a net income of $6,539,000 in 1946. Stock in the company, which had sold for $65 in 1946, was selling for $4.50 in the summer of 1953.

To pull the magazines out of their trouble, the company installed Paul C. Smith as its president in December, 1953. Smith had come to the company as a vice-president eight months earlier to analyze its difficulties. Before that, he had been general manager of the San Francisco *Chronicle* for seventeen years. The histories of the magazines he dealt with for four years before their suspension are a study in the fortunes of publishing.

When Knapp bought it, *Collier's* was so sickly senile that for a long time it seemed kinder to kill it than to nurse it along. Weak to begin with, it had suffered through, in quick succession, a paper shortage, a general strike of printers, and the hard times of 1920. For four consecutive weeks, it failed to appear. Advertising revenues dropped from $4,806,000 in 1920 to $960,000 in 1922, a year in which the *Saturday Evening Post* carried more than $28,000,000 in advertising. For a half-dozen years, *Collier's* moped along under three different editors whose tenure seemed so insecure that George Creel, refusing to wait twenty minutes for an appointment with one, explained, "I don't know who the editor will be twenty minutes from now." [5]

But Thomas H. Beck, who had urged its purchase, kept trying to get the weekly on its feet. He got help from William L. Chenery, who took over as editor in 1925. To his staff Chenery added a lively crew, including Walter Davenport, John T. Flynn, W. B. Courtney, and Kyle Crichton. The crew was so high spirited in fact, that it once moved Chenery to step from his office and remark, "Gentlemen, may I suggest the staff get drunk in shifts?" [6]

The new spirit began showing itself in the editorial content. Collier's opened 1925 with a serial, "Bobbed Hair," begun by Carolyn Wells and continued by nineteen other authors, including Alexander Woollcott, Dorothy Parker, Louis Bromfield, Elsie Janis, Sophie Kerr, Kermit Roosevelt, and Rube Goldberg. Its staff in 1925 began exposing the evils of Prohibition, a taboo subject in many magazines. The magazine continued to exploit its All-America Football Teams, a feature that Walter Camp had conducted in Collier's since 1897 and that Grantland Rice conducted for twenty-seven years after Camp's death in 1925. The magazine evolved its stable and staple editorial formula consisting of a balance of politics, economics, amusement, sports, serials, and short stories, one of them a short-short; and it hit upon a tone and brevity that distinguished it from its rival, the Saturday Evening Post.

Collier's became well known for its brevity. Even famous contributors—and the magazine attracted such contributors as President Franklin D. Roosevelt and Secretary of the Navy Frank Knox— had to make every word do full duty. Dr. S. Parkes Cadman once insisted that Collier's run all 10,000 words of a contribution; he finally approved a version one-fourth that length. On occasion Winston Churchill had to rewrite his contributions before they satisfied the editors.

In sparking up their magazine, Collier's editors depended on a network of correspondents to keep them informed of news and gossip in various localities. Writing under the name "Mr. X," each correspondent sent the managing editor a detailed but informal

---

[5] Hickman Powell, "Collier's," Scribner's, 105 (May, 1939) 20.
[6] Powell, p. 21.

memorandum on public sentiment, business, politics, and so on from his section.

As the magazine began to hit its stride, both circulation and advertising revenues moved upward. Circulation, just a shade over a million in 1924, was about twice that in 1929. From $1,729,000 in 1924, gross advertising revenues rose to $3,065,000 in 1927, when, nonetheless, they were still far behind the $53,145,000 of the *Saturday Evening Post*. Yet *Collier's* continued to operate at a loss. By 1927 the company had spent some $10,000,000 on the magazine, and some of its stockholders were wondering if *Collier's* were not an expensive blunder. Not so Knapp, however. Predicting that the magazine would be on its feet within three years, he said that he would be glad to buy out any stockholder who wanted to quit. Within the three years that Knapp had predicted, *Collier's* had started to break even; it had cost the company $15,000,000 to get it there. Between 1926 and 1934, its advertising income increased 147 per cent—from $2,910,000 to $7,200,000. Its gross advertising revenues, from 1937 through 1956, exceeded those of all other Crowell-Collier magazines combined.

During and after World War II, *Collier's* had a rapid turnover among its top editorial personnel. It had seven different editors in the twelve years after William L. Chenery quit to become publisher in 1943. Subeditors also came and went. The editor who had perhaps the most impact on the magazine was Louis Ruppel, who came to Crowell-Collier in March, 1949, from the executive editorship of Hearst's Chicago *American*. At the same time, Chenery retired as publisher but stayed on as vice-president of the company. His job as publisher went to Edward Anthony, for the preceding six years publisher of *Woman's Home Companion*.

In his first week at *Collier's*, Ruppel fired the articles editor and the art director; the fiction editor resigned. Chafing at the five-week gap between deadline and publication date, Ruppel tried to run the magazine like a newspaper. With an "exposé a week" and controversial "inside stories" by reporters on large dailies, he hoped to give the magazine a new life; and indeed, a reader who had known only Chenery's *Collier's* of the thirties would scarcely have recognized the jazzed-up *Collier's* Ruppel put together. But the changes were more dramatic than successful. Ruppel resigned in May, 1952, and in May, 1953, *Collier's* changed from weekly to

biweekly publication to cut costs and to make the magazine more attractive to advertisers by increasing the number of pages.

The rapid changes on the staff of *Collier's* seem to have been both a cause and an effect of an insecure magazine. Although *Collier's* appears to have had a healthy growth for fifteen or so years after it began showing a profit, it came upon hard times in 1949 and 1950. Its circulation in 1950 was but 6 per cent more than that of 1941, whereas some other weeklies had shown much greater gains in that same decade—*Time* 86 per cent, for instance, *Life* 62 per cent, and the *Saturday Evening Post* 23 per cent. Worse, advertising revenue dropped from $22,691,000 in 1947 to $17,048,000 in 1949. In 1950 its competitor *Look* nosed it out in gross advertising, $17,765,000 to $17,351,000, and thereafter continued to outpace it. After the end came, an advertising man recalled, "We'd go along with a company's sales manager when he was holding his annual sales meeting. If he got up and announced that this year his company was making its big advertising push in *Collier's*, the salesmen just sat there. If he said *Life*, they'd get up on their feet and cheer."

When *Collier's* ended publication, Cowles Magazines, Inc., bought the title and unexpired subscriptions and thereby hoped to pick up a million new subscribers for *Look*. The Curtis Publishing Company bought the third and final installment of a serial—"Doom Cliff" by Luke Short—which *Collier's* had begun but never concluded, for a February issue of the *Saturday Evening Post*.

Two competitors were likewise waiting to pick up the unexpired subscriptions to *Woman's Home Companion* when it died. After a thorough study of the list, *Ladies' Home Journal* and *McCall's* announced that they expected to add 390,679 new subscribers each to their own circulations.

For most of its life as a Crowell-Collier magazine, *Woman's Home Companion* was the editorial product of Gertrude Battles Lane, who joined its staff at $18 a week in 1903 and who was earning $52,000 a year and was a vice-president and director of the company when she died in 1941. As a young woman, Miss Lane spent her last $10 to get from Boston, where she had been a stenographer for a publishing house and spare-time editor of a small magazine, to New York, where she found work as household editor of *Woman's Home Companion*. In 1912, a half-dozen years after Knapp had taken over the magazine, she was promoted to editor. In the next twenty-nine years, she pushed *Woman's Home Companion* to the top of the highly competitive field of women's magazines where, during the decade before her death, it jockeyed with Curtis' *Ladies' Home Journal* for first position.

Miss Lane served her readers the established women's magazine fare: fiction by well-known authors, articles about food and fashion, articles giving practical assistance to the homemaker, articles with an element of do-goodism and uplift. She ran the high-priced stories of such authors as Edna Ferber, Dorothy Canfield Fisher, and Kathleen Norris. She established a Better Baby Bureau to stimulate interest in child health. She crusaded for packaged groceries. She paid $25,000 for the unpublished letters of Robert and Elizabeth Barrett Browning. She set up a department to give advice to consumers. To keep her magazine in tune with readers' interests, the company in 1935 organized a panel of 2,000 readers who were queried on a variety of subjects each month.

Meanwhile, *Woman's Home Companion* grew in circulation and advertising. When Miss Lane became editor in 1912, circulation was 737,000 and advertising revenues $1,019,000. In 1930, when circulation was 2,598,000, revenues were at a peak of $8,500,000. In the late thirties, advertising revenues slipped, and they were down to $5,935,000 in 1941, the year in which Miss Lane died.

In 1943 when Edward Anthony became publisher, he set about altering the editorial formula which, virtually unchanged even after Miss Lane's death, had kept *Woman's Home Companion* successful for decades. Granting that the functions of a women's magazine are to entertain and to serve, he concluded that the *Woman's Home Companion* could help its readers with their minds as well as with foods, fashions, and family. Since he thought that articles give a magazine its personality, he sought a new approach for the service nonfiction in *Woman's Home Companion*. Before long the magazine was running articles on juvenile delinquency and racial and religious prejudice, was urging its readers to support the United Nations. But both Anthony and W. A. Birnie, the editor who later replaced him as publisher, thought they had developed a new editorial approach to such subjects. A good women's magazine, according to Birnie, should differ from other magazines in this respect: "that the article, the subject to be treated, must be something that offers an opportunity for the woman to do something about it." [7] To that end, *Woman's Home Companion* developed what Roger Dakin, then its articles editor, called "the chocolate cake approach": "Show someone a chocolate cake and you don't have to argue him into wanting a piece. In dealing with problems that affect all communities, for example, show vividly how one community solved it, how the women in that community benefited by the solution. Report, don't sermonize. There will come a point in the article when the reader will feel: 'Why can't my town do it too?' That's the time to tell her how it can, and what she can do to get started." [8]

Although the new approach can scarcely be given full credit, the *Woman's Home Companion* for a time seemed to do well under it. Circulation climbed from 3,728,000 in 1946 to 4,343,000 in 1953, and advertising revenues in the same period rose from $9,084,000 to $11,955,000. But *McCall's* had already edged it out for second place to *Ladies' Home Journal* in the women's field, and revenues slid swiftly downward again—to $9,026,000 in 1956. Woodrow Wirsig, who succeeded Birnie as editor in 1953, was himself succeeded by Theodore Strauss three years later. Those last years were ones of mounting losses and corporate problems, and with its issue of January, 1957, the *Woman's Home Companion* vanished.

When Joseph Palmer Knapp acquired the *American*, he thought it had possibilities as a magazine for men, a counterbalance to *Woman's Home Companion*. The man who made the *American* a magazine for men was John Siddall, its editor from 1915 to 1923. The editorial policy of the *American*, Siddall once said, was based on victory—"victory for the individual over the odds that beset him." "There are all kinds of odds: sickness, lack of education, or opportunity, or money; unfortunate environment, bad habits, absurd weakness, every sort of mental, physical, and spiritual barrier. What we do in the magazine is to stand at the hard places in the road and cry, 'You can come through; you can win!' " [9] To inspire his readers to victory, Siddall used what he called the "personal angle," an approach that filled the *American* with articles telling how financially successful men made the grade.

[7] William A. Birnie, interviewed by Quincy Howe, on "You and Magazines," broadcast over station WCBS, Feb. 1, 1950.

[8] *Tide*, 20 (Oct. 25, 1946) 21.

[9] Quoted in John E. Drewry, "The American Magazine Adopts a New Success Slant," *Writer*, 48 (Sept., 1935) 344-45.

Merle Crowell, who became editor on the death of Siddall in 1923, continued the success formula of his predecessor. The popularity of the *American*, Crowell said, was based on "the universal desire of man to improve himself." His editorial policy was "to give such true human experiences, such wise counsel out of the mouths of practical men and women, such adventures of mind and soul as will be new . . . sound and intimate." [10]

Under Crowell, the *American* grew. By the time he resigned because of ill health in 1929, he had added 350,000 new readers and had put the *American* into sixth place in circulation of all magazines in the United States. To take Crowell's place as editor, the company engaged Sumner Blossom, a former editor of the New York *Daily News* and of *Popular Science Monthly*. He was still holding the job when Crowell-Collier suspended the magazine in 1956.

The crash of 1929, which almost coincided with Blossom's joining the *American*, made incongruous the optimistic success stories on which the magazine had flourished in the twenties. Blossom sent his staff a memorandum which said, "Horatio Alger doesn't work here any more." Then, by redesigning its editorial approach, he slowly changed the *American* from a man's magazine into a family magazine. Although he did not entirely scrap the success formula, he changed the magazine's definition of success. Personal success, Blossom thought, was not as important as the successful idea or achievement which improved the welfare of large numbers of persons.[11] He tried to make the magazine an authoritative interpreter of contemporary life. To encourage new fiction writers and to discourage his staff from being blinded by famous names, he ordered mailroom clerks to mask the author's name on all unsolicited pieces of fiction. The staff learned the author's identity only after it had decided to accept or reject a manuscript.

Like *Collier's*, the *American* sank into a decline after World War II. Although its sale of copies gained slightly, its advertising revenues fell from $5,802,000 in 1946 to less than half that amount in 1955. In July, 1956, since the magazine showed less promise than the other two Crowell-Collier publications, the company announced that it was suspending the publication with the August issue.

---

[10] Drewry, p. 345.
[11] John E. Drewry, "Writing for *American* Magazine," *Writer,* 50 (Aug., 1937) 256.

The Crowell-Collier magazines, then, were uncertainties when Paul Smith took over as president in 1953, but he spoke hopefully of saving them. For a time, he did in fact cut their disastrous drain on resources; the losses of *Collier's* dropped from $7,000,000 in 1953 to $4,500,000 the next year, and the company under Smith briefly moved into the black. In July, 1954, he relieved the three magazines of their individual publishers and took over their management himself. He reorganized their staffs, instituted various economies, reviewed editorial policies, and, as editor-in-chief, even approved their covers and major features.

From the first, he brought in financial help. Between the time he took over and the deaths of the magazines, some $10,000,000 in new capital went into the company. Working with Edward L. Elliott, a New York broker, Smith in 1955 negotiated large sums from a group of New York and Chicago financiers, who took over working control of the company. Early in 1956, the company announced plans to branch out into broadcasting, newspaper publishing, and other communications ventures. During the year, it did acquire four record clubs and a radio station, although its plans to acquire a string of radio and television stations fell through for want of funds.

Meanwhile, Smith tried to put down rumors that the magazines were dying. One major advertiser, after reading the company's 1953 financial statement, canceled a million dollars' worth of advertising in the *Woman's Home Companion* because he saw no sense in placing it in such a precarious publication. Smith managed to save most of that business. Just nine days before the end came, Smith was still fighting rumors. "I have no intention at the present of suspending the magazines or selling them," he said. For the sixth time, he said, he had encountered a "rugged cash problem," and he had explored with Cowles Magazines and Time Inc. the possibilities of their taking over his unexpired subscriptions if he could not solve it.[12] As it happened, he could not solve it.

The end of the magazines, which had lost nearly $8,000,000 in their final year, did not mean an end of the Crowell-Collier company. It sold its printing plant in Springfield, Ohio, to the R. R. Donnelley and Sons Company of Chicago, a major magazine printer, for $3,894,374.[13] Cowles Magazines acquired the company's sub-

---

[12] *Advertising Age*, 27 (Dec. 10, 1956) 1.
[13] *Advertising Age*, 28 (March 25, 1957) 108.

scription-selling subsidiary and its educational division. Other publishers helped to absorb its jobless employees. The Securities and Exchange Commission investigated stock trading that had preceded the deaths of the magazines but took no action against the company, although it did penalize three brokerage firms. Both the company and its broker contended that the transactions were private and thus the debentures were exempt from the commission's registration.[14] Smith left the company on February 15, 1957, and about a year later, after a rest in Tahiti, Brazil, and Venezuela, became vice-president and treasurer of American Export Lines. Free of its magazines, Crowell-Collier expanded its book-publishing activities, added broadcast stations, and regularly reported an annual profit.

Although the mass media treated Cowell-Collier's withdrawal from magazine publishing as news of national importance, esteemed magazines had been quietly vanishing since the century was young —indeed, since the first magazine appeared. Among those to which the twentieth century brought an end were many magazines of high literary quality, journals of comment and opinion, and weeklies and monthlies backgrounding and analyzing current affairs. One by one, during the thirties and forties, magazines such as the *North American Review, Living Age, Forum,* and *Independent* disappeared. The publisher of a sick magazine usually tried to prolong its life by merging it with a moribund rival, thereby decreasing its immediate competition and strengthening it temporarily by an increased circulation. In time, however, a magazine which had taken over its competitors was invariably swallowed by a stronger magazine. Thus, for instance, *World's Work* was absorbed by the *Review of Reviews,* which was absorbed by the *Literary Digest,* which on its deathbed was absorbed by *Time.*

No doubt some of the magazines of quality died because their audience was limited. True, advances in education increased the number of Americans who could read and write, but schools were not producing the sort of educated reader that the best nineteenth-century magazines were edited for, the man at home in all ages and all lands; rather they were producing persons whose interests were best served by the popular weeklies and monthlies. Readers themselves could support but few quality magazines. And such

---

[14] *Advertising Age,* 28 (Jan. 21, 1957) 1, 85; (Aug. 19, 1957) 38; 29 (May 19, 1958) 69.

publications were not attractive to advertisers, who, with the growth of a mass market for consumer goods and services, could much more economically reach their potential customers through the organs of mass circulation.

Because of their small circulations, the quality publications could not share in the economies of mass production, and they had to compete with the affluent mass-circulation periodicals for authors. In the nineteenth century, before the development of advertising, magazines could buy the works of Mark Twain for two cents a word; in the twentieth century, magazines spent thousands of dollars on works they wanted, as when *Collier's* paid $50,000 for James Farley's history of the New Deal, when *Reader's Digest* reportedly paid Eric Johnston $25,000 plus a $15,000 bonus for an account of his wartime interview with Stalin, and when *Life* paid $500,000 to the first seven U.S. astronauts for exclusive stories of their training and flights into space. The best authors still wrote for periodicals of small circulation, but they wrote for the mass-circulation magazines as well. Moreover, the copyright agreements between the United States and Great Britain after 1891 closed an inexpensive source of material to the quality magazines—British periodicals, from which many nineteenth-century American magazines had clipped freely without paying royalties to the authors.

Two quality magazines that had been among the most respected in the United States, *North American Review* and *Living Age*, died on the eve of America's entry into World War II. Their last publisher was Joseph Hilton Smyth, who pleaded guilty in 1942 to serving as an agent of the Japanese government without registering with the State Department. Two other men who also received pay from the Japanese were involved with Smyth in his publishing activities.[15]

Between June, 1938, and December, 1941, the Japanese government had provided Smyth and his associates with more than $125,000 to establish or buy publications as vehicles for Japanese propaganda. Smyth acquired *Living Age* in June, 1938, and *North American Review* the following September. He also was involved with *Scribner's Commentator*, a strongly pro-isolationist magazine, but it seems to have taken its policies not from him but from others associated with it.

When the *North American Review* suspended publication in

[15] *Editor & Publisher*, 75 (Sept. 12, 1942) 8; *Time*, 40 (Sept. 14, 1942) 46.

1940, it was one of the oldest magazines in America. In its century and a quarter of existence, it had had such distinguished editors as Richard H. Dana, James Russell Lowell, Henry Adams, and Henry Cabot Lodge, and its contributors had included some of the world's most famous writers. Bryant's "Thanatopsis" first appeared in it, and so did Alan Seeger's "I Have a Rendezvous with Death"; Mark Twain, a regular contributor, prepared chapters of his autobiography for it, and in it Henry James serialized his *The Ambassadors.*

Although the *North American Review* was a ponderous and somewhat provincially New England magazine for the first sixty years after its founding in 1815, it became a lively journal with a wide range of subject matter in the late 1870's. In 1891, when its circulation was at a peak of 76,000, *Review of Reviews* wrote of it: "It is unquestionably true that the *North American Review* is regarded by more people, in all parts of the country, as at once the highest and most impartial platform upon which current public issues can be discussed, than is any other magazine or review." [16]

In 1899 Colonel George Harvey, a former managing editor of Joseph Pulitzer's New York *World* who had made a fortune in electric railways, bought control of the *North American Review.* As editor until 1921, when he was appointed ambassador to the Court of St. James's, Colonel Harvey upheld the distinction which the magazine had achieved in the late nineteenth century and made it a political influence. On his return to the United States in 1924, he again took over the active editorship and, finding the circulation at a low of 13,000, changed the magazine to a quarterly.

Colonel Harvey sold the magazine in the fall of 1926 to Walter Butler Mahony, a corporation lawyer. Under the new owner, the magazine announced that it would become more sprightly and timely, and it again became a monthly. Mahony's ownership continued into the 1930's, and the magazine maintained high standards, although it slipped far from the leadership it had once held. Smyth bought the magazine in September, 1938.

Like the *North American Review*, *Living Age* was an old and respected magazine when Smyth became its publisher. Eliakim Littell founded the magazine in Boston in 1844 as *Littell's Living Age,* and each week he filled it with material clipped from British publications. After he died in 1870, his son Robert continued the

---

[16] Frank Luther Mott, *A History of American Magazines 1850-1865* (Cambridge, 1938), p. 255.

magazine under the same policies until his own death in 1896. Then Frank Foxcroft took control, dropped the word "Littell's" from the title, and somewhat broadened its scope by adding sections on American books and authors.

The Atlantic Monthly Press bought the weekly in 1919, and Ellery Sedgwick, longtime editor of the *Atlantic*, served briefly as its editor. In 1924 the publishers dressed up the cover and typography and promised readers to bring out an occasional issue carrying longer articles of enduring significance. But the magazine continued to be chiefly a repository of ably selected material from foreign publications. It went from weekly to monthly publication in 1927. The following year a new company, World Topics Corporation, took over the magazine and gave it a new format and a new editor, John Bakeless, former managing editor of *Forum* and late of the infant *Time*. Smyth bought into *Living Age* in 1938 when the Japanese government supplied $15,000 for the initial purchase and $2,500 a month to underwrite losses. The magazine stopped publication in 1941.

Scribner's Commentator, which began steering a strongly pro-isolationist course in mid-1940 and then vanished under a cloud of suspicion and distrust, had little resemblance except in name to the monthly magazine that once had proudly carried the title *Scribner's*. It was a merger of the titles of *Commentator*, a pocket-sized monthly, and *Scribner's*, a magazine of quality which to all purposes had already died.

Scribner's had passed its fiftieth anniversary when it ceased publication in 1939. In 1886 Charles Scribner of the book-publishing house decided to bring out a new illustrated magazine of general interest. Some years before he had lent his name to the magazine which eventually became the *Century*, and when he had withdrawn from that periodical, he had agreed that no magazine should bear his name for five years. When the five years were up, he had E. L. Burlingame put together a new magazine in an office over the Scribner bookstore on Broadway. The first issue of the new *Scribner's* appeared in January, 1887. Burlingame and Robert Bridges, who succeeded him as editor in 1914, solidly established the reputation of *Scribner's* for literary excellence. It ran the early works of many well-known authors, among them Thomas Wolfe and Ernest Hemingway, and published dozens of short stories and novels that have endured, among them Richard Harding Davis'

"Gallagher" and "The Bar Sinister," Hemingway's "The Killers," Stephen Crane's "The Open Boat," Edith Wharton's *Ethan Frome*, James Barrie's *Sentimental Tommy*, and Robert Louis Stevenson's *The Master of Ballantrae*.

On Bridges' retirement in 1930, Alfred Dashiell held the editorship until 1936 when he joined the *Reader's Digest*. Circulation of *Scribner's* had once reached 200,000; but the magazine was unable or unwilling to compete with livelier popular journals, and fewer and fewer persons bought copies, which still bore the ugly anachronistic yellow cover that Stanford White had designed for its first issue. In 1936 when Dashiell quit, sales were down to 43,000.

As its new editor, the publisher hired Harlan Logan, a former teacher of English who had drifted into the business of analyzing magazines to help them rebuild sagging circulations. The magazine was divorced from the Scribner book-publishing firm, which, however, held a controlling interest in the new publishing company. Logan, believing that the day of the small circulation class magazine was over, aimed at a circulation of a quarter of a million. To get it, he enlarged *Scribner's* and broadened its editorial appeal. Although he more than doubled its circulation and cut operating losses from $2,500 to $700 a month, he could not make the magazine show a profit, and it ceased publication in May, 1939. David Smart of Esquire, Inc., bought its circulation of 80,000 for a reported $11,000. The pocket-sized *Commentator* acquired its name.

Commentator had first appeared in January, 1937, with Lowell Thomas, the radio commentator, as editor. When the magazine telescoped the name *Scribner's* with its own, Thomas left, and the magazine underwent changes in financial backing, staff, and policy. By mid-1940 *Scribner's Commentator* had emerged as a vigorously pro-isolationist journal. In 1942, the year that it died, one of its staff members, Ralph Townsend of San Francisco, pleaded guilty to serving as an unregistered agent of the Japanese government, and the magazine itself was listed by the Attorney General of the United States in connection with a sedition conspiracy for which twenty-eight persons were indicted, a case ending in mistrial because of the death of the presiding judge.

So died the *North American Review*, *Living Age*, and *Scribner's*, all magazines of quality in their day. *Scribner's* had survived by a decade an earlier quality magazine which had carried the same name. The name of the earlier *Scribner's* had been changed to

Century in 1881. As *Century*, the magazine was a giant in prestige and a comparative giant in advertising linage in the decade before Munsey and McClure began publishing their popular magazines.

The first *Scribner's* was conceived by Roswell Smith and Dr. Josiah Gilbert Holland, a well-known literary man, who met in Switzerland in 1869 and talked about the magazine they would like to publish on their return home. Back in the United States, they took their plans to Charles Scribner, who bought four-tenths of the stock in the magazine and lent it his name to inspire confidence. Some 40,000 readers received copies of the first issue in November, 1870. Under Holland's editorship, *Scribner's* ran serials by such authors as Frances Hodgson Burnett, Henry James, and Bret Harte, and short stories by Hans Christian Andersen, Frank Stockton, and Helen Hunt Jackson. Circulation mounted, and by 1880 it was more than 100,000.

In 1881 both the Scribner publishing firm and Holland withdrew from ownership of *Scribner's*, and Roswell Smith took control. As part of the transaction, Smith agreed to change the name of the magazine, which he altered to *Century;* the Scribner firm agreed not to publish another magazine for five years, after which time it did publish the *Scribner's* that died in 1939.

Holland lived to edit but one number of the *Century;* his successor was Richard Watson Gilder, who served as editor until 1909. *Century* reached its zenith under Gilder. It ran a remarkable series on the Civil War by important participants, including Generals Grant, McClellan, Longstreet, and Beauregard, and the articles plus the book growing out of them earned the Century Company more than a million dollars. The magazine published, as a sequel, a serial life of Lincoln by Nicolay and Hay.

Circulation rolled upward to a peak of 200,000 in the late 1880's, and the magazine was packed with advertisements in the 1890's. On Gilder's death in 1909, the *Century* got new editors in fairly rapid succession, considering Gilder's tenure of twenty-eight years —five editors in a dozen years. In 1921 Glenn Frank took over as editor, changed the cover, raised the newsstand price from thirty-five to fifty cents, and tried to inject vitality into the magazine, but he never quite succeeded in striking the editorial formula requisite for a healthy circulation. When Frank resigned in 1925 to become president of the University of Wisconsin, he was succeeded by

Hewitt H. Howland, for many years literary adviser to the Bobbs-Merrill Company.

In 1929, a lush year for magazines generally, the *Century* was sick in circulation and ailing in advertising. After sixty years as a monthly, Howland announced, *Century* would appear quarterly because the world was going at "too fast a pace" and he wanted to give people a longer time to read the magazine. But the switch to quarterly publication was no more effective in holding readers than had been an attempt to make the magazine journalistic in 1913. Despite the policy changes as editor succeeded editor, circulation and advertising volume slid gently but steadily downward. Sales dropped from 150,000 in 1906 to 20,000 in 1930; advertising volume slumped from fifty pages an issue in the 1880's and double that in the 1890's to but five pages in the final issue in the spring of 1930. *Forum*, a competitor, bought *Century's* name, but eventually even that disappeared.

It was on the *Forum* that Walter Hines Page established his reputation as an editor. In 1887, when Page was working for a New York newspaper, he was approached by a stranger who offered him the job of putting *Forum* on its feet. An infant publication, a review founded in the hope that it would become a major influence in art, literature, politics, and science, the *Forum* until then had shown little but a propensity for losing its founders' money. Page joined the magazine, first as manager, then as editor, and he stayed with it until the summer of 1895.

The purpose of *Forum*, in Page's words, was "to provide discussion about subjects of contemporary interest, in which the magazine is not partisan, but merely the instrument." [17] To make the magazine timely, Page held open its pages until a week before the day of publication; to make the magazine authoritative, he sought articles from men famous in their fields, Theodore Roosevelt, Woodrow Wilson, William Graham Sumner; to make the magazine measure to high standards, he often threw away contributions for which he had paid.

Although the influence of *Forum* was probably far greater than its circulation indicated, Page did succeed in attracting some 30,000 subscribers, a good showing considering the type of magazine; and

---

[17] Burton J. Hendrick, *The Life and Letters of Walter H. Page* (Garden City, N.Y., 1922), I, 49.

before he resigned, the magazine was making a profit. A succession of editors followed Page. When *Forum* took over *Century* in 1930, its editor was Henry Goddard Leach, who had trebled the highest circulation that Page had achieved.

A decade after *Forum* swallowed *Century*, it in turn was swallowed by *Current History*, which annexed its title with the issue for July, 1940, and for about a year published under the name *Current History and Forum*. Still in existence in 1963, *Current History* was established by the New York Times Company in 1914 to carry source news on the war and on the international situation. In 1936, disposing of two of its special publications, the New York Times Company sold the magazine to M. E. Tracy, who for many years had been associated with the Scripps-Howard newspapers. Tracy released the staff writers of the magazine because he thought them too stuffy. One of the deposed men, Spencer Brodney, the former editor of *Current History*, began his own magazine, *Events*, in 1937, and in it he sought to perpetuate the policies of *Current History*. His offshoot lasted but a few years. In 1941, *Current History and Forum* took over *Events* to become *Current History*, "Incorporating *Events, Forum* and *Century*."

Throughout the twentieth century, one quality magazine after another swallowed its shaky competitors, just as *Forum* swallowed the *Century* and in turn was taken over by *Current History*. After more than thirty years of publication, *World's Work* vanished into *Review of Reviews*. A few years later *Review of Reviews* was merged with the *Literary Digest*, and later still the *Literary Digest* sold its name to *Time*, which once a year thereafter ran the nameplate, "*Time*, Incorporating the *Literary Digest*," to preserve its legal claim to the title.

In 1900 the young publishing firm of Doubleday, Page and Company decided to bring out a new magazine, *World's Work*, devoted to the "activities of the newly organized world, its problems and even its romances." Its editor from the start was Walter Hines Page, a partner in the firm, and he guided the magazine until he was appointed ambassador to the Court of St. James's in 1913.

World's Work scored its first great scoop in 1907 when it published the reminiscences of John D. Rockefeller, Sr., in a series of six articles. When Page relinquished the editorship, he was succeeded by his son, Arthur Wilson Page. Arthur Page displayed his initiative as editor when war broke out in 1914. Halting the issue already on the presses, he quickly replaced it with a war manual which contained a thorough picture of the international scene. That issue just about trebled the magazine's circulation of 100,000.

A number of editors followed Arthur Page: Burton J. Hendrick, Edgar F. Strother, Barton W. Currie, Russell Doubleday, and Alan C. Collins. By 1929, when Russell Doubleday took over as editor, even the publishers admitted that the magazine had fallen by the wayside and promised a renewed vigor. Advertising volume had been slipping throughout the twenties. It plummeted from $510,000 in 1929 to $219,760 in 1932, when circulation was about 77,000. In July, 1932, *Review of Reviews* announced that with the August issue it would carry the name *World's Work* besides its own on the cover but that its own policies would remain unchanged.

Review of Reviews was founded in 1891 by Dr. Albert Shaw, Sr., who edited the magazine until it became buried in the *Literary Digest* in 1937. Shaw, a former editorial writer for the Minneapolis *Tribune*, decided that readers had to plow through far too many magazines to keep well informed about world affairs. To simplify the job for them, he rounded up a staff of editors and set them to condensing material for a publication he called *Review of Reviews*. He himself wrote the lead editorial, "The Progress of the World," and he continued to write editorials for virtually every issue in the forty-six years that the magazine existed.

Review of Reviews had its greatest influence and circulation during World War I, when its sales were about 250,000 copies. During the twenties, its advertising revenues slipped steadily—from $670,-902 in 1920 to $461,040 in 1927. When it absorbed *World's Work* in 1932, *Review of Reviews* had advertising revenues of $195,000, a circulation of 167,000.

In the 1930's, the *Literary Digest* also was ailing; and when it became known that the publishers wanted to dispose of it, the magazine industry buzzed with rumors that William Randolph Hearst would buy it, that George Hecht of *Parents'* would buy it. The purchaser, however, was Albert Shaw, Jr., president of the Review of Reviews Corporation, who paid a reported $200,000 for it in June, 1937. The Shaws merged the *Literary Digest* with their *Review of Reviews* and on July 17, 1937, brought out the result of the union, *The Digest*, a weekly that proposed to give a summary of the news of the week, eight pages of "stories in pictures," a digest of books, and a digest of magazine articles in important United States and foreign publications. *The Digest* started out bravely with an initial press run of 600,000, but it lasted only until the following autumn. In November it vanished, and in its place re-emerged the *Literary Digest* with a new set of owners. The new owners, who paid about $200,000 to the Shaws for the Review of Reviews Corporation, were headed by George F. Havell, who had once been circulation manager, business manager, and later managing editor of *Forum*. The Shaws had called him in to help start *The Digest,* and he had invested in the venture. When *The Digest* failed to find an audience, Havell and a group of others bought it to revive the *Literary Digest*. But Havell's revived *Literary Digest* lived only about six months; then the magazine finally died, and its name was bought by Time Inc.

The *Literary Digest* was founded in 1890 by Dr. Isaac K. Funk and Adam W. Wagnalls, both former Lutheran ministers. Wagnalls had been pastor of a church in Kansas City for two years, then city clerk in Atchison, Kansas, for another two years before he went to New York to join Funk in a book-publishing company. In 1878 Wagnalls became a partner in Funk and Company; in 1891 the firm became Funk and Wagnalls Company. Its output depended heavily on reprints of European authors, dictionaries, encyclopedias, and religious works. Funk died in 1912, his partner in 1924.

In 1890 the two publishers brought out a magazine that they thought would be especially helpful to educators and ministers— the *Literary Digest,* "a repository of contemporaneous thought and research as presented in the periodical literature of the world." The magazine extended its editorial scope to cover general news and comment in 1905. The same year William Seaver Woods, a minister's son, became editor, a post he held until 1933.

The man who probably did most to guide the *Literary Digest* into becoming a national institution was Robert J. Cuddihy, its publisher from 1905 to 1937. Cuddihy had joined the company in 1878 as an office boy, and eventually he came to own 60 per cent of the stock in the company. Mailing out barrage after barrage of subscription offers to names in telephone directories and on other lists, plowing profits back into the business, Cuddihy pushed up both circulation and profits. Beginning with the 1920 election, the *Literary Digest* conducted its famous straw votes, which provided it with thousands of new subscribers as well as prestige and good editorial copy. The magazine mailed out millions of ballots—

20,000,000 in 1932, half that many in 1936—and from the returns accurately foretold the major election results in 1920, 1924, 1928, and 1932. Subscription offers accompanied the ballots. The magazine acquired 70,000 new subscribers from a poll on the Prohibition question in the spring of 1930.

In 1920 the *Literary Digest*, with gross revenues of $12,720,000 from its linage, was second only to the *Saturday Evening Post* in dollar volume of national advertising. Although its revenues dropped to $7,866,000 in 1925, it remained among the leaders in advertising. In 1925 the magazine was able to buy out a minor rival, *Current Opinion*, for a rumored $250,000. Annual profits reached an estimated $2,000,000. Just before the crash of 1929, Cuddihy is said to have unsuccessfully offered $5,000,000 to Wilfred J. Funk, son of the cofounder, for his share in the company.

Circulation slid downward through the 1920's and early 1930's, although it remained above the million mark. The magazine tried a number of devices to keep up its sales. It offered gift premiums to subscribers; for a dollar more than the usual subscription price, subscribers in 1930 could get an accident insurance policy.

In 1933, when circulation had sagged to 978,000, and when Woods resigned, the publishers let the new editor, Arthur Draper, make some changes in the tradition-bound magazine. Draper brightened the typography, threw out some old features and added some new ones, introduced signed contributions on current affairs, and made other changes. But circulation dropped to 686,000 in 1936, when the circulation guarantee was the lowest since 1917. Draper resigned as editor in 1935 because of differences over matters of policy. Morton Savell briefly followed him as editor and then was replaced by Wilfred Funk.

There is a popular notion that the *Literary Digest* died because it incorrectly forecast the Presidential election in 1936 when its straw poll showed 1,293,669 votes for Alfred Landon and 972,897 for Franklin Roosevelt; but the ill health of the magazine in the years before suggests that the poll was but the blow that finished an already tottering publication. Despite the efforts of the Shaws of the *Review of Reviews* and of George Havell to revive the moribund magazine, it finally had to cease publication in February, 1938, when it laid off all but twenty of its 200 employees. The magazine never reappeared, although George Havell said he hoped to resume publication within sixty days. He got some revenue by renting the mailing lists of the magazine to advertisers, while he scouted for new working capital, and he appealed to subscribers to send in a dollar apiece to keep alive "an American institution." Other publishers who had sold subscriptions to the magazine in combination with their own objected to the appeal to subscribers, and the Audit Bureau of Circulations reproved the managers of the *Digest,* who returned the contributions they had received.

In March, 1938, the publishers petitioned the United States District Court for permission to reorganize under the bankruptcy act. For a magazine that had been valued at millions of dollars in its prime, the publishers listed liabilities of $1,492,067.67 and assets of $850,923.72. Since the suspension of the *Digest* in February, Time Inc. had been negotiating with Havell for its purchase. With its issue of May 23, 1938, *Time* added the name of the *Literary Digest* to its own and began fulfilling the 250,000 subscriptions on the books of the defunct publication.

Again and again the process was repeated: on its deathbed, an old magazine of quality sought to regain its vitality by devouring its faltering competitors but instead of fattening, died with them. The *Outlook,* edited in its early years by Henry Ward Beecher and in its last years by Alfred E. Smith, the defeated Presidential candidate, absorbed the older *Independent*—and even a stripling as well, the *International Interpreter*—but within a few years after the mergers it was dead.

When the *Outlook* first appeared in 1867, it was a Baptist paper called the *Church Union.* Its circulation dropped from 16,000 to 2,000 within a few years, and its debt-saddled owner gave the publication to J. B. Ford and Company, publishers of Henry Ward Beecher. They installed Beecher as editor and on his advice changed its name to *Christian Union,* which it retained until 1893.

The publication was changed from a specialized religious paper into a general family weekly with sermons, essays, fiction, puzzles, and jokes. By giving away premiums and by sending out door-to-door canvassers, the publishers between 1870 and 1873 built for it the largest circulation that a religious publication had ever attained, more than 130,000. A series of misfortunes drove the circulation down to 10,000 in 1877, and it stayed at about twice that figure throughout most of the 1880's.

After several changes of ownership, *Christian Union* appeared in July, 1893, under a new name—*Outlook*—and with a new policy:

it became a regular journal of opinion rather than a family publication with a religious emphasis. The magazine attracted important contributors and important works. Theodore Roosevelt, after leaving the Presidency, became a contributing editor for a time, and the weekly carried such serials as Booker T. Washington's *Up from Slavery* and Jacob A. Riis's *The Making of an American*.

From the turn of the century until after World War I, a period during which its circulation played between 100,000 and 125,000, the *Outlook* had its greatest prestige and prosperity. Its golden age closed in 1923 with the death of Lyman Abbott, its editor for forty-seven years and its principal owner for thirty-two.

To bolster its slipping circulation—105,000 in 1920, 84,000 in 1925—the *Outlook* took over two other publications. In June, 1924, *Outlook* absorbed the *International Interpreter*, founded two years and two months earlier, as it said, "to foster amity among nations; cooperation between Capital and Labor; equal opportunity for all; and liberty under law and order." *International Interpreter* bequeathed *Outlook* a circulation of 10,000.

In October, 1928, the *Outlook* merged with the eighty-year-old *Independent*. Like the *Outlook*, the *Independent* had been established as a religious paper, had shifted to content of more general scope, and had once been edited by Henry Ward Beecher. The *Independent*, credited with playing an important part in developing American sentiment in favor of the League of Nations, had been in difficult straits since 1919. In February, 1924, when an involuntary petition in bankruptcy was filed against its publishers, its estimated liabilities were $230,000, its assets $58,000. Although a reorganization followed, the new venture also failed.

The *Outlook and Independent*, as the magazine was called after *Outlook* and *Independent* joined forces in 1928, was little strengthened by the merger. Its circulation was down to about 85,000 even before the depression struck. In March, 1932, feeling the pinch of the depression, it went from weekly to monthly publication; and fattened by the change in periodicity, it sought to increase its newsstand sales.

The change failed to help. *Outlook* and *Independent* suspended publication in May, 1932, and was put on auction by a bankruptcy referee. Among those interested in acquiring it was Funk and Wagnalls, which bid $2,000 to get its subscription list for the *Literary Digest*. The new owner, however, was Frank A. Tichenor, publisher of *Aero Digest, Sportsman Pilot, Spur, Port,* and *Plumbers' and Heating Contractors' Trade Journal.* He got *Outlook and Independent* for $12,500 and sought to recapture for it the political influence it had enjoyed in Theodore Roosevelt's time.

In August, 1932, Tichenor hired Alfred E. Smith, the defeated Presidential candidate in 1928, as editor. Smith was to help set the policies of the *New Outlook* and to contribute editorials and articles; Francis Walton, the managing editor, planned to have much of the magazine's comment on world affairs written by newsmen on the spot instead of at second-hand. Smith held the editorship until March, 1934, when he resigned, ostensibly because of other business interests, although he was said to have differed with Tichenor on matters of policy. Walton replaced him as editor-in-chief. The magazine never regained its onetime prestige, however, and it died with its issue of June, 1935.

Quality magazines, journals of comment and opinion, reviews— they have traditionally had a difficult time surviving in America. It is perhaps less surprising that they faded away one by one than that a number of weekly and monthly magazines of general interest also died. Some were among the circulation giants that had survived from the nineteenth century into the twentieth, *Leslie's Weekly, McClure's, Munsey's;* others, like *Liberty,* were founded in the twentieth century, achieved large circulations, but never quite succeeded financially.

Leslie's Weekly, established in 1855, lasted until the 1920's. A pioneer news-in-pictures publication, it ran up a circulation of 100,000 within a short time of its founding, and it occasionally doubled or trebled sales during the next decade or so when it made the most of an exciting sports event or sensational crime. It gave a good pictorial record of the Civil War—at one time it had twelve correspondents at the front—and of the Spanish-American War. For a time, in the first years of the twentieth century, it had a circulation as large as any in its heyday. From 75,000 in 1900, its circulation mounted to 379,000 in 1914. After World War I, it came upon hard times, and died in June, 1922.

McClure's, one of the first of the low-priced national magazines, flourished only briefly in the new century. Decay set in after several of its outstanding staff members, Ray Stannard Baker, Lincoln Steffens, Ida M. Tarbell, John Siddall, and Albert Boyden, resigned in March, 1906, as a result of disagreements with S. S. McClure.

The trouble, according to Ida Tarbell, stemmed from McClure's plan to correct the abuses of society by forming a model community and a string of commercial enterprises, including a bank, a life insurance company, and a company for publishing school books. The plan became an obsession with McClure; his associates looked upon it with a good deal less than enthusiasm. Eventually the plan split McClure and his partner, John S. Phillips. When Phillips left McClure's, several of the editorial staff also resigned, and soon afterward they were reunited on the *American*.[18]

A few years later, McClure disposed of the magazine that bore his name, and thereafter it had several owners, none of whom appears to have made much of a success of it. Several times it suspended publication—for a half-year after October, 1921, for eight months in 1924-25, and for six months in 1926. McClure himself bought the magazine again in 1924, supposedly with financial assistance from Lewis E. Myers, a manufacturer of toys. But the fire was gone from *McClure's*, and after that last brief try for a comeback, its founder left the magazine to others, narrowed his world to the musty Murray Hill Hotel and the Union League Library, and worked on a history of freedom and other books until he died of a heart attack in 1949 at the age of ninety-two.

William Randolph Hearst purchased *McClure's* in 1926 and in June brought it out with the subtitle, "The Magazine of Romance." A little more than a year later, the publication dropped the subtitle and got a new editor, Arthur S. Hoffman, who had built *Adventure* into one of the top men's magazines. Hoffman stayed with *McClure's* for about a year. In April, 1928, Hearst sold the magazine to James R. Quirk, publisher of *Photoplay* and *Opportunity*. Degenerated into a magazine of snappy stories, merged with *Smart Set*, the once proud, once excellent *McClure's* died for good in 1933. Ida Tarbell, remembering the magazine as it had been in its youth, not in its senility, wrote its valedictory: "It was a magazine which from the first put quality above everything else. . . ."[19]

The twentieth century saw the eclipse of three outstanding satirical weeklies, *Puck*, *Life*, and *Judge*. *Puck*, which had commented on the American scene with sharp words and pointed cartoons since its founding in 1877, died at the close of World War I. *Life* and *Judge* were growing while *Puck* was dying. They hit

---

[18] Ida M. Tarbell, *All in the Day's Work* (New York, 1939), pp. 256-59.
[19] Tarbell, p. 257.

their peak circulations, about a quarter of a million, in the early 1920's. *Life*, after a long decline, died in 1936, when it sold its name to Henry Luce's new picture magazine. *Judge* struggled on alone, impoverished, dying and being revived, a ghost of its former self.

It is hard to say why they died, but certainly their position was weakened by competition from the *New Yorker* after 1925, from *Esquire* after 1933, and from *Ballyhoo* and *Hooey*, magazines of crude burlesque, during the depression. Conceivably the ubiquitous radio comedian diminished the demand for their editorial offerings; conceivably their drawings lost some of their appeal after general magazines began sprinkling cartoons throughout their pages. Whatever the reason, their decline was inexorable.

Puck entered the new century with a circulation of 90,000 and with Harry Leon Wilson as editor. Editors following Wilson were John Kendrick Bangs, the well-known humorist, and Arthur Hamilton Folwell, the first for a couple of years, the latter for more than a decade. Before World War I, *Puck* was a lively weekly, brightened by the work of George Jean Nathan, John Held, Jr., Franklin P. Adams, Arthur Guiterman, and others. William Randolph Hearst bought the weekly in 1917, and, no doubt with his eye on its declining circulation, he changed it first to a fortnightly and then to a monthly publication. He discontinued it entirely in September, 1918, although at midcentury its name still appeared on a newspaper comic section.

When Time Inc. bought the name *Life* for its new picture magazine in 1936, Clair Maxwell, the former owner, remarked: "We cannot claim, like Mr. Tunney, that we resigned our championship undefeated in our prime. But at least we hope to retire gracefully from a world still friendly." [20] *Life* indeed had passed its prime almost a decade earlier, but the world was still friendly; even as *Life* ceased publication, it was still earning a small profit.

Life began its fifty-three years as a satirical weekly on January 4, 1883, the product of three Harvard men—John Ames Mitchell, an artist who rashly sank a legacy of $10,000 into the magazine to have a medium for his pictures; Edward Sanford Martin, a former editor of the *Harvard Lampoon* with literary aspirations; and Andrew Miller, who became business manager of the new magazine

---

[20] *Time*, 28 (Oct. 19, 1936) 63.

shortly before the first issue. Henry Holt, the book publisher, who had warned Mitchell against starting a magazine in a field in which *Puck* and *Judge* were already established, skeptically dubbed the first issue *Short Life*. For a time it looked as if *Life* would be short. Three-fourths of the second issue and practically all of the third were returned from the stands unsold. Worse, the publishers discovered with alarm that returned copies of the fourth and fifth issues exceeded by 2,000 the number of copies they had had printed —until they noticed that the extra copies were from previous issues.[21]

As *Life* began to show promise, ill health forced Edward S. Martin out as part owner and away from the magazine for a few years. But he returned to the staff, and for the next forty years he contributed editorials to the magazine. Mitchell and Miller published *Life* as partners until Mitchell's death in 1918.

Under them, *Life* attracted some impressive literary and artistic talent. John Kendrick Bangs joined the staff as literary editor, and James Whitcomb Riley was a contributor. In 1887 *Life* paid a youth named Charles Dana Gibson $4 for a drawing, his first sale to a magazine; in a few years Gibson became perhaps the most important contributor to *Life*. Week after week his Gibson girl and Gibson man adorned the pages of *Life*, and thousands of young women and young blades aped their dress and carriage.

Setting *Life* apart from *Puck* and *Judge* were its crusades, some of them quixotic. It got in licks against trusts, rigid Sabbatarians, serums, Anthony Comstock, "dudes," Christian Science, and vivisection, among other things. From the start of World War I, *Life* took up the Allied cause. Both Mitchell and Gibson were ardent Francophiles who, as the writer of *Life*'s obituary in *Time* put it, "took it as a personal affront when Germany invaded Belgium." In 1916 *Life* appealed to the United States to arm, and it showed little restraint in trying to gain sympathy for the Allied cause. Mitchell lived long enough to see that his last great crusade culminated in the declaration of war by the United States, but not long enough to see the armistice. He died in July, 1918; Miller died the following year.

Charles Dana Gibson bought a controlling interest in the com-

---

[21] Frank Luther Mott, "Fifty Years of Life: The Story of a Satirical Weekly," *Journalism Quarterly*, 25 (Sept., 1948) 226.

pany in 1920 for a sum which press accounts said was $1,000,000. Early in 1925, Miller's widow asked the court to appoint a receiver for the company and to set a "reasonable" salary for Gibson, who was said to be drawing $30,000 a year for his contributions to the magazine and $20,000 as president. She withdrew the suit almost immediately.[22]

Meanwhile, Robert Sherwood had become editor. There was a luster to the roster of contributors: Franklin P. Adams, Robert Benchley, Percy Crosby, Will James, Rollin Kirby, Dorothy Parker, Frank Sullivan, and Gluyas Williams. In 1929 Norman Hume Anthony quit the editorship of *Judge* to succeed Sherwood as editor of *Life*.

Thereafter changes came to *Life* in quick succession. Anthony's tenure was brief—he left to establish *Ballyhoo*, which had a short but highly successful existence—but in his stay on *Life* he threw out some old features, added new ones, and in general changed the tone of the magazine. Replacing him as editor was Bolton Mallory, soon succeeded by George Eggleston. Presumably because circulation was slipping—it dropped from 227,000 in 1922 to less than half that in 1930—*Life* switched to monthly publication late in 1931. Charles Dana Gibson, who had given up the presidency in 1928, retired from the company in 1932, and full ownership passed to Clair Maxwell, Henry Richter, and Frederick Francis.

But *Life* was beyond recall. In 1936 its publishers jumped at the chance to sell its name to Time Inc. for $92,000, and its list of subscribers to *Judge*.

A running mate of *Life* and a dozen years older, *Judge* began existence in October, 1881, by announcing editorially that it was "started . . . for fun" and that "money is no object." Fun the first issues were; but circulation remained low, and money became an object, money to stay alive. The Republican party, having recognized the value of a satirical weekly in political campaigning, in 1885 gave substantial aid to William J. Arkell, who reorganized the Judge Company. *Judge* is generally given credit for coining the "full dinner pail" slogan in the McKinley-Bryan Presidential campaign of 1896. A close affiliation with the Republican party existed until 1910, when the company again reorganized.

Judge began the new century with a circulation of 85,000. Like

Life, it hit its circulation peak in the early 1920's, a happy time for humor magazines; its high point was 25,000 copies in 1922.

Norman Hume Anthony assumed the editorship of *Judge* in 1922, the same year that the magazine absorbed *Leslie's Weekly*, and held it until he went to *Life* at the start of 1929. Among the talented crew contributing to *Judge* were Heywood Broun, Walter Prichard Eaton, John Held, Jr., Ring Lardner, George Jean Nathan, and, for a short time as editorial writer, William Allen White.

The depression hit *Judge* as it hit *Life*. Circulation dropped to 172,000 in 1930. In March, 1932, with liabilities of $500,000, *Judge* went bankrupt. Although Clair Maxwell of *Life* and George T. Delacorte, Jr., of *Ballyhoo* both hoped to acquire *Judge* at bankruptcy proceedings, members of its own staff, headed by Fred L. Rogan, a former advertising man for Curtis Publishing Company, raised $17,000 and bought the magazine, which they continued as a monthly.

But *Judge* was up against a good deal of competition, and not only from its old rival *Life*. The *New Yorker* had established itself as a weekly of urbanity and wit. A flock of magazines of earthy humor followed in the wake of *Ballyhoo*, which under Anthony had quickly acquired almost 2,000,000 readers with its parodies of advertisements and its cartoons with sex rampant. *Judge* had neither the quality and sophistication of the *New Yorker* nor the slapstick appeal of *Ballyhoo* and its imitators.

In 1936 *Judge* was ready for a new publisher and found one in Monte Bourjaily, a former executive of United Features Syndicate who also was trying to make a success of the waning picture magazine *Mid-Week Pictorial*. Bourjaily bought title to *Judge* from the Kable Brothers Printing Company, which had taken over stock control of the magazine to satisfy a printing bill. The magazine got a slight boost when it acquired the subscription lists of *Life* and simultaneously lost a major competitor, but it never again exhibited its old vitality. After a year of *Judge*, Bourjaily withdrew and ownership reverted to the printers. They found a new publisher in Harry M. Newman, a former publisher of *Fourth Estate*, a trade paper for newspapermen. But Newman could not get *Judge* back onto a successful course. After he left, the magazine periodically died and was periodically revived but never with more than a modest circulation.

There were shifting fortunes among the women's magazines, too, and some of the largest of them merged with others or died. Theirs was a highly competitive segment of the industry. Their basic aim was to help the reader manage her household, and since they relied on the same general formula of fashion, foods, family, and fiction, there was little to distinguish one magazine from the others. As "trade papers" for the homemaker, they made the home their world until the mid-thirties, when they broadened their editorial scope to pull out of a slump. With so many publications offering such similar editorial material and reaching an identical consumer market, it is not surprising that some of the magazines were weeded out.

In 1928 the Butterick Publishing Company merged its *Designer* with *Delineator*, which was among the top five women's magazines in circulation and in advertising revenue. The *Delineator*, still fifth among women's magazines, in turn was absorbed in 1937 by *Pictorial Review*, which achieved a circulation of more than 3,000,000 as a result of the merger, one of the first magazines to reach so high a figure. Although its circulation slipped, it was still selling more than 2,500,000 copies when it ceased publication in 1939.

After Ebenezer Butterick devised the first tissue paper pattern in 1863, he began publishing a little magazine to promote the sale of his patterns. He called his magazine *Ladies' Quarterly Review of Broadway Fashions,* and he later brought out a similar publication, *Metropolitan.* Out of a merger of those two publications in 1873 came the *Delineator,* which devoted itself to fashions for the next thirty years. In 1894 it broadened its editorial appeal; in 1897 it ran its first fiction; and in the first years of the new century, fashions, which once had accounted for three-fourths of the contents, gave way to home departments, general articles, and fiction.

The company was reorganized in 1902—Butterick himself had withdrawn in 1899—so that the Butterick Company devoted itself to patterns and the Butterick Publishing Company to periodicals. Within a short time the Butterick Publishing Company, which issued thirty-two periodicals, ranked as one of the largest magazine publishers in the United States.

Meanwhile the *Delineator* flourished. Its circulation mounted from 480,000 in 1900 to slightly more than a million in 1920. By 1929 it was more than 2,000,000, a level it held until 1935, when it began to fall. Throughout the 1920's, gross advertising revenues varied, but they were generally between $2,000,000 and $3,500,000 a year, a highly creditable showing for a women's magazine during that period.

Theodore Dreiser, who had already published *Sister Carrie* and was working on *Jennie Gerhardt,* edited *Delineator* from 1907 until 1910, when he left to devote himself to his literary work. He set out to corral "name" authors and attracted, among others, Arthur Conan Doyle, Rudyard Kipling, Oscar Hammerstein, and Woodrow Wilson. The editor during World War I and until 1921 was Honore Willsie Morrow, later well known as a novelist, who was followed by Mrs. William Brown Meloney, the editor who later guided *This Week,* the Sunday newspaper supplement, to success.

Like other women's magazines, *Delineator* had its share of causes. It raised $100,000 to get a gram of radium for Madame Curie, placed 21,000 children for adoption in its Child Rescue Campaign, and conducted a Better Homes Campaign. During World War I, it carried on a campaign to aid war victims in France; after the armistice, it helped to rehabilitate French towns ruined in the war.

Crusading was diminished after 1926, and *Delineator* strove for an air of sophistication and exclusiveness. The exclusiveness became even more apparent in April, 1935, when, according to Oscar Graeve, its last editor, *Delineator* "decided to abandon the mad struggle for the largest circulation claim and limit its circulation to women who really wanted it." To this end, the magazine raised its circulation price and keyed its copy "to the modern scene, the modern woman, and her staccato mood" by running shorter articles, stories, and serials, and by striving for greater variety.[23]

With almost no warning, *Delineator* ceased publication with its issue for April, 1937. It was merged the next month with William Randolph Hearst's *Pictorial Review,* in which its identity was completely lost.

Pictorial Review, like *Delineator,* originated as an offshoot of a dress pattern business. It was founded in 1899 by William Paul Ahnelt, a German immigrant who set up his dress pattern business in the United States on a capital of $13, a sum he symbolized by incorporating the figure thirteen in his trademark.

Pictorial Review dealt mainly in fashions until 1908, but then its editor, Arthur T. Vance, started attracting writers of good fiction

---

[23] Oscar Graeve, "Speaking of Delineator," *Quill,* 25 (Jan., 1937) 10.

away from the general magazines. In time, a number of stories from *Pictorial Review* were appearing in the collections of best short stories selected by Edward J. O'Brien, and a number of its serials were later appearing in book form, among them Donn Byrne's *Hangman's House*, Edith Wharton's *Age of Innocence*, Booth Tarkington's *Alice Adams*, as well as works by Emil Ludwig, Carl Sandburg, Gertrude Atherton, Joseph Conrad, and others.

Following the lead of *Ladies' Home Journal*, the *Pictorial Review* adopted some special projects and engaged in some crusading. For a number of years it annually presented its achievement award of $5,000 to the American woman who had made the greatest contribution of the year to American culture. It was an early champion of woman's suffrage and of women's clubs. In 1937, after a survey of readers showed that they wanted frank discussions of medical problems, it ran a series on abortions, the menopause, syphilis, and even troubles of the prostate gland.

During the 1920's, *Pictorial Review* ranked among the top women's magazines in advertising revenue and in circulation. In 1920 its gross advertising revenues of $6,908,000 put it fourth of all magazines in the United States in dollar volume of advertising and second in the women's field only to *Ladies' Home Journal*. In circulation, too, it was near the top. From 1922 until the magazine died, circulation never dropped below 2,000,000, and in 1929 it hit a high point of 2,511,000.

The founder of *Pictorial Review*, Ahnelt, sold it in January, 1932, to George S. Fowler, an advertising man who had been a vice-president in the company since the preceding April, and Lee Ellmaker, formerly general manager of Macfadden Publications and onetime publisher of *Liberty*. About two and a half years later, William Randolph Hearst bought *Pictorial Review* as well as the Pictorial Review Pattern Company and Excella Patterns, subsidiaries of the magazine. Hearst is said to have acquired the magazine from its printer and its paper supplier under an arrangement which allowed him to write off its back debts unless it showed a profit. The first issue of *Pictorial Review* under Hearst ownership was for January, 1935, and with it Herbert Mayes replaced Percy Waxman as editor.

Although circulation had stayed at more than 2,500,000 in 1930 and 1931, it had thereafter slipped to barely more than 2,000,000 in 1934, from which it moved up only slightly under Hearst ownership. When *Pictorial Review* took over *Delineator* in 1937, its circulation jumped to more than 3,000,000. But advertising revenues lagged, and in January, 1939, the Hearst organization killed *Pictorial Review*. It was the biggest magazine to die up until that time. In 1938, the year before it folded, circulation was more than 2,862,000; and on its books were an estimated $1,000,000 worth of unfulfilled subscriptions.

Still another women's magazine that lost its separate identity if not its name was *Farmer's Wife*, which perennially turned up among magazines with circulations of a million or more in the twenties and thirties. The only magazine written and edited exclusively for farm women, a sort of rural *Delineator*, the magazine grew rapidly after Dr. Ella S. Webb, the missionary-trained sister of the publisher, Edward A. Webb, took over as editor early in the century. *Farmer's Wife* was published in St. Paul and had its greatest circulation in the Midwest and Great Lakes states. In the late 1930's it had annual revenues of $1,200,000 and a circulation of 1,150,000. In 1939 the magazine was taken over by *Farm Journal* of Philadelphia, which supposedly wanted its readers in order to attract advertising for baby foods, cosmetics, and home appliances. *Farmer's Wife* lost its separate existence with the change in ownership and became a section in *Farm Journal*.

Apart from comic books, which first appeared in the 1930's, and apart from Sunday school papers, magazines for children had a difficult time in the twentieth century. One by one the oldest of them died off until only a sparse handful remained. The *Youth's Companion*, which had delighted children and their elders for more than a century, was merged in 1939 with *American Boy*; but as so often happened, the merger was its death, for the *American Boy* retained its own name and editorial policy until it in turn died in 1941. *St. Nicholas*, another perennial favorite, languished in the thirties and died in the forties. This decline of magazines edited primarily for readers between the ages of, say, nine and sixteen was followed by a rise of publications for children between the ages of two and twelve—periodicals such as *Jack and Jill* of Curtis Publishing Company, *Humpty Dumpty's Magazine* and *Children's Digest* of the Parents' Magazine Press, Inc., and a number of twenty-five-cent story books which were sold in drugstores and supermarkets. Some of these publications began to appear in the thirties, but their boom seems to have been after World War II.

Magazines for children had their heyday before radio and television programs and Saturday afternoon movies made their play for

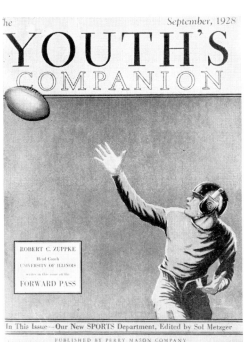

September, 1928

YOUTH'S
COMPANION

ROBERT C. ZUPPKE
Head Coach
UNIVERSITY OF ILLINOIS
writes in this issue on the
FORWARD PASS

In This Issue—Our New SPORTS Department, Edited by Sol Metzger

PUBLISHED BY PERRY MASON COMPANY

CENTS A COPY   Established 1827 $1.00 A YEAR

ST. NICHOLAS FOR BOYS and GIRLS

Beginning a new
SMILEY ADAMS serial—
"The Whip", by R. J. Burrough

November 1934

youthful audiences; and, perhaps significantly, two of them folded shortly after comic books had begun to snowball to success, although they had run into troubles before then. A common explanation for the failure of such magazines is that children were not a good market for advertisers, therefore the publishers could count on little advertising support. That explanation does not seem invalidated by the number of radio programs for children in the thirties and afterwards, for such shows were usually sponsored by manufacturers of low-cost items such as breakfast foods, and their advertising no doubt reached their mass market at lower unit cost through radio than through magazines. Magazines for small children, such as *Jack and Jill* and others, did not depend on advertising for support.

Youth's Companion was founded in Boston in 1827 by Nathaniel Willis and his partner Asa Rand to entertain and instruct young people, to "warn against the ways of transgression," to encourage "virtue and piety"; and to that end, it served several generations a wholesome diet of outdoor adventure stories, historical articles, anecdotes, contests, travel articles, and editorials. Its editorial fare was often by well-known persons—Theodore Roosevelt, Booker T. Washington, Jack London, Grover Cleveland. Even Henry L. Mencken appeared in it with a short story in 1926, although perhaps somewhat to his chagrin. The editors discovered a manuscript that Mencken had sold to the magazine in 1900 when he was still a young reporter in Baltimore, and blowing the dust off this previously unpublished story, they ran it.

For years the *Youth's Companion* was famous for its premiums offered for new subscriptions, and its premium plan helped to push circulation to about 500,000 in the 1890's and to slightly more than that in the years before World War I. Another reason for the large circulation of *Youth's Companion* may have been that its content appealed to the whole family, not to youth alone, and many persons continued to read the magazine long after they had reached adulthood.

After World War I, circulation began to decline, and by 1928 it was down to 250,000. In 1927, ostensibly to observe its hundredth anniversary, the magazine changed from weekly to monthly publication and enlarged itself. But the magazine lived only two years beyond the century mark. In August, 1929, its owners sold *Youth's Companion* to its biggest rival, *American Boy*. Its publisher explained that because juvenile magazines had a "thin market" it was inevitable that one of the two largest should take over the other.

The *American Boy* that absorbed the *Youth's Companion* was founded in 1899 as a quiet protest against the *Companion* and other reading matter for young people. When a ten-year-old boy named Willie Sprague was ill, he complained that the reading fare allowed to him was too sissified and too dull. With Willie in mind, his uncle, Griffin Ogden Ellis, designed a lively new magazine for boys; and Sprague Publications, Inc.—formed by Willie's father, W. C. Sprague, J. Cotner, Jr., and Ellis—began publishing it in Detroit in 1899. Ellis edited the *American Boy* for Willie, and after the real Willie died in World War I, he edited for an imaginary high school sophomore he called Skeeter Bennett.

In 1929, when it took over the *Youth's Companion*, the *American Boy* was healthy. Its circulation was 360,000 and its advertising revenue was about $750,000. But the depression hit it hard. Circulation slid to only 329,000 in 1933, but advertising revenues dropped to about $200,000 and stayed there until the magazine died.

After forty years as editor, Ellis sold the *American Boy* in 1939 to Elmer P. Grierson, its business manager, whom he had picked many years earlier as his successor. A little more than a year later, in the summer of 1940, Grierson sold a half-interest in the magazine to George F. Pierrot, who had joined the *American Boy* as assistant managing editor in 1922, had become managing editor two years later, and had held that position until 1936 when he resigned to devote full time to a lecture series he had formed. The following spring Grierson and Pierrot tried to promote additional working capital of $150,000. When they failed to raise it, Sprague Publications, Inc., went into bankruptcy, and the magazine published its last issue in July, 1941. Lack of advertising was given as the reason for its death.

At bankruptcy proceedings, the Curtis Publishing Company bought the *American Boy* subscription list for $1,800, and James A. Humberstone, a former editor of a house organ for the Ford Motor Company, bought the good will and title. Humberstone sought to raise $50,000 to resume publication, but the magazine never reappeared.

But the name *American Boy* lived on in other publications. Ted Kesting, editor of *Sports Afield*, acquired the title and merged it with his *Mark Trail*, a magazine of outdoors for young people. In the spring of 1953, Kesting sold *American Boy-Mark Trail* to the publishers of *Open Road,* a boys' magazine begun by three young Harvard graduates in 1919. One of the three, Clayton Holt Ernst, resigned as an editor of *Youth's Companion* to help start the new publication. He and his partners, casting about for a title for their magazine, found one in a phrase from Walt Whitman's "Song of the Open Road." Ernst was editor of *Open Road* until his death in 1945. *Open Road* promoted correspondence between American boys and young people in foreign countries, and it sponsored several exchange trips for them during the summers. It started a Pioneers' Club in 1927 to encourage boys to learn about nature and to become woodsmen. In July, 1953, the magazine became *American Boy-Open Road.* It suspended publication in October, 1954. George Hecht of *Parents'* magazine acquired the title but did not resume publication.

The same Roswell Smith who helped to start the *Scribner's* magazine that later became *Century* also established *St. Nicholas,* a monthly magazine for boys and girls. The first issue appeared in 1873, and the editor for the first thirty-two years was Mary Mapes Dodge, author of *Hans Brinker or the Silver Skates.*

St. Nicholas seems to have inspired a loyalty bordering on fanaticism in its young readers. May Lamberton Becker, a subscriber of *St. Nicholas* as a child and its editor in the early 1930's, once said that she had seen no piece of furniture as hard to pass as the bookcase full of bound volumes in her office: "Men and women who came on business would stop short, search the shelves for the year when they used to 'take *St. Nicholas*,' pull out the time-worn volume and lose themselves in its pages. Famous authors whose first appearance in print had been in the St. Nicholas League for Young Contributors, founded in 1899, would turn to poems that won silver badges or names in its roll of honor. . . . Children as young as I was when first I came under its spell were enchanted by these volumes in just the same way." [24]

Well might *St. Nicholas* have enchanted children. Rudyard Kipling contributed his *Jungle Book* stories to it, Mark Twain his *Tom Sawyer Abroad,* and Frances Hodgson Burnett *Little Lord Fauntleroy.* Frank Stockton, associate editor for its first two years, was a regular contributor; other authors included Kate Douglas Wiggin,

---

[24] In Henry Steele Commager, editor, *The St. Nicholas Anthology* (New York, 1948), p. xvi.

Mayne Reid, Louisa May Alcott—just about everyone with a reputation as a children's author. Young subscribers, too, were encouraged to send drawings and short bits of prose and verse for prizes. Youthful contributors who later became famous included Edna St. Vincent Millay, Robert Benchley, Ring Lardner, William Rose Benet, Stephen Vincent Benet, Rachel Field, William Faulkner, Sterling North, and Babette Deutsch.

In the reorganization that resulted in the renaming of *Scribner's* as *Century* in 1881, *St. Nicholas* passed from Scribner and Company to the Century Company, which published it until 1930. When the Century Company withdrew from magazine publishing in 1930, it sold *St. Nicholas* to the publishers of *Scholastic*, a fortnightly begun in 1920 for young people. In late 1934 title to the magazine was acquired by Roy Walker of the Educational Publishing Corporation, who wanted *St. Nicholas* as an adjunct to his magazine for teachers, *Grade Teacher*. Such old-time contributors and subscribers as Struthers Burt, Fannie Hurst, Burton Rascoe, and Henry Seidel Canby flocked to a cocktail party early in 1935 to celebrate the revival of *St. Nicholas* under Walker, who said he wanted to elevate the magazine to its old standards so that a new generation of children would grow up with really first-rate prose, verse, and illustrations.

A few years later, however, the old *St. Nicholas* could not be recognized in the new one, which aimed at successively younger readers as circulation declined. In 1939 the F. W. Woolworth chain arranged for distribution of *St. Nicholas*, by then edited for elementary school children, in 112 of its stores. Although the publisher of *St. Nicholas* was at first optimistic about the arrangement with Woolworth, he sold the magazine in March, 1940, to Mrs. J. David Stern, wife of the publisher of the Philadelphia *Record*, who had offered her financial help in its revival in 1935. Mrs. Stern's ambition was to recapture the glory of the days when Mary Mapes Dodge was editor. She announced that *St. Nicholas* would suspend publication until September, 1940. The war interfered with her plan to revive the magazine, however, and not until 1943 did it appear briefly under her auspices before it vanished completely.

Why did they die, those magazines of age and quality? No one really knows; there can be only guesses. If magazine men knew why some magazines prosper while others fail, they undoubtedly would be far more successful in prescribing the regimen, medicine, or surgical operations necessary for keeping their publications in good health. But even the reasons for success are elusive. Henry Luce once called together a group of his executives to help him explain why Time Inc. had fared so well in the commercial world. After rejecting a dozen possible reasons that occurred to him, he asked, "Could it be because, as a group, we are more than average clever in some ways?" Slowly he studied each of the faces around the table. "No," he said sadly, shaking his head, "I'm sure *that* isn't why." [25]

Success and failure do seem related. In the rise and fall of magazines, one editor has seen a law of natural selection at work. William Nichols, editor of *This Week,* in a talk in 1952, noted that circulation and advertising figures show "a steady rhythm of birth, adaptation, and death among magazines" with major shifts occurring every twenty-five years, most recently in the twenties when *Time,* the *New Yorker,* and *Reader's Digest* were founded. Interesting as Nichols' thesis is, it is more descriptive than explanatory. There are, however, several possible general explanations, some of them closely interrelated, for magazine mortality.

One is that publishers were reluctant to alter their editorial formulas even when changing times and changing interests outmoded them. Since no magazine could strike a balance of editorial ingredients that would hold its readers forever, the fortunate publishers were those whose editors anticipated changes in public taste and subtly adapted their publications to them without losing readers along the way. Some editors did just that for varying lengths of time. But editors are mortal, and they are fallible; even George Horace Lorimer finally lost touch with the readers of the *Saturday Evening Post.* More frequently than they anticipated change, magazines depended on their tried editorial patterns until too late. No doubt publishers found it difficult to believe that an editorial approach which had brought them success had finally lost its appeal. Instead of reworking their basic editorial formula, then, they sought to recapture readers by tinkering with incidentals—by sparking up the typography, for instance, or by redesigning the cover.

Even if a publisher recognized that his editorial approach was outmoded, he still had to discover a new formula at least as successful as his old one. Some publishers succeeded in doing so. As

---

[25] Eric Hodgins, *The Span of Time* (New York, 1946), p. 11.

a later chapter will show, several publishing companies which retained the same magazines over the years changed their publications so thoroughly from time to time that only the names remained. Their magazines survived not only because their publishers scrapped worn-out editorial formulas but also because they were astute or lucky enough to hit upon successful new ones. But many publishers were not so fortunate. Several publishers whose magazines failed also completely abandoned their old editorial slants and sought new ones, but their publications succumbed while they were still groping for a successful new formula. Part of the trouble was that magazines had to do some of their experimenting in public. Trying one unsuccessful editorial approach after another, as *Collier's* did in its last years, they communicated their uncertainties to readers and advertisers.

Many publishers lacked economic resources to keep their magazines afloat while they devised a new editorial approach. Some magazines undergoing editorial revision probably died for want of funds before their new policies gained reader and advertiser acceptance. Probably even more often, the risk of financial loss deterred the publisher from abandoning an old editorial formula that was slipping. Often his profit margin was narrow, and if by changing his content he lost more old readers than he gained new ones, his publication might well die. Better then to risk slow death than suicide.

Closely related to the reluctance of publishers to alter outmoded editorial formulas is another probable reason for magazine mortality: the ease with which the new publisher could enter the industry. Many of the phenomenally successful companies established after World War I, as later chapters will show, were innovators. They introduced new types of magazines or brought fresh treatment to existing types, as Time Inc. did with the news magazine and picture magazine and the Reader's Digest Association did with the digest magazine. Their magazines were experiments that turned out successfully. The nature of the industry encouraged such experimentation. For in trying new ideas, the newcomer often risked less and had more to gain than established publishers. When readers grew weary of the *Literary Digest's* sometimes ponderous treatment of current events, for instance, its publishers would have been jeopardizing an investment of several million dollars if they had abandoned its basic editorial formula; for $86,000 Briton Hadden and Henry Luce discovered a new way of reporting current events which contributed to the death of the *Digest*.

The smallness of their publishers' operations no doubt kept many magazines from surviving. True, many of the newcomers rapidly grew from small businesses into large ones. But many of the magazines that failed were the only publications of their publishers. They lacked several obvious advantages of the large publisher in the struggle for survival. Usually the large publisher owned more than one magazine, and in times of adversity his strong publications could support the weak ones. The large publisher could benefit from quantity buying and mass production. He had funds to attract the most popular artists and authors and to promote his magazines.

Finally, some magazines died because they failed to strike that difficult, delicate balance of circulation and advertising volume, of income and expense, that had become a condition of survival since the 1890's. Some no doubt had lost whatever advertising reason for existence they had once possessed. Advertisers could reach the audiences they served more economically through other media, and reader support alone was insufficient to keep them going.

The Troubled Giant 7

In June, 1933, within a few days of his eighty-third birthday anniversary, Cyrus H. K. Curtis died peacefully at Lyndon, his estate near Philadelphia. He was the second of a mighty triumvirate to die. Edward W. Bok, who had won for the *Ladies' Home Journal* the largest circulation of any magazine in the world, had been laid to rest three and a half years earlier in the bell tower of the sanctuary he had established at Iron Mountain, Florida. George Horace Lorimer, editor of the *Saturday Evening Post* in its early lean years and in its fattest and successor to Curtis as head of the Curtis magazine empire, survived his former employer by four and a half years. Then in October, 1937, less than a year after his retirement, he too died. And so, a few years apart, they all went, the publisher with the golden touch and his two successful editors.

Together they had built the Curtis Publishing Company into a giant that for a time took in $2 out of every $5 spent on national advertising in magazines, and in doing so they had contributed immensely to the development of the low-priced, mass-circulation periodical. Curtis had demonstrated more vividly than any other publisher the principle on which most large circulations of the twentieth century were based: that by selling a magazine for less than its cost of production, a publisher could become wealthy on the advertising which a large circulation attracted. Bok and Lorimer, editorial midwives at the birth of the national magazine in the late nineteenth century, attracted audiences vaster than publishers had ever before dreamed possible. Their magazines influenced not only the reading tastes of middle-class America but even the very size of rural mailboxes.

The company they left behind seemed impregnable. On into the fifties it stood, proud and prosperous, its income among the largest of any magazine-publishing house. Then in the last years of the decade, trouble came. In 1961, for the first time in its history, the company failed to make money. Its losses that year came to $4,-194,000, and the next year they were far worse, $18,917,000.

Even before outsiders learned the full extent of the trouble, they knew that Curtis was having a hard time. Rival *Look* had shot up rapidly and passed the *Saturday Evening Post*. Although the *Post* remained among the circulation leaders, a position maintained in part by extensive use of bargain-rate subscriptions, its advertising linage in 1960 was only about 60 per cent of what it had been a decade earlier, and the magazine became a heavy drain on the company. *McCall's* had set out with determination in 1958 to topple *Ladies' Home Journal* from first place among the women's magazines, and a fierce and costly battle had not stopped it from doing so. Rumors said that the magazines were about to die, that the company itself was for sale. Curtis tried to pull the *Post* from its slump with a drastic, highly publicized redesigning in mid-1961, but its losses continued, and so did those of the *Journal*.

President Robert MacNeal tried to halt the decline. In March, 1962, he cut the weekly *Post* to forty-five issues a year, the monthly *Journal* to ten. At the same time, both magazines got new editors, and the *Post* forsook its new format for yet another. Retrenchments instituted by MacNeal saved the company about $13,000,000 that year.

But in July a new bloc on the board of directors replaced him with Matthew J. Culligan, an energetic, forty-four-year-old salesman, widely regarded as a corporate alchemist whose touch transformed red ink into black. Culligan immediately charged off on his mission to save the company. In his first year, he got rid of one in every five employees on the payroll, 2,000 in all, and consolidated departments. He made changes in top level personnel. He mapped out elaborate sales campaigns for the magazines, and he traveled 80,000 miles to visit personally with 180 business leaders to convince them that the Curtis publications were stable ones, worthy

THE LADIES' HOME JOURNAL

Saint Valentine Story Number

The New Skating Dance
From a Painting by Lester Ralph

FEBRUARY 1915
FIFTEEN CENTS
THE CURTIS PUBLISHING
COMPANY PHILADELPHIA

LADIES' HOME — THE MAGAZINE WOMEN BELIEVE IN — SUMMER 1962 35¢

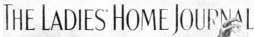

JOURNAL

FEMININITY: What is it? Who has it? Do you? ❧ BETTE DAVIS: The Hollywood Male Ego ❧
17 Boys From Good Families: WHY DID THEY STEAL? ❧ How to Live with a Tyrannical Husband
THE CHILD WITH ONE PARENT: Dr. Spock ❧ THE PARIS LOOK ❧ Outstanding Condensed Novel
Luscious Summer Foods ❧ PHYLLIS McGINLEY–Profession: Housewife ❧ 9 WAYS TO LIVE LONGER

of their advertising. From time to time, he spoke confidently of building Curtis into a billion-dollar empire encompassing not only magazines but radio, television, and newspapers as well.

Actually, the corporation that Culligan took over was already a sizable empire. Bit by bit over the years, it had grown into probably the only self-contained magazine-publishing company in the United States. Through its subsidiaries, it controlled every step of its magazine production from raising trees for paper to distributing copies to newsstands in the United States and Canada.

Wood for making the paper in Curtis magazines came from 139,000 acres of woodland in Pennsylvania and 123,000 in Ontario. Most of the wood fiber paper came from subsidiaries that processed the wood in their own pulp mills, made their own chemicals used in the pulping process, and manufactured the paper itself in three mills.

Curtis magazines were printed in Philadelphia. The main offices of the company were housed in a twelve-story building fronting on Independence Square, although some of its operations had moved to New York early in 1962. In its thirty acres of building space at Independence Square, the company had its own composition rooms, press rooms, and bindery. It owned another plant, at Sharon Hill, Pennsylvania, to which it planned to transfer all of its printing in 1963. A large part of the electrotype plates used in the printing came from a subsidiary, dissolved in 1963.

Other subsidiaries conducted market research and sold magazine subscriptions. National Analysis, Inc., made market surveys and prepared statistical studies. The Moore-Cottrell Subscription Agencies, Inc., and Keystone Readers Service solicited magazine subscriptions for Curtis and other publications. Premium Service, Inc., ran a premium merchandise business.

Still another subsidiary, the Curtis Circulation Company, distributed magazines for Curtis and other publishers in the United States and Canada and solicited subscriptions for them. The company also owned a half-interest in the National Magazine Service, Inc., formed in 1950 with the S-M News Company to distribute magazines directly to retail outlets not served by the truck runs of regular wholesalers. In addition, Curtis had owned 30 per cent of three book companies, for which it handled distribution: Bantam Books, a paperback firm, and Treasure Books and Wonder Books, publishers of children's books. However, the company announced in February, 1964, that it had sold its interest to the other owner, Grosset and Dunlap, Inc., so that it would be free to enter other book-publishing fields.

The growth of the Curtis Publishing Company into a giant of that size probably resulted from a happy meeting of the times and the men. The company was established in the late nineteenth century when increased industrialization, changes in marketing, and the growth of advertising, among other things, made the times propitious for the magazine industry. The men complemented one another. Curtis' genius was on the business side, in publishing as distinct from editing; the brillance of Bok and Lorimer was primarily in editing, although both men had a keen business sense. Curtis provided the atmosphere in which Bok and Lorimer could best exercise their capabilities.

One quality that helped to make Curtis a successful publisher was his ability to sense the market for new publications. He did so with the *Ladies' Home Journal*. Detecting the interest in the women's page of his *Tribune and Farmer,* he overruled the wishes of his junior partner in expanding that department into an eight-page supplement which, under the editorship of Mrs. Curtis, was a popular success as the *Ladies' Home Journal* even before Bok became editor. The partner, who chose to stick with *Tribune and Farmer,* was out of business within a few months. Curtis also sensed the market for the *Saturday Evening Post,* although business associates and advertising men warned that it would break him and journalists told him that the day of the weekly was past. But Curtis was convinced that American men would buy a magazine edited for them, as the *Ladies' Home Journal* was edited for women. The *Saturday Evening Post* which he brought out—at a time when the businessman and industrialist were assuming importance in the American scene, and the public was interested in them—did not compete editorially with existing weekly magazines; and even in an era of inexpensive magazines, its five-cent price was, some observers thought, ruinously low. Curtis again sensed the market when he bought *Country Gentleman* in 1911. The few national farm magazines did not cover the business side of farming, he noted; yet farming, because of the agricultural colleges, was becoming even more businesslike and scientific. A business magazine for farmers could succeed, he thought, just as the *Post* had succeeded among businessmen.

Perhaps of even greater consequence to his company than his ability to pick markets was Curtis' recognition of the important part that advertising was to play in the American economy. The pioneer work done in market research by the Curtis Publishing Company was evidence of that recognition. The five-cent price of the *Post* was a gamble on the capacity of the weekly to attract a tremendous volume of advertising. Curtis himself had a profound faith in advertising. The day after the company treasurer complained that the *Saturday Evening Post* had lost $800,000 and still showed few signs of making a profit, Curtis began a $200,000 advertising campaign for the magazine. Once when a potential advertiser refused to listen to a Curtis advertising salesman, Curtis, the story goes, bought a full-page advertisement in the New York *Sun* to get his sales message to the advertiser's attention.

Curtis had a rare faculty for choosing capable editors, then leaving them alone. Edward W. Bok once summed up Curtis' attitude toward his editors thusly: "The editor is the pivot. Get the right editor and you'll have the right magazine. Then it's only a selling proposition." [1] One of the few attempts Curtis ever made to interfere with Lorimer on the *Post* was to protest a short story. "My wife doesn't think it's a very good piece to be in the *Post*," Curtis remarked. Lorimer replied, "I'm not editing the *Saturday Evening Post* for your wife." Curtis said no more. [2] When Bok wanted to discuss sex in the *Ladies' Home Journal*, he realized that the magazine would lose advertising and at least 100,000 readers. He told Curtis so. Curtis advised him to run the articles anyway. When advertisers, subscribers, and friends put pressure on Curtis to stop the articles, he gave them all the same reply: "Go and talk to Mr. Bok about it. He is the editor." [3] Curtis treated Lorimer much the same way. "I take down the profits, but the *Post* really belongs to Lorimer," he once said. "I would no more think of telling him how to run it, what to print and what not to print, than I would think of telling Commodore Bennett how to run the New York *Herald*." [4]

---

[1] Edward W. Bok, *A Man from Maine* (New York, 1923), p. 169.
[2] John Tebbel, *George Horace Lorimer and the Saturday Evening Post* (Garden City, N.Y., 1948), p. 25.
[3] Bok, pp. 167-68.
[4] Tebbel, p. 40.

The support Curtis gave his editors was material as well as moral. "Give him what he wants," he used to say. "A man can't work unless he has the tools." What his editors wanted, they got. He approved Bok's request for new four-color printing presses costing $800,000 without even bothering to read the statement about them that Bok had prepared for him.[5]

Growing rapidly after 1900, especially after 1908, the Curtis Publishing Company had one of the largest gross incomes of any magazine-publishing house by World War I. During the twenties, the company grew more and more prosperous. Obviously its success was not the result of the editorial staff alone. The advertising and research departments shared credit for the pages of advertising that made Curtis magazines valuable properties. The company acquired its own organizations for selling its magazines as well as those of other publishers and for distributing them to newsstands. Field workers with well-developed sales talks went from door to door across the United States selling subscriptions to householders, and until World War II no magazine in the nation had as many boy salesmen as the *Post.*

In his thirty years as editor of the *Ladies' Home Journal,* Bok hit upon most of the ideas that later editors of women's magazines were to adopt. Chain-smoking Sweet Caporals or his private blend from Benson and Hedges, suffering quietly the pain of his ulcer, he edited with a cold logic and with some paradox, for he was a man who understood women but disdained most of them, who appreciated the uses of humor but was incapable of spontaneous wit, who proclaimed his Americanization but was governed by his Dutch sense of neatness and thrift. Although he resigned in 1919 and turned the editorship over to other hands, the *Journal* continued to lead all other women's magazines in advertising and circulation for most of the twenties.

The *Saturday Evening Post,* still untouched by competition from radio, the major weekly magazine in the United States, a magazine read by women now as well as by men, grew even more prosperous under Lorimer, who, as Wesley W. Stout remarked, "set out to interpret America to itself, always readably, but constructively."

The America he interpreted was an average middle-class America, for that was his audience. On his covers, he gave it Norman Rock-

well; in fiction, he gave it Harry Leon Wilson, Mary Roberts Rinehart, Emerson Hough, and Octavus Roy Cohen; in his editorials,
he gave it conservatism and a strong admiration for material success; in articles, he gave it a conservative and sometimes prolix
discussion of its problems, not always its transitory ones. That was
the essence of the *Post*, but there were important breaks with that
pattern. For instance, F. Scott Fitzgerald, whose writing scarcely
represented the middle-class complacency of the twenties, contributed almost seventy stories to the *Post*, virtually all of them in
Lorimer's time, and they were by no means all potboilers. "Babylon
Revisited" and "Family in the Wind," sometimes regarded as two
of his finest stories, were published in the *Post* in 1931 and 1932
respectively. The *Post* under Lorimer was the first mass-circulation
magazine to publish the stories of William Faulkner, and for more
than a decade the only one. But the *Post* seldom went far beyond
the tastes of the millions who settled in an easy chair with it each
Thursday evening. Lorimer's formula, well in tune with his audience, was a successful one.

Its success, like that of the *Ladies' Home Journal*, was reflected
in the ledgers of the company. In 1925 Curtis stockholders voted
themselves one of the largest stock dividends ever declared when
they approved a plan to increase the preferred stock from 200,000
to 900,000 shares, worth $70,000,000, and to distribute them among
the holders of the 900,000 shares of common stock outstanding. The
peak earnings came in 1929. In that year the company reported a
net of $21,534,000, the highest that any publishing enterprise had
ever achieved up until then.

The thirties brought relatively hard times to the Curtis Publishing
Company. Compared with other publishers, Curtis still did well,
but compared with the company's prosperity since World War I,
its showing throughout the thirties was poor. Net income, for instance, dropped from $19,121,000 in 1930 to $5,568,000 in 1932 and
$5,906,000 in 1934.

There were a number of reasons for the slump. First, of course,
the depression curtailed expenditures on national advertising in
magazines generally; the dollar volume in 1933 was roughly half
of what it had been in 1929, and Curtis magazines suffered with
the rest. Second, network radio had emerged as a potent competitor for the dollars that advertisers were spending during those
hard times. While magazine advertising was falling, the dollar

volume of advertising on radio networks was growing; it rose from about $19,000,000 in 1929 to $33,000,000 in 1933, and it climbed steadily thereafter. The weekly *Saturday Evening Post* with its large circulation certainly must have been affected. Third, while the *Post* had once stood alone as a major weekly advertising medium, other weekly magazines of general interest—*Collier's, Liberty,* and after 1936, *Life*—had begun to cut into its field. It was probably newsstand competition from *Collier's* and *Liberty,* which dated their issues a week in advance, that caused the *Post* in 1931 to change its publication date from Thursday to Tuesday and thus gain an extra two sales days a week.

Then, too, in the last years before his death in 1933, Cyrus Curtis had left the affairs of his magazines to others. As early as 1926, he had remarked, "I'm not giving a thought to my magazines now. They are in capable hands." [6] He played a decreasing part in the operations of his company. For a time he peacefully sailed the Atlantic Coast in his yacht *Lyndonia* and summered at Camden, Maine; but, suffering from a heart ailment, he became less and less active.

Curtis had once remarked, "When a man feels he can't leave the organization he has built up, it proves him to be a poor organizer." [7] There was nothing wrong with the Curtis organization, as such, in the thirties; but its magazines were growing out of touch with the times. The *Ladies' Home Journal* had fallen into the rut that many another women's magazine had fallen into. The *Saturday Evening Post* was still living in the world of yesterday in which it had grown to glory. The times were changing, but the Curtis magazines did not change with them. George Horace Lorimer, president of the company, refused to accept the change.

Lorimer became president of the Curtis Publishing Company in 1932, the year that Franklin D. Roosevelt was elected President of the United States. Almost from the start, Lorimer opposed Roosevelt and his New Deal. In the winter of 1933, he told a friend, "I'll fight this New Deal if it's the last thing I ever do." [8] Fighting the New Deal continually, he changed the *Post* from an organ of entertainment and enlightenment into a weapon of political warfare; and in a sense, it was the last thing he ever did, for the

---

[6] *Editor & Publisher,* 59 (July 10, 1926) 11.
[7] Bok, p. 103.
[8] Tebbel, pp. 198-99.

endorsement of the New Deal at the polls in 1936 left him crushed and bewildered, a stranger in a land he loved and had understood so well for more than three decades. He had not expected Landon to win, although he had supported him; but he had thought that in opposing the New Deal he had spoken for a large share of voters. In the 1936 election, the people turned their backs on all he had battled for; he realized that somewhere America had turned a corner that he had missed and that his world was ended. Two months after the elections, on January 1, 1937, he resigned from Curtis to live a more leisurely life. He died October 27, 1939.

In 1934, to offset rumors that its attacks on the New Deal were costing it readers, the *Post* took full-page newspaper advertisements to report that its sales were increasing because readers "honored a magazine . . . that has the courage of its convictions." In truth, however, its conservatism seems to have cost the *Post* dearly. For years, many readers had regarded its political discussions as authoritative. Nine presidents of the United States had written for it, and Lorimer had been a friend of some of them. When the *Post* lost touch with the mood of the American people in the thirties, then, its lapse was underscored; its prestige suffered. Moreover, Lorimer's conservatism extended beyond politics into the whole character of the magazine. The *Post* still used the outmoded headline type that had been designed for it in 1904, and with the type went antiquated layouts. The articles were often boringly long. The magazine was stuffy, and its anachronisms were made all the more striking by the lively makeup and content of its major competitors —*Life,* for example.

It took more than one man to replace Lorimer. Walter D. Fuller became president. Wesley W. Stout, who had been on the staff since 1922, took the job that Lorimer had trained him for, the editorship of the *Post*. Although he introduced a few minor changes, such as photographic covers, a taboo under Lorimer, Stout produced a *Post* scarcely distinguishable from his predecessor's. A continuation of Lorimer's editorial formula evidently was not the prescription for the ailing magazine, for its gross advertising revenues dropped from $26,602,000 in Stout's first year as editor to $22,341,000 in his second. For five years, Stout continued as editor. Then, in March, 1942, at odds with the management, he resigned. The public explanations of his resignation were vague. Stout himself said, "There was not one point of disagreement but several." Walter

POST

The Saturday Evening

Nov. 18, 1961

20¢

EXCLUSIVE

★★★ AT LAST
THE FULL STORY
OF PRESIDENT
JOHN KENNEDY'S
WORLD WAR II
ADVENTURES AS
A TORPEDO-BOAT
SKIPPER ★★★

D. Fuller said, "It has been speculated that our differences rose from political viewpoints. That was not the case." [9] A probable reason, advanced in the advertising trade press, was that management had pressured Stout to do something about the threat of *Life,* by then a serious competitor of the *Post* in circulation and advertising, a difficult task for any editor who had worked for fourteen years with Lorimer as closely as Stout had.

Changes came rapidly to the *Post* after Ben Hibbs was transferred to its editorship from the editorship of *Country Gentleman.* For the first time in forty-five years, the *Post* appeared without Benjamin Franklin's picture on the cover, perhaps a symbolic break with the past. The old-fashioned typography and layouts disappeared. The amount of fiction decreased, the amount of nonfiction rose. And the average length of articles dropped nearly 30 per cent—from 5,825 words to 4,217—between 1941 and 1945, and the trend toward brevity continued. The subjects those words dealt with, especially after the war, were lighter than those that Lorimer's *Post* had usually carried. By broadening the editorial base of the *Post,* Hibbs aimed at increasing the number of young persons in its audience, a move that offered new markets to the advertising and circulation departments. If Lorimer in his editing had relied upon empathy with his readers, Hibbs relied on empathy plus research; twenty-six times a year readers were polled on their reading preferences, and Hibbs used the results in getting out his magazine, as for example, in inaugurating a series about "Cities of America," which the staff first vetoed as having too limited an appeal. The promotion department, which moved into new quarters in 1946 because of its expansion in the preceding two years, had a budget of $2,500,000 for advertising the magazine.

Circulation and advertising responded to the changes in the *Post,* although wartime shortages, both of paper and of the goods usually advertised in the *Post,* no doubt kept the magazine from gaining ground as rapidly as it might have. During the war, circulation did not increase greatly, but after 1945 it gained rapidly and in the winter of 1947 climbed to more than 4,000,000. After the war, advertising revenues also marched steadily past the records of Lorimer's best years.

Revitalization of the *Ladies' Home Journal* had come earlier than that of the *Saturday Evening Post.* After Bok left it, the

[9] *Time,* 34 (March 23, 1942) 40.

magazine eventually fell into a steady decline, and none of the three editors who followed him could pull it out. The *Journal* achieved such minor triumphs as getting exclusive rights to publish the latest fashions of seventeen Paris designers, a scoop which failed to stir its competitors, although it may have reminded them of Bok's campaign, years earlier, to cause American women to spurn French fashions for American designs. But the middle-aged *Journal* had settled down to an editorial formula of fiction and service articles which did little to set it apart from other women's magazines; and in the late twenties and early thirties, its circulation settled down to about 2,500,000. Even before the depression its advertising had dropped slightly, and after the crash of 1929, revenues plunged abruptly. From a peak of $16,627,000 in 1929, gross advertising revenue fell to a low of $7,242,000 in 1935.

In 1935 Lorimer put the *Journal* under the editorship of the husband-and-wife team that rescued it, Bruce and Beatrice Blackmar Gould. Classmates at the State University of Iowa, they had married in 1923, had worked on New York newspapers, and had collaborated on a successful Broadway play. For some time Lorimer had had his eye on Bruce Gould, then a staff member of the *Saturday Evening Post*, a man so independent in his thinking and so frequently in disagreement with his editor that Lorimer had observed, "Bruce Gould isn't just an associate editor—he's an editor." [10] When Lorimer suggested the joint editorship, Mrs. Gould accepted reluctantly because of her duties as wife and mother, but she did consent to spend three days a week at the office.

The Goulds, without forsaking the home-service features which formed the backbone of the women's magazines, nevertheless insisted that "a woman's world is a good deal broader than the kitchen." They gave the *Journal* some of the freshness and frankness it had had under Bok. In 1937, in article and in short story, they revived the campaign against venereal disease that Bok had waged thirty-two years earlier. They discussed birth control, and they ran articles about the sexual problems of teen-agers. They polled their readers on just causes of divorce, and in their columns they counseled the unhappily wed. Public health, mental illness, alcoholism, slum clearance, American architecture—they gave their readers articles about such subjects, along with Henry Stimson's memoirs, Joseph Stilwell's diary, and Eleanor Roosevelt's auto-

[10] Tebbel, pp. 212-13.

biography. They inaugurated a seemingly interminable series on "How America Lives," in which they reported on the home lives, domestic problems, budgets, and similar personal affairs of "typical" American families.

The *Journal* responded to their touch. In 1941 the company took full-page advertisements in metropolitan newspapers to trumpet the *Journal's* circulation of 4,000,000, a record held previously by only the *Reader's Digest*. In 1957 it still led all other women's magazines with a circulation of 5,449,000; the closest to it was *McCall's* with 4,931,000. Nor could other women's magazines outpace it in advertising volume. In 1947, its peak year until 1957, it grossed $25,627,000 in advertising, more than the combined grosses of its competitors *Good Housekeeping* and *McCall's*. Advertising revenues in 1957 had risen to $29,506,000—still some $8,019,000 more than those of *Good Housekeeping* and $7,775,000 more than those of *McCall's*.

During the forties and early fifties, Curtis rebuilt its gross income to figures that compared favorably with those of earlier days, although its net in 1954 was less than a fourth of what it had been in 1929 when production costs were lower and taxes took a smaller share. Robert MacNeal became president in 1950, when Walter Fuller advanced to the chairmanship. Seven years later Fuller, who had been with the company for almost a half-century, resigned as chairman and the position was left vacant because, as MacNeal said, no one could really replace him.

After 1938 the company started or acquired several new magazines and experimented with others, although not always with success. First of the new publications was *Jack and Jill*, a monthly magazine without advertising, for children under ten. Begun as an experiment in November, 1938, with a press run of 40,000, *Jack and Jill* flourished under its editor, Ada Campbell Rose, and in the mid-fifties its circulation was 702,000.

A second experiment undertaken by Curtis after World War II did not come off. It was *Magazine X*, which trade gossip said would be a slick picture magazine seeking the largest readership in the United States, a competitor of *Life* and *Look*. After some two years of experimentation, Curtis suspended work on the project in March, 1947, and disbanded its staff of thirty.

Some of the staff members of *Magazine X* went to *Holiday*, the second new Curtis magazine, which had made its debut, amidst a fanfare of promotion, with its issue of March, 1946. A glossy, colorful, picture-filled travel magazine selling for fifty cents a copy, *Holiday* quickly rolled up a sale of 450,000 copies. Although advertising in it had reportedly been sold out a year in advance before the first issue appeared, President Walter D. Fuller said at the outset that he did not expect the magazine to make money for five years. Nor did it. Curtis poured money into it. When newsstand sales faltered a few months after the first issue, the original editor was replaced by Ted Patrick, editor of *Magazine X*. With the issue of January, 1948, *Holiday* began to accept liquor advertising, the first Curtis publication ever to do so. Transformed by Patrick, *Holiday* began to gain the acceptance of readers and advertisers. On its fifth birthday, the company announced, it was a "definite asset" which had "developed into an even more important publishing property" than Curtis had hoped for.[11] From then on, year after year, *Holiday* gained in circulation and advertising. In the early sixties, it had a circulation of 939,000 and a gross advertising income of more than $10,000,000.

In 1954, when *Holiday* was well established, Curtis bought a 60 per cent interest in *Science and Mechanics*, a fourteen-year-old magazine for the hobbyist and home craftsman. Five years later it sold the magazine to Davis Publications.

In 1954, too, Curtis laid plans for a program guide for the televiewer. Production costs of *TV Program Week* exceeded original estimates, however, according to the company, and it suspended the publication in 1955 after the circulation of its first eight issues declined precipitously. The company formed a separate corporation in 1955 to publish *Bride-To-Be*. In February, 1956, after it had published three issues, Curtis sold the quarterly to *Bride's* magazine.

Besides adding to its holdings, Curtis disposed of one of its old properties in June, 1955. For years *Country Gentleman* had competed with *Farm Journal* for top position as one of the two truly national farm magazines in the United States, but in the forties and fifties it began to fall behind. From 1948 on, its advertising dropped off steadily, although it was still considerably higher than in prewar years. With the issue of January, 1955, Curtis changed the name of *Country Gentleman* to *Better Farming* because the new title, it said, more nearly represented the mission of the mag-

---

[11] *Tide*, 25 (March 2, 1951) 44.

azine. Five months later, Curtis sold *Country Gentleman* to its old rival *Farm Journal.*

In commenting on the sale, Robert MacNeal, president of Curtis, said, "Aside from the fact that *Farm Journal* made us a very attractive offer, we see definite advantages in concentrating our efforts on the other magazines of the Curtis line, in which newsstand sales are an important factor. . . . We believe that the change will result in more effective utilization of resources and facilities essential to the strength of our company position." [12]

Soon after the sale was announced, the Federal Trade Commission filed a complaint under the Clayton Anti-trust Act on the grounds that the merger of the two magazines would "lessen competition" and "tend to create monopoly" by giving *Farm Journal* about 51 per cent of the total net paid circulation among the six largest competitors in the farm magazine field. In September, the circuit court of appeals in Philadelphia denied the F.T.C.'s petition for an injunction to prevent the merger.

In November, 1958, when Capper Publications of Topeka suspended its *Household,* a home magazine with a circulation of more than 2,600,000, primarily in small towns, Curtis acquired the subscription list to divide among its own magazines.

That same year it entered the home-service field by buying the voting stock in *American Home* from W. H. Eaton and Mrs. Jean Austin. "Sooner or later the book had to be sold—after all I'm not going to live forever," Eaton said. "Also, I've had a feeling for a long time that these days it's foolish to paddle along with one book." [13] Eaton died five years later, in April, 1963, and he had paddled along with *American Home* since the thirties.

American Home began life early in the century as *Garden Magazine,* which told readers how to tend their lawns, fruit trees, flowers, and vegetables. It was only moderately successful, and Doubleday, Doran, its publisher, converted it into a general home-service magazine in 1928. Eaton, circulation director for all of the Doubleday magazines, was deeply involved in its transformation into *American Home;* he was convinced that there was room for a monthly magazine which could serve the middle class just as the company's *Country Life* served the well-to-do. The first years of its new life were lean ones. In 1932 *Country Life* and *American*

---

[12] *Advertising Age,* 26 (June 13, 1955) 58.
[13] *Advertising Age,* 29 (April 29, 1958) 3.

HOLIDAY

JULY 1962 ▪ 60c

FEATURING:

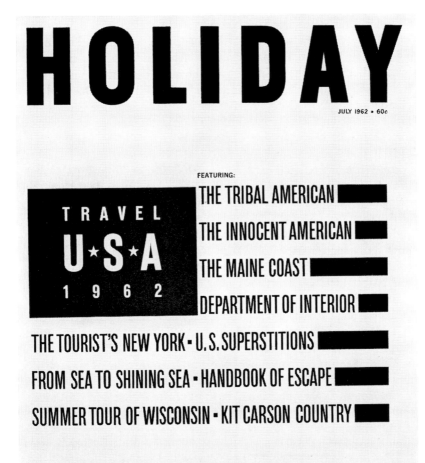

TRAVEL
U★S★A
1 9 6 2

THE TRIBAL AMERICAN

THE INNOCENT AMERICAN

THE MAINE COAST

DEPARTMENT OF INTERIOR

THE TOURIST'S NEW YORK ▪ U.S. SUPERSTITIONS

FROM SEA TO SHINING SEA ▪ HANDBOOK OF ESCAPE

SUMMER TOUR OF WISCONSIN ▪ KIT CARSON COUNTRY

ANNUAL U. S. RESTAURANT AWARDS

OGDEN NASH ▪ CLIFTON FADIMAN ▪ WILLIAM MANCHESTER ▪ ALISTAIR COOKE ▪ SILAS SPITZER ▪ JOHN D. WEAVER

Home were losing about $60,000 a month, and *American Home* accounted for most of it. In December, 1932, after he had blocked a move by the company to sell the magazine to an outsider, Eaton arranged to lease both magazines for five years with an option to buy. Taking over the business side, he put editorial direction into the hands of Mrs. Jean Austin, who had worked on Doubleday's circulation staff. In October, 1935, he and his associates bought the magazines from Doubleday. *Country Life* continued on as an organ for the luxury trade until it ceased publication in the early forties after it had been merged into *Polo* and the *Sportsman*.

American Home had cost Eaton $400,000, and during the first five years he got more than $1,000,000 in credit to build up the magazine. It flourished even during the depression; in its first decade under Eaton's control, it increased its circulation by more than eight times, from 283,000 to 2,303,000. Mrs. Austin remained editor for twenty-seven years. John Mack Carter, who had edited *Household*, ran the magazine for a few years before joining *McCall's*, and Hubbard Cobb then took over the editorship.

In its first year under Curtis, *American Home* gained about a million dollars in gross advertising revenues, and Robert MacNeal had other good news when he reported the company's progress during 1959. The gross operating income of $343,044,000 was $125,973,000 more than that of the previous year, he said, and the net income of $3,961,000 was $1,448,000 more.

But some disturbing signs must have tempered any optimism that MacNeal felt. Since 1950 the *Saturday Evening Post* had fallen steadily in number of advertising pages, although its revenues had grown as a result of its rising circulation. *Look*, fattened in circulation by the subscription list of *Collier's* and by its own sales campaigns and also revitalized editorially, had joined *Life* as a strong competitor out to grab advertising away from the *Post*. Indeed, although a biweekly, it carried 70 per cent as many advertising pages as the weekly *Post* in 1961 and was ahead of it the following year. Herbert Mayes in 1958 had taken over *McCall's*, revolutionized its design, poured money into it, and relentlessly set out to get a major share of the $80,000,000 that advertisers were spending on women's magazines and to claim a large share of their 19,000,000 readers.

Meanwhile, too, magazines had become involved in the race for circulations that critics called the numbers game. Mailing out millions of offers of bargain subscriptions, taking over the lists of defunct publications, as Curtis itself had taken over the list of *Household*, they tried to outrun one another; it was a costly race, and the Curtis magazines sprinted along with the rest, although not as rapidly. *McCall's* picked up almost a million new readers in little more than a year. It narrowed the lead that *Ladies' Home Journal* had long held, then in 1960 nosed it out in circulation and outran it in advertising by $2,600,000.

Publicly the Goulds disparaged the swift rise of *McCall's*. Advertising men always liked to see a trend before it was there, they said, although they had been temporarily caught "off guard promotionally." Mayes was letting his art director run his magazine and was trying to impress the advertising agencies; they were still concerned with rapport with the reader. "If Madison Avenue were run by women," they said, "we'd get so much advertising that we couldn't take it all." [14] Privately, they prepared for their approaching retirement by choosing their successor, Curtiss Anderson of *Better Homes and Gardens*, and training him for the job.

The warfare led to an almost unprecedented public name-calling match in 1961 when *McCall's* announced that it would guarantee advertisers a circulation of 7,000,000 and would pledge them another million as bonus. Robert MacNeal told the press that advertising rates among women's magazines were already unprofitably low and that *McCall's* announcement represented "a form of ego satisfaction, rather than a sound publishing practice, and we see no virtue in winning a race to the poorhouse." A. Edward Miller, publisher of *McCall's*, replied that the financial position of his magazine spoke for itself: in the first seven months of 1961, its advertising revenues were 87.9 per cent over those of 1959; those of the *Journal* were down by 14.9 per cent.[15] A few days later MacNeal called Miller's rebuttal misleading, certain of its claims hilarious, and Miller in turn described MacNeal's reaction as a petulant outburst.[16] The following month MacNeal, reporting losses to his stockholders, sharply criticized the cut-rate subscription offers with which publishers were flooding the mails while complaining they could not afford higher postal rates. If the Audit Bureau of Circulations did not take measures to stop the movement, which was

---

[14] *Advertising Age*, 32 (May 8, 1961) 154.
[15] *Advertising Age*, 32 (July 24, 1961) 3.
[16] *Advertising Age*, 32 (July 31, 1961) 3.

seriously affecting magazine profits, he said, the Post Office Department should.[17]

In some ways, MacNeal must have found Curtis difficult to adapt to the intensified competition that threatened its two oldest magazines. It was a tradition-bound company, proud of its past and slow to change its ways of thinking and doing; and because it was self-contained, it had enormous fixed costs. The *Post* was a heavy financial burden. As a general magazine of large circulation it was perhaps more vulnerable to the competition of television than specialized publications. From the sidelines, observers counseled MacNeal to make the magazine a biweekly and cited the record of *Look* as encouraging evidence. Yet the *Post* was the flagship of the company, one of the oldest publications in the nation, and retrenchment would have been an obvious signal of distress. Moreover, cutting it to biweekly publication doubtlessly would have meant the sacrifice of advertising already contracted for and, more important, the heavy costs of production facilities left idle unless the company could keep them profitably occupied with other business.

The *Post* was the first magazine to undergo change. In the summer of 1961, 200 advertising men got a preview of a revamping that had been in the planning for almost a year, the first abrupt change in nearly twenty years. What they saw, and what readers saw with the issue of September 16, was a magazine that broke strikingly with its past in cover, logotype, interior design, editorial features, and grouping of content. Advertisers professed to be excited about the changes, and the company budgeted $1,250,000 to publicize them. Responsible for the redesign was Robert Fuoss, who had worked closely with Ben Hibbs since 1942 and who was to take over the editorship when Hibbs retired on January 1, 1962. By the time readers saw the new *Post*, Curtis had become fair game for second-guessers, who found fault on two counts: the company had been obsequious to advertisers in letting them see the redesigned magazine before readers did, and it had handicapped itself by publicizing the changes too far in advance.

In the next half-year or so, MacNeal announced a succession of important changes. By March of 1962 Fuoss was gone, and so were many of the innovations he had introduced into the *Post*. Robert Sherrod moved up to the editorship, and a number of staff members changed offices. The *Post* was cut to forty-five issues a year.

---

[17] *Advertising Age,* 32 (Aug. 28, 1961) 194.

The *Ladies' Home Journal* and *American Home* were cut to ten issues, their circulation guarantees lowered, and the printing of *American Home* was transferred from Cuneo Press to the Curtis plant. "We have now put our house in order with a multi-million dollar cost reduction program," MacNeal said, "and each property is either 'in the black' or can satisfactorily lower its break-even point." [18]

At the same time MacNeal said that the board had been increased to accommodate two new directors—Robert McLean Stewart, partner in an investment firm, and Milton Gould, partner in a New York law firm. As a practical matter, working control of the company had rested with the daughter of Cyrus Curtis, the widow of Edward Bok, Mrs. Mary Zimbalist, who owned 32 per cent of the stock and whose father's estate held another 17 per cent. As early as 1960, some other publishers had been considering the investment possibilities of the company, and in the spring of the following year there had been a heavy trade in Curtis stock. Before long three brokerage firms—Carl M. Loeb, Rhoades and Company; J. R. Williston and Beane; and Treves and Company—had asked for representatives on the board and had put up Stewart and Gould as their candidates.

In that turbulent spring of 1962, the Goulds retired after twenty-seven years with the *Journal,* and Curtiss Anderson took over as editor.

From then on changes came to Curtis so swiftly that one employee was moved to suggest that the company mimeograph its directory of executives for daily distribution. The board, influenced by the newcomers, dismissed MacNeal from his $131,700-a-year position and installed Matthew J. Culligan, who later became chairman as well as president. When MacNeal left, so did a number of top editors.

Almost at once, Culligan began hacking away at what he regarded as an overloaded payroll, getting rid of key personnel and bringing in new, proclaiming his faith in the company to whoever would listen, and trying to persuade advertisers to give Curtis their business. He publicly diagnosed the troubles of the company as resulting, in part, from its decision years earlier to "integrate with a squirrel-like instinct," its failure to have gone into broadcasting, its avoiding the growing fields of the news weeklies and special interest magazines, its susceptibility to "knife-in-the-back assassin

---

[18] Philadelphia *Evening Bulletin,* March 27, 1962, p. 10.

attacks" by competitors, and its overcorrecting when it belatedly restyled the *Saturday Evening Post.* [19]

Since Culligan, too, regarded the *Post* as the flagship of the company, he gave it his special attention. "To some extent the magazine got into the hands of the Bohemians and finger painters," he said. "We're going back, within reason, to what the *Saturday Evening Post* used to be." [20] The *Post* did not return to its traditional ways, as Culligan suggested it would, however. It kept a modern design, less iconoclastic than that of Fuoss, less conservative than that of Hibbs. It got a new editor-in-chief, its fourth in twenty months, Clay Blair, Jr., who set the *Post* on a course of what he called "sophisticated muckraking." Because of the size and reach of magazines, they had a special responsibility to awaken a lethargic America, he said: "The first question we ask here is 'does it matter?' and if it does we print it without fear." [21]

If the new policy did not frighten the editors, it shocked some old subscribers and involved the magazine in controversy and litigation. The *Post* in December, 1962, reported a top-secret meeting at which high government officials had discussed government policy toward the build-up of missile bases in Cuba; Ambassador Adlai Stevenson, the article said, had wanted a soft policy, a Munich. What gave the article special impact was one of its authors, Charles Bartlett, a close friend of President Kennedy. The article touched off a counter article in *Life,* an indignant report in the *New Republic,* questions at a Presidential press conference, and scores of newspaper stories and editorials. Then in August, 1963, a jury in Atlanta found that a former football coach at the University of Alabama had been defamed by a *Post* article, "The Story of a College Football Fix." The jury awarded the coach, Wallace Butts, $3,000,000 in punitive damages and $60,000 in actual damages, one of the largest libel judgments in legal history. Calling the amount "grossly excessive," the trial judge in January, 1964, ruled that Butts must accept a $460,000 settlement or have the case retried. In February, 1964, Curtis made a $300,000 settlement with another coach who had filed suit for $10,000,000 on the basis of the same article. Altogether, the *Post* had $27,060,000 in libel suits filed against it at the end of 1963.

Meanwhile, for efficiency, Curtis had moved its editorial offices

---

[19] *Advertising Age,* 33 (Oct. 15, 1962) 3, 83.
[20] St. Louis *Post-Dispatch,* Sept. 23, 1962, p. 3G.
[21] *News Workshop* of New York University, 14 (May, 1963) 1.

from their long-time home on Independence Square to New York, the literary and advertising capital; and as part of a move toward centralization, it had made Blair editorial director of all Curtis magazines.

Meanwhile, too, Curtiss Anderson had been quietly making changes in the *Ladies' Home Journal,* increasing the amount of text, dropping some of the regular features that the Goulds had used and running others less frequently, adding features of his own, pacing the magazine differently. However, the movement toward centralization brought what Anderson regarded as interference with his proper domain and a threat to the individuality of his magazine. When he was not sustained in protests against inroads on his autonomy, he left the magazine, and several of his key editors left with him. Anderson went to *McCall's,* then to edit Cowles' new *Venture.* In a few months after his departure, the *Journal* had had two other new editors. Early in 1964 the company announced that starting in July the magazine would again publish twelve issues a year instead of ten.

Compared with the changes in the *Post* and *Journal,* those in the profitable *Jack and Jill* were minor. It opened its pages to advertising for the first time in October, 1962, and at the same time the company retained Dr. Frances Horwich, who had conducted a children's program on network television, as director of children's activities. So successful was *Jack and Jill* that the company announced it was contemplating another children's magazine and eventually might add a third.

By early 1964 Culligan had conducted an intensive campaign to get advertising for all Curtis magazines, had reduced operating costs, had slowed the rate of loss, and had arranged a refinancing plan that raised the debt limit of the company and provided additional credit for working capital. He repeated his assertions that the company did not intend to liquidate itself or to sell its magazines. Even so, in publishing and advertising offices, there was still speculation over whether or not he could really save the company. One of the new executives he had brought into the company expressed the doubts of many: "When we took over Curtis was headed for certain disaster. We've made all the right moves and pulled all the right levers in order to change our course. I think we're going to make it. But whether there's too much inertia to overcome we don't know yet for sure." [22]

---

[22] *Wall Street Journal,* June 11, 1963, p. 26.

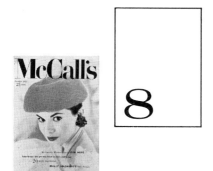

The Old Leaders That Survived

One day in 1905 Ormond Smith of Street & Smith decided to publish a magazine for "the John Smiths of America" because, as he observed, there were so many of them. He named it *Smith's Magazine,* not after himself but after its intended audience, and he hired a young writer from Indiana, Theodore Dreiser, to edit it. Within two years, the magazine had a loyal following of 200,000.

When Street & Smith brought out *Smith's,* the company was already fifty years old, and it had prospered by providing all of the John Smiths of America and their families with a variety of inexpensive reading matter—dime novels and story papers which chronicled the adventures of Nick Carter, Diamond Dick, Buffalo Bill, and Frank Merriwell, and which numbered Ned Buntline, Horatio Alger, Jr., and Burt Standish among their authors; reprints of books by popular foreign writers such as Rudyard Kipling, Conan Doyle, Robert Louis Stevenson, and Victor Hugo; periodicals such as *Ainslie's,* which lived for nearly thirty years after it was launched in 1898 as "the magazine that entertains," and the *Popular Magazine,* which was started in 1903.

The company remained under the continuous control of the families that founded it until 1959, when Condé Nast Publications bought it. In the twenties and thirties, the company was a major publisher of pulp magazines, and in the forties it added a line

of comic books. It moved into quality publishing in 1935 with
Mademoiselle, which it followed with *Charm* in 1941 and *Living
for Young Homemakers* in 1947. It dropped its surviving pulps and
the last of its comics in 1949. Quentin Reynolds, in an informal
history, once called the company a "fiction factory" and attributed
its long life to two basic principles—diversity and killing off publications as soon as their popularity began to wane.[1]

In the cycle of life and death in the magazine industry, a few
publishing companies that were born before or just after 1900
managed to survive as Street & Smith did. The old publishers had
to endure fierce competition, for in the twenties and after a large
number of new publishers entered the field and rapidly emerged
as leaders in circulation, revenue, and prestige. Two of those newcomers, Time Inc. and the Reader's Digest Association, rose to
the top of the industry. But near the top were two oldtimers, the
McCall Corporation and the Hearst Corporation, the subjects of
this chapter.

Twice in its lifetime the McCall Corporation underwent dramatic revivals—once in 1919 when William Bishop Warner was
called in to pull it out of a decline, again almost forty years later
when new owners and new management took over and toppled
the *Ladies' Home Journal* from the supremacy it had enjoyed in
the women's field for a quarter-century.

Like the Butterick publishing house, which Dreiser joined when
he left Street & Smith, the McCall Corporation evolved from a
company which originally manufactured paper patterns for wom-
en's dresses. It remained a minor publishing company until after
World War I. Its founder was James McCall, who never lived to
see the magazine which bore his name. A Scottish tailor, he emi-
grated to America and set up a pattern business in New York in
1870. There seems to be no record of just when he added publishing to his patternmaking, but in 1884, the year he died, his company was publishing the *Queen,* a small magazine of fashion notes
which then was reaching about 300,000 women.

In the decade after McCall's death, the company underwent
several changes in ownership. McCall's widow served as president
of it for a half-dozen years. The firm was reorganized in 1890 as
the McCall Publishing Company, with George H. Bladsworth as

---

[1] Quentin Reynolds, *The Fiction Factory, or from Pulp Row to Quality Street*
(New York, 1955), pp. 268-69.

president. Page and Ringot purchased the company a year or two later, and a short time afterward Page sold out to his partner, who formed J. H. Ringot and Company. The McCall Company was incorporated in New York in 1893, and for the next twenty years it built up the circulation of its magazine by giving premiums with subscriptions.

Meanwhile the magazine had been renamed the *Queen of Fashion*. It had fattened, sometimes to twenty pages, and in 1894 it ran its first fiction, a story it had awarded $10 in a contest. The magazine changed in other ways. Its issue of July, 1896, appeared with a photographic cover, its first; and the next month it carried its first full-page advertisement, for "Alma, the Leading Canadian College for Women." In September, 1897, the magazine appeared as *McCall's Magazine,* with the subtitle, "The Queen of Fashion," which it subsequently dropped. The circulation of *McCall's* hovered around 200,000 at the turn of the century but had grown to more than a million by 1910.

The modern phase of the McCall organization began in 1913 when the banking firm of White, Weld and Company bought the company from James A. Ottley, but the most impressive expansion began a half-dozen years later. In 1919 *McCall's* was in poor shape. The magazine had a circulation of 1,163,000, but it had attracted so many subscribers with patterns and rose bushes as premiums that its circulation failed to impress advertisers. Advertisers, who perhaps noticed that *McCall's* could sell only about 20,000 copies on the newsstands, spent but $951,000 on it in 1919 as compared with $8,775,000 on the *Ladies' Home Journal.*

The owners of the company installed William Bishop Warner as president in 1919 to put the company on its feet. He remained as head until four months before his death in 1946, when Marvin Pierce succeeded him. Warner was forty-five when he came to the publishing house from Detroit, where he had been president of a department store. One of his first tactics was to pour money into *McCall's* to improve its editorial content. Both revenues and circulation jumped upward. In 1920 the magazine carried $2,494,000 in advertising, more than two and a half times that of the previous year. In 1927 the sale of copies exceeded 2,000,000, and advertising income was $6,265,000. *McCall's* became and stayed one of the major women's magazines.

Much of the editorial revitalization of *McCall's* was the work of

THE
QUEEN OF FASHION

THE BEST LADIES' FASHION JOURNAL PUBLISHED.

NEW YORK, JUNE, 1896.

A STYLISH AND SERVICEABLE CYCLING COSTUME.

First Magazine for Women

McCall's

May 1962
35 cents

"Dearly Beloved"- a New Novel by
ANNE MORROW LINDBERGH

Special Presentation
Complete in This Issue

Prettiest Section Ever
**PLAIN AND FANCY
TABLE SETTINGS**

Actress of the century?
**ANNE BANCROFT:
MIRACLE WORKER**

**SIX SUMMER
HAIRDOS**
and the permanents
that make them

CHILDREN IN THE WHITE HOUSE by TYLER A. KENNEDY

Otis L. Wiese, who was only twenty-three years old when he assumed the editorship in 1928. A graduate of the University of Wisconsin, he had come to New York searching for an editorial job and had been hired by Harry Payne Burton, editor of *McCall's*. When Burton quit, Warner asked Wiese for a report on how the magazine could be improved. On the strength of his recommendations, he was appointed editor.

Wiese's changes were so iconoclastic that he was fired a half-dozen times in his first year. He broke with the Gene Stratton Porter and Harold Bell Wright schools of fiction, scouted out heavier fare for his articles, redesigned the makeup, and made increased use of color printing. He converted *McCall's* into "three magazines in one" in 1932 by giving it separate sections for "news and fiction," "homemaking," and "style and beauty," each with its separate cover, a form of departmentalization used on through the forties. He began running a full-length novel in each issue in December, 1937. In 1949 he captured Eleanor Roosevelt away from his old rival, *Ladies' Home Journal,* which had serialized the first volume of her memoirs and had carried her monthly column for several years. Wiese splashed Mrs. Roosevelt's picture across *McCall's* cover, the next volume of her memoirs across its pages, and spent $120,000 calling attention to his coup through newspapers, radio, and television. The following year he redesigned *McCall's* makeup to break away from its rigid departmentalization; and he stirred interest in the magazine by printing a picture of a cake on the covers of half its copies, a picture of a pretty girl on the other half, then inviting readers to vote for their preferences. In 1950, too, *McCall's* opened branch editorial offices on the West Coast, the first national women's service magazine to do so. Wiese announced a fundamental change in policy for *McCall's* in May, 1954. No longer would the magazine be exclusively for women, he said; henceforth it would be directed at women and their families. The new editorial pitch was based on what Wiese called "togetherness"—a family's living not as isolated members but as a unit sharing experiences.

In the fall of 1958, when "togetherness" was a household word, Wiese and several key staff members resigned in protest over the policies of a new management. A group of West Coast financiers headed by Norton Simon, who controlled Hunt Foods and the Ohio Match Company, began buying stock in the company in 1953. By late 1956 they occupied half of the seats on the board. They chose Arthur Langlie, a former governor of Washington, as president to succeed Marvin Pierce, who was elected chairman. Wiese and the others left when they thought they saw business-office domination of editorial policies under the new management.

To succeed Wiese as editor, the new group brought in Herbert R. Mayes, editor of *Good Housekeeping* since the late thirties. Mayes had been fired over policy differences with other Hearst executives only a few weeks earlier. In his last years with the Hearst organization, he had chafed under what he thought was interference with his editorial domain; on joining *McCall's*, he publicly announced that he intended to run the magazine in his own fashion.[2] He had the understanding of an able publisher in A. Edward Miller of *Life*, who teamed up with him in the fall of 1959.

When Norton Simon and his associates took control of the company, there was speculation in the industry that they would liquidate the magazines, as Crowell-Collier had recently done, and concentrate on the profitable printing end of the business. Simon quickly put an end to the rumors by pouring money into the company for expansion, and Mayes, by precipitating a battle with *Ladies' Home Journal* which one advertising man called "the most dramatic thing in publishing" in a quarter of a century.

Redesigning the magazine, using dramatic layouts and generous splashes of color, spraying the cover with plastic to give it a sheen, spending lavishly for editorial features, Mayes worked sixty-five hours a week to make *McCall's* the leading women's magazine. He threw out $400,000 worth of manuscripts on file and went after features he thought his readers would prefer—columns by Clare Booth Luce and the Duchess of Windsor, fiction by John Steinbeck, biographies and autobiographies of celebrities, the memoirs of Anthony Eden, former British prime minister, for which he paid $100,000. He thought women were bored by cooking, so he glamorized food with pictures and text. He hired top photographers to illustrate his features on fashions, foods, and decor. He paid Salvador Dali $6,000 for a two-page illustration for a story. Increasing the number of pages, he tried to give his readers more editorial matter than they could get from any of his competitors.

All of those changes and heavy expenditures on promotion

---

[2] *Advertising Age*, 29 (Nov. 10, 1958) 102.

helped to make *McCall's* one of the most talked-about magazines in the advertising business. By the end of 1960, it was more than $3,000,000 ahead of the *Ladies' Home Journal* in advertising revenues and a short lap ahead in distribution. Circulation, aided by mass-mailings of bargain subscription offers, soared from 5,350,000 in 1958, when Mayes took over, to 8,221,000 in 1963, when he thought the magazine was still far from having achieved its full sales potential, although it was some 1,500,000 ahead of the *Journal*. Advertising revenues jumped from $18,391,000 in 1958 to $41,868,000 in 1963, when the *Journal* took in about two-thirds as much. In the last quarter of 1962, Mayes announced, the magazine had shown a profit for the first time since World War II, and it was continuing to earn money throughout the next year.

Mayes was made president and chief executive officer of the company in August, 1961, when Langlie became chairman. Although he initially retained the editorship of *McCall's,* he eventually turned its direction over to John Mack Carter, who had come to the staff by way of *Better Homes and Gardens* and *American Home.*

The company had expanded in various directions under William Bishop Warner, and the expansion continued under the managements that came after his retirement. The McCall Corporation and the Popular Science Publishing Company in 1919 formed the S-M News Company, an organization for distributing magazines to newsstands. The McCall firm built a new printing plant in Dayton, Ohio, in 1923, an addition for pattern production in 1927. The plant in Dayton was enlarged in 1928, again in 1929, and periodically thereafter; a multicolor department was created in 1939 with the installation of five high-speed, double, five-color presses. The company began its commercial printing operations in 1930 when it took over the printing of *Popular Science Monthly.* It was printing more than fifty magazines for other publishers at its plant in Dayton in the early sixties; among them were *Newsweek, U.S. News and World Report,* and most of the domestic edition of the *Reader's Digest.* Growth of the company was reflected in the number of employees. When the *Queen of Fashion* began to grow in 1894, the company had thirteen workers on the payroll. In 1925, after the Dayton plant went into production, the number was 535, and in 1955, a decade after a $11,000,000 expansion program had been inaugurated, the company was employing 4,430. That number had grown to 6,000 by the start of 1963. Besides its operations in

October 1917 THE RED BOOK MAGAZINE Price 20 Cents

a new novel

"The Unpardonable Sin" by RUPERT HUGHES

eman Tilden
FlemingWilson
ene Manlove Rhodes
na Katharine Green

Donn Byrne
Ida M.Evans
Roy Norton
Royal Brown

Z.Pljikolaki

he Bull Called Emily" by IRVIN S. COBB

REDBOOK

35 CENTS • THE MAGAZINE FOR YOUNG ADULTS

The world's busiest mothers: How they find enough time and money

Prince Charles: A classmate's view of a lonely boy

Will school psychologists help or hurt your child?

Full report on the new summer make-up

Must reading for expectant mothers: How safe is induced labor?

Margaret Mead: What I owe other women

8 pages of vacation ideas

Dayton, the company had pattern factories in Toronto, Sydney, and London.

In October, 1962, the McCall organization bought the National Publishing Company of Washington, D.C., a printer of fifty magazines and newspapers, and eight months later for $6,280,375 it acquired Foote and Davies of Atlanta, a printer of hardbound books, magazines, catalogs, maps, and forms.

For nearly sixty years the company published only periodicals for women, *McCall's* and its predecessors, and pattern and sewing publications. It broadened its market in 1929 by buying out the Consolidated Magazines Corporation, publishers of *Red Book* and *Blue Book*. *Redbook* and *Bluebook*—McCall telescoped the words in their titles—were survivors of a trio of magazines which were established in Chicago at the turn of the century as vehicles for light fiction and articles about the theater. The third member of the trio, *Green Book*, had concentrated exclusively on the theater. It had been hit hard when movies diminished popular interest in the theater, and it had died in the depression of 1921 after a premature attempt to convert it into a magazine for career girls. Ray Long had edited all three magazines for a half-dozen years before he joined the Hearst magazines in 1919.

For twenty years after the McCall company took over *Redbook*, its editor, Edwin Balmer, made it a general interest monthly with a heavy load of light fiction for men and women. Although sales increased steadily and passed the million mark in 1937, *Redbook* still lagged behind its two major competitors, the *American* of Crowell-Collier and *Cosmopolitan* of Hearst. Some editorial changes were made in the forties—the ratio of fact to fiction was increased, for instance—but the company decided on even more drastic changes after the magazine lost $400,000 in 1948. The following year it brought in a new editor, Wade Nichols, who had made a reputation by driving up the circulations of *Click* and *Modern Screen*. Nichols gradually but completely overhauled *Redbook* and aimed it at young married couples, an entirely different audience from the old one. Circulation reached 2,000,000 in 1950, and *Redbook* officially acknowledged the changeover in audience in 1951 by adding the subtitle, "The Magazine for Young Adults." The magazine was awarded the Benjamin Franklin Magazine Award gold medal for public service for three articles published in 1954. The articles, dealing with security risks, academic freedom, and racial segregation, were called a "courageous effort to bring controversial issues before a mass audience."

When Mayes joined *McCall's* in 1958, Nichols left to take his position as editor of *Good Housekeeping*. His successor, Robert Stein, continued to beam *Redbook* at an audience between the ages of eighteen and thirty-five. The magazine carried $10,249,000 worth of advertising in 1963, more than triple the amount of a half-dozen years earlier, and circulation had climbed to 3,699,000.

Bluebook, which did not depend upon advertising for support, was largely a fiction magazine. In its early years, it ran stories by Mary Roberts Rinehart, James Oliver Curwood, Donn Byrne, and Rider Haggard. In 1925, sensing a popular interest in fact pieces, its editors began to run articles of exciting personal experience and serialized autobiography. Admiral Richard E. Byrd, André Maurois, and Sir Hubert Wilkins were among its contributors. *Bluebook* began to call itself a "magazine for men" early in World War II; it was changed into a general magazine for men, with an increased ratio of fact to fiction, during the boom in men's magazines after the war. Donald Kennicott, who had been with the magazine for forty-two years when he retired, ran the magazine virtually without editorial assistance from 1927 to 1952. The magazine was losing money in the early fifties, however, and the company suspended it with its issue of May, 1956.

That same month the firm also killed *Better Living*, a store-distributed women's magazine started in 1951. Although the magazine had achieved a circulation of more than 2,000,000, it had fared poorly in advertising in its competition against *Family Circle* and *Woman's Day*; in consequence, company officials said, they would concentrate their energies on their other magazines.

In 1961, when it was on the lookout for new properties, the McCall Corporation paid $3,000,000 in stock for a lively weekly devoted to literature, politics, science, education, and the popular arts. The magazine was the *Saturday Review*, which had grown at a tremendous rate in the preceding decade, and largest of its twelve stockholders were its editor Norman Cousins and its publisher J. R. Cominsky.

As the *Saturday Review of Literature*, the magazine had grown out of a literary supplement that Henry Seidel Canby, Amy Loveman, Christopher Morley, and William Rose Benet had edited for the New York *Evening Post*. When Cyrus Curtis bought the *Post*, they left to start an independent literary weekly of their own. Their first issue came out in August, 1924. They had wanted to call the magazine just *Saturday Review;* but as a British publication had legal claim to that name, they called it *Saturday Review of Literature*, its title until 1952, when it dropped the "of Literature" without fear of litigation.

In the beginning, Time Inc. had an interest in the *Saturday Review of Literature*. Canby was a former Yale professor, and he had befriended Hadden and Luce when they were trying to start *Time*. When they learned of his plans to found a literary journal, Time Inc. bought substantial stock in the new magazine; its editors were invited to share *Time's* offices; and Roy E. Larsen, *Time's* circulation manager, conducted its circulation and promotional campaign, which included a two-page advertisement in *Time*. The two magazines amicably severed most of their ties in 1925 when *Time* moved to Cleveland, although Time Inc. was listed as publisher of the *Saturday Review* for a few issues in 1926 and Larsen remained a vice-president in its company until 1932.

In the twelve years that Canby was editor and in the two that Bernard DeVoto held the position, the *Saturday Review* carried conscientious book reviews and literary discussions by well-known authors alongside its editorials, its erudite and whimsical columns, its evaluations of detective stories, and its famous column of personal advertisements in which the lonely sought pen pals, the unemployed sought situations, and sellers of unconventional goods and services sought buyers. Friends of the magazine, among them Thomas Lamont, made up its losses. Harrison Smith, a book and magazine publisher, bought the publication in 1938 but sold it four years later to Saturday Review Associates, Inc., in which he remained a stockholder.

The big change in policy came after the early forties when Norman Cousins joined the magazine as editor. Cousins added articles on politics, business, travel, music, and mass communications to the traditional literary discussions, and inaugurated special supplements devoted to phonograph recordings, science, and education. From time to time, the magazine engaged in crusades and appeals to the public conscience. An article by its science editor in 1959 resulted in the Federal Trade Commission's filing a complaint against a pharmaceutical company for the advertising

Hearst's International combined with

Cosmopolitan

February
35 Cents

Beginning –
"WAR NURSE"
An American Woman Who Lived, Loved and
Suffered on the WESTERN FRONT

Good Housekeeping

AUGUST, 1927   25 CENTS
35 CENTS IN CANADA

Beginning A NEW NOVEL *of* FAR ADVENTURE
By Edison Marshall
And THE FIRST WOMAN GOVERNOR'S STORY
By Nellie Tayloe Ross

COSMOPOLITAN
APRIL 1964•35c

EXCLUSIVE FORUM:
7 SENATE WIVES
SPEAK OUT

World's Richest
Family From the new book:
The duPonts of Delaware

DALLAS REVISITED
THE LESSON LEARNED

Natalie Wood
The winsome
psychologist in
Sex and the Single Girl

ROYAL FLUSH
CONDENSED
NOVEL BY WILLIAM
DRYDEN

Good Housekeeping
May 1964•35c

Behind the headlines
– Reassuring facts
about the breast
cancer controversy!

"Our First 90 Days
in the White House,"
as Lady Bird lived
and recalls them

Exciting 14-page
first preview of our
WORLD'S FAIR
MODEL HOME

it circulated among physicians and in the resignation of a division chief in the Food and Drug Administration.

Like some other magazines appealing to the better educated segments of the population, the *Saturday Review* enjoyed a rapid expansion in the age of television. Circulation in 1963 was 339,000, triple what it was in 1950, and advertising revenues had quadrupled in a decade to reach $2,741,000 in 1963.

The McCall Corporation created a book-publishing division in 1961, added a modest line of trade and business magazines, which Mayes planned to expand as a source of small but steady profit, took over the small-circulation *Bridge World* in 1963, and apparently remained alert to other ventures.

In the sixties the Hearst Corporation, too, was looking for new magazine properties, according to company officials. For sixty years, it had shown a greater interest in buying up magazines started by others than in launching new ones of its own. William Randolph Hearst entered magazine publishing in 1903 after he had already put together the first links in his newspaper chain. While he was visiting in London, he came across a British periodical, *The Car;* it interested him so much that he fired off a cable to one of his executives in New York: "Have decided to start a magazine devoted to motor interests. . . ."[3] That magazine, his first, was *Motor*. For twenty-one years *Motor* was a magazine for automobilists. It promoted traffic laws and good roads, covered the auto shows, and had correspondents who reported the progress of motoring abroad. Then in 1924 the magazine changed its editorial pitch and its audience; it became a business publication for manufacturers and dealers of automobiles.

Soon after Hearst had started *Motor*, he began adding magazines to his growing empire. According to George d'Utassay, one of his executives, he acquired them by using his credit with printers and paper manufacturers and by giving bonds, which he redeemed from the profits of his other magazines.[4]

At his peak in 1935, Hearst owned thirteen magazines, but more than that passed through his hands. Some he merged, some he killed, and some he sold. The Hearst empire melted considerably

[3] John R. Winkler, *W. R. Hearst, an American Phenomenon* (New York, 1928), p. 244.
[4] Mrs. Fremont Older, *William Randolph Hearst, American* (New York, 1936), p. 256.

after 1935; but in 1963, a dozen years after the death of its founder, the company still published eleven American magazines— *American Druggist, Cosmopolitan, Good Housekeeping, Harper's Bazaar, House Beautiful, Motor, Motor Boating, New Medical Materials, Popular Mechanics, Sports Afield,* and *Town and Country.* It published another six in Britain, three of them editions of its American magazines.

Although Hearst's newspapers were aimed at the lowest of common denominators, several of his magazines were edited for upper-class or highly specialized markets. With two possible exceptions, the American magazines published by the Hearst Corporation in 1963 were for narrowly defined audiences. However much Hearst used his newspapers to promote his ideas and causes, he left the editorial policies of his magazines pretty much alone, according to an editor who worked for him for more than two decades; although he asked that they not oppose his campaigns, he did not ask that they champion them.

One of the magazines with a broad market was *Cosmopolitan,* which Hearst acquired in 1905. Despite its large circulation, however, the staff prided itself on the quality of its audience. *Cosmopolitan* sold for thirty-five cents during the twenties, a high price for a popular magazine, and the staff recalled President Coolidge's remark when he chose it to publish his autobiography, "Yes, when you pay thirty-five cents for a magazine, that magazine takes on in your eyes the nature of a book and you treat it accordingly." [5]

Cosmopolitan, carrying the motto, "The world is my country and all mankind are my countrymen," was born in Rochester, New York, in 1886, and Schlicht and Fields were its parents. Its editorial content in the first year was as cosmopolitan as the title implied. The monthly ran articles on such diversified subjects as downtown New York, how ancient peoples lived, up and down Vesuvius, Gladstone, and young Mozart.

After a struggle in Rochester, the publishers moved *Cosmopolitan* to New York, where John Brisben Walker purchased it in 1889. Walker believed that a magazine should be "a university of the mind," and he gave *Cosmopolitan* a heavily educational accent. For its time, the magazine had a large circulation—about 400,000 in the mid-nineties.

---

[5] *Time,* 13 (March 18, 1929) 46.

Cosmopolitan, under Hearst, was the magazine which carried Ray Long to glory. For twenty years, Long tensely walked the precarious tightrope across the peak of the magazine arena. In 1929, fortune's child, he owned forty suits, five automobiles, and the reputation of being one of the highest paid editors in the world, his reward for an uncanny ability to sense public taste and to move with it.

After growing up in a small town in Indiana, Long had worked on newspapers in Indianapolis, Cincinnati, and Cleveland, then had edited *Hampton's, Blue Book, Green Book,* and *Red Book.* Hearst hired him late in 1918 to edit *Cosmopolitan.* He ran it well. Hearst raised his salary by a third after four months, then by a fourth, and made him president and editor-in-chief of the International Magazine Company.

When Long assumed direction of *Cosmopolitan* in January, 1919, it had a circulation of about a million; he added 700,000 to that figure and, in doing so, more than doubled advertising rates. His editorial policy was to pick up ideas which had outgrown their original intellectual coteries, adapt them for a larger and less intellectual circle, and forsake them before they had lost their freshness. He kept a half-pace ahead of his readers. When they began to tire of stories about high society, he gave them Peter B. Kyne and James Oliver Curwood; when they wanted doses of culture, he gave them Will Durant.[6] He once attributed his editorial success to having the tastes of an average American. The public does not know what it wants, he said; finding out is the task of the editor: "But if he is alert and intelligent, interested in life and people, if he mixes with enough folks to keep his wits sharpened, he can feel safe in buying and putting into his magazines those stories and features which interest or stimulate him." [7]

In 1925 *Cosmopolitan* absorbed *Hearst's International,* a sister publication. *Hearst's International* was the outgrowth of a magazine founded in 1901. When Hearst bought it in 1911, it was called *World Today.* Hearst was advised that the magazine could never achieve a circulation of more than 200,000 under its current editorial policies, so he converted it into *Hearst's International,* a monthly which carried an increasingly heavier load of fiction, usually of a slightly lower caliber than that in *Cosmopolitan.*

[6] "The *Cosmopolitan* of Ray Long," *Fortune,* 3 (March, 1931) 49-55.
[7] Ray Long, "Introduction," *Twenty Best Short Stories in Ray Long's Twenty Years as an Editor* (New York, 1932), p. xi.

Cosmopolitan was primarily a fiction magazine while Long was editor and for several years after he resigned in 1931. For a long time he had been afraid that he was going stale, and a large number of Russian stories he had bought on a trip to Russia fell flat with his readers. An authoritarian man who had come to enjoy power, he had made his share of enemies. On leaving the Hearst organization, he formed a publishing house with Richard Smith, then drifted to the West Coast and to one job after another— manuscript editor for Columbia Pictures, editor of *Photoplay,* subeditor of *Liberty.* In 1935 he was found dead in his bedroom in Beverly Hills, a rifle at his side.

Harry Payne Burton, who had once edited *McCall's,* steered *Cosmopolitan* for more than a decade after Long's resignation. Just after World War II, in 1946, the magazine underwent a major change in direction when Arthur Gordon was appointed editor. Gordon, a Rhodes scholar, thought that the mass-circulation magazines had lagged behind the intellectual curiosity of their audiences, and as editor of *Cosmopolitan* he strove for the provocative. Readers responded to his formula with insufficient enthusiasm, however, and Herbert Mayes, editor of *Good Housekeeping,* for a time took over the editorial side of both magazines. In 1952 *Cosmopolitan* was given another overhaul, but both its circulation and advertising revenues skidded. The Hearst organization applied an iconoclastic remedy in 1953. In the hope of making a profit from the higher margin on single-copy sales, it dropped the magazine's promotion budget, which had once been a million dollars a year, let subscriptions lapse on expiration, and concentrated on newsstand distribution. Circulation, which was 1,703,000, dropped off by half, but by 1963 it had climbed back to 890,000, about 97 per cent of it single-copy. Under its editors in the late fifties and early sixties, *Cosmopolitan* carried a heavy balance of fiction, including complete novels, articles of general appeal, and some service features. From time to time, it devoted an entire issue to a single subject—the movies, for instance, or new talent on Broadway.

A second magazine with which Hearst sought a wide audience was *Good Housekeeping.* Like *Cosmopolitan,* it was already a fairly old publication when he added it to his fold in 1911. George W. Bryan had published its first issue, "conducted in the interests of higher life in the household," as he put it, at Holyoke, Massachusetts, in May, 1885. After Bryan died in 1898, his *Good Housekeeping* passed from one owner to another—from John Pettigrew to George C. Chamberlain to the Phelps Publishing Company. When the century opened, it was advising homemakers on preparing Sunday dinners, canning fruits, simplified housekeeping, fashions, and rearing children.

Early in the century, the Phelps Publishing Company set up the Good Housekeeping Experiment Station to provide tested information on home economics subjects. Out of the experiment station grew the Good Housekeeping Bureau and the Good Housekeeping Institute, which in laboratories and kitchens tested consumer products of many kinds and issued seals of approval to their manufacturers whether or not they advertised in the magazine. During an investigation by the Federal Trade Commission in 1940, Richard H. Waldo, who had helped to establish the institute, testified that *Good Housekeeping* rejected $196,000 in advertising out of a year's total of $240,000 in the institute's first year of existence.[8] The bureau and the institute were sources of a heavy proportion of articles in the magazine from the time of their founding onward.

Good Housekeeping expanded after Hearst acquired it in 1911, and so did its conception of service to the reader, but the basic editorial pattern of fiction and service still remained in the early sixties. In the mid-thirties, a typical issue carried eight stories, three of them serials, four articles, poems, children's stories, and advice on architecture, home furnishings, fashions, and beauty— essentially the ingredients of issues of a decade earlier. Some twenty-five years later, in the early sixties, the magazine carried features on foods, beauty, needlework, fashions, decorating, appliances, and health, articles of general interest to women, a lesser amount of fiction, and a special insert, "The Better Way," which ran short pieces on such practical concerns as children's camps, snow removal, and plant foods.

When *McCall's* and *Ladies' Home Journal* fought for first place in the women's field during the late fifties and early sixties, *Good Housekeeping* professed to stand aloof from the battle. Taking advertisements in the advertising trade press to proclaim that it was not a party to the "fanfare or frenzy" of the circulation race, it claimed its gains to be an "honest accumulation of those women who care most about what this magazine is best able to give them." Even so, its circulation had grown to 5,269,000 in 1963, a gain of more than 50 per cent in the previous decade, and advertisers were

---

[8] *Editor & Publisher*, 73 (Feb. 10, 1940) 8.

spending more than $25,000,000 annually on its pages. During the forties and most of the fifties, the magazine reportedly earned a profit of $2,000,000 a year.

At one time or another in the twenties and thirties, Hearst owned other magazines of popular appeal—*McClure's, Smart Set,* and *Pictorial Review.* In 1963, however, the remainder of its magazines were special interest and class publications. *Motor Boating,* edited for persons interested in small pleasure craft, was two years old when Hearst interests acquired control of it in 1909. *American Druggist,* a trade publication which Hearst bought in 1927, had begun in 1871 under the title *New Remedies.* Three magazines for upper-class audiences, *House Beautiful, Town and Country,* and *Harper's Bazaar,* also had long pasts when they were brought under Hearst ownership. *Bride and Home* was begun in 1956, *New Medical Materials* in 1959 as a continuing product guide for physicians. In the fifties, the company bought two long-established magazines —*Sports Afield* and *Popular Mechanics.*

A Chicago civil engineer, Eugene Klapp, began *House Beautiful* in 1896 to spread his conviction that beauty in architecture and home decoration demanded simplicity. When his magazine was in its second year, he turned it over to Herbert Stone, a Chicago publisher with kindred ideas. Along with its articles telling readers how to raise squab, dress a four-poster bed, collect beer steins, and repair a smoking chimney, *House Beautiful* in 1904 ran a series called "The Poor Taste of the Rich." The articles were illustrated with photographs of interiors of homes of the wealthy, whom the magazine identified, and their purpose was to show "that wealth is not essential to the decoration of a house, and that the homes of many of our richest citizens are furnished in execrable taste." The magazine succeeded well enough to swallow up *Indoors and Out* in 1908, *Modern Homes* in 1909, and *American Suburbs* in 1912.

The Atlantic Monthly Company purchased *House Beautiful* in 1913 and published it for the next twenty years. Then Hearst bought it for $35,000 to merge with *Home and Field,* a competing magazine which he had owned for five years. *House Beautiful* addressed itself to an audience of somewhat higher income than most of the other home service magazines. Its large gains in circulation and revenue came after World War II. In the early sixties, when its circulation was 912,000, it was bringing in some $7,000,000 worth of advertising a year.

Town and Country was one of the oldest periodicals in America when Hearst bought it in 1925. The magazine had begun its life in 1846 as *Home Journal*, designed as a cultured weekly for "the upper ten thousand composed of the well-born, the rich and the able" to give them the "cream and substance of the week's wilderness of newspaper reading." *Home Journal* was the offspring of Nathaniel Parker Willis, an esthete and dandy with some reputation as essayist and poet, who set its tone, and George Pope Morris, a popular song writer and author of "Woodman, Spare That Tree," who tended its business side. Their periodical carried news of society, borrowings from foreign publications, poetry and ballads, and literary miscellany. After a succession of editors and owners, during which it retained its cosmopolitan flavor, *Home Journal* became *Town and Country* in 1901. In its later years, the magazine acquainted its readers with Ludwig Bemelmans, Evelyn Waugh, Oliver St. John Gogarty, and Salvador Dali, just as it had acquainted them in its earlier years with Swinburne, Alfred de Musset, George Sand, and Balzac. Under Hearst ownership, the magazine continued to seek an audience of means and taste; its production was elegant, its tone sophisticated.

Almost twenty years after the upper 10,000 had buzzed over the first issue of *Home Journal*, the Harper brothers issued the initial number of *Harper's Bazaar*, which Hearst purchased in 1913. Soon after the end of the Civil War, Fletcher Harper, of the book-publishing firm, urged his brothers to join him in bringing out a women's periodical modeled after *Der Bazar* in Berlin. The brothers were already publishing two successful periodicals, *Harper's Monthly* and *Harper's Weekly*, and they were not inclined to start another. If the firm would not undertake the new magazine, Fletcher told them, he would publish it by himself. "No, you will not," responded one of his partners. "We'll defer to your judgment, and you shall have your *Bazar*." [9]

The first number of the new periodical gave readers an idea of what the Harper brothers had in store for them. "*Harper's Bazar* is designed to be a Family Journal, in the true sense of the word," an editorial said, "and it is hoped that its literary merit will equal its practical utility. Serials, novelettes, poems, literary and art miscellany, familiar science, aesthetics, the current literature, new books, amusements, gardening, architecture, household literature— in short all that is likely to interest the home circle will receive due

[9] J. Henry Harper, *The House of Harper* (New York, 1912), pp. 252-53.

notice." [10] In addition, the new publication promised to carry advance news of fashions. It had arranged for *Der Bazar*, "which supplies the fashions to the newspapers of Paris," to ship it electrotypes and proofs of its fashion materials, and its own staff covered New York styles.

The Harper company published the *Bazar* as a weekly until 1901 when it converted it into a monthly magazine. Although the *Bazar* was highly successful at first, it had been losing money for a number of years before Hearst purchased it.

As a Hearst publication, *Harper's Bazar* became a thick, glossy, chic, lavishly illustrated monthly devoted to fashions, beauty, fiction, and belles-lettres, its advertising scarcely distinguishable from its editorial content. Its tone was set by Henry B. Sell, who edited it from 1920 to 1926 and who returned to the Hearst organization in 1949 as editor of *Town and Country*. For the remainder of the twenties, the *Bazar's* editor was Charles Hanson Towne. He had successively edited the *Designer*, *Smart Set*, and *McClure's*, and he sometimes spoke of the encouragement he had given O. Henry, James Branch Cabell, and Theodore Dreiser. The title of the magazine was modified in 1929 by the addition of a second "a" to *Bazaar*.

Carmel Snow, who had been trained under Edna Woolman Chase of *Vogue*, caused a stir in the silk-and-taffeta fashion world in 1932 when she resigned from *Vogue* and joined its archrival, *Harper's Bazaar*. For two years she handled its fashions and other features while its editor, Arthur Samuels, gave his attention to his major interest, fiction. Then she moved up to the editorship, and until her retirement at the end of 1957 she *was* the *Bazaar* in salons, ateliers, and the minds of her readers. For a time after World War II, she edited a *Junior Bazaar*, which she hoped to make a serious competitor of *Mademoiselle* and *Seventeen* but which the company merged into the parent magazine in 1948 on the grounds that it was diverting too much of her energy. She died in May, 1961. After her retirement, her associate Nancy White had become editor of the *Bazaar*.

The *Bazaar's* world of haute couture and luxury was remote from the woodsy world of hunting and fishing trips, canoe expeditions, and simple outdoor pleasures depicted by another Hearst

---

[10] *Harper's Bazar*, 1 (Nov. 2, 1867) 2.

magazine. *Sports Afield* was oldest of the three leading magazines for outdoorsmen when the Hearst organization acquired it in the fifties, and it had endured many seasons when its bag was lean. Although sportsmen had been reading it since 1887, it trailed far behind *Outdoor Life* and *Field and Stream* in the twenties. In the thirties, when the magazine was having a difficult time financially, its editor paid $10 for a manuscript submitted by M. J. Bell, Sr., a wealthy lumber man. Bell became so interested in the magazine that he invested more than $50,000 to keep it going. Guided by Bell and Walter F. Taylor, *Sports Afield* had moved to the forefront of the outdoor magazines by 1935, when its circulation of 161,000 was more than five times greater than a decade earlier. Ted Kesting, a sportsman trained in magazine work on *Country Gentleman*, took over the editorship in the mid-forties. For a time, by competing for name authors and livening the content, he steered *Sports Afield* to first place among the outdoor magazines; but the lead was a shifting thing, and in the early sixties, the publication lagged slightly behind its two chief competitors.

Millions of men were also familiar with *Popular Mechanics*, a monthly that the Hearst organization bought in 1958. It had begun life in January, 1902, as a skimpy weekly which went to five subscribers and a few hundred curious readers who paid their nickels for copies at the newsstand.

Its founder was Henry H. Windsor, Sr., an Iowa minister's son who believed that the age of science and mechanics needed interpretation for the average man. He had worked for a short time as city editor of a newspaper in Marshalltown, Iowa, before holding positions with two public transportation companies. His work as secretary of the Chicago City Railway Company in the eighties led him to start a trade magazine, *Street Railway Review*, which he edited from 1892 to 1901.

Then he got the idea for *Popular Mechanics*. He personally wrote every word of copy and sold every advertisement which appeared in the first issue. His only help was a bookkeeper and a mail clerk, and neither had enough work to keep busy for several months.

By September, 1903, *Popular Mechanics* had become successful enough for Windsor to change it from a sixteen-page weekly into a hundred-page monthly. Soon Windsor struck upon the editorial pattern which characterized the magazine long after its issues had swollen to 300 pages—a section of news and general features about science and technology, a section for shop mechanics, and a section of how-to-do-it articles for the home craftsman.

Windsor died in 1924, but the magazine remained in his family. His son, Henry H. Windsor, Jr., who acquired full control of the company in the mid-forties, became editor and president, and his grandson, Henry H. Windsor, III, a vice-president in the organization. In the mid-forties, the company shook off the complacency which had begun to overtake it. It adopted more aggressive editorial policies, increased its promotional and research activities, and expanded its market by publishing foreign editions in French, Spanish, Danish, and Swedish. For nearly a year before Hearst bought the magazine, however, the Windsor family had been trying to sell it. Hearst moved the divisions of the magazine from Chicago to New York in 1962.

In 1963 the Hearst organization was among the largest communications empires in the world. The parent company and its two dozen subsidiaries at home and abroad had interests in or owned, among other properties, ten daily newspapers, six radio and television stations, a paperback book-publishing house, a subscription solicitation agency, an advertising firm, newspaper feature syndicates, a movie newsreel, two companies dealing in musical compositions, and such other diversified enterprises as paper mills, power and dam sites, and real estate. The organization was in good financial shape, according to Gerhard O. Markuson, its general manager. "We don't owe a nickel to anybody," he said. "We're looking for new properties if we can find the right things. They may be newspapers, preferably, or TV stations, or magazines, and we're ready to pay cash." [11]

---

[11] New York *Times,* Oct. 20, 1963, p. 10F.

New Leaders: The Missionaries

9

In 1937 David A. Smart, a former advertising man who had drifted into magazine publishing, is said to have remarked, "Why didn't somebody tell me about this publishing business before? It's a cinch."

Not many publishers would have agreed with Smart that the publishing business was a cinch; its uncertainties were too evident, its failures too numerous. Yet several publishers who started their businesses in the twenties would have conceded that they had succeeded beyond all expectation. The publishing companies which they formed, usually on little capital, grew into large businesses. The magazines which they founded attracted large followings within comparatively short periods, became the foremost carriers of advertising, and displaced such old favorites as the *Literary Digest* and the *North American Review*.

In the years immediately after World War I, a number of young men not long discharged from military service arrived in New York with big ideas for magazines in their heads and little money in their pockets. They arrived at a good time. The twenties, apart from a brief period of doubt and a year of discouragement, were a time of growing prosperity for American business and industry. The rapidly expanding automotive industry, which directly or indirectly created an estimated 4,000,000 new jobs, was pumping dollars into the whole economy; and construction workers were kept busy laying down new highways over which motorists could travel. Radios and household appliances were becoming necessities instead of curiosities or luxuries, and to a lesser degree than the automobile, they contributed to the prosperity of the period. Manufacturers of many commodities were adapting the assembly-line techniques of the automobile makers and were putting science to work for them. The salesman was becoming an ubiquitous figure, and the consumer was making heavy use of the installment plan. The mounting sums allocated to advertising were both a partial cause and an effect of the vast expenditures for consumer goods.

But economic prosperity alone did not account for the success of the new magazines which hopeful young men offered to the reading public; some of them first appeared in years of recession or depression. There were other factors as well. One was a widening market of persons who could read and who bought the goods that advertisers sold. Another was technological advances in the graphic arts industries which enabled publishers to mass produce magazines at high speed. Still another was a happy meeting between what the publishers originated and what the reading public wanted. Several of the publishers read the barometer of public taste so accurately that the magazines they founded were forerunners of whole new classes of magazines—the digest magazines, for instance, and the news magazines.

The founders of new magazines after World War I can be grouped into two loosely defined categories—the "missionaries" and the "merchants." The terms should not be taken in a strictly literal sense, however, and they imply no disrespect for publishers in either class. The missionaries did not necessarily propagate a religious gospel, although a few of them came from ministers' families and there were evangelical overtones to two or three of their publications; but they did propagate a faith—a faith in a Better America, for instance, a faith in a way of life, a faith in the American Century. The merchants, on the other hand, were not primarily champions of points of view or causes. They were men who quite evidently regarded magazine publishing as strictly a business enterprise to be operated at a profit. They were interested mainly in discovering what readers wanted and then giving it to them. The merchants' approach to magazine publishing, it should be emphasized, was a perfectly legitimate one, one in accord with the Anglo-

American theory of the press. For that theory, like the "invisible hand" theory of Adam Smith, assumed that a publisher working in his own self-interest would inevitably work in the interests of the community. According to the theory, the need for the press to be financially self-sufficient assured readers of a press attuned to their wants and needs. As readers voted with their coins at the newsstand and with their subscriptions by mail, so the theory went, the publications they did not want would die for lack of support; the ones they favored would flourish.

The missionaries were businessmen as well as disseminators of some secular gospel. Some of them founded and edited magazines which were among the most successful in the market place. Indeed, some merchants followed where the missionaries led by imitating their successful editorial products.

This chapter will trace the development of four commercially successful publishing houses established by missionaries after World War I. They were missionaries of widely divergent types: DeWitt Wallace of the Reader's Digest Association, Inc., who preached optimism, the simple life, faith in a Better America; Henry Luce of Time Inc., who regarded even photographs as vehicles of information and education and who proclaimed the American Century; Harold Ross of the *New Yorker*, who taught the gospel of perfection; and Bernarr Macfadden of Macfadden Publications, Inc., who crusaded for healthful living. All of them originated publications which resulted in the emergence of new categories of magazines.

Both the Reader's Digest Association, Inc., and Time Inc. were founded by, and in their early years staffed by, persons without previous magazine experience. Both companies were established on relatively small investments, a circumstance made possible in part because their publications did not originate editorial copy but merely condensed, simplified, and brightened up material which had first appeared in other publications. Both companies were among the largest magazine-publishing enterprises in the world in the early sixties.

For several years before the *Reader's Digest* sent out its first 5,000 pocket-sized copies in February, 1922, DeWitt Wallace had had the idea for a magazine which he thought might eventually earn him $5,000 a year. Wallace was born in St. Paul, Minnesota, where his father, Dr. James Wallace, a Presbyterian minister and scholar of Greek and Latin, was president of Macalester College, a Presbyterian school. After attending Macalester and the University of California, Wallace worked in St. Paul for the Webb Publishing Company, a publisher of farm magazines and textbooks, and as a salesman for Brown and Bigelow, a large printer of calendars and advertising specialties.

By the time he joined the Webb Publishing Company to handle correspondence in its book department, he had his idea for the *Reader's Digest*. Many people wanted to be well informed, he thought, but no reader had the time or money to scout out the material of lasting interest buried deep in the thousands of magazines issued each month. Wallace proposed to sift out such worthwhile articles, condense them for easy reading, and gather them into a handy publication which could be saved. While he was in the hospital recovering from shrapnel wounds that he had suffered as an infantry sergeant during the Meuse-Argonne offensive, Wallace experimented with his idea by clipping out dozens of magazine articles and editing them for brevity without sacrificing their meaning. Back in St. Paul, he spent six months copying and pruning articles from old magazines in the public library. He collected thirty-one of them into a sample pocket-sized magazine called the *Reader's Digest*, had 200 copies printed, and mailed copies to a dozen New York publishers and other potential backers. No one was interested.

In 1921, laid off from a job in the publicity department of the Westinghouse Electric Company, Wallace spent three months writing promotional circulars for his projected magazine. He borrowed money from friends until he had accumulated a capital of $5,000 and he took on a partner—his fiancée, Lila Bell Acheson, the daughter of a Presbyterian minister. During World War I, Lila Acheson had traveled about the country with her parents doing morale work in war plants for the Presbyterian church; after the war, with her brother Barclay, she went to Constantinople to work for Near East Relief. She became engaged to Wallace, whom she had known for several years, on her return to the United States in 1921. They rented an office in a basement under a speakeasy in Greenwich Village, formed the Reader's Digest Association, clipped and condensed innumerable articles, and prepared a mimeographed circular soliciting subscriptions. On their wedding day, October 15, 1921, they mailed out thousands of circulars advertising their

magazine, and when they returned from their honeymoon they found 1,500 charter subscriptions at $3 each. They set to work on their first issue, dated February, 1922.

At first the Wallaces intended their *Reader's Digest* primarily for women. They soon added men to their audience, and they developed the editorial formula which made the *Digest* one of the most commercially successful magazines in all history. Their slogan expressed their aim, "An article a day from leading magazines in condensed, permanent booklet form." They were guided by three criteria in choosing features. The first was "applicability"; the reader should feel that the subject concerned him. The second was "lasting interest"; an article should be worth reading a year hence (the *Digest* often reprinted articles from its own earlier issues). The third was "constructiveness," which led the *Digest* to shun articles reflecting defeatism and to favor those featuring optimism and good works.

After World War II, although he had long since changed his ways of obtaining copy, DeWitt Wallace was still choosing material according to the pattern he had worked out in the twenties. He described his formula this way: "Primarily, we are looking for articles of lasting interest which will appeal to a large audience, articles that come within the range of interests, experience, and conversation of the average person. The over-all emphasis, for twenty-one years, has been a more or less conscious effort to find articles that tend to promote a Better America, with capital letters, with a fuller life for all, and with a place for the United States of increasing influence and respect in world affairs." [1] A critic, in an exceedingly unfriendly study of the magazine, found more specific ingredients of the formula. They were dogmatism, optimism, and "simplism," that is, the "appearance, if not the actual quality, of simplicity." [2]

At the end of the first year, the Wallaces moved their office from Greenwich Village to Pleasantville, forty miles north of New York. There, for $25 a month, they rented a single room in the garage of Pendleton Dudley, a public relations counsel, and used it for living quarters and office. They later rented a pony shed adjoining the garage for another $10 a month. In 1926, after three years in the

---

[1] Kenneth Stewart, "Meet the Editor and Fifty-two Per Cent Owner of 'Reader's Digest,'" *PM*, 4 (March 12, 1944) m4.

[2] John Bainbridge, *Little Wonder, or the Reader's Digest and How It Grew* (New York, 1946), pp. 135-43.

garage and pony shed, they built a home on property next to Dud-
ley's and edited the *Digest* from their study. The *Digest* eventually
outgrew the study, and they rented office space in two bank buildings. In 1939 the *Digest* moved into a $1,500,000 building of its own
at Chappaqua, near Pleasantville.

In the garage and pony shed days, the Wallaces could publish
the *Digest* with help from just a couple of clerks; but as the circulation grew, so did their staff. It was a staff of amateurs until
the mid-thirties; only two of the thirty-two staff members in 1936
had ever worked for a magazine before. Two of the top editors
were former clergymen, and one was a former missionary. The first
professional editor to join the *Digest* staff was Kenneth W. Payne,
who had once edited the *North American Review* and who moved
to the *Digest* in 1930. A number of men who had edited other
magazines took positions with the *Digest* in the mid-thirties after
it ceased being strictly a magazine of reprints, among them Alfred
S. Dashiell of *Scribner's*, Howard Florance of *Review of Reviews*
and the *Literary Digest*, Merle Crowell of the *American*, Fulton
Oursler of *Liberty*, Paul Palmer of *American Mercury*, and Marc
Rose of *Business Week*. Albert L. Cole, who had been publisher of
Popular Science and who had advised Wallace on business matters
for several years, became full-time general business manager in
1939.

Although Wallace tried to hide the success of the *Digest* by
keeping its circulation a secret until 1936, numerous imitators
sprang up in the late twenties. None of them seriously threatened
the *Reader's Digest* in editorial capability or in circulation, but
they affected the *Digest* in its means of distribution and in its means
of obtaining editorial material.

Wallace originally distributed the *Digest* entirely by subscription
for fear that it would not sell well on the newsstand. When imitators achieved large sales on the stands, Wallace recognized that
he had been wrong, and in 1929 he arranged for the S-M News
Company to sell the *Digest* through retail outlets.

At first the *Digest* easily obtained permission to reprint articles
without payment since magazines were gratified by the publicity
and since Wallace was no competitor for advertising. After a few
years, however, some editors began viewing the *Digest* as a parasite
which fed on their copy and ate into their circulation. Wallace,
with the help of Kenneth W. Payne, then on the staff of the *North*

American Review, convinced editors that the *Digest* actually stimulated magazine reading.

But when imitators started to pester editors for permission to reprint and even began to reprint without permission, Wallace realized that the whole idea of the digest magazine was highly vulnerable. What if the leading magazines should deny him reprint rights?

His fears were partly justified, then and later. The Hearst magazines, Crowell-Collier, and Curtis all refused to enter reprint agreements. Although Crowell-Collier and Curtis later signed contracts, Curtis would not renew its contract in 1938 and closed its magazines as a source of copy until 1943. The *New Yorker*, after five years of cooperation, broke off relations in 1944.

In the early thirties, Wallace set about assuring the *Digest* a steady flow of material. As the *Digest* was both the leader and the most affluent of the reprint magazines, he could get exclusive reprint rights from most of the magazines he approached. The rates Wallace paid magazines for using their articles rose steadily. In the early days, it was perhaps $100 an article. In 1933 Wallace reportedly paid a top price of about $10,000 for use of material over a three-year period. The payments provided for in three-year contracts after World War II were said to range from $3,500 to $50,000.[3]

As insurance against boycott by his source, Wallace began to run original articles in 1933. Another reason for this fundamental change in policy, Wallace said, was that he could not find enough articles of lasting interest and of the wide variety he desired to fill the magazine. The *Digest* carried fifteen original articles in 1933, but no one seemed to notice the change to original material until 1935 when it ran "—And Sudden Death" by J. C. Furnas, a grisly account of automobile accidents which Wallace hoped would make motorists safety-conscious. Hundreds of newspapers and magazines picked up the article, radio stations broadcast it, government officials passed out reprints, judges read it in court or had traffic violators copy it. In three months, the *Digest* sent out 4,000,000 copies to more than 8,000 business firms and organizations. The response made editors aware that Wallace was not just a "second-guess editor," as some had called him, but one with a keen sense of what the reading public wanted.

---

[3] Bainbridge, pp. 49-50.

Although an increasing amount of copy was originating in its own offices, the *Reader's Digest* kept the appearance of a digest by a controversial system. In the mid-thirties, having money to commission the sort of nonfiction he wanted, Wallace began offering articles to other publications in exchange for the right to "condense" and reprint them. Wallace and his staff provided the ideas, assigned writers to the articles, and paid for them. Critics called them "planted articles"; the *Digest* called them "cooperatively planned."

Some magazines with small budgets welcomed articles they could not otherwise afford. A dozen, among them *Scribner's, North American Review, American Mercury,* and *Rotarian,* printed about sixty such articles in the first year and a half. According to John Bainbridge, a critic of the arrangement, 682 of the 1,908 major articles in the *Digest* from 1939 through 1943 were ones made available to other publications and then reprinted. They had appeared originally in more than sixty periodicals, including *Harper's, Atlantic, Yale Review, Nation, New Republic, Survey Graphic,* and *Hygeia.*[4]

When the *New Yorker* ended its reprint agreement, it attacked the system as "a threat to the free flow of ideas and to the independent spirit." In a letter to contributors, it said that "the *Digest* is beginning to generate a considerable fraction of the contents of American magazines. . . . The fact seems to be that some publications are already as good as subsidized by the *Digest.*" If the *Digest* wanted to become a magazine of original content, the letter continued, it should have done so directly; it should not have operated through other media to maintain the "reprint myth."[5] Other individuals and magazines were less fearful than Bainbridge and the *New Yorker,* in which his study of the *Reader's Digest* first appeared. Dixon Wecter in a review of Bainbridge's book said, "One finds it rather hard to share Mr. Bainbridge's shocked feeling that this trend, developing over the past ten years, is somehow perfidious and sinister, though of course it does do violence to the magazine's original aim and title." Yet the matter, Wecter thought, was "chiefly the business of the parties concerned."[6] In May, 1944, *Esquire* defended the *Digest* in a full-page editorial attacking the *New Yorker* for its harsh words. While the *New Yorker* was within its rights in ending its reprint agreement, *Esquire* said, its letter to

---

[4] Bainbridge, pp. 60-62.
[5] *Tide,* 18 (March 1, 1944) 42, 44.
[6] Dixon Wecter, "The Bean Stalk of Pleasantville," *Saturday Review of Literature,* 29 (June 15, 1946) 15.

contributors was "dangerous loose talk" about other people's business and could stimulate rumors of governmental action against the *Digest* on charges of monopoly or unfair competition. Whatever can be said for or against the practice, the *Reader's Digest* continued it throughout the fifties and on into the sixties.

Since the *Reader's Digest* was the property of just DeWitt Wallace and Lila Acheson Wallace, its financial affairs have seldom been made public; but one can sketch a little of its financial history from the various speculations made from time to time. Judging from circulation figures, the *Digest* probably grossed $60,000 annually while its headquarters were the garage in Pleasantville and $327,000 a year just before it was sold on newsstands in 1929. Its revenues were $2,178,000 in 1935, according to *Fortune;*[7] and for 1951, *Time* estimated its gross at between $25,000,000 and $30,000,000, its net at about $1,500,000.[8]

So long as the *Digest* carried no advertising in its domestic edition, it did not have to make its circulation available. Its circulation was revealed for the first time in 1936 by *Fortune.* Although records for the early years were unreliable, *Fortune* put sales at 7,000 at the end of the magazine's first year, at 20,000 by 1925, and 109,000 just before the *Digest* sought newsstand sales in 1929. Doubling in the two years after 1932, they had passed the million mark by 1935. The magazine itself has given its distribution as 3,471,000 in 1940, as 8,769,000 in 1945, and as 9,132,000 in 1950. Even before then it had become the largest selling magazine in the United States; in 1963 its circulation of 14,523,000 was more than 5,000,000 greater than that of *TV Guide,* its runner-up.

The magazine that had been loath to seek newsstand sales began to expand its circulation into foreign lands with an edition for Britain in 1938. From then on new international editions appeared in rapid succession. In 1963 the *Digest* had major offices in twenty-five countries outside the United States and was circulated in all of the noncommunist countries of the world. In all, it had twenty-nine basic international editions published in thirteen languages, and their total circulation was 10,415,000. Four of the editions— the British, French, German, and Canadian-English—had sales of more than a million a month. The world circulation of the *Digest,* including the domestic edition, was almost 25,000,000.

[7] "The Reader's Digest," *Fortune,* 14 (Nov., 1936) 131.
[8] *Time,* 58 (Dec. 10, 1951) 64

When Wallace started his international editions, he found that most foreign readers could not afford to pay the equivalent of twenty-five cents for the *Digest*, its cost at home. He cut the price of his foreign issues to fifteen cents and opened his international editions to advertising. Circulation and advertising linage grew, and some foreign editions showed a small profit, but revenue from international operations as a whole did not keep up with rising production costs. At the end of 1950, the *Reader's Digest* for the first time broke even on its international operations.

The domestic edition of the *Digest* carried no paid advertising in its first thirty-three years. However, it sometimes reprinted advertisements that its editors thought noteworthy; and from 1929 on, it carried a number of "consumer articles" that evaluated widely distributed products and that no doubt affected the buying habits of thousands of Americans. Over the years the *Digest* assessed such products as ammoniated toothpastes, automobile waxes, detergents, and leading brands of cigarettes. Like a nagging wife it periodically warned of the dangers of smoking. Indeed, the agency handling its advertising account of $1,250,000 canceled the contract in 1957 because an article conflicted with the interests of another client, a tobacco company.

Many advertisers quoted the consumer articles, sometimes misleadingly, and used the *Digest* name as a seal of approval. The magazine tried to stop them, and it repeatedly explained to its readers that it never granted permission to use its name but had no legal power to keep advertisers from doing so. Advertisers capitalized on its consumer articles so extensively that in late 1950 *Tide*, the advertising trade magazine, devoted three pages to reviewing abuses of *Digest* copy. An editorial called the practice "short-term thinking, opportunistic operating and gray-area advertising." [9]

The *Reader's Digest* broke its long policy against advertising with its issue of April, 1955. Rising costs had made it impossible to operate on revenue from readers alone, according to Wallace, and a survey of readers had indicated that they preferred advertising to an increase in the price of the magazine. Wallace held advertising to thirty-two pages an issue for the first year; but since advertisers found that restriction too arbitrary for their fluctuating needs, he thereafter set a limit that varied with the number of

---

[9] *Tide*, 24 (Dec. 15, 1950) 13-15.

editorial pages. The *Digest* fattened under a heavy load of advertising, which brought in $11,700,000 the first year, $59,035,000 in 1963. However, the company said that readers continued to contribute a sizable part of its income. They paid an average of 18.3 cents a copy in 1954, the last year the magazine was without advertising, and an average of 24.3 cents in 1962.

Drawing on its subscribers as an initial market, the company started the Reader's Digest Condensed Book Club in 1950. In the late fifties, the company was remarkably successful in selling two phonograph records by direct-mail to its subscribers; and in 1961 a new subsidiary, Reader's Digest Music, Inc., bought out the R.C.A. Victor Record Clubs.

The alacrity with which advertisers quoted the *Reader's Digest* and rushed to its pages when it first opened them to advertising was a testimonial to the influence of the magazine. Thousands of middle-class Americans put a good deal of faith in the magazine. They found it a wholesome, conservative magazine, as inspiring as a good sermon. Interesting and informative, it praised the simple life, the life of neighborliness and good works, and its optimism never faltered. It was a secular magazine, but its overtones of evangelism were unmistakable.

Like the founders of the Reader's Digest Association, the young men who established Time Inc. in 1922 were without professional magazine experience and so were the editors who staffed the publication on which the company was built. Even after Time Inc. had grown into one of the largest magazine-publishing houses in the world and had many experienced professionals on its staff, one could still detect traces of amateurishness in its open-minded approach to publishing problems and procedures. Like the Wallaces of *Reader's Digest*, the founders of Time Inc. had a strong streak of the missionary; indeed, one of them was the son of a missionary to China. As the *Reader's Digest* generated a whole new class of magazines, two publications of Time Inc. were responsible for new classes—the news magazines and the picture magazines. The stories of those innovators, *Time* and *Life*, are told in a subsequent chapter which treats the classes of publications they inspired. In this chapter, the emphasis will be on the story of Time Inc. as a publishing company, although obviously the stories of the company and its magazines cannot be sharply separated.

The men with a sense of mission who founded Time Inc. in 1922 were Briton Hadden and Henry R. Luce, both then twenty-four years old. Hadden, born in Brooklyn of well-to-do parents, had been interested in journalism since childhood, when he had entertained his family with epic poems and his schoolmates with a newspaper, the *Daily Glonk.* Educated at Hotchkiss and Yale, he had got a job on the New York *World* after telling Herbert Bayard Swope, who had tried to get rid of him, "Mr. Swope, you're interfering with my destiny." His destiny, as he explained it, was to start a publication of his own; the job on the *World* was to provide him with experience for starting it.[10]

Luce was born in Shantung, China, the son of Dr. Henry Winters Luce, a Presbyterian missionary who had founded two American universities in China and who required each member of his family to spend at least an hour a day in useful effort. Luce went to school in China, then to Hotchkiss and Yale. After a year at Oxford, he took a job as a legman and researcher for Ben Hecht, then a columnist for the Chicago *News.*

The idea for what became *Time* was conceived by Hadden and Luce at Yale, where they collaborated on managing the undergraduate newspaper. They nurtured the idea during service together at an officers' training camp in World War I, and they developed it further while working on Frank Munsey's Baltimore *News.* Early in 1922 they quit their jobs on the *News* (with the understanding that they could return if their project failed) and set about raising money for a "paper" of their own which they referred to as *Facts.* That "paper" became *Time,* and they founded it on $86,000 raised with the help of friends and acquaintances.

Although Hadden and Luce had no magazine experience before the first issue of *Time* appeared in March, 1923, they had picked up a knowledge of publishing on their jobs and from persons in the business. As they sought advice on how to go about getting their publication to press, they appeared so inexperienced that people were glad to help them. A banker assisted in capitalizing their company; William Herbert Eaton, then circulation manager of *World's Work,* taught them the secrets of building a subscription list by direct-mail advertising, a system which Time Inc. developed successfully and was still using in the sixties.

And yet an amateurishness characterized the early years of *Time.*

---

[10] Noel Busch, *Briton Hadden: A Biography of the Co-Founder of Time* (New York, 1949), pp. 44-45.

None of the small staff was more than three years out of college. The foreign news editor, Thomas J. C. Martyn, who later founded *Newsweek*, did his first professional writing for the initial issue of *Time;* Hadden and Luce, erroneously thinking him a foreign correspondent, had lured him from Rome at a salary larger than either of their own. Roy Larsen, the circulation manager, had been out of college but a year. His assistants were debutantes working for a lark; they mixed up their mailing lists so badly that some subscribers got three copies of the first issue, none for the next two.

In appearance, too, *Time* was amateurish in its first few years. "Its printing standards," one executive of the company wrote years later, "were approximately those of a French provincial newspaper in 1910 and its pictures, in the words of the late Robert Benchley, looked as if they had been engraved on pieces of bread." [11] Early issues of *Time* carried few photographs because they were expensive, and the magazine was not printed on slick paper until near the end of the first year. Even then it appeared in monotonous black and white; the first red-bordered cover and the first color advertising came just before its fourth anniversary.

The unprepossessing appearance of *Time* was partly the result of economy, for there was seldom enough money for comfort in those early years. Once, near the end of the second year, cash on hand shrank to $5,000, enough for only a few days' operations. And one evening when *Time* was nearly three years old, Luce walked for two hours in Bryant Park debating with a friend whether or not he and Hadden could afford to raise their own salaries to $50 a week.

Perhaps one reason *Time* managed to survive was that Hadden and Luce, who took turns editing and managing business affairs, got their raw news from an exceedingly inexpensive source—the daily newspapers, especially the New York *Times*. They clipped the papers and passed the items along to their staff for rewriting. Their staff was small. At times two men wrote 50 to 70 per cent of the magazine, and the entire full-time staff needed only a single taxi for the ride to the printer at press time.

In September, 1925, to economize, Hadden and Luce moved Time Inc. from New York, where it shared space in an East Side loft building with the infant *Saturday Review of Literature*, to Cleveland, Ohio, where rent and clerical help were cheaper. But

[11] Eric Hodgins, *The Span of Time* (New York, 1946), p. 3.

they returned to New York in August, 1927. For one thing, they missed the supply of adventuresome young intellectuals whom they could hire for comparatively small salaries in New York. For another, they missed up-to-date copies of the New York *Times*, indispensable to their coverage of the news.

Meanwhile, Time Inc. was growing, and its founders plowed its profits back into the business. In 1927 circulation of *Time*, 136,000, was about a third higher than that of the year before; gross advertising revenue, $501,000, was about 77 per cent higher. The next year circulation went up by almost another third, gross advertising revenue by about 54 per cent. There was no doubt about the success of Time Inc. by 1930, when the company grossed more than $3,000,000 in advertising and paid stockholders their first dividend on preferred stock.

But in 1929, Time Inc. lost one of the men who had helped to make it a success. On February 27, 1929, after an illness of two months, Briton Hadden died. What had he contributed to the new company? The estimate of his cousin and biographer, Noel Busch, himself a writer and editor for Time Inc., seems fair enough: "Time was, first of all, an invention pure and simple; and Hadden had a large part in designing it. Secondly, *Time* was a daring and well-organized business venture; and Hadden played an important part in that. . . . Finally, and perhaps most important of all, Hadden was a great editor. Notable performance in one such line of effort is much more than most people attain in a full lifetime. He attained notable performance in all three in less than half that space." [12]

As *Time* prospered, the company experimented with other publications. Before Hadden's death, it had started *Tide*, the advertising trade magazine. Hadden, serving his turn as business manager, thought there was a need for a magazine which would summarize the news of advertising as *Time* summarized general news. In April, 1927, the company bought out *Tide*, which resembled *Time* in format and news presentation. After Hadden's death, the executives of the company were too concerned with another new magazine, *Fortune*, to give *Tide* the attention it demanded. Time Inc. sold it in late 1930 to Raymond Rubicam, cofounder of the Young and Rubicam advertising agency. He sold it to four of its executives in 1948. After four other changes of ownership, *Tide* died in 1959.

The idea for *Fortune* came from Henry Luce, who also contrib-

---

[12] Busch, p. 107.

uted its name. The business section of *Time* was necessarily too small to carry all of the material its staff produced. Luce suggested that the company start a magazine of restricted circulation to use the material being crowded out of *Time's* business pages. Time Inc. established an experimental department in 1928 to work out plans for the new magazine, and by late 1929 the department had produced a dummy. "Business," the original prospectus said, "is the greatest single common denominator of interest among the active leading citizens of the U.S. . . . *Fortune's* purpose is to reflect Industrial Life in ink and paper and word and picture as the finest skyscraper reflects it in steel and architecture."

As Time Inc. planned publication of *Fortune* for early 1930 and set its price at an unprecedented dollar a copy, the big bull market of the twenties collapsed. A few days after the market crash, executives of Time Inc. met to decide whether or not readers and advertisers would accept a lush magazine dedicated to business, which was patently in trouble. They decided to proceed with the magazine. "But we will not be over-optimistic," they said; "we will recognize that this business slump may last as long as an entire year."[13] And so the first issue of *Fortune,* dated February, 1930, was mailed to 30,000 subscribers.

Despite the depression, *Fortune* gained in circulation and in advertising. Subscriptions increased from 34,000 in 1930 to 139,000 in 1936. In the same period, gross advertising revenues more than tripled; they rose from $427,000 in 1930 to $1,963,000 in 1936. The gains continued throughout the forties and fifties. In the early sixties, circulation was about 383,000, and the advertising revenues of $11,996,000 in 1962 were the second largest in history.

Nevertheless, *Fortune,* while a publication of some prestige, contributed only a small part to the total income of Time Inc. The company has seldom revealed the profits from *Fortune,* but one writer who studied the publication, William Lydgate, has estimated its earnings during the thirties.[14] In its first eight years, he estimated, *Fortune* earned a net of about $1,300,000, approximately 15 per cent of the income of Time Inc. from its publications in that period. His figures, all approximations, showed that the magazine lost $150,000 in 1930, earned $30,000 in 1931, lost $30,000 in 1932, and broke even in 1933. For the remaining four years covered by

[13] William A. Lydgate, "Romantic Business," *Scribner's,* 104 (Sept., 1938) 18.
[14] Lydgate, p. 18.

his study, the magazine showed a profit: more than $200,000 in 1934, more than $400,000 in 1935, not quite $400,000 in 1936, and $498,000 in 1937. In the fifties, at least for a time, the magazine was said to have been losing money.

Fortune was an expensive magazine to produce. From its first issue, the company took pride in its fine printing, its many excellent illustrations, its carefully written and carefully researched articles. Confident of its accuracy, the editors in May, 1937, offered readers $5 for every error of fact they could find. When the amount was raised to $10, the editors received nearly a thousand letters. The editors allowed two "major errors," twenty-three "minor ones," and forty "small points." They paid out $4,000, then withdrew their offer because of the time wasted in reading, checking, and answering the letters from readers.

The editorial approach of *Fortune* was influenced by Henry Luce. In the early thirties, he read a book by A. A. Berle and G. C. Means, *The Modern Corporation and Private Property,* which contended that all business, per se, was invested with a public interest. From that thesis, Luce developed *Fortune's* editorial approach, which sought to hold all business to constant public scrutiny.

One article type in which *Fortune* pioneered in the thirties was the detailed analysis of the policies, problems, structure, and finances of a single corporation. In time such articles became a standard feature of business magazines like *Forbes* and *Business Week.* Although *Fortune* did not entirely discontinue the corporation story, it sought fresher approaches to covering business and industry. And soon after its founding, *Fortune* moved from an examination of big business to an examination of politics, government, and social questions in general. Dwight Macdonald, a former *Fortune* writer, believed that the magazine pushed leftward during the New Deal for several reasons. One was that Luce recognized that the New Deal was big news and that big business, for the time being, was not. Another was that many of the talented *Fortune* writers were liberals. Still another was that as writers dug for facts, they became increasingly liberal even if they had not been at the start.[15] In the late thirties, a typical issue of *Fortune* dealt with such subjects as a single corporation, an entire industry, a wealthy or influential family, a foreign country, and a specific American locality.

---

[15] Dwight Macdonald, " 'Fortune Magazine,' " *Nation,* 144 (May 8, 1937) 528.

Early in 1948 Luce outlined a plan for changing the familiar format and editorial pattern of the magazine. Redesigned in typography and layout, the "new" *Fortune* that appeared the following October carried several new departments, including a "Business Roundup" which summarized and evaluated the leading developments of the past thirty days in American business, and more and shorter articles. It experimented with group biography, a single article about several leading businessmen or industrialists, and it viewed with perceptive eyes such subjects as executives' wives, industrial communications, and the rise of suburbia. With its issue of January, 1956, *Fortune* underwent additional changes. The cover was redesigned, the table of contents restyled, and the layout of the inside pages altered.

Fortune was devoted to business and industry in general; in April, 1932, Time Inc. acquired a magazine devoted to a single industry. *Architectural Forum* had begun publication as the *Bricklayer* in 1892 and had been renamed *Architectural Forum* in 1917. It was a professional journal exclusively for architects when Time Inc. took it over. The inspiration for buying it came to Luce from Marriner Eccles, a financier who held positions in the Treasury Department and in the Federal Reserve System under President Franklin D. Roosevelt.

"Eccles said that the main line of attack against the depression would be in housing," Luce explained a dozen years later. "*Fortune* had been started as a magazine for general business with a pull toward the over-all picture, and we thought we ought to have a magazine for a particular industry. Building was the biggest single industry in America, with tremendous potentialities. That was why we bought *Arch Forum*—at least that was the rationale. But it just didn't work out that way, and we never fully realized our ambitions." [16]

The original mission of *Architectural Forum* under Time Inc., as its publishers expressed it in their prospectus, was "to bring together, around the central art and science of architecture, all the influences which will build the new America." Gradually the magazine widened its editorial scope so that it covered not only architecture but all branches of the construction industry. As the purpose of the magazine broadened, its audience came to include

[16] Kenneth Stewart, "The Education of Henry Luce," *PM*, 5 (Aug. 27, 1944) m9.

builders, realtors, building owners, bankers, and government officials. Consequently the name was changed in 1950 to *The Magazine of Building.* In January, 1952, the magazine was subdivided
into two distinct publications. One, *Architectural Forum,* was edited for the heavy building industry. The other, *House and Home,*
was edited for builders of residential homes, architects, and mortgage lenders.

In 1936 Time Inc. developed *Life,* a picture magazine, the history of which is sketched in a later chapter, and in 1952 it began
publication of *Life en Español,* a fortnightly Spanish-language edition of *Life.* After World War II, Luce and his associates experimented with what they called a "think-magazine." Although they
did not know exactly what they wanted it to be like, they had
general notions of a publication of high intellectual caliber on the
order of the old *Dial* or the contemporary *Partisan Review.* As described to stockholders in 1947, the proposed magazine would
carry high quality articles about politics, philosophy, religion, and
the arts in general. If the magazine were really good, Luce became
convinced, it could find a six-figure audience, not one of just the
15,000 originally intended. But Luce and his staff were not satisfied with the experiment and they put the project in abeyance.
They had "fussed" with it so much, Luce said, that they went stale.

The next new magazine was *Sports Illustrated,* a weekly reporter
of "the wonderful world of sports," which first appeared in August,
1954, after more than a year of intensive experimentation. Originally the magazine was intended to cover the whole field of recreation; but that conception had been changed before the first
trial dummy went to press, and for months staff members referred
to their forthcoming magazine as "Muscles."

Time Inc. planned *Sports Illustrated* as a magazine for well-edu-
cated, upper-income readers and set a circulation goal of 450,000.
An advanced promotion campaign brought in 250,000 subscribers
even before the magazine had a name, however, and sales at the
end of six months' publication were some 575,000 an issue. Its
growth thereafter was rapid. In less than a decade after its founding, it had attracted a following of more than a million; in the six
years after 1957, its advertising revenues considerably more than
doubled to reach $17,985,000.

Sports Illustrated not only covered the usual spectator sports—
football, basketball, baseball, boxing—but also took its readers, by

word and picture, on mountain-climbing expeditions, fox hunts, big-game hunts, and field trials. It counseled them on skiing, golf, boating, swimming, snorkel-diving, riding, and even bridge. Since its staff believed that sports had never got proper visual treatment, it made extensive use of color photography and sent artists out to record sports events on canvas.

At first the editors had thought they could buy more than half of their material from newspaper sports writers, but they soon discovered that the reporters were too busy or too undisciplined for the sort of writing they wanted. Therefore, they leaned heavily on their own staff, but they also commissioned articles from such well-known writers as Catherine Drinker Bowen, William Saroyan, and Robert Frost. William Faulkner covered hockey and the eighty-first Kentucky Derby; John P. Marquand contributed a satirical series on country clubs; John Steinbeck wrote about fishing; and President-elect John F. Kennedy decried "the soft American." The magazine exposed the connection between racketeering and boxing, crusaded for safe driving, and argued for conservation. Its approach seemed to attract a devoted circle of readers. Yet some of the missionary zeal which had characterized the early *Time* and *Life* seemed absent.

During World War II and in the postwar years, Time Inc., in the words of its staff, grew from "a big little business" into "a little big business." Judged by its net income, the company was a small operation indeed during the late twenties and early thirties. Its net was only $3,860 in 1927, the year it returned to New York from Cleveland; $125,787 in 1928; $325,412 in 1929; and $818,936 in 1930. Its net had grown to more than $1,000,000 by 1933, to more than $2,000,000 by 1935.

In 1963 Time Inc. with its subsidiaries was the largest publisher of magazines in the United States. Besides its magazines, which accounted for about three-fourths of its revenues, the company published general and text books; operated radio and television stations in the United States and had interests in foreign television stations, especially in Latin America; conducted a large export business in magazines; maintained an organization doing research in the graphic arts and another for selling technical developments to the printing trades; was part owner of magazine subscription and distribution agencies; ran pulp and paper mills; and owned 610,000 acres of Texas timberland and other real estate. One of its magazines, *Life*, led all American magazines in gross advertising revenues in 1963 with $143,875,000; another, *Time*, was third with $61,276,000. The gross revenue of the corporation in 1962 was $326 million, and its net income was $10,190,000, the third largest in its history. The company employed 6,700 persons. It had moved from the Chrysler Building to the Time and Life Building in Rockefeller Center in the spring of 1938. Cramped there after a half-dozen years, it had moved to another new building of its own early in 1960.

Before 1941 Time Inc. had no correspondents or photographers of its own abroad, no staff members overseas except a few March of Time people in London and Paris. As a result of its expanded coverage and publishing activities abroad during World War II, it formed Time-Life International in 1945 as a division to administer foreign news coverage and to distribute *Time* and *Life* outside of the United States. The company published five international weekly editions of *Time*, one fortnightly international edition of *Life*, and a fortnightly edition of *Life en Español*. With Arnoldo Mondadori Editore as copublisher, Time Inc. launched a new monthly magazine in Italy, *Panorama*, in October, 1962. With an Argentine publisher, it brought out a Spanish-language edition of the magazine the following June. And with a Japanese publisher, it started a Japanese counterpart of *Fortune*, a monthly called *President*, in May, 1963.

As Time Inc. expanded into a global operation and took the world for its beat, another missionary was deliberately cultivating a relatively small following and was focusing his editorial attention on a single city. Harold Ross and his *New Yorker* kept their eyes on New York; and although they regularly peered across the ocean at Europe and occasionally looked across the United States at Hollywood, they largely ignored the America west of the Hudson. Yet Ross's *New Yorker* was an influential magazine. It changed the character of American humor, introduced a new approach to magazine biography, set high standards of reporting, and thereby influenced the course of American journalism in general.

In 1952 when Dale Kramer published a book about Harold Ross and his *New Yorker*, some of the persons most closely associated with the magazine disavowed the book on principle. No outsider, they insisted, could possibly handle the subject adequately. A number of writers before Kramer, some of them staff members of the

New Yorker, had tried to tell what Ross was like. "Unfortunately, it is a story which nobody is able to tell," Russell Maloney, who had worked with Ross for eleven years, admitted in his own attempt in 1947. "No man . . . has been the subject of so much analysis, interpretation, and explanation with so little concrete results." [17]

For twenty-six years, from the first issue in February, 1925, until his death in December, 1951, the *New Yorker* was unmistakably the product of Harold Ross. He worked on every piece of copy which went into the magazine, apart from a few sports columns and foreign newsletters which came in over the weekend, Maloney recalled; and he stalked "through the dirty corridors of his editorial domain, gaunt, gap-toothed, his black hair tousled and his mouth agape like that of a man who has just established contact with a bad oyster, watching the next issue grow and arguing minute points of fact, taste, punctuation, or policy."

By all accounts, Ross was aloof, tactless, rude, given to outbursts of temper and profanity, a man with relatively few friends. Yet the friends he had were remarkably loyal; and he was indisputably a demanding editor, a meticulous one, a great one. The *New Yorker* reflected Ross's personality; but, curiously, his personality and that of the urbane, witty, sometimes acid *New Yorker* were totally unalike.

Harold Ross was not a native New Yorker, not even an Easterner. He was born in Aspen, Colorado, in November, 1892, and moved to Salt Lake City with his family when he was seven. He never completed high school. At the end of his sophomore year, he quit to take a job with the Salt Lake City *Tribune;* and as a young man of college age, he was a tramp newspaperman whose driftings took him to Sacramento, Atlanta, Panama City, New Orleans, and San Francisco. His biographer has described him as a "happy-go-lucky, poker-playing, hard-swearing" reporter, competent but not outstanding.[18] His newspaper associates in San Francisco nicknamed him "Rough House."

In 1917 Ross enlisted in the railway engineers' corps, was among the first American troops to arrive in France, and went to an officers' training camp there. But when he learned that a newspaper for enlisted men was to be published in Paris, he went absent

---

[17] Russell Maloney, "A Profile of the *New Yorker*," *Saturday Review of Literature,* 30 (Aug. 30, 1947) 8.
[18] Dale Kramer, *Ross and the New Yorker* (Garden City, N.Y., 1951), p. 9.

without leave to get a job on it. He became editor of that newspaper, *Stars and Stripes*, after leading a revolt which deposed the officer in charge of publication. The journalists with whom he worked on the paper and spent his off-duty hours at a restaurant in Montmartre included Alexander Woollcott, Franklin P. Adams, John Winterich, and Grantland Rice.

After the war, Ross edited *Home Sector*, a short-lived veterans' magazine staffed by former *Stars and Stripes* men, which tried unsuccessfully to capitalize on the wartime popularity of *Stars and Stripes* among the troops. From *Home Sector* he went to the editorship of the official publication of the *American Legion,* which he left for a brief term as editor of *Judge*. Meanwhile he was planning a magazine of his own. Meanwhile, too, he was admitted into the select circle of wits who lunched at the famous Round Table in the Algonquin Hotel—Dorothy Parker, Robert Benchley, Marc Connelly, Franklin P. Adams, Edna Ferber, and a few others— and played poker with some of them on Saturday nights.

At one of the poker games Ross met Raoul Fleischmann, whose family had made a fortune from a bakery and yeast business. Fleischmann agreed to help finance Ross's projected magazine, a weekly of high quality humor and satire. The idea for the magazine seems to have grown out of Ross's experiences on *Stars and Stripes* and *Judge,* tempered by his association with the Round Table sophisticates. Just as *Stars and Stripes* had been written by enlisted men for enlisted men and had shown no respect for officialdom, so the new magazine would be written by the urbane for the urbane and would make no concessions to a mass audience. The humor in *Judge* was broad and obvious because the magazine was addressed to a large audience, and it was often stale because of the big spread between deadline and publication date. By seeking a New York audience, the new magazine could be produced fast enough to preserve the freshness of its humor and commentary; more than that, it could publish what Ross thought was the most successful type of humor, humor with a local flavor like that in Franklin P. Adams' newspaper column.

Ross put his ideas for his magazine into a prospectus which, as it turned out, was a good description of the *New Yorker* during the twenty-six years of his editorship:

The *New Yorker* will be a reflection in word and picture of metropolitan life. It will be human. Its general tenor will be one of gaiety, wit and satire, but it will be more than a jester. It will not be what is commonly called radical or highbrow. It will be what is commonly called sophisticated, in that it will assume a reasonable degree of enlightenment on the part of its readers. It will hate bunk.

As compared to the newspaper, the *New Yorker* will be interpretive rather than stenographic. It will print facts that it will have to go behind the scenes to get, but it will not deal in scandal for the sake of scandal nor sensation for the sake of sensation. Its integrity will be above suspicion. It hopes to be so entertaining and informative as to be a necessity for the person who knows his way about or wants to.

. . . .

The *New Yorker* will be the magazine which is not edited for the old lady in Dubuque. It will not be concerned in what she is thinking about. This is not meant in disrespect, but the *New Yorker* is a magazine avowedly published for a metropolitan audience and thereby will escape an influence which hampers most national publications. It expects a considerable national circulation, but this will come from persons who have a metropolitan interest.

Since Ross's interests were primarily editorial, his biographers have disagreed over whether or not he foresaw the commercial possibilities of his metropolitan magazine. There was no good reason that he should have overlooked them. In retrospect, the idea was simple enough: through a local magazine, an advertiser could reach a sizable number of well-to-do consumers in the New York area with far less expense and waste circulation than he could through metropolitan newspapers or through national magazines. After readers outside of the city came to far outnumber those in New York, the magazine offered advertisers a screened circulation; and even then, advertisers could still buy space in only a special New York edition until 1960, when it was discontinued as anachronistic. Simple as the idea seemed, it failed when publishers tried it in other large cities in imitation of the *New Yorker*, as a later chapter will show.

The idea almost failed for Ross at first. He set to work translating his prospectus into the words and drawings of a first issue, and to help him he had a staff consisting only of Philip Wylie, Tyler Bliss, an advertising salesman, two secretaries, and a telephone switchboard operator. The first issue appeared on February 19, 1925. By general agreement, it was terrible. Ross knew little about New York, lacked the sort of material he wanted to publish, and did not have the ability to write it himself. He hoped for an eventual circulation of 50,000 to 70,000. His first issue sold 15,000 copies, his third 12,000, his fourth 10,500. Circulation had dropped to 8,000 by April, and the magazine was losing $8,000 a week. In May, Fleischmann, who was covering the losses, held a conference on the fate of the magazine. He decided to kill it. But as he walked away from the meeting, he overheard an associate remark that "it is like killing a living thing." He was so bothered by the idea that he told Ross he would keep the magazine going a little longer while he sought new capital.

Ross had originally estimated that the *New Yorker* could be started on $50,000. He had contributed $20,000 and had drawn only a third of his salary; Fleischmann had furnished $25,000. Their first issues, scanty of advertising as well as of circulation, rapidly depleted their initial capital. Its backers invested $225,000 in the *New Yorker* during its first year of publication, and Fleischmann provided all but $35,000 of it. A total of $710,000—$550,000 from Fleischmann alone—went into the *New Yorker* before it began paying its own way in 1928. Thereafter it made a profit every year.

When Fleischmann gave the *New Yorker* its reprieve, Ross, aware that his Round Table friends could not fill the magazine in their leisure time, began building up a staff which, as it enlarged, included Ralph Ingersoll, who later went to Time Inc. and then on to the newspaper *PM;* Morris Markey, whom Ross lured away from *Collier's;* Joseph Moncure March; Lois Long; and Corey Ford, a frequent contributor to *Vanity Fair.* Getting the sort of staff he wanted was a frantic business; Ross is said to have fired about a hundred staff members in the first year and a half of the magazine's existence. The week after the first issue appeared, Fleischmann had sought assistance from John Hanrahan, a publishers' consultant and "magazine doctor," who offered to help manage the *New Yorker* in exchange for stock in the company. Hanrahan has been credited with recruiting personnel for all departments other than editorial and with having a strong hand in a series of advertisements which promoted the *New Yorker* among advertising men in the fall of 1925.

At that time there were signs that the *New Yorker* would survive. Legend credits a series of articles by Ellin Mackay, a young society woman, with establishing the success of the magazine. Miss Mackay was the rebellious daughter of Clarence H. Mackay, president of Postal Telegraph, and she had decided to become a writer.

She sent the *New Yorker* a manuscript written in longhand and impressively bound in leather. Ross had staff members rewrite the article, then ran it under the title "Why We Go to Cabarets," with the subtitle "A Post-Debutante Explains." Miss Mackay's explanation was that society girls frequented cabarets to escape the stag lines of society affairs. Newspapers reprinted parts of the article because it was somewhat iconoclastic and because its author was a member of high society, and the result was a good deal of publicity for the *New Yorker*. Miss Mackay wrote additional articles for the magazine before she caused another stir by marrying Irving Berlin, the song writer, against her father's wishes. Her articles supposedly brought the *New Yorker* to the attention of the Park Avenue set. Whether they did or not, the *New Yorker* ended 1925 with a rising circulation and a growing number of advertising contracts.

In its early years the *New Yorker* acquired some of the staff members whose names were associated with it at midcentury. E. B. White, a graduate of Cornell who had served unhappily in an advertising agency, joined the staff in 1926. James Thurber, a native of Columbus, Ohio, was hired away from a newspaper in 1927 and thereafter brightened the pages of the *New Yorker* with prose and sketches. By ruthless hiring and firing, Ross found the other editors, writers, and artists he wanted: Katherine Angell, who married E. B. White in 1929, Alva Johnston, Wolcott Gibbs, John O'Hara, S. J. Perelman, Ogden Nash, Helen Hokinson, O. Soglow, Peter Arno.

It was a staff whose escapades provided an unending succession of anecdotes about the *New Yorker*. Ross, intrigued by the weekly editorial teas of *Punch*, established a private speakeasy to create a bond between the *New Yorker* and its contributors. One morning the employee who opened it discovered two contributors of opposite sexes stretched out in a stupor, and Ross permanently closed down the establishment. Another day Ross was acquainting a new managing editor with office routine. "I am surrounded by idiots and children!" he complained. Just then a copy boy rushed in shouting, "Mr. Thurber is standing on a ledge outside the window threatening to commit suicide." Ross turned to the new editor. "See?" A man in the financial district once submitted an essay by Stephen Leacock as his own contribution. The *New Yorker* published it without recognizing it as Leacock's. Ross and Wolcott

Gibbs soon learned of the plagiarism, but they took no legal action against the offender. Instead they requested that he write a financial letter each week. They returned each contribution with a note saying that the article was not quite what they wanted but that he was getting close.

Working for the *New Yorker* as editor or staff writer, Russell Maloney concluded after eleven years of it, was "physically debilitating, mentally exhausting, and a form of social suicide." It was not just the escapades which made it so; it was Ross's insistence upon perfection. For Ross, perfection was "not a goal or an ideal, but something that belongs to him, like his watch or his hat." [19]

Ross's mania for perfection was exemplified in the Profile, a term registered by the *New Yorker* to designate its probing biographical studies. The Profiles developed from casual sketches of Manhattan personalities into detailed dissections of character and motives. Their development, Wolcott Gibbs once observed, was "the story of Ross' ferocious curiosity about people—struggling against the mechanical limitations of a fifteen-cent magazine and the lethargy of authors generally. . . ." [20] The Profile became a distinctive form of biography. Clifton Fadiman suggested that the Profile was perhaps no less specific a form of composition than the familiar essay, the sonnet, or the one-act play.[21]

Profiles in the early years were, as the term literally suggests, offhand impressions of the subject which an author could report and write in a few days. As Ross sought perfection, the Profile became increasingly long and complex. By the end of World War II, a reporter sometimes devoted five months to preparing one—three months to collecting his facts, a month to writing his article, and another month to revising it for publication. Ross was no longer content with mere outlines of character; he demanded "a family history, bank references, urinalysis, catalogue of household possessions, names of all living relatives, business connections, political affiliations." [22]

The Profiles, without doubt, helped to improve the quality of magazine biography generally and demonstrated that a person need

[19] Maloney, p. 29.

[20] Quoted in John Drewry, "A Study of *New Yorker* Profiles of Famous Journalists," *Journalism Quarterly*, 23 (Dec., 1946) 372.

[21] Clifton Fadiman, "Introduction," *Profiles from the New Yorker* (New York, 1938), p. vi.

[22] Maloney, p. 30.

be neither successful nor significant to be worthy of treatment. Before the *New Yorker*, magazines had run biographies of successful businessmen, the lives of historical figures, sentimental sketches of lovable characters; but the *New Yorker* gave attention to persons who, in Clifton Fadiman's words, had "made a success, not of their bank-balances, but of their personalities." [23] Subjects of the Profiles were sometimes eminent citizens, sometimes raffish characters from New York's byways, sometimes persons of accomplishment, sometimes persons of doubtful integrity; but all of them, as Fadiman noted, had one common quality: their personalities were literally outstanding. Reporters conveyed not just a surface impression but explored deep into their characters in a manner of which Plutarch would have approved.

Because of Ross's obsession for completeness, accuracy, and lucidity, the *New Yorker* established a checking system comparable perhaps only to the research department of Time Inc. Checkers examined and re-examined every fact that went into the magazine. Writing that satisfied Ross could not be done hastily. In the mid-twenties, Fillmore Hyde could write the entire 3,000 words of the "Talk of the Town" department in a single afternoon; in 1947 four reporters devoted their entire working week to it.

To what seemed the perpetual astonishment of its executives, the *New Yorker* prospered handsomely. A share of its stock valued at about $30 in 1925 was worth $1,440 in 1960. The magazine had to ration advertising because it attracted so much. Its profit record was one of the best in the industry. Its income of $2,028,186 on gross revenues of $19,843,337 in 1962 came to 10.2 per cent as compared with an average of less than 2 per cent for many other major publishers. With virtually no bargain offers, it kept its circulation growing at a faster rate than the population after 1950.

Inevitably perhaps, the *New Yorker* became a regular target for critics as it grew old and wealthy. On the ninth anniversary of Ross's death, *Time* took a page to complain that the magazine was not what it once had been. No brilliant writers had replaced its original crew, who had died, retired, or become infrequent contributors, *Time* said, and its editorial formula of the twenties and thirties sat ill with the sixties. Its shapeless, plotless fiction was pedestrian, its cartoons trite.[24] A reviewer noted that the signifi-

---

[23] Fadiman, p. vi.
[24] *Time*, 75 (May 16, 1960) 73-74.

cant young writers, almost without exception, rarely appeared in it. Its Profiles had deteriorated, and although the other nonfiction was of high quality, one read it out of a nagging sense of duty instead out of any provocation to thought.[25] When James Baldwin contributed an angry essay on the degradation of the Negro, another reviewer remarked on the irony of its appearing amidst advertisements for $1,300 chinchilla furs and $18,500 diamond clips and bracelets.[26] Even James Thurber had his say. He worried, he said, about the increase in size, wealth, and "matronly girth": "We have got into a thing that Ross dreaded all his life—the magazine is turning grim and long."[27]

Such complaints had some validity, but it was easy to exaggerate their basis. Executives of the *New Yorker*, wearing their success with an air of pleasant disbelief mingled with constant apprehension, did seem uneasy about changing an extremely profitable pattern. Indeed, after World War II, the magazine was probably more notable for innovations in advertising than in editorial matter. Editorial copy did trickle in slender streams between mountains of advertising, as critics charged, and flowed on at sometimes inordinate length. The magazine did show signs of greater preoccupation with remote regions of Asia and obscure English villages than with the New York scene.

On the other hand, William Shawn followed an editor who had become almost an institution, and any comparison of his magazine with Ross's was bound to be tinged with nostalgia. Some of the developments that critics complained of, in fact, had begun while Ross was still editor. By any standard, the *New Yorker* was still an excellent, provocative magazine in the fifties and sixties. It first carried Rachel Carson's warning about the dangers of pesticides, which in 1962 touched off a national debate and a governmental investigation, for instance, and Hannah Arendt's significant series on the Eichmann trial, which engaged intellectuals in controversy in 1963.

Certainly over the years the *New Yorker* influenced American journalism all out of proportion to its relatively small circulation, about 468,000 in 1963. Perhaps no other magazine in a similar pe-

---

[25] Peter Salmon, "The *New Yorker's* Golden Age," *New Republic,* 140 (June 29, 1959) 19-20.

[26] John Seelye, "Black on White," *New Republic,* 147 (Dec. 29, 1962) 21-23.

[27] Henry Brandon, "'Everybody is Getting Very Serious,'" *New Republic,* 138 (May 26, 1958) 15-16.

riod published as many articles, stories, cartoons, and verses that later appeared in book form. Any listing of such books—and each year brought a fresh dozen or so—would be purely arbitrary; but among them were Clarence Day's *Life with Father,* James Thurber's *My Life and Hard Times,* Sally Benson's *Junior Miss,* Ruth McKenney's *My Sister Eileen,* John O'Hara's *Pal Joey,* John Hersey's *Hiroshima,* to which the magazine unprecedentedly devoted an entire issue in 1946, John Updike's *Pigeon Feathers,* Rachel Carson's *Silent Spring,* and Alan Moorehead's *The Blue Nile.* At one time in 1941 four comedies based on *New Yorker* pieces were simultaneously hits on Broadway: *Mr. and Mrs. North, Pal Joey, Life with Father,* and *My Sister Eileen.*

Although the *New Yorker* was not a "funny" magazine, it raised the level of American humor. It showed that humor could take other forms than the traditional "he-she" jokes. Ross's prejudice against that sort of humor was so strong that he published one joke, its lines transposed, in each anniversary issue:

Pop: A man who thinks he can make it in par.

Johnny: What is an optimist, pop?

The *New Yorker* helped to popularize the cartoon with caption intimately related to picture. Cartoons in *Judge* and the old *Life* were merely appendages to two-line jokes which could have stood without illustration. Ross developed the one-line caption, made pointed by rewriting, and he insisted that readers know at a glance which character in the picture was speaking.

In less apparent fashion, the conscientious reporting by Rebecca West, Alva Johnston, Joseph Mitchell, Richard Rovere, St. Clair McKelway, Lillian Ross, A. J. Liebling, Daniel Lang, E. J. Kahn, Jr., and others surely affected the standards of American journalism. Richard Watts, Jr., succinctly expressed the essence of the *New Yorker's* reportage:

It doesn't encourage the stuffed shirts and it has a warm place in its heart for the more amiable misfits; it certainly isn't radical, but it can give the reactionaries an expert dressing down; it is often annoyingly supercilious, but it likewise can be perceptive and understanding. Best of all, it not only has a frequent kind of frank honesty which the newspapers too often lack, but it is so professionally skillful that it impresses the journalistic journeymen it tends to despise and serves as a good example for them. I suspect it of being the most forceful influence in American newspaper writing today.[28]

[28] Richard Watts, Jr., "Reporters at Large," *New Republic,* 117 (Aug. 25, 1947) 28.

Another missionary who influenced American journalism, although not in the same sense that Ross did, established Macfadden Publications, Inc. The company had its origins in a magazine published before the century opened, but the firm did not flourish until after World War I, a few years before Wallace, Luce, and other missionaries started their publications. Its founder was Bernarr Macfadden, a curious combination of missionary and merchant—a zealot who contended that man could live to the age of 125 if he followed the Macfadden doctrines of healthful living, which he ardently practiced and tempestuously publicized; a merchant of magazines and newspapers who had a rare genius for discerning latent mass tastes and satisfying them with superficialities, sex, and sensation.

To propagate his principles of healthful living, Macfadden established the Bernarr Macfadden Foundation, Inc., with a grant of $5,000,000. Its properties, which he directed as unsalaried president, in 1950 included a physical culture hotel, a sanitarium, several summer camps, a military academy, and other holdings. In 1931 he opened five Penny Restaurants in New York, Washington, and Chicago at which diners could buy complete health-giving dinners for a dime and individual dishes for a penny.

As a merchant of magazines and newspapers, Macfadden originated the confession magazine and true detective magazine; he poured upon newsstands a stream of periodicals bearing such titles as *True Story, True Romances, True Experiences, True Ghost Stories, True Proposals, True Strange Stories, Dream World, Brain Power, Muscle Builder, Modern Marriage, Radio Stories, True Lovers, Dance, Movie Weekly,* and *Midnight,* several of which reformers and critics charged with prurience and literary incompetence; and he gave New York its most blatantly sensational tabloid newspaper in an era of blatant sensationalism, the *Graphic,* which New Yorkers nicknamed "the Pornographic."

With some justification, one could categorize Bernarr Macfadden the publisher as merchant rather than as missionary. Yet Macfadden himself saw no cleavage between his roles of crusader and publisher. "My publications, my sanitariums, all my plans and projects have been directed toward one purpose," he told lecture audiences, "to bring health and joy through exercise, diet and the simple life." [29] He used his publications as vehicles for his views

[29] Robert Lewis Taylor, "Physical Culture: I," *New Yorker,* 26 (Oct. 14, 1950) 46.

on health, and he used their profits to advance his cause. Minority stockholders instituted suits in 1940 to recover funds that Macfadden, as president and chairman of the board, had allegedly spent on the Bernarr Macfadden Foundation and on other activities not directly related to the company. As a result, Macfadden withdrew from the company the following year, and a group of employees took control of it. At the time friends said Macfadden had regarded his publishing business and other activities so closely interrelated that he thought funds from one might justifiably be spent on the other.

Macfadden listed his occupation in *Who's Who* as "physical culturist," not as publisher; but he used his publications as organs for carrying his convictions to the large audience they attracted. And his audience was vast; the total circulation of his magazines in 1935 was 7,355,000, greater than the total magazine circulation of Crowell, Curtis, or Hearst. Macfadden urged his system of healthful living on his readers in articles and editorials which he turned out prolifically. He was interested in his readers' politics as well as in their physiques. He bought *Liberty* in 1931 and publicized Franklin D. Roosevelt as a Presidential candidate by running seventeen articles about him within a year. (Later he himself aspired to the Presidency.) In 1932 he launched a short-lived magazine for young parents, *Babies: Just Babies*, with Mrs. Eleanor Roosevelt and her daughter as editors. His choice of editors, according to Mary Macfadden, who was then his wife, was governed by his hope that Mrs. Roosevelt would use her influence to help him achieve a long-held ambition, the creation of a Secretary of Health in the Cabinet.[30] Even in his sensational tabloid, the *Graphic*, he advocated his principles of physical culture, which dictated matters of basic policy.

Bernarr Macfadden was born of impoverished parents on a run-down farm near Mill Spring, Missouri, in 1868. He was a scrawny child, given to fits of coughing and to running high temperatures. His childhood was one of toil, he recalled in 1950, and he seldom had enough to eat. His sisters were sent off to live with neighbors or relatives. He was packed off to a small boarding school as miserable as anything in Dickens, and then, after a period of heavy

---

[30] Mary Macfadden and Emile Gauvreau, *Dumbbells and Carrot Strips* (New York, 1953), pp. 299-300.

work at home on the farm, was sent away to Illinois to help out at a hotel run by relatives of his mother. For some time he worked long hours carrying luggage, emptying slops, blackening shoes. Then his relatives bound him out as a laborer to a farmer in the vicinity. His work was heavy, his hours long, his employer niggardly and unsympathetic; but Macfadden grew in strength on the farm. He ran away when he was twelve.

Macfadden became fascinated by a gymnasium in St. Louis, where he was working while still a boy. He was too poor to patronize it, but it inspired him to buy a set of dumbbells and exercise in his room. From then on Macfadden dedicated his life to health. In later years he gloried in exhibiting his physical prowess by dictating while standing on his head; by walking barefoot from his home to office, sometimes toting a forty-pound bag of sand; by parachuting from an airplane to celebrate his eighty-first, eighty-third, and eighty-fourth birthdays.

The Macfadden publishing company grew from a small magazine which Macfadden brought out in March, 1899. Its slogan was "Weakness Is a Crime: Don't Be a Criminal," and its cover bore photographs of "Prof. B. Macfadden in Classical Poses." Macfadden had conceived the magazine a few months earlier while he was touring England demonstrating his physique and lecturing on physical culture. He had hawked a four-page booklet on health, and so many customers had asked if it were a periodical that he had concluded that a magazine about physical fitness had commercial possibilities.

Physical Culture, the magazine, which Macfadden wrote entirely by himself at first, took the line that exercise and diet could cure any illness. It fought such "terrible evils" as prudery, corsets, muscular inactivity, gluttony, drugs, alcohol, and tobacco. Reformers and crusaders against vice assailed the magazine, and the medical profession from time to time denounced it as a pernicious influence. *Hygeia,* a popular magazine published by the American Medical Association, in its issue of November, 1924, for instance, declared that *Physical Culture* was "an outstanding example of the money that is to be made from catering to ignorance" and called it a magazine "devoted to fantastic and bizarre fads."

Physical Culture sold well despite such attacks, perhaps because of them, for they called attention to the magazine. Three years after the magazine first appeared, Macfadden reported a circulation of 150,000, which had grown by only about a thousand in 1919 when Macfadden struck riches by bringing out *True Story*.

Of all the publications which Macfadden owned, *Physical Culture* seems to have been the closest to his heart. It remained true to his principles of health as long as he owned it, although it underwent several metamorphoses; and it was the one magazine which he repurchased after he parted with the company he had formed.

The editorial approach and even the name of *Physical Culture* were changed several times in its history. In the early twenties, the magazine concentrated on stories telling how famous persons kept fit. It enlarged its appeal in the late twenties by adding fiction and departments on homemaking, foods, and beauty. In the early thirties, it aped the general monthlies and ran fiction by popular authors like Warwick Deeping and Harold Bell Wright, although it still clung to its original mission of health. The title was changed to *Beauty and Health* in 1941, after Macfadden had left the company, and the publication was transformed into a women's magazine which forsook its traditional hostility to medical science. The company suspended the magazine shortly thereafter because of the war. Macfadden soon bought it back and reissued it in pocket size in 1943 as *Physical Culture*. In 1950 he changed its name to *Bernarr Macfadden's Health Review*, its policy to "Not Merely Muscles, but Health." Trade directories in 1963 still listed the magazine as being published under the title of *Physical Culture Reports*, with Felix May as editor and publisher.

In 1919 Macfadden fathered *True Story*, first of the confession magazines, as related in a subsequent chapter; and as it brought money pouring into the company, he tried out one new magazine after another. Macfadden was publishing ten magazines and ten newspapers at his peak in about 1930, and his fortune was estimated at roughly $30,000,000. He made big use of the melodrama on which *True Story* was based in most of his magazines, which were directed, as company officials said, at wage earners, not at the salaried class.

Although it had been highly profitable, Macfadden Publications, Inc., began running in the red in 1938 when it showed a deficit of some $200,000. Its losses were reported as $518,775 in 1940. That same year stockholders filed suits against Bernarr Macfadden; and the following year, under an agreement approved by the court, he retired from management and was succeeded as president by O. J. Elder, an associate since 1903. When Elder took over, current assets were about $2,800,000, liabilities $2,350,000, and working capital $450,000. In 1944 he rearranged the capital stock of the company. After 1943 the company ceased to run at a loss, although its net income fluctuated during the forties and fifties.

The company came under new management in early 1951. Irving S. Manheimer, who had made a fortune exporting old magazines abroad and who had formed the Publishers Distributing Corporation in 1939, had been quietly buying up Macfadden stock for the previous year and a half; and in February, 1951, along with three other stockholders, he emerged with working control of the company. Elder resigned as president. Manheimer dismissed 170 employees, instituted a number of economies, and reviewed the policies and potentialities of the various Macfadden magazines.

A decade later Manheimer and a management group sold a controlling interest in the company to the Bartell Broadcasting Corporation for $1,500,000. Seven Macfadden stockholders took legal action to prevent the merger, but the court approved a settlement in December, 1962, and the corporate name was changed to Macfadden-Bartell Corporation.

The company and its subsidiaries in 1963 owned a sizable communications empire. The organization published fourteen magazines, which earned more than $5,000,000 a year: *Climax, Master Detective, Motion Picture, Pageant, Photoplay, Saga, Sport, True Confessions, True Detective, True Experience, True Love, True Romance, True Story,* and *TV-Radio Mirror.* Its other properties, which brought in another $17,000,000 a year, included a line of paperback books published under the names of Macfadden and Hillman, an agency for distributing its own paperback books and magazines as well as those of other publishers in the United States and abroad, three radio stations, an interest in a television station in Curacao, and an interest in the Teleglobe Pay-TV System.

When Bernarr Macfadden left the company, he agreed not to enter into direct competition with its magazines for five years. He began publishing *Physical Culture* in 1943, as noted; and in 1946, at the end of the stipulated period, he was full of plans for magazines which would form a new publishing company in which his two sons would be associates—a detective magazine, a love story magazine, a radio magazine. His new magazine empire failed to blossom. So did a vast chain of hotels which he had intended to forge when he bought the Arrowhead Springs Hotel in California in 1950. But almost until his death, Macfadden was as active as ever. At the age of eighty, he remarried, only to become estranged from his wife a few years later, and at eighty-two he was taking singing lessons. He died in October, 1955, at eighty-seven.

In seeking reasons for the success of those four publishing companies, one might look for common denominators in their histories. First, the magazines which led to the formation of those four companies were all designed for markets that had been previously overlooked or inadequately served. *Reader's Digest* and *Time* were established on the assumption that the busy and thoughtful reader of the fast-paced twenties would appreciate a magazine which condensed and simplified for him the ever mounting mass of printed communications. The *New Yorker* was established on the assumption that a small group of discriminating people would appreciate a magazine written by persons of their own kind and that advertisers would welcome an economical means of reaching such a market. *True Story* pioneered among persons who probably had seldom read magazines before. Advertisers were not especially interested in reaching them, as their purchasing power was low, and publishers largely ignored them.

Second, those magazines strongly reflected the personalities of their publishers. The *Reader's Digest* clearly mirrored the personality of DeWitt Wallace, who once remarked, "I simply hunt for things that interest me, and if they do, I print them." [31] Even after Time Inc. had grown into a large company, its publications bore the stamp of Henry Luce, who expected his employees to agree with him on fundamentals, for, as he said in a speech in February, 1953: "When basic differences of conviction are made clear, the men who wish to be both honorable and free will part company. We are called to be the servants of truth: Let us serve it together when we can, and separately when we must." The *New Yorker* showed the hand of Harold Ross, who worked over almost every word that went into it. The touch of Bernarr Macfadden was evident in all his magazines.

Third, those magazines, except perhaps the *Reader's Digest*, changed constantly as conditions and reading tastes changed.

[31] *Time*, 58 (Dec. 10, 1951) 64.

James Linen, a key official of *Time,* remarked in 1953, "*Time* to-day is completely different from *Time* in the forties. That *Time* was totally different from *Time* in the thirties. And so on back." Ernest Havemann, a writer for *Life,* said, "There is no such thing as a *Life* magazine. There have been eight or nine of them." [32] So it was with *Physical Culture, True Story,* and to a lesser extent, the *New Yorker.*

Fourth, most of these enterprises were characterized by good business management. If the founders themselves were not especially interested in the business side of publishing, they became associated with men who were.

Finally, promotional activities played roles of varying importance in the rapid growth of the companies. The *New Yorker* first won acceptance after a series of newspaper advertisements, for instance, and was promoted consistently if somewhat quietly thereafter. The promotional activities of Time Inc. were extensive, and the company turned even misfortune into prestige advertising—the $5,000,000 that it lost when the circulation of *Life* outran advertising rates. The exploits of Bernarr Macfadden constantly kept his periodicals before the public.

Apart from those common denominators, those companies no doubt benefited from conditions beneficial to the magazine industry as a whole. One was the emergence of advertising as a major tool of business. The *New Yorker, Reader's Digest,* and *Time* were all founded within a few years of one another in the twenties when expenditures on advertising in magazines were more than triple what they had been before America entered World War I. Another was the upsurge in education. The appearance of *Time* and the *New Yorker* coincided with the enlarged college enrollments after World War I, and the *Reader's Digest* and *Life* no doubt drew much of their audience from the increasing number of high school graduates. Finally, success probably bred success for each of those companies. As a publication began to succeed, advertisers and readers were attracted to it and its success increased.

---

[32] "Life with Time," *Forbes,* 72 (Aug. 15, 1953) 15.

10 | New Leaders: The Merchants

Advertisers were canceling their schedules in even magazines addressed to affluent readers during the depression, and the advertising manager of *House and Garden* cast about for a publication that would be truly depression-proof. For several years, Wells Drorbaugh had been intrigued by the principle of publishing for a selective market. What he hoped to hit upon was a magazine for his conception of "primary prospects"—people already on the verge of buying the products of certain advertisers.

He got his idea from an article in *Fortune*, "Budget for a Bride," which said that more than a million American women had become married in 1932, a bleak depression year. On the back of an envelope, Drorbaugh jotted down a few points justifying a new magazine: in good times and bad, women were getting married and in sufficient numbers to constitute a volume market. Since they were without many possessions, they were buying everything new and spending more money than at any other single occasion in their lives. They needed help from a service magazine, but none existed.

The idea seemed almost too simple. For a year, Drorbaugh tried to find fault with it. When he did decide to publish the magazine for brides, he ran into a major problem—how to get copies into the hands of women immediately after they had become engaged. At first his plan was to scout out newly engaged women through announcements on the society pages of newspapers and to mail them free copies. In time, after the magazine became known, he eliminated free distribution and sold it on newsstands and by subscription.

The first issue of his *Bride's Magazine* went to press in September, 1934, with only New York, New Jersey, and Connecticut as its market. The magazine reached out for a national distribution five years later. It was still being published in the early sixties, when advertisers were spending more than $2,000,000 a year to reach its 220,000 readers.

Like Drorbaugh, perhaps most publishers who founded magazines in the twentieth century were essentially merchants. Unlike the missionaries of the preceding chapter, they championed no causes, secular or religious. For them, magazine publishing was a business, no more, and their primary aim was profit, a legitimate goal.

They pursued their goal with different degrees of commercialism and with different degrees of social responsibility. Some of them published magazines of high quality; others published almost anything which turned a quick profit.

They sought their profit by different methods. Some of them, like Condé Nast and David Smart, looked for it in the advertising that could be attracted by sleekly elegant magazines addressed to a relatively small number of luxury-loving readers. Others, like Gardner Cowles, Jr., sought it in the volume of advertising that could be captured by magazines for a mass audience. Still others, like the Fawcetts and George T. Delacorte, Jr., hoped for profit from magazines that were edited at a low level of sophistication and that depended on circulation almost as much as on advertising for their revenues.

Some of the merchants developed only a few magazines and built them into stable properties. Others were among the most prolific of publishers. They brought out one new magazine after another, watched every fluctuation in sales on the newsstands, promoted the magazines which showed promise of success, and abruptly killed the ones which did not.

Some of the merchants were blessed with originality, but many of them—probably most—were not. Since their primary ambition was profit, they preferred the tried to the untried; they were in-

clined to be highly imitative, to copy the successful innovations of
the missionaries and of one another.

In this chapter, we will study the operations of five publishing
companies which grew into prominence after World War I: Condé
Nast Publications, Inc.; Esquire, Inc.; Cowles Magazines and
Broadcasting, Inc.; Fawcett Publications, Inc.; and the Dell Publishing Company.

The companies no more resembled one another than those of
the missionaries in the preceding chapter, yet all of them seem to
have had one common characteristic: they were guided by men
who were merchants.

One must set Condé Nast apart from the other merchant publishers. Through his magazines, he coached Americans in high
fashion and gracious living for more than thirty years before he
died in his twenty-room penthouse on Park Avenue in September,
1942. His magazines, *Vogue, Vanity Fair,* and *House and Garden,*
went out to a relatively few discriminating readers, in contrast to
the confession and movie magazines with which some merchants
sought their fortunes among a mass audience. In his private life,
he lived in a world far from the balance sheets of business. A
worldly wise esthete, he moved in a circle of royalty, statesmen,
socialites, and artists. A courtly host, he entertained hundreds of
persons at a time at elaborate parties, dances, and dinners in his
luxurious apartment. There was something almost regal about his
gestures. He once hid gold coins, $500 in all, under the chocolates
in a box of candy he sent Edna Woolman Chase of *Vogue* as a
Christmas gift. Another time he dropped Mrs. Chase a note saying
that in appreciation of her work he had set aside $100,000 "to use
for embroidery" on the home she was building, although Mrs.
Chase collected but $25,000 before Nast's financial reverses during
the depression.

In his private life and in publishing, Condé Nast was a perfec-
tionist. He himself planned the most minute details of his apartment; he invariably asked his golf partners to call his defects to
his attention, and he once had a movie made of himself so he
could analyze the shortcomings of his slice. He often worked a
full weekend at his office to overcome some minor problem of
layout. He spent $350,000 landscaping the grounds of his printing
plant in Connecticut. He surrounded himself with cultured editors

VOGUE

60¢
MARCH 1

Paris:
straight
talk on
the new
French
clothes

The U.S.
fashion
pulse:
dresses
with a
new pitch
for chic

BACKSTAGE NOTES AT
TWO FAMOUS
AMERICAN COLLECTIONS

who could endow his publications with smartness and quality. He offered his readers the prose of Gertrude Stein, William Bolitho, Ferenc Molnar, and Willa Cather; the photography of Edward Steichen and Cecil Beaton; the paintings of Seurat and Modigliani.

And yet for Condé Nast, magazine publishing was frankly a business, not a crusade. As a publisher, he once remarked, he was but a name broker who attracted a selected audience with his editorial fare and sold advertisers access to it. What he and his editors did, he said, was to "bait the editorial pages in such a way as to lift out of all the millions of Americans just the hundred thousand cultivated persons who can buy these quality goods." [1]

Condé Nast was born in New York in March, 1874, and reared in St. Louis. He earned his bachelor's and master's degrees at Georgetown University and a law degree at Washington University. He had been a classmate of Robert J. Collier at Georgetown; in 1901, while he was still trying to decide whether or not to practice law, Collier gave him a job at $12 a week as advertising manager of *Collier's,* then a skimpy weekly with a circulation of 170,000. Under Nast, who had a flair for promotion, advertising income shot from $5,500 a year to $1,000,000 a year in less than a decade. Nast was business manager of *Collier's* at a salary of $40,000 a year in 1907 when he quit to go into business for himself.

While still at *Collier's,* as a personal venture, he organized the Home Pattern Company to manufacture and sell dress patterns under an arrangement with the *Ladies' Home Journal.* The company was soon successful, but it was not Nast's idea of the way to make a fortune.

He became a magazine publisher in 1909 when he bought *Vogue,* a weekly of 22,500 circulation, and *House and Garden,* a publication devoted to architecture, decoration, and horticulture. *Vogue* had begun publication in December, 1892, as a weekly magazine of fashion, society, and "the ceremonial side of life" for a small circle of socially elite New Yorkers, and its fifty-six backers included Cornelius Vanderbilt, Mrs. Stuyvesant Fish, and Mrs. William D. Sloan. Its founder was Arthur Baldwin Turnure, a socialite. The magazine was taking in some $100,000 a year in advertising when Nast bought it, but it was probably operating at a slight loss.

Nast saw in *Vogue* a chance to test his theory, developed while he was an advertising man, that money could be made from a

---

[1] *Time,* 40 (Sept. 28, 1942) 51-52.

medium which efficiently brought together the buyers and sellers of luxury goods. Most publishers of his time were after large circulations; he was after a selective one, which he described by analogy: "If you had a tray with 2,000,000 needles on it and only 150,000 of these had gold tips which you wanted, it would be an endless and costly process to weed them out. Moreover, the 1,850,000 which were not gold tipped would be of no use to you, they couldn't help you, but if you could get a magnet that would draw out only the gold ones what a saving!" [2] *Vogue* was to be such a magnet.

Nast made little change in *Vogue* in his first years of ownership apart from converting it to semimonthly publication. His idea was to retain its appeal to the wealthy and socially elite but to widen its services, to improve its physical appearance, and to improve the caliber of its content. In the thirties, he said that the basic approach of *Vogue* had changed little since 1909. "Our proportion of fashion to society material hasn't changed very much," he said. "What I did, if anything, was to get better artists and better writers." [3]

Nast inaugurated editions of *Vogue* in France and Britain. The French edition was suspended when the Germans occupied Paris during World War II, but it was revived in January, 1945. An attempt to establish an edition in Germany in the late twenties was unsuccessful. The magazine had counterparts in five countries in 1962, when the company formed a subsidiary in Milan to publish *Novita*, a similar class publication for Italian women.

The editor of *Vogue* from 1914 until 1952 was Edna Woolman Chase, an astute judge of fashion trends who had been on the staff before Nast acquired the publication. Under her direction *Vogue*, along with its major competitor, Hearst's *Harper's Bazaar*, became an arbiter of high fashion, and the appearance of Mrs. Chase at a couturier's showing of new gowns was an event of major importance. *Vogue* anticipated new fashions by learning what the designers planned to produce; it presented them in alluring photographs and sketches in a setting which bespoke opulence and cosmopolitanism. Its tone was frankly snobbish.

The world depicted by *Vogue* was a strange one to outlanders. George Orwell, the British literary critic and satirist, tried to

---

[2] Edna Woolman Chase and Ilka Chase, *Always in Vogue* (Garden City, N.Y., 1954), p. 66.
[3] Henry Pringle, "High Hat," *Scribner's,* 104 (July, 1938) 19.

describe it in 1946. "The magazine," he said,

consists of 325 large quarto pages, of which no less than 15 are given up to articles on world politics, literature, etc. The rest consists entirely of pictures, with a little letterpress creeping around their edges: pictures of ball dresses, mink coats, step-ins, panties, brassieres, silk stockings, slippers, perfumes, lipsticks, nail polish—and, of course, of the women, unrelievedly beautiful, who wear them or make use of them.

One striking thing, when one looks at these pictures, is the overbred, exhausted, even decadent style of beauty that now seems to be striven after. Nearly all of these women are immensely elongated. A thin-boned, ancient-Egyptian type of face seems to predominate: narrow hips are general, and slender, non-prehensile hands like those of a lizard are quite universal. . . .

Another striking thing is the prose style of the advertisements, an extraordinary mixture of sheer lushness with clipped and sometimes very expensive technical jargon. Words like suave-mannered, custom-finished, contour-conforming, mitt-back, innersole, backdip, midriff, swoosh, swash, curvaceous, slenderize and pet-smooth are flung about with evident full expectation that the reader will understand them at a glance. . . .[4]

Vogue continued its elegant course throughout the fifties and into the sixties. It had begun the twenties with a circulation of about 137,000 and an advertising income of $2,178,000. Its number of readers had grown to some 500,000 by 1963, when its advertising revenues were $8,466,000.

In April, 1939, Condé Nast brought out a little sister of *Vogue*, a monthly called *Glamour*, which was edited for the young woman with a job. Street & Smith had already demonstrated the potentialities of such a fashion magazine for the young woman far lower on the economic scale than the reader of *Vogue*. Four years earlier, in February, 1935, it had introduced *Mademoiselle*, edited for women aged seventeen to thirty, and had developed it into one of its most lucrative properties. Nast's *Glamour* quite obviously expected its readers to make some of their own dresses instead of commissioning them from Fath or Dior. It advised its readers on such things as fashions, beauty, careers, travel, and the arts, in a breezy, extroverted, conversational style. When Condé Nast Publications bought out Street & Smith in 1959, it combined *Glamour* and one of its acquisitions, *Charm*, a magazine for young working women. Given a boost by the merger, *Glamour* had a circulation of more than a million in the early sixties.

The editorial copy in *Vogue* and *Glamour*, like that in *Harper's*

---

[4] George Orwell, "It Looks Different from Abroad," *New Republic*, 115 (Dec. 2, 1946) 726.

Bazaar and *Mademoiselle,* was hard to find amid the advertisements; but then women probably bought them as much for their advertising as for their editorial features. And yet while it was easy to satirize their chi-chi advertising, as Orwell did, all four magazines ran material by authors of stature. The artistic level of their prose and illustration was generally high; and at least one of the four, *Mademoiselle,* was well known for the encouragement it gave to unknown young writers of promise.

Nast's *House and Garden,* like *Vogue,* was intended for the economically secure. Founded in 1901, it had a circulation of about 34,000 when Nast bought it in 1909. Richardson Wright became its editor in June, 1914. He had served as Sunday editor of the *Knickerbocker News* in Albany, as a correspondent in Siberia and Manchuria for a string of American newspapers in 1911-12, and as literary critic for the New York *Times.* He was president of the Food and Wine Society and chairman of the Horticulture Society of New York, and he wrote some two dozen books with titles as divergent as *Hawkers and Walkers of Early America* and *The Bed-Book of Eating and Drinking.*

During his thirty-five years as editor, Wright made *House and Garden* a magazine of architecture, decoration, and gardening for readers in the above-average income brackets. The magazine more than doubled its circulation in the first decade of Nast's ownership. After Wright retired in 1949—he died in 1961—his successors steered the magazine in the same general direction in which he had pointed it.

House and Garden showed large gains in advertising after World War II when home service magazines enjoyed a boom as a result of increases in home construction and home ownership. Its gross advertising revenues in 1947 were $2,396,000, a long climb from the $419,000 of 1921 and an increase of more than 37 per cent over 1946. Mounting during the fifties, they made a sharp jump of 47 per cent between 1961 and 1962 to reach $8,166,000 and to put the magazine ahead of its long-time competitor, Hearst's *House Beautiful.* Circulation by then had passed the million mark.

At least three magazines called *Vanity Fair* were published at different periods in the nineteenth century. Nast's *Vanity Fair* was a continuation of a magazine of that name established in December, 1892, to cover sports, music, and drama. Nast brought out his version in September, 1913, and for the first four issues he called it *Dress and Vanity Fair.* Dissatisfied with it, he showed a copy to his old friend Frank Crowninshield, who had a suggestion: "There is no magazine which covers the things people talk about at parties —the arts, sports, humor, and so forth." From then until *Vanity Fair* was submerged in *Vogue* in 1936, Crowninshield as editor tried to make it just such a magazine.

Crowninshield, who had worked for the *Bookman, Century,* and *Munsey's* and for a couple of years was Frank Munsey's literary agent in London, was a wit, a connoisseur of art and letters, and an exponent of gracious living. His friends were many and influential; his wide circle of acquaintances, as Nast once said, had beneficent results upon his publishing activities: "It was always, for example, easy for him to persuade Joseph H. Choate to write for us, or Irene Castle to pose for photographs, or John Sargent to permit our use of his sketches, or Aldous Huxley to work on our staff, or Joe Louis to pass an hour or two before the cameras in our studio, or persuade August Belmont and Harry Payne Whitney to cooperate in photographing their horses in their stables, or Isadora Duncan to help in a benefit dance recital, or Geraldine Farrar to do us any order of favor." [5] Crowninshield himself, in a moment of self-analysis, said, "My interest in society—at times so pronounced that the word 'snob' comes a little to mind—derives from the fact that I like an immense number of things which society, money, and position bring in their train: painting, tapestries, rare books, smart dresses, dances, gardens, country houses, correct cuisine, and pretty women." [6]

His interests were reflected in *Vanity Fair*, a chic monthly which gave attention to art, the theater, literature, to a wide span of subjects. For it Edmund Lester Pearson and Alexander Woollcott recalled classic American crimes, Corey Ford and Robert Benchley polished their little satires, and Paul Gallico and Grantland Rice reported on sports. For it Gertrude Stein, T. S. Eliot, e. e. cummings, and Elinor Wylie wrote their poems, Ferenc Molnar wrote plays, Gilbert Seldes and Robert Sherwood assessed the cinema, and Edward Steichen and Cecil Beaton took their photographs. From it, many Americans no doubt learned of Picasso, Rouault, Matisse, and Gauguin, whose works were reproduced on its pages. In a nostalgic tribute to what they called "America's most memorable magazine," Cleveland Amory and Frederic Bradlee collected

---

[5] Geoffrey T. Hellman, "That Was New York: Crowninshield," *New Yorker*, 23 (Feb. 14, 1948) 72.
[6] Hellman, p. 72.

a sampling from its pages in a book, *Vanity Fair*, published in 1960.

In 1932 Condé Nast decided that *Vanity Fair* was lacking in substance, and he hired John Franklin Carter, Jr. (who wrote on politics under the name of Jay Franklin) and Henry Pringle as part-time editorial advisers to give the magazine a serious note. Clare Boothe Luce, an editor of *Vanity Fair* at the time, has described Crowninshield's reaction to the change in policy:

'Twixt card tricks and African sculpture, Mr. Crowninshield laid glibly before the editors, for their distracted consideration, the serious articles on labor, politics, and science which Mr. Nast was then ordering from Jay Franklin, Walter Lippmann, and Matthew Woll, in the days when not only *Vanity Fair* was dying but the very world it stood for. Mr. Crowninshield, alas, was not the man to outflank the world of Mrs. Astor and Mrs. Van Rensselaer, even with the help of Matthew Woll. He was spiritually, if not intellectually, too much a part of that world.[7]

It was addressed to a narrow circle, *Vanity Fair*, and its circulation was never large. It opened the twenties with a circulation of about 99,000 and closed them with 86,000. When it vanished into *Vogue* in 1936, it had a sale of about 90,000. Nor was its advertising income large. In the early twenties *Vanity Fair* took in a half-million dollars in advertising a year, more or less, and in 1935 only $292,895. According to one report, the magazine had shown a profit in only one year of its existence.[8] The company gave declining advertising revenues as the reason for the merger of *Vanity Fair* with *Vogue*. Among its mourners were many advertisers who had never bothered to support it when it was alive.

A perennial competitor of Nast was William Randolph Hearst, who published several magazines aiming at the wealthy and fastidious readers whom Nast had chosen for his market. *Harper's Bazaar*, established in 1867 and acquired by Hearst in the early twenties, was the foremost competitor of *Vogue*, although it never overtook it in circulation or advertising. Unlike *Vogue*, the *Bazaar* ran fiction —fiction by authors such as Christopher Isherwood, Virginia Woolf, Eudora Welty, Colette, and Jean Stafford—but it was essentially a magazine of high fashion. The Hearst competitors of *House and Garden* were first *Home and Field,* then *House Beautiful.* Another Hearst publication, *Town and Country,* circulated among persons of taste and wealth, as *Vanity Fair* did.

There were skirmishes between Hearst and Nast from time to

---

[7] Hellman, p. 72.
[8] *Newsweek*, 7 (Jan. 4, 1936) 31.

time. In 1923 Nast bought a full-page advertisement in *Printers'
Ink*, the advertising trade magazine, to deny a story which ran in
several Hearst newspapers. The story said that Nast had given up
trying to start an English edition of *Vogue* and had sold it to a
British publisher, but that Hearst's *Good Housekeeping* had become
"in two short years the leading women's magazine in England,
excepting only *Nash's Magazine*, which also belongs to Mr.
Hearst."[9] In 1930 Hearst bought *Smart Set* back from James R.
Quirk, to whom he had sold it two years earlier, with the intention
of converting it into a smart competitor of *Vanity Fair*. He had
hired Arthur Samuels of the *New Yorker* as editor of the transformed magazine; the project fell through, however, and Samuels
served briefly as editor of *Harper's Bazaar*.

During the depression, just about the time he was planning to
retire, Nast lost much of his personal fortune on the stock market,
and his company suffered financial difficulties as well. Gross revenues of the company dropped from $10,251,000 in 1929 to
$5,558,000 in 1933, net income from $320,000 to a deficit of $501,000.
Lord Camrose, a British press lord, invested in the company to
help put it on its feet. Nast spent the thirties rebuilding his personal
and corporate fortunes. He was succeeded after his death in 1942
by Iva Patcévitch, his executive assistant since 1928, who continued to improve the financial health of the corporation throughout the forties. Gross revenues in the late forties were more than
$20,000,000 a year and net income well over $1,000,000. During
the fifties, net profits fell, and the firm ran at a loss for the last four
years of the decade.

In January, 1959, the company bought *Bride's Magazine* from
Wells Drorbaugh, who continued as chief executive officer of the
publication.

But that same month, Patcévitch was weighing bids for control
of his own company. In March, S. I. Newhouse, owner of a coast-
to-coast empire of newspapers and broadcasting stations, paid
$5,000,000 to Amalgamated Press Ltd. of London for enough shares
to give him near-control of Condé Nast Publications. Besides its
magazines and pattern books, the property included a large printing plant at Greenwich, Connecticut, where the company printed
its magazines and those of other publishers. Patcévitch, next to

---

[9] *Printers' Ink*, 124 (Sept. 20, 1923) 35.

Newhouse the largest stockholder, remained as publisher and president.

The following August, Condé Nast Publications bought out Street & Smith, a major competitor which had been under continuous control of the same families since its founding more than a century earlier. Although the price was not disclosed, trade reports put it at $4,000,000 in cash plus stock options. By taking over Street & Smith, officials at Condé Nast felt that they had substantially strengthened their competitive advantage in the field of women's magazines. They combined *Charm* with their *Glamour* at once, *Living for Young Homemakers* with their *House and Garden* in January, 1962. In the transaction, they also acquired *Astounding Science Fiction, Air Progress,* and *Hobbies for Young Men.*

In the early sixties, Condé Nast was earning a profit—a net of $1,010,000 in 1960, of $702,000 in 1961, and $1,476,000 in 1962. It disposed of its unprofitable pattern operations in 1961 by permitting Butterick Company to manufacture *Vogue* patterns and to publish the *Vogue Pattern Book* under a licensing agreement. Early in 1963 the Condé Nast printing plant lost $4,500,000 in contracts representing 40 per cent of its volume when the *New Yorker* and *Scientific American* transferred their printing to R. R. Donnelley and Sons, Chicago.

Although Condé Nast showed that there was a market for a fashion magazine for women of means, there was no similar magazine for men. Then in 1933, out of a trade publication for retailers of men's clothing, there emerged a magazine of fashion and entertainment for men, a glossy magazine which circulated in an upper-income market. The magazine was *Esquire;* with it as a foundation, David A. Smart and his associates built a fairly large magazine publishing company, Esquire, Inc.

David A. Smart and his brother Alfred Smart, both of whom had been in the advertising business, joined forces with William H. Weintraub in 1927 to publish a trade paper for the men's clothing industry. They hired a young advertising man named Arnold Gingrich to edit it because some copy he had written for Kuppenheimer clothing advertisements had greatly impressed David Smart. The magazine, *National Men's Wear Salesman,* did rather well, and they followed it with a succession of lavishly illustrated style guides which they syndicated to retailers of men's furnishings.

Retailers who bought the service had their names imprinted on the booklets, which had such titles as *Gentlemen's Quarterly, Club and Campus,* and the *Observer,* but which were in effect consumer house organs to promote the sale of men's clothing.

In 1930 Smart and his partners decided to expand their fashion coverage by photographing celebrities who attended opening nights at New York theaters and sending the pictures by telephoto to men's clothing stores, which could use them as window displays. They tried out the idea at the opening of Ziegfeld's *Smiles* in November, 1930. The photo service ran into opposition almost at once, but it led indirectly to one of the most spectacularly successful magazines of the decade, *Esquire.* The publisher of the leading trade paper in the men's wear field accused the Smarts and Weintraub of sending out faked photographs—pictures of models who posed long before the actual opening. Weintraub, angered by the attack, suggested that they retaliate by starting a publication in direct competition with the publisher's. But there were other reasons than retaliation for starting the magazine. The depression had hit the clothing industry, and retailers were no longer able to afford the expensive catalogs that the partners had been syndicating.

The new publication was *Apparel Arts,* a handsome quarterly for the men's clothing trade, and it was the immediate inspiration for *Esquire.* It first appeared on October 15, 1931, with Arnold Gingrich as editor. In format, paper stock, use of art work, and even somewhat in the development of its articles, it had been unashamedly influenced by *Fortune.* Retailers who could not afford to stock all of the merchandise pictured in the magazine left copies on their counters and ordered whatever their customers chose. As intended, customers picked up the copies and leafed through them, but they further demonstrated their interest by walking off with them. When the magazine was about a year old, Rogers Peet let the publishers know it was interested in an inexpensive giveaway for Christmas, a publication like the ones they had once syndicated, and wondered if they could work something out of *Apparel Arts.*

Cutting up copies of *Apparel Arts,* Gingrich and the others assembled dummies of a fashion magazine they could sell for a dime. None of their attempts satisfied them, although the projected price gradually rose to forty cents. The version they liked best would have to sell for a prohibitive fifty cents, and they named it *Trend.* But when they sent the name to a Washington patent attorney for checking, he wrote them that it had already been taken. So had their next three favorites: *Stag, Beau,* and *Trim.* One day when they were working up a list of other possibilities, they noticed the abbreviation "Esq." on the attorney's latest letter. Without much enthusiasm, they took *Esquire* as their working title. Gingrich kept it despite a last-minute attempt to change the name to *Town and Campus.*[10]

The *Esquire* that came out in October, 1933, was an oversized quarterly on glossy paper, about a third of its 116 pages in color. Experts had predicted that a fifty-cent magazine could sell no more than 25,000 copies. The publishers had printed 105,000; clothing stores had taken 100,000, and a distributor had reluctantly agreed to put the remainder on newsstands. Demand was so great that the publishers had to retrieve all but 5,000 of their copies from the clothing stores for newsstand sale. One metropolitan newsdealer, originally allocated a hundred copies, sold 2,000 in the first week. Because of demand, the magazine switched to monthly publication with its second issue, dated January, 1934.

A number of impressive names turned up under bylines in the first issue. Ernest Hemingway, John Dos Passos, William McFee, Erskine Caldwell, Manuel Komroff, Morley Callaghan, and Dashiell Hammett all had articles or stories in it, and there were sports pieces by Gene Tunney, Bobby Jones, and Benny Leonard.

By shrewd buying, Gingrich was able to land such authors at comparatively little cost. He had signed up Hemingway early in planning the first issue. Using Hemingway's name as bait to gain entree, he had offered authors payment that was immediate although small. He also had written several mass-circulation magazines to ask if they had any manuscripts by well-known writers which, on second thought, seemed too daring or too different for them to use. For a few hundred dollars he was able to get manuscripts that had cost thousands. Once the magazine was launched, he continued to publish well-known writers on a comparatively low editorial budget. For one thing, he offered prompt payment, an important incentive in the depression years. For another thing, he cared little for formula writing, and he no doubt attracted some authors for that reason.

Esquire was a magazine of literary distinction for most of its first decade. Thomas Mann wrote for it; so did D. H. Lawrence,

<hr>

[10] "Thirty Years Hath Esquire," *Esquire,* 30 (Oct., 1963) 8 ff.

Ezra Pound, Andre Maurois, Thomas Wolfe, and George Jean Nathan. Ernest Hemingway, a regular contributor, first published his "The Snows of Kilimanjaro" in it. F. Scott Fitzgerald, with rare introspection, explored the disintegration of an artist in a series of sensitive articles that Edmund Wilson later collected into book form under the title of the first article, *The Crack-Up*.

Alongside its stories, articles, and essays, *Esquire* ran scores of cartoons, many full page, many in color, most based on smoking-car humor. Probably no American magazine had ever been so laden with art work. One regular feature, the Petty girl, a creature of curves, inordinately long limbs, and gossamer clothing, became as familiar as the earlier Gibson girl.

In the forties, *Esquire* underwent revisions of content, typography, and makeup. Arnold Gingrich had gone abroad to live for several years, and editorial direction was in other hands. "From, roughly '42 to '52, or approximately the second decade, our grapes weren't tended as carefully as they had been before and have been since," he confessed in 1958. "Some of us turned our backs on the vineyard for too long a time, and thought the vines would tend themselves." [11]

When Gingrich returned to *Esquire* in 1952, he scrapped thousands of dollars worth of manuscript inventory and, aided by a young art director and a young fiction editor, set out to recapture the magazine's lost distinction. *Esquire* abandoned its youthful preoccupation with sex, a concern soon to be taken up by its youthful imitator, *Playboy*, and adopted a new seriousness of purpose. A new generation of writers contributed to it—Philip Roth, Vance Bourjaily, Anthony West, Howard Nemerov—but some of the older hands remained. Arthur Miller wrote "The Misfits" for it, and William Inge and Tennessee Williams contributed the texts of new plays. Norman Mailer covered a political convention, and Arthur Schlesinger, Jr., assessed the course of national politics. Its content fell into no easy pattern. It could carry an article about the world's worst poetess and a memoir of a type designer, but it could also carry the battle plans of the Congress on Racial Equality, prose sketches of Alger Hiss and Roy Cohn in juxtaposition, and a piece telling what had become of the Lincoln Brigade which had fought in the Spanish Civil War. A sense of social consciousness some-

[11] "Preface," *The Armchair Esquire,* Arnold Gingrich and L. Rust Hills, editors (New York, 1958), p. 19.

JANUARY

NOW ISSUED EVERY MONTH
PRICE FIFTY CENTS

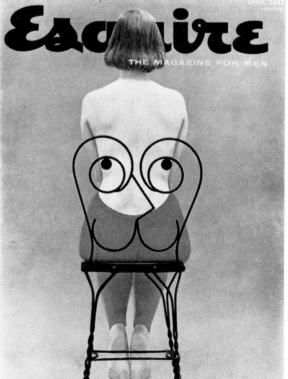

times shone through its pages. A decade after Gingrich had returned to the magazine its circulation had grown to about 884,000, its gross advertising revenues to about $7,470,000.

Arnold Gingrich once said that he had no complicated formula for *Esquire*. He had always wanted to give the reader as big a money's worth as possible, and he held to the dictum "he who edits best edits least." What he did want was a breadth of editorial pattern: "We wanted, always, to feel that the reader could never feel sure, as he turned from one page to the next and from one issue to the next, of what might be coming up." [12]

Esquire, Inc., expanded in the thirties. In 1936 it began to publish *Coronet,* which is discussed in another chapter, and it branched out into the production of instructional and training films, an aspect of the business that grew rapidly during World War II. In 1937 David Smart impulsively purchased the defunct French art magazine *Minotaur* and thus acquired the services of its French-based Greek editor, E. Teriade; Gingrich worked out the publishing arrangements and format for the succeeding art review, *Verve,* for which Teriade obtained original artwork and cover designs by Matisse, Chagall, Rouault, Braque, Gris, and Miro. Esquire-Coronet, as the company was then called, distributed the first four issues in America at $2.50 a copy, a fraction of the price they were later to command as collector's items.

For about eighteen months before the outbreak of World War II in Europe, the company experimented unprofitably with a magazine that set out hopefully to tap a reservoir of liberalism by presenting background stories of events as insiders saw them. Smart and Gingrich, in what seems to have been a spirit of contagious idealism, began laying plans for the magazine in March, 1937. Before the first half-million copies of *Ken* appeared a year later, however, commercial pressures cramped their idealism and forced them to change their plans several times.

At first during its gestation period they saw *Ken* as a magazine that Lincoln Steffens would have been at home with, a magazine that would expose intrigue and corruption, print the things that other publications did not dare to print. Politically, it was to be a rallying point for liberals and progressives, a champion of the under-privileged, and a militant foe of fascism. Many liberals of

---

[12] Arnold Gingrich, "Introduction," *The Esquire Treasury* (New York, 1953), pp. xiii-xv.

the time were worried about the threat of fascism at home—Sinclair Lewis had made it the theme of *It Can't Happen Here* two years earlier—and the foreign staffs of American newspapers were recording its sweep across Europe.

From friends Smart and Gingrich had learned of Jay Cooke Allen, a foreign correspondent for the Chicago *Tribune*, whose dispatches from Europe had impressed them. They engaged him as editor and gave him $30,000 to hire a staff and to prepare a dummy. When the money was gone, they felt they had nothing to show for it. Allen left the venture in October, and they dismissed virtually all of his staff at the same time. But the liberal mission attracted others, and Smart and Gingrich moved the magazine toward publication.

Meanwhile, however, they began to realize how woefully they had miscalculated the reaction of advertisers. In its original conception, *Ken* had little promise of attracting advertising; worse, some advertisers threatened to retaliate by pulling their business out of the profitable *Esquire*. Even in the planning stage, the magazine departed more and more from its original prospectus, according to George Seldes, who served briefly as one of its editors.[13]

When the first issue came out in March, 1938, Ken was not as far to the left as some of its staff had hoped it would be. Among the editors listed in that first issue were Paul de Kruif, George Grosz, Raymond Gram Swing, John Spivak, and George Seldes. By the fourth issue, they had been dropped from the masthead as editors; and although some remained on for a time as contributors, they gradually drifted away. Ernest Hemingway had learned the general aims of the magazine from Gingrich and had asked to be listed as an active editor; later he was disturbed by conflicting reports about it that reached him in Spain, and at his request a note in the first issue said he was not an editor, that he had taken no part in setting policies, and that he was simply a contributor. Some of the staff members who had rejoiced over the original plans complained that *Ken* found it safer to expose conditions abroad than at home and that it had become anticommunist as well as antifascist to appease business interests.[14]

Ken, in fact, was much concerned with the foreign scene, and

[13] George Seldes, " 'Ken'—The Inside Story," *Nation,* 146 (April 30, 1938) 497.
[14] Seldes, p. 499; *Time,* 31 (March 21, 1938) 54-55.

its statement of purpose said it was against dictatorships of either the left or right. Many of the men first associated with it were foreign correspondents, and foreign coverage had been a part of the plan from the beginning. Events abroad provided the material for many of *Ken's* "inside stories"—the dictatorships of Europe and South America, political maneuvering on the checkerboard of Europe, preparations for war, indeed, war itself. Hemingway wrote on the fighting in Spain, John Malone on the sack of Nanking. But the magazine looked at the domestic scene, too, with articles about the cotton economy of the South, the difficulties encountered by social workers, the plight of migratory workers in California, the dangers of water pollution, the rehabilitation of ex-convicts. Alongside the reportage there were human interest articles and occasional lapses into sensationalism, as in a picture sequence of a man dying of rabies. The magazine made rich use of photographs, many full page and in stark documentary style.

Ken sold an average of a quarter of a million copies an issue for a while, but it gradually lost the fifty pages of advertising it had started with. Its publishers changed it from semimonthly to weekly publication in April, 1939, in an effort to reach the total monthly circulation guaranteed to advertisers. Two months later they cut the price from twenty-five to ten cents. Neither method was effective, and Arnold Gingrich announced that *Ken* would cease publication with its issue of August 3, 1939. The publishers, he said, were ready "to admit that 'they had backed the wrong horse.'" [15]

Four years later the company encountered difficulties that could have meant the end of *Esquire* itself. Frank C. Walker, the Postmaster General, revoked second-class mailing privileges of *Esquire* in September, 1943, on the grounds that the magazine did not meet one of the tests of eligibility for that preferential rate. Walker said that *Esquire* was not, as the law required, "published for the dissemination of information of a public character, or devoted to literature, the sciences, arts or some special industry." Although *Esquire* could have still used the mails, the fourth-class rate would have added approximately $500,000 a year to its postal bill.

While the publishers of *Esquire* spent $40,000 to advertise their side in forty-one newspapers across the United States, their attorneys filed suit to restrain the Postmaster General's action. The United States Supreme Court in an unanimous decision restored

---

[15] *Time*, 34 (July 10, 1939) 33.

second-class privileges to *Esquire* after two years of litigation. Meanwhile the magazine had continued to use second-class with the understanding that it would repay the Post Office Department the difference between second and fourth-class rates if the Postmaster General's revocation were upheld.

In 1941 William Weintraub, one of the founders, sold out his interest in the company and left to form an advertising agency. David Smart died in 1952, a year after the death of his brother Alfred. His younger brother John then moved into the presidency and later to chairmanship of the board. The company they had founded was still operating in the black in the early sixties. Besides *Esquire*, it published the *Gentlemen's Quarterly*, a fashion magazine that grew out of *Apparel Arts* in 1957, and operated a broadcasting station in Atlanta. Other diversifications were the acquisition of the Scott Stamp Albums, a product of a century-old company specializing in philately; the Wide-Lite Corporation of Houston, Texas, a company furnishing outdoor lighting installations; and the establishment with the A. C. Nielsen Company of Neo-Data, Inc., utilizing the company's subscription fulfillment center at Boulder, Colorado. At that center Esquire, Inc., by the end of 1963 was servicing the subscription fulfillment of twenty-one magazines in addition to its own publications.

From 1950 onward Esquire, Inc., shared a building on Madison Avenue with the company that Gardner Cowles, Jr., had built on the success of *Look*. Indeed, there had been a brief era of ill feelings when Esquire, Inc., on moving in, discovered that the landlord had permitted it to be called the Look Building.

The Cowles family had been newspaper publishers in Iowa since shortly after the turn of the century. Gardner Cowles, Sr., a small-town banker and former superintendent of schools, bought the debt-ridden Des Moines *Register* in 1903 for $300,000. In time, after combining it with the *Tribune*, he made it the only daily in the city and the dominant one in the state. Two of his sons, Gardner, Jr., and John, joined him in the business, and they expanded it by branching out into Minneapolis in the thirties and making their dailies the only ones there, too.

From experiments with photographs in the *Register* and *Tribune*, the brothers had got the idea for the picture magazine that became *Look*. Their father had little faith in it, but the brothers did; and while John supervised their newspapers, Gardner, Jr., concentrated on the magazine. As a publication that condensed its predecessors, *Look*, like another Cowles magazine, *Quick*, will get a somewhat more detailed treatment in a later chapter. To begin with it was, as Gardner Cowles, Jr., saw it, chiefly a vehicle for exploiting pictures for their own sake. "During the first fifteen years of *Look*, I greatly underestimated the intelligence and taste of the American public," he admitted in 1963.[16]

Look grew rapidly, and Cowles moved its editorial and advertising offices from Des Moines to New York in 1940. It remained the sole magazine of the company until 1949. Then, just a few months apart, Cowles tried out two unconventional publications: *Quick*, a miniature weekly that squeezed reports of current happenings into capsules of no more than six sentences, and *Flair*, a monthly so elegant that five printing firms were needed to produce it. *Quick* found a mass audience, *Flair* a select one, but production costs of both far outran income. Cowles sold *Quick* after four years and killed off *Flair* after one.

In its short, luxurious existence, *Flair* achieved its objective of being "spectacularly different, completely unconventional." Its editor was Fleur Fenton Cowles, wife of Gardner Cowles, Jr.; and in her script, reproduced in gold ink on blue paper, its first issue in February, 1950, outlined its promise. Capitalizing on recent "adventures" in graphic design, *Flair* would be "a magazine which combines, for the first time under one set of covers, the best in the arts: literature, fashion, humor, decoration, travel and entertainment." What readers seemed most impressed with, however, was the design; perhaps never before had a magazine had so many different papers, inserts, gatefolds, pullouts, and peepholes. *Flair* sold about 200,000 copies an issue, but it carried only 180 pages of advertising during the entire year.

Some of the basic appeal of *Quick* was revived in the *Insider's Newsletter*, which Cowles began issuing in the spring of 1959. Mailed in sealed envelopes, carrying no advertising, the newsletter was intended as a private report to subscribers on matters of importance, the publishers said, and it took only twelve minutes a week to read. Although *Quick* had sold for ten cents a copy, the newsletter sold for $31.20 a year. It had picked up more than 100,000 subscribers by mid-1962.

The next Cowles magazine was thirty years old when the company

---

[16] New York *Times*, Oct. 23, 1963, sec. L, p. 64.

took it over in 1962. *Family Circle* had been one of the very first of the store-distributed magazines. It had swallowed up a competitor in 1958 to become *Everywoman's Family Circle*, had more than doubled its circulation in the sixties, and as a leading home service magazine had earned $760,000 in the year before Cowles bought it.

When the old *Life* was undergoing one of its periodic readjustments, its managing editor, Harry Evans, joined with Charles Merrill, a financier with an interest in grocery chains, to start a magazine that would be distributed free but that would carry advertising. The first issue of the rotogravure tabloid weekly, containing articles about food, fashions, beauty, movies, and radio, appeared on the counters of 1,275 grocery chain stores in 1932. Its circulation was only about 350,000, but Evans had great hopes of eventually raising it to 3,000,000. Advertisers were making a big mistake in ignoring giveaway magazines, he said; after all, radio programs were broadcast free to the listener.[17]

However, *Family Circle* did not have its great expansion until after World War II. In 1946 it changed from weekly to monthly publication and began selling its copies for five cents. Three years later it achieved national distribution when the Kroger stores joined the other chains handling it. Just about that time the field became overcrowded and fiercely competitive. The Great Atlantic and Pacific Tea Company had been selling *Woman's Day* for more than a decade. The McCall Corporation began issuing *Better Living* through stores belonging to the Super Market Institute and guaranteed it a circulation of 1,500,000 from its first issue in early 1951. Several food chains and John Cuneo of the Cuneo printing firm purchased *Everywoman's* and set out to give it a new life in early 1951 by distributing it through twenty-five food chains. *Better Living* quit the field in 1956; during its five years, it and *Everywoman's* had struggled for position by raiding one another's distribution outlets and by sneering at one another's claims. *Everywoman's* was left weakened by the fight. When it was merged with *Family Circle* in 1958, the combined *Everywoman's Family Circle* emerged with a circulation of 5,000,000 and access to 12,657 grocery stores in the United States and Canada—1,000,000 circulation and 5,367 stores from *Everywoman's*, 4,000,000 and 7,290 stores from *Family Circle*.

---

[17] *Time,* 20 (Oct. 3, 1932) 19.

Meanwhile there had been changes at *Family Circle*. P. K. Leberman, its publisher since 1936, had bought a majority interest in 1954, although Evans, Merrill, and others associated with the magazine retained some stock in it. The editor for eighteen years, Robert Endicott, left that same year after policy differences and was succeeded by Robert Jones, who came from *Better Homes and Gardens* and who held the magazine in close harmony with the homemaking interests of its audience.

After six months of negotiation, the Cowles company acquired *Everywoman's Family Circle* in December, 1962, for an exchange of stock valued at $4,300,000. The company did not alter the basic policies of the magazine, which had increased its circulation to about 7,000,000 by 1963.

Cowles broadcasting stations and magazines were combined in 1960 into Cowles Magazines and Broadcasting, Inc., which the following year offered stock for public sale. Besides its magazines, its properties in 1963 included radio and television stations in Des Moines and Memphis, two newspapers in Florida and one in Puerto Rico, six subscription agencies, a book and encyclopedia division, and real estate in Florida. It had plans for a new travel magazine, *Venture*, to appear in March, 1964, with a circulation of 250,000 restricted to holders of American Express credit cards.

Two publishing companies built by merchants were keen competitors of Bernarr Macfadden, the missionary with a strong streak of merchant. The men who established and operated them were not missionaries like Macfadden. Although they made some innovations of their own, they borrowed ideas from Macfadden and others. The two companies were Fawcett Publications, founded by Wilford H. Fawcett, and Dell Publishing Company, founded by George T. Delacorte, Jr.

Wilford H. Fawcett and his sons parlayed a mimeographed sheet of risqué jokes into a large company that published magazines and paperback books, operated a printing plant, and ran a distribution agency. The company, a family affair, reported in 1956 that over the previous fifteen years its earnings before taxes had totaled more than $20,600,000 and in 1961 that it had taken in $21,000,000 in the past year.

Back home in Minneapolis after service as a captain in World War I, Fawcett, a former police reporter for the Minneapolis *Journal*, sat down to a borrowed typewriter and amused himself by turning out a collection of off-color jokes and verses which he mimeographed for distribution among ex-servicemen. He called the sheet *Captain Billy's Whiz Bang*, and it was in such great demand that he found a small printing company willing to take a chance on bringing it out as a magazine.

Whiz Bang, a pocket-sized magazine selling for twenty-five cents, consisted of broad, earthy jokes and drawings which may have tried the patience of the postal authorities, who, nonetheless, never actually barred an issue from the mails. *Whiz Bang* found its humor in the predicaments of the farmer's daughter whose virtue was constantly in peril, in pictures of privies, and in the escapades of Pedro, the *Whiz Bang* bull. Captain Billy's monthly editorial was called "Drippings from the Fawcett."

Whiz Bang had a large sale among persons who liked their humor unsophisticated. It claimed a circulation of 425,000 by 1923, and it was earning Fawcett from $35,000 to $40,000 a month, although it carried no advertising. It was far too profitable to remain without imitators. Fawcett himself started one in 1926, *Smokehouse Monthly*, which grew out of a column of verse in *Whiz Bang*. When Fawcett and his wife Antoinette Fisher Fawcett were divorced in 1932, she used her alimony to buy out another imitator, the *Calgary Eye Opener*, also published in Minneapolis. But by then readers had tired of *Whiz Bang* and its competitors. The circulation of *Whiz Bang* had dropped to 150,000 in 1930. The next year, in 1931, Dell Publishing Company introduced *Ballyhoo*, a different sort of humor magazine which in six months had reached a circulation of nearly 2,000,000 among persons whose tastes in humor were scarcely more sophisticated. Perhaps because *Ballyhoo* usurped what remained of its audience, *Whiz Bang* died in 1932.

Meanwhile, with his earnings from *Whiz Bang* and help from his brothers Roscoe and Harvey, Fawcett had started several other magazines, most of them copies of competitors' publications which had demonstrated their popularity on the newsstands. In 1922 he introduced *True Confessions*, which at first consisted of stories of persons involved in crime and notoriety but which soon became a confession magazine in imitation of Bernarr Macfadden's *True Story*. He followed it, at a time when the pulp magazine was burgeoning, with *Triple X*, variously a war story magazine, an aviation magazine, a crime story magazine, and a Western story magazine, depending on which type sold the best. In 1926 Fawcett added *Battle Stories* and *Screen Secrets,* which was converted into the movie fan magazine *Screen Play* in 1930. Probably because both Wilford and Roscoe Fawcett were sportsmen—the former had coached the United States trapshooting team in the 1924 Olympics, the latter was a onetime state champion golfer—the company brought out *Amateur Golfer and Sportsman* in 1927. In 1928 the company purchased *Jim Jam Jems,* a rival of *Whiz Bang;* and the same year, it launched *Modern Mechanics,* an imitation of *Popular Mechanics. Modern Mechanics* was rechristened *Mechanix Illustrated* after the publishers of *Popular Mechanics* complained that its original title infringed on their own. When the success of Dell's *Ballyhoo* was the talk of the publishing industry in 1931, Fawcett cashed in on its popularity with an imitation, *Hooey.* According to Roscoe Fawcett, the company had been urged by independent distributors of magazines to bring out a competitor of *Ballyhoo,* which was distributed by American News, and although the firm had at first hesitated, it had decided to proceed when it learned that Bernarr Macfadden also was planning to issue one.

The company spawned new magazines so rapidly that a complete listing would be tedious. At one time, before World War II, Fawcett was publishing sixty-three different magazines. For the most part, the company officials apparently attempted to duplicate the successes of other publishers. Thus when *Esquire* was one of the fastest-selling magazines of the mid-thirties, Fawcett came out with *For Men,* a pocket magazine full of articles and cartoons somewhat in the *Esquire* vein. When the demand for *Life* exceeded the supply, Fawcett appeared with *Spot,* a picture magazine. When such self-help and inspirational books as Dale Carnegie's *How to Win Friends and Influence People* and Dorothea Brande's *Wake Up and Live!* were on the best-seller lists in the mid-thirties, Fawcett brought out *Photo-Facts,* a pocket magazine of "useful information." When Superman became one of the most popular of comic book heroes, Fawcett introduced Captain Marvel, clearly patterned after Superman.

The Fawcetts concentrated on publications which promised large sales on the newsstand; they discouraged subscriptions. Their policy for years was to kill off magazines which did not make money and to promote the ones which did. During World War II, when paper supplies were limited, the company suspended forty-nine of its sixty-three prewar magazines and strengthened the remaining fourteen.

As the company expanded, it moved its headquarters from the Midwest to the centers of publishing in the East and branched out from magazine publishing into the allied fields of distribution and printing. It moved its general offices from Minneapolis to Greenwich, Connecticut, in 1935. There the business and circulation offices remained, but in 1946 the company bought a twenty-one-story building in Manhattan to house its editorial, advertising, and managerial offices, previously scattered about New York. To put their own publications and those of certain other publishers onto newsstands across the United States, the Fawcetts founded the Fawcett Distributing Corporation. Early in 1944 Fawcett Publications purchased the C. T. Dearing Printing Company of Louisville, Kentucky, which had long done most of its printing. The purchase, at a price reportedly close to a million dollars, included two holdings of the Dearing company—the Louisville Colorgravure Company and the Frankfort State Journal Company, which published a daily newspaper in Frankfort, Kentucky, and the *State Legislative Digest*.

Roscoe Fawcett died in 1935, Wilford H. in 1940. Management of the company then passed to Wilford's four sons, who all had been associated with it since they had wrapped and delivered copies of *Whiz Bang* as young boys. W. H. Fawcett, Jr., became president; Roger Fawcett, general manager; Gordon Fawcett, secretary-treasurer; and Roscoe Fawcett, circulation director.

During and after World War II, the four brothers continued to introduce new publications and to experiment with old ones. They entered trade-paper publishing in 1946 with a weekly, *Cosmetic and Drug Preview*, which they summarily discontinued after three months. They converted one of their pulp magazines into a slick publication for men, *True*, and, as a later chapter will show, thereby contributed to the development of a new type of magazine. They toned down the stories of sexual adventure in their *True Confessions* and gave the magazine respectability by publishing such contributors as Eleanor Roosevelt.

In 1945, casting about for another stable publishing property, the Fawcetts decided to enter the competitive field of women's service magazines with one designed for women between the ages of eighteen and thirty-five. They had concluded from their research that existing service magazines circulated chiefly among older women, and they were confident that they could attract a young audience, "the most responsive section of the service magazine readers," they said, "and the section with the most clearly defined selfish interests for editors to appeal to." [18]

They gradually changed the editorial balance of one of their confession magazines, *Life Story*, and brought it out as a full-fledged women's service magazine in November, 1945, under the title of *Today's Woman*. Whereas *Life Story* had run such pieces as "Cheater's Reward," *Today's Woman* carried articles and stories by Clare Boothe Luce, Wilbur Daniel Steele, Mary Heaton Vorse, and James Street. It was able to guarantee advertisers a circulation of 1,000,000 by July, 1948. The Fawcetts expected the magazine to lose money for a time, and it did, although the trade press reported constant gains in circulation and advertising linage for it. It still had not developed into a profitable property when the Fawcetts suspended it in mid-1954.

Four years later the Fawcett company got its women's magazine by buying *Woman's Day*, a store-distributed monthly which it had been printing for some time. The Great Atlantic and Pacific Tea Company had introduced *Woman's Day* to its customers in October, 1937. The magazine was an outgrowth of a slim rotogravure giveaway dealing with food, the *A & P Menu Sheet*, which had become increasingly expensive to produce. The company formed a subsidiary to publish a true women's service magazine, and those first 815,000 copies of *Woman's Day* bore a three-cent price tag and carried advertising, although chiefly for products stocked by A and P stores.

The magazine was sold only in A and P stores, except in Colorado, where the chain had no outlets. It was stored in A and P warehouses and distributed by A and P trucks, like any other product. Yet from the beginning, it had been conceived of as more than a company house organ, and advertising salesmen made a special point of telling advertisers they would get no preferential treatment from the chain if they bought space in it. Like *Family Circle*, it developed into a first-rate service magazine for women.

When Fawcett bought *Woman's Day* in the fall of 1958, the magazine had been involved in antitrust litigation for the past

[18] *Tide*, 23 (Oct. 7, 1949) 48.

THE FAMILY CIRCLE
RADIO · MOVIES · HUMOR · RECIPES · STYLE
SEPTEMBER 12th, 1932

JOAN MARSH displays her favorite evening gown. (Description and other Styles on Page 7.)

JOAN AND DOUG . . . Will be regular readers of The Family Circle. See their letter to the Editor on Page 2!

BING CROSBY . . . "Broadway doubted him, so he pointed to the sign and got the shirt." (Story and other Radio Personalities on Page 14.)

JOLLY BILL tells JANE his favorite story . . . Tune in on pages 12 and 13 and you will find it there with other humorous stories and pictures.

HOW YOU CAN AID THE CAUSE OF PEACE · By President John F. Kennedy

Family Circle
Nov. 1962

THE DISCIPLINE DILEMMA
What can a parent believe?

GIFTS TO BUY, GIFTS TO MAKE
Over 300 cream-of-the-crop ideas

FOR SHOWY HOLIDAY DINNERS
Appetizers, roasts, desserts

How to protect your family from sniffles and sore throats

15 cents

thirty months. Twenty-three retail grocers and two wholesalers in the Chicago area had charged three major food companies with spending substantial amounts in the magazine but making no discounts, rebates, or similar benefits to competitors of A and P; the practice was a discriminatory one costing them business, they said, and the magazine a device for building store traffic and a captive audience of consumers. A federal judge dismissed the suit in July, 1957, but his decision was reversed thirteen months later.

While the suit was in progress, several agencies refrained from placing advertising in the magazine. Advertising revenues slipped from $9,280,000 in 1955 to $7,200,000 in 1956 and to $5,558,000 in 1957. Meanwhile, in May, 1958, its publishers offered the magazine to any grocery, drugstore, or newsstand wishing to sell it. By the time Fawcett purchased the magazine, it was being distributed by 400 wholesalers to thousands of retail outlets. Its circulation was 6,444,000 in 1963, and its gross advertising revenues had climbed to $13,929,000.

When *True* was approaching a circulation of 2,000,000, Fawcett decided the men's market was large enough to support a running mate for it; and in 1952 the company introduced *Cavalier*, a bimonthly, which sought an audience among men interested in true adventure, the outdoors, sports, and crime served under such titles as "I Bossed the Danish Underground" and "How We Pioneered the Tamiami Trail." After a decade, it abruptly changed its pitch from action and adventure to sophistication. Under Frederic A. Birmingham, who had edited *Esquire* in the fifties, it followed a pattern much like that of Hugh Hefner's *Playboy*, with fiction, satire, pinups, and features about fashions, drink, and travel.

The history and operations of the Dell Publishing Company paralleled those of Fawcett Publications, Inc., in several ways. Dell Publishing Company belonged to George T. Delacorte, Jr., who began publishing in 1921 with one magazine and three employees and who could say by the mid-fifties that in the intervening years he had issued more titles than Curtis, Crowell-Collier, Hearst, and Macfadden combined. As he and his family owned the company, it was not obliged to reveal its finances. However, in the midfifties he said that it had taken in $40,000 in its first year and had never failed to make a profit since; its gross in 1953 was $38,700,000.[19] His company was perhaps the largest one concentrating on news-

---

[19] *Advertising Age*, 25 (July 12, 1954) 38.

stand distribution in 1963, when its magazines included *Hairdo, Ingenue, Modern Screen, Modern Romances, Screen Stories, Inside Detective,* and a group of comic books with a multimillion circulation. By that time, Delacorte had left much of the operation of the company to others; in 1957 his son Albert Delacorte became chairman of the company and Mrs. Helen Meyer president and general manager.

Delacorte, born in 1894, was educated at Harvard and Columbia. He broke into magazine publishing after stretches as a freelance solicitor of advertising and as a circulation man. He formed the Dell Publishing Company in 1921 in partnership with William A. Johnston, for many years Sunday editor of the New York *World,* but the company belonged solely to him after Johnston's death the following year. At first Dell's only publications were ten-cent pamphlets on character analysis, horoscopes, birthdays, and kindred subjects.

The first magazine that Dell published was *Sweetheart Stories,* and from its inception Delacorte seems to have followed five practices which probably accounted for the commercial success of his company. First, he practiced rigid economy. He had to, for his company began in the tail end of the depression of 1921 on a capitalization of only a few thousand dollars. Second, like Fawcett, he concentrated on newsstand sales. About 95 per cent of Dell's circulation in 1955 was in single-copy sales, and the ratio was perhaps not far below that in 1963, if one includes comics and annuals. Even among its regular magazines in 1963, single-copy sales accounted for perhaps 45 per cent. Third, Delacorte looked to circulation rather than to advertising for his revenue. True, advertising became increasingly important to his operation after 1930, when he first diligently sought it for some of his publications. However, he declined advertising for his comic books as late as 1949 because he believed he could sell more copies by keeping their covers free for full-color illustrations. However, he began accepting advertising in his comics in late 1951 when high production costs forced him to cut some issues from their usual forty-eight pages to thirty-two. Fourth, he never based his hopes on a single magazine but always published a number of titles. His practice, like that of many another merchant, was to sell space not in single publications but in groups of his magazines—the Modern Magazine Group, for instance, and the Dell Detective Group. Fifth, he quickly buried magazines that did not catch on; he rarely nursed along weak publications in the hope of retrieving losses, as many other publishers did. A common practice was to test the market with a one-shot publication; if it had an unusually good reception, it would be continued as a periodical as long as the demand lasted. In the late forties, for instance, a sports album had a promising sale. Borrowing the title *Sports Illustrated* from Stuart Sheftel, who later sold it to Time Inc., Dell essayed a slick sports monthly, born in 1949 but killed that same year after it had lost $250,000. The company had better fortune a decade later. A one-shot called *1,000 Hints for Teens* did so well on the stands that the company used it as the basis for a new magazine in 1959, *Ingenue*, which four years later was selling about 602,000 copies a month.

Delacorte originated nearly three dozen magazines and abandoned well over half of them in his first decade as a magazine publisher; in 1931 he owned fourteen magazines, most of them pulps, confession publications, and movie fan magazines with such titles as *War Stories, Western Romances, Cupid's Diary, I Confess, Modern Romances,* and *Modern Screen.*

On his twenty-fifth anniversary as a publisher, Delacorte recalled some of the economies which had enabled him to stay in business in his first years. He got inexpensive manuscripts for his first four magazines by going to England, buying enough stories at low rates to fill his magazines for two or three years, then assigning them to rewrite men who changed the characters and situations into American ones. To build demand for his magazines, he often passed out free sample copies, and he introduced pulps to retail at the low price of ten cents. At that price he could not risk a hazard which publishers of pulps accepted as inevitable, a large proportion of unsold copies, so he numbered his issues instead of dating them. Then he put them on sale only east of the Rockies and south of Canada. When dealers from that region returned their unsold copies, Delacorte trimmed the yellowed edges and marketed the magazines west of the Rockies and in Canada.[20]

In 1931 Delacorte and Norman Hume Anthony, a past editor of *Judge,* were responsible for a humor magazine which zoomed to an incredible commercial success in its first issues. *Ballyhoo* fizzled out, like a spent rocket, within two years; but at its peak it had a newsstand sale of more than 2,000,000 copies, more than any other magazine until the forties, when its record was surpassed by *Life*

[20] *Tide,* 21 (Jan. 3, 1947) 32.

and *Woman's Day;* it sent competitors hurrying to slap together imitations; it begat "Ballyhoo" dresses, neckties, scarves, rings, cuff links, scarf pins, games, songs, greeting cards, and night clubs; and its editor wrote a musical show named *Ballyhoo* which had some of the success of its namesake.

Ballyhoo was conceived by Anthony, to whom Delacorte gave a free hand. Its humor, much of it deriving from the bathroom or sex, much of it in questionable taste, was broad and audacious. Anthony had said that a magazine could dare to be funny only if it carried no advertising, and *Ballyhoo* was without advertising. Much of its popularity resulted from its burlesques of familiar advertising slogans, and a few advertisers actually paid large sums to have their advertisements lampooned on its pages.

Delacorte said that he was going against his best judgment for the first time when he underwrote *Ballyhoo,* a fortnightly, but he thought he could make money on a sale of 100,000 copies an issue. Although the circulation figures are unreliable, the first issue of 150,000 copies was said to have sold out in five days; the second issue sold 450,000 copies, the third 675,000, and the fourth more than 1,000,000. In a few months circulation exceeded 2,000,000. On the second birthday of the magazine, however, sales had fallen to about 300,000, and as circulation dropped off, the magazine shrank to pocket size and became a quarterly. It died altogether in 1939.

Delacorte turned from *Ballyhoo* to other projects which promised a good return. He was one of the first publishers of comic books. His company accounted for more than a third of all comics sold in 1957, when it celebrated publication of its four billionth copy, and it was still publishing a large share of them in 1963. He introduced a line of paperbound books in the early forties and emerged as one of the major publishers of them; his company ordered a prepublication press run of 3,000,000 when it acquired rights to *Peyton Place* in 1957. Even in 1963 his company kept a number of books of horoscopes, crossword puzzles, and jokes on its list. One suspects that Delacorte would have nodded in agreement at a remark made by Mrs. Helen Meyer, who had joined the company soon after its founding: "All we are, really, are gamblers in ideas. We don't own printing plants or paper mills or enough office equipment to fill five zeroes. Ideas are all we have to sell, and the thing we respond to most." [21]

---

[21] Kirk Polking, "What's Doing at Dell," *Writer's Digest,* 37 (Oct., 1957) 14.

11

Success by Imitation

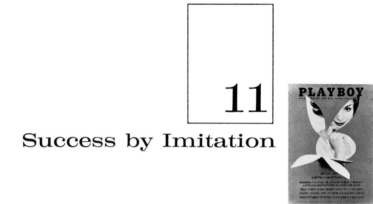

In May, 1919, Bernarr Macfadden, an energetic crusader for health-ful living who had been publishing *Physical Culture* for twenty years, brought out a new magazine which he called *True Story*. Its cover bore the motto, "Truth is stranger than fiction," and the line, "We Offer $1,000 for Your Life Romance." The cover illustra-tion of a man and woman gazing tenderly at one another was cap-tioned, "And their love turned to hatred."

Thousands of American women paid twenty cents a copy for *True Story* to read such pieces as "How I Learned to Hate My Parents" and "My Battle with John Barleycorn," which were illus-trated with posed photographs intended to heighten their veracity and emotional intensity. The number of buyers increased from issue to issue; by 1926 *True Story* had the then astounding circula-tion of 2,000,000, almost all of it on the newsstand, and advertising revenues of $3,000,000.

It was impossible for Macfadden to hide his good fortune from other publishers, who got together similar magazines of their own. Macfadden himself started other magazines to provide readers more of the content they were getting in *True Story*. Thus the con-fession magazine emerged as a distinct category of American mag-azines.

Several other categories of magazines came about in similar

fashion during the twentieth century. Time and again a publisher struck upon a new idea for a magazine or gave a new slant to an old idea, and as his publication became successful, other publishers copied it.

The new classes of magazines which resulted, especially after World War I, seemed to reflect the changes in American life. Life in the twentieth century moved at a faster pace than it had in the nineteenth. Improvements in transportation and communication wiped out distances. The political and economic systems became increasingly complex; and as citizen and as consumer, the typical American was called upon to make more decisions than ever before. Illiteracy declined, and schools and colleges sent forth a mounting number of graduates. Women gained the right to vote and competed for jobs that had once been the prerogative of men. Psychology became a catch-word. Sex was no longer a subject discussed in whispers, and gossip became a multimillion-dollar business. The printed media reached more persons than ever before; they were joined by new, powerful media which assailed the ear as well as the eye: movies, radio, and television.

The new kinds of magazines that arose were the products of their times, and they helped to shape them. The confession magazines could have gained the acceptance they did only in a time when sex was talked about frankly. And by reaching millions of persons who could never have understood the language of Freud, they well may have helped to influence the popular attitudes toward sex. The magazines for movie, radio, and television fans reported the most intimate affairs of the folk heroes created by three new mass media, and in doing so, glorified them further. The pulp magazine furnished inexpensive escape from a humdrum world to persons for whom the frontier was closed and the West won, to persons who could read but who, for the time being at least, were not disposed to think. One of their successors, the adventure magazine, reaffirmed faith in the individual and his accomplishments when mass society was ascendant.

In a fast-paced world, many of the new types of magazines built their success on condensing traditional fare in word and picture. The news magazine came along to sift the glut of news, to put it into convenient compartments, and to tell the hurried reader what it meant. The digest magazines, which grew up alongside the news magazines, tried to distill, in simple language, the vast outpourings of busy presses for the reader on the run; and their generally un-restrained optimism gave him reassurance in times of prosperity, solace in times of despair. The modern picture magazine and the comic book, which paralleled one another in their development, abbreviated even more than the digests, for they did so by picture instead of by text.

This chapter will discuss some of the categories of magazines that came about in the twentieth century, most of them after World War I—the confession magazines, the factual detective magazines, the fan magazines, the pulp magazines, the men's mag-azines, and the local magazines. The next chapter will cover the news magazines, the digests, the picture magazines, and the comic books.

Bernarr Macfadden was responsible for the birth of two distinct classes of magazines shortly after World War I, the confession magazines and the factual detective magazines, the latter of which seems a natural outgrowth of the former. An official of the Ameri-can News Company once remarked, "Macfadden had the first new idea in the publishing field in the last fifty years," but Macfadden was actually more a rediscoverer than a discoverer. Publishers had been exploiting the popular appeal of sex and crime almost from the time printing was introduced into England. Even before the first newspaper came along, presses had sent forth thousands of broad-sides in artless prose and amateurish poesy that told of serving maids seduced by naval officers and of mistresses murdered by their paramours. The anonymous hacks who scribbled such broad-sides for the scullery maid and apprentice often told their stories in the first person and with a strongly moralizing tone.

Bernarr Macfadden simply rediscovered what publishers had known for centuries and applied it to the magazine field. He found that a narrative of a true, highly emotional experience—a seduc-tion, a murder—had tremendous reader appeal, especially when told in the first person. If it pointed up some lofty moral, so much the better. His emotionally charged editorial matter, he also found, attracted thousands of persons who probably had never read mag-azines before, persons with little education and little purchasing power, persons whom other publishers had neglected because they were not the sort that advertisers were especially interested in reaching. The nature of their audience does much to explain why

the confession, detective, and movie magazines rarely attracted large amounts of advertising.

In his confession magazines, in his detective magazines, in his tabloid newspaper, the New York *Daily Graphic*, Macfadden exploited his findings; as he did, he strongly influenced the editorial content of certain types of magazines. His rivals not only copied his confession and detective magazines; they also applied some or all of his basic formula to the movie magazines, the sports magazines, and, after World War II, the men's magazines.

There are conflicting versions of how Bernarr Macfadden got the idea for *True Story*, the first of the confession magazines, but all of them agree that the publication grew out of *Physical Culture*. According to one account, Macfadden conducted a column of advice to women in *Physical Culture*. It took far too much time for a single department, but it was a highly popular feature, so he thought it might be the basis for a new magazine.[1] According to another account, he got the idea for *True Story* as he brooded over a mounting pile of letters from readers of *Physical Culture* who poured out details about their personal problems and asked for advice.[2] In still another account, his former wife Mary took credit for originating the magazine. His only hope for success, she told him, was in branching out from his physical culture enterprises into the regular publishing business. Most of the manuscripts for *Physical Culture* and the letters from readers were about true experiences. Many readers wanted to write about their love affairs, personal problems, and intimate experiences, but the magazine restricted them to accounts of physical development and prowess. Why not, Mary Macfadden suggested, get out an entertainment magazine of true stories written by its own readers in the first person?[3]

Whatever its origins, *True Story* was the keystone of Macfadden's publishing business and for years was its most profitable magazine, although Macfadden seems to have given his greatest affection to *Physical Culture*. Business affairs of *True Story* were handled by Orr J. Elder, a long-time associate of Macfadden who succeeded him as head of Macfadden Publications in 1941. First editor was John Brennan of *Physical Culture*.

[1] Robert Lewis Taylor, "Physical Culture," *New Yorker,* 26 (Oct. 28, 1950) 42.
[2] Harland Manchester, "True Stories," *Scribner's,* 104 (Aug., 1938) 25.
[3] Mary Macfadden and Emile Gauvreau, *Dumbbells and Carrot Strips* (New York, 1953), pp. 218-19.

The staff worked hard to keep professionalism out of *True Story*. "We want stories only from the common people," Macfadden said. "We've got to keep out 'writing writers' who want to make a business of it." Amateur "consultants" passed judgment on the 70,000 to 100,000 manuscripts that came to the magazine each year, and Macfadden often asked the head elevator operator what he thought of contributions. The narratives had to be completely serious, true to life, and told in the first person in simple, homely language, and they had to teach a strong moral lesson. Macfadden announced that contributors were required to sign affadavits swearing their stories were authentic and periodically threatened to prosecute those who broke faith, but only the naive took him seriously. A board of New York clergymen served as "censors" of the magazine. Members of the editor's family were models for the early photographic illustrations, but the magazine was able to draw on professionals when young actors and actresses began to realize the publicity value of the pictures. Among the models who later became stars were Norma Shearer, Frederic March, Jean Arthur, Anita Louise, Madge Evans, and Bebe Daniels.

As editor of *True Story* from 1926 until 1942, William Jordan Rapp guided it through several changes in policy which he summed up as from "sex to social significance in twenty years." [4] Rapp gradually rid the magazine of its blatant amateurishness while retaining its personal flavor. As his readers' tastes changed, he changed the content. Sex was rampant in the confession magazines when he took over the editorship. Early in 1927 he diluted the amount of sex in *True Story* because he thought his readers had begun to prefer virtue and heart throbs to outright seduction. As his readers became older, he chose stories discussing the problems of marriage instead of the problems of courtship. During the depression and the war which followed it, the stories he selected gave increasing attention to social problems. By the end of World War II, *True Story* had begun to show some interest in departments and features dealing with homemaking, child care, medicine, and national affairs, although its forte was still confession.

Competitors who hoped to duplicate the success of *True Story* were quick to bring out imitations. They registered scores of titles including the words "revealing," "true," "secrets," "romance," "intimate," and "personal"; and they filled their magazines with hun-

---

[4] *Tide,* 16 (Feb. 1, 1942) 21.

dreds of stories with such titles as "That First Sin," "Slave of Desire," "Because I Was Easy," and "My Dude Ranch Love Affair." George T. Delacorte, Jr., of Dell Publishing Company brought out *I Confess,* which suspended publication, although another publisher was publishing a magazine with the same title after World War II. Dell launched *Modern Romances* in 1930 and built it into one of the leaders in the confession field. In 1931 Dell introduced *My Story* but killed it abruptly when Macfadden threatened to undersell it with a new publication called *Your Story.* Fawcett Publications launched *True Confessions* in August, 1922; and although it lagged behind *True Story,* it had the second largest sale of any confession magazines for years, and after 1937 periodically appeared on lists of magazines with circulations of a million or more. Fawcett sold the magazine, along with *Motion Picture,* to the Macfadden organization in mid-1963 for $2,000,000 cash and other considerations. In 1931 Alfred Cohen, a publisher of movie fan magazines, revived *Everybody's,* as "the magazine of real life stories." *Everybody's* had been one of the first crusading journals at the turn of the century but had been discontinued in January, 1930.

Even Macfadden himself brought out imitations of *True Story.* He launched *True Experiences* in 1922 and followed it with *Love and Romance,* both of which continued to deal in the affairs of courtship while *True Story* turned to problems of marriage and family. Over the years, new titles issued by various publishers appeared on the newsstands as the confession magazine became an important item in the reading fare of American women: *True Marriage Stories* and *True Love Stories* in 1924, *Secrets* in 1936, *Personal Romances* in 1937, *Intimate Story* in 1948, and *Revealing Romances* in 1949.

The confession magazine was born amidst the revolution in manners and morals in the decade after World War I. Indeed, it was both a result of and a contribution to that revolution, according to Frederick Lewis Allen, an historian of the period. As the message of Sigmund Freud circulated among the lay public after the war, Allen has suggested, many educated men and women found "scientific" reasons for believing that universal moral codes lacked validity, that sex was the prime force which moved mankind, and that one needed an uninhibited sex life to be well and happy.[5] The

---

[5] Frederick Lewis Allen, *Only Yesterday* (New York, 1946), pp. 117-22.

free discussion of sex created an atmosphere conducive to the birth of the confession magazine. The confession magazine, in turn, he said, influenced attitudes toward sex among many readers who had never heard of Freud and the libido.

The satisfactions that women got from confession magazines may have been similar to those they got from radio and television soap opera. They could vicariously enjoy love experiences which circumstance denied them. They could find what they regarded as help in solving their personal problems. In 1955, in an unpublished study, "The World of the Confession Magazine," Wilbur Schramm put it this way:

A woman can . . . turn to these magazines for reassurance that other people have problems like hers—in fact, many of them have much more severe problems of the same kind. Furthermore, a reader can turn to these magazines for good advice on some of the problems. Ought she confess that episode out of her past? How can she handle a husband who always wants to sit at home in the evenings? And so forth. And still more important, the reader can get from these magazines a comforting sense that this is not a world of chance or caprice, but rather of order and justice. If she makes a mistake, she can do something to rectify it. Her neighbor, who seems to be getting by with murder, will be caught up with in good time; nobody is "getting by" with anything. But neither is anyone foredoomed to unhappiness, providing he is willing to do something about it. It is a comforting pattern of justice and free will.

In the fifties and sixties, some of the confession publications called themselves "family behavior magazines" and made much of the instruction, guidance, and help they offered their readers. A large share of their audience consisted of young housewives in working-class families whose values, outlook, conflicts, and anxieties were distinctly different from those of the middle class. They were women not reached to any appreciable extent by the middle-class service magazines such as *McCall's* and *Ladies' Home Journal* or, for that matter, by *Reader's Digest* and *Life*. The mission of the confession magazines then was to deal with their problems and to give them information, entertainment, guidance, and reassurance in a manner which they would accept as realistic and with which they could identify. Thus, the publishers said, confession magazines in contrast to the service magazines dealt with stark reality instead of the superficial problem, the practical instead of the academic, the fact instead of the make-believe. A service magazine might run "Built-in Baby Sitter," an entertaining account of a superficial problem; a confession magazine would run "I Killed My Child," the stark story of a young mother who saw her child killed by an automobile. A service magazine might run "Girl on the Outside," the story of a young girl overshadowed by her older sister's popularity; a confession magazine would run "Let's Live It Up," the story of a teenager who had to decide how far she would go to be popular.[6] Not all of the confession magazines were directed at married women, however; some—*Real Confessions,* for instance, and *My Secret Story*—appealed to girls in their teens, who often wrote the editors for advice.

Certainly the confession magazines reached a sizable audience that other publications had chosen to ignore. Perhaps no magazine until then had grown as rapidly as *True Story.* Almost every year from 1926 through 1963 it had a circulation of at least 2,000,000. Although it is hard to estimate the total audience of the confession magazines, the major ones in 1963 had an aggregate circulation of more than 8,500,000. There were probably fewer purchasers than that, however; one editor thought that each of her readers bought about three confession magazines a month.

As a class, confession magazines never fared as well in advertising as the service magazines for women, although a number of large national advertisers used them extensively during World War II when paper rationing limited advertising space in the home service publications. Advertising revenues grew to a peak in the mid-fifties, then began to decline. *True Story,* the leader among confession magazines, carried about $3,214,000 in advertising in 1963. Its showing was impressive against the $258,000 in *True Confessions,* the $247,000 in *Modern Romances,* the $26,000 in *True Experiences,* but it was far behind such service magazines as *McCall's* with $41,868,000 and *Good Housekeeping* with $28,-419,000. And it was a good distance behind its own $5,624,000 in 1957.

Like *True Story,* a few confession magazines added homemaking features to their first-person stories of transgression and atonement after World War II. But the service features were a relatively insignificant part of the confession magazines as a whole, which remained dominated by their "true" narratives of actual experiences.

---

[6] Although this material came from booklets issued by the True Story Group, the subject is treated by George Gerbner, "The Social Role of the Confession Magazine," *Social Problems* 6 (Summer, 1958) 29-40.

The world of the confession magazines was one in which sex was a prime motivating force and in which making and maintaining a happy marriage was the central problem. It was, in the words of Wilbur Schramm, "a woman's world, a young person's world, an urban middle class world, characterized by violence, overpowering sex drives, and broken homes. It is ruled by a code of ideal justice which demands and accepts payment for all transgressions against the code of accepted behavior. Therefore, the spectre of punishment hangs over these stories."

The factual detective magazines, which first appeared in 1924 when tabloid newspapers and gang warfare were making the public acutely aware of murder and mayhem, seem to have been a natural outgrowth of the confession magazines. Like the confession magazines, they exploited sin. Like the confession magazines, they featured true stories. Like the confession magazines, they reported factual material in the suspenseful narrative of fiction. "The essence of the best stories for *True Detective*," the editor once wrote, "lies in the actual fact detail given in sequence, one action of the investigators leading to the next, thus evolving a clearly pictured development of events; recreating in all its details what actually happened months or years before. . . ." [7] At times the detective magazines used the first-person approach, although much less than the confession magazines, for their accounts were usually written in the third person by police reporters instead of by participants.

Actually, the confession magazines had dabbled in crime from the start. The first issue of *True Story* had carried a story about "An Ex-Convict's Climb to Millions"; and for later issues, Jack Grey, a retired safecracker, had written his "Confessions of a Bank Burglar." When Fawcett's *True Confessions* first appeared in 1922, it concentrated on actual confessions of criminals and ran such articles as "Memoirs of a Con Man" and "Revelations of a District Attorney" before it settled down to the usual fare of the confession magazines.

Despite Fawcett's brief excursion into crime with *True Confessions*, the father of the factual detective magazine as it evolved in the second quarter of the twentieth century was Bernarr Macfadden. In 1924 he began *True Detective Mysteries*, which attempted

---

[7] John Shuttleworth, *Hints to T. D. Writers: Stories Needed for True Detective Magazine* (New York, 1944), p 18.

to prove that true crime mysteries could be as engrossing as the fiction mysteries of the pulps. *True Detective* never had the spectacular success of *True Story*, but it developed into a durable property. After it caught on, Macfadden followed it with *Master Detective* in 1929, just as he had capitalized on the popularity of *True Story* by starting *True Experiences*. Rival publishers copied *True Detective* as they had *True Story*, and scores of detective magazines, some of them highly sensational, sprang up over the ensuing years. Probably the best written and best edited of the lot were Macfadden's *True Detective Mysteries* and Annenberg's *Official Detective Stories*, established in 1934, and they led the others in sales. Actually, the audience for the factual detective magazine was comparatively small. *True Detective* had sales of about 300,000 in 1963, and the combined circulations of the major ones was slightly more than 2,000,000.

Magazines for movie fans began to appear when motion pictures moved from the shady atmosphere of the nickelodeon into grand palaces of their own, when the star system evolved and moviegoers became interested in Mary Pickford, Mabel Normand, Dustin Farnum, and Milton Sills offstage as well as on. Although the movie magazine antedated the confession magazine, the two types seem to have risen to popularity side by side. They had much in common. Both types were usually produced by the same publishers. Both types offered escape by giving the reader a glimpse into someone else's most intimate affairs. Both types went to the same class of readers, and they attracted the same kinds of advertising; in fact, it became customary for a publisher of several confession and movie magazines to sell space in them as a group.

Although a few publications may have been issued even before then, movie magazines seem to have proliferated after 1910. *Photoplay*, which by midcentury had grown modestly prosperous by glamorizing Hollywood and which had long led the field, was started in 1911 and struggled along for its first years as a skimpy little pamphlet. *Picture Play*, another of the early fan magazines with a long life span, began publication in 1915. Several others, long since forgotten, also appeared before World War I.

After World War I the movie publications grew rapidly in numbers and in circulation. Throughout the twenties, thirties, and forties, new titles were forever appearing on the newsstands: *Screenland* in 1920, *Screen Play* in 1925, *Screenbook* in 1928, *Screen*

Stories and *Screen Romances* in 1929, *Modern Screen* and *Movies* in 1930, *Movie Mirror* and *Romantic Movie Stories* in 1933, *Movie Life* in 1937, *Movie Stars Parade* in 1940, and *Movieland* in 1942, to name a few. As old titles dropped from the stands, new ones took their places.

The fan magazines probably resulted from and helped to perpetuate the star system of the movies. They created a picture of the "real" life of the movie stars, of the "real" Hollywood, as synthetic as the world that the movies themselves portrayed. But for the typical reader, there was nothing artificial about such articles as "Happiness Comes Again to Arline Judge," "That Man Menjou," "Kim Novak's Man Problem," "Why Brando Fascinates Women," and "Why Ava Gardner Quit Hollywood." From articles like those, the reader knew what his favorite stars were "really like," how they spent their money and their spare time, how they stayed handsome or beautiful, what they looked for in a mate.

In the early sixties, there were about two dozen fan magazines with a total circulation of perhaps 8,000,000, but a change had come over them, according to Lawrence J. Quirk, who had withdrawn from publishing fan magazines when their "cheapness and scurrility" alienated him. In the twenties and thirties, he said, they were a highly respected medium that reached an audience of 3,000,000 adults who were enthralled by films and who wanted wholesome information about them. After the mid-thirties, the magazines went through a transformation. They began aiming at a younger audience and, finding that their content was beginning to pall, they increasingly sought sensational revelations about the stars. The success of *Confidential* in the mid-fifties hastened the trend.[8] So, probably, did the fact that general magazines were carrying a good many articles of the sort that had once been the staple of the fan publication. In the early sixties, when even President John F. Kennedy's family was a subject for their covers and articles, the fan magazines heard considerable public criticism, and some movie stars responded to their editorial treatment by filing libel suits against them.

Radio and television, like the movies, were responsible for the creation of fan magazines which carried articles about the stars, program listings, and similar material. The radio publications were

---

[8] Lawrence J. Quirk, "Fan Magazines: The Pros and Cons," *Variety*, Jan. 9, 1963, pp. 36, 41.

never as numerous or as widely circulated as the movie magazines, but several of them were published from the thirties onward, new ones replacing those which died. There was a ready market for magazines carrying radio program schedules as long as many newspapers refused to list them because of their feud with the new medium. For instance, Annenberg's *Radio Guide* in 1936 sold 420,000 copies of its seventeen regional editions with program listings. As newspapers began running the schedules, *Radio Guide* lost circulation and broadened its scope to cover movies as well as radio. Annenberg killed *Radio-Movie Guide* in November, 1943, to obtain additional paper for other magazines. When television boomed after World War II, at least one of the oldest radio magazines put its emphasis on the new medium. It was *TV Radio Mirror,* which had begun life in 1933 as *Radio Mirror* and which in the sixties was one of the oldest magazines of its type.

At least a dozen magazines listing television programs and carrying articles about television personalities sprang up in the late forties and early fifties, and their titles indicated their slant: *TV Forecast, TV Index, TV Prevue, TV People and Pictures, TV Fan, TV Star Parade.* One of the earliest was *TV Guide,* which Lee Wagner established in 1948 for a New York audience but later distributed nationally. Less than two years after Walter Annenberg's Triangle Publications took over *TV Guide* in 1953, the magazine had twenty-seven different editions and a total circulation of 2,222,000. Early in 1962 it announced that it had become the first weekly to achieve a circulation of 8,000,000, and later that same year it increased its number of regional editions to seventy.

The pulp magazine, a descendant of the dime novels and yellow-back weeklies of the nineteenth century, was born in 1896. Frank Munsey, tinkering with his *Argosy,* made it an all-fiction magazine and switched to a rough wood-pulp paper because he thought the story was more important than what it was printed on. Publishers of cheap fiction may have seen that the pulp could save postage. As single publications, dime novels were not eligible for the low second-class postal rates granted to periodicals; the pulp magazine was. Sent on its way by Munsey and by Street & Smith, a publisher of dime novels since 1855, the pulp magazine grew in numbers, divided, amoeba-like, into a variety of subtypes, and furnished inexpensive reading for 10,000,000 Americans for many years. During World War II pulp publishers were hit hard by ris-

ing production costs and, somewhat ironically in view of the forerunners of the pulp, by twenty-five cent paperbound books. Certainly they also faced serious competition from the comic books,
which gave the reader much the same content in visual form.

Traditionally, the pulp ran little advertising. It depended on its
sales for revenue and was produced so economically that a publisher could make a profit even if he sold just half of the copies he
printed. The editor bought fiction at low rates—three or four cents
a word in the boom twenties, a penny a word in the thirties—and
printed it with little adornment.

At first all pulps were general adventure magazines, but eventually three other broad categories emerged: love, detective, and
Western. Those new types resulted as other publishers imitated
three successful magazines originated by Street & Smith, *Love
Story, Detective Story,* and *Western Story.* One instance illustrates
this point. Although pulps had sometimes previously published
love stories, the first love pulp appeared in May, 1921. Its origina-
tor was Amita Fairgrieve, a young woman whom Street & Smith
had assigned to develop a new magazine. She holed up in an office
during the winter of 1920-21 and pored through a stack of old
dime novels. The magazine she emerged with was *Love Story.*
First a quarterly, next a semimonthly, then a weekly, *Love Story*
was so widely imitated that in 1938 there were eighteen love pulps
selling about 3,000,000 copies a month.[9]

For more than twenty years, the editor of *Love Story* was Daisy
Bacon, a descendant of William Bradford, governor of Plymouth
Colony. She had come to New York from Pennsylvania in the late
twenties, and she had got her job on *Love Story* by answering a
classified ad in the New York *Times.* She became editor in 1928.
In the fashion of the business, she edited a number of other pulps
for varying periods while keeping one hand on *Love Story—Real
Love, Ainslie's, True Love Stories, Pocket Love, Romantic Range,*
and *Detective Story.*

The appeal of the love pulps was not illicit sex; their heroines
assiduously preserved their virginity even though they drank and
sometimes spent the night in a bachelor's apartment. The fiction
differed from that of the women's slick-paper magazines mainly in
the writing, which was usually of lower quality and always sur-
charged with emotion. But pulp publishers early discovered the

---

[9] Thomas H. Uzzell, "The Love Pulps," *Scribner's,* 103 (April, 1938) 36.

sales appeal of sex. Long before World War I, old timers like Courtland Young with his *Breezy Stories* and *Young's Magazine* were publishing stories that titillated readers without being pornographic. The trade made a clear distinction between such "snappy stories" and "sexy stories." According to one veteran editor, there was as much difference between "snappy" and "sexy" in pulp connotations as between Western and adventure. The pulps dealing with raw sex appeared about 1922 when publishers took advantage of the new frankness in discussions of sex that followed the war.[10]

In the competition after World War I, pulp publishers broke the four main categories—adventure, love, detective, and Western—into subcategories. For instance, they issued magazines dealing exclusively with stories that had been but a part of the general adventure pulp and thus flooded the stands with titles such as *Sea Stories, Spy Stories, Sport Stories,* and *Air Stories.* George Delacorte, Jr., of Dell Publishing Company originated the war story pulp, Harold Hersey and W. M. Clayton the pulp of Western love. Hersey also has taken credit for originating the gangster and jungle pulps.[11]

The first pulp devoted entirely to science fiction appeared in April, 1926, when Hugo Gernsback brought out *Amazing Stories.* Four years later he issued another, *Wonder Stories,* and lined up a staff of authorities including William J. Luyten of Harvard Observatory and Clyde Fisher of the American Museum of Natural History, New York, to check his stories for factual accuracy. Fifteen years before *Amazing Stories,* Gernsback had written and published the first science-fiction story to appear in a magazine, a piece about the adventures of one Ralph 124C41 that appeared in *Modern Electrics,* April, 1911. But the antecedents of the science-fiction pulp were earlier than even that. The first pulps of the nineties, Munsey's *Argosy* and others, had run tales based on supernatural phenomena, and before World War I pulps had run stories of interplanetary travel. But the father of pulp fiction with a scientific or pseudo-scientific background was Gernsback. Interest in science fiction grew; by 1939 about a dozen pulps were entirely filled with it, and its fans had formed their own organization, New Fandom, which met in convention. Science fiction in book and magazine attracted a hard core of perhaps 20,000 dedicated fans

---

[10] Harold B. Hersey, *Pulpwood Editor* (New York, 1937), pp. 159-60.
[11] Hersey, p. 163.

after World War II. The twenty-five or so magazines devoted to it in the early fifties included some publications of quality such as *Astounding Science Fiction, Fantasy & Science Fiction,* and *Galaxy Science Fiction,* as well as lesser publications which simply moved the scenes of traditional pulp tales from the West to outer space. Judging from listings in directories, the number had fallen off by the early sixties, when the paperback was a popular medium for the tales; but a few were still around, and *Astounding Science Fiction,* perhaps anticipating the age of the computer, changed its name to *Analog.*

And so the pulp grew and spread. In 1935 one major publisher of pulps, A. A. Wyn, released some figures on the size of the industry. Each year 125 pulps shipped out 2,000 carloads of magazines for 10,000,000 fans. In producing them, they used $500,000 worth of art and engravings and $1,500,000 worth of manuscripts, printed at a cost of $2,000,000 on $1,250,000 worth of paper.[12]

Yet a little more than a decade later the pulp was virtually extinct. The paperback book had offered itself as an alternative; the comic book, and later television, provided the same sort of romantic and adventurous escape in a form that required less effort and attention. Then, too, during and immediately after World War II, publishers of pulps were hit especially hard by swiftly rising production costs, which increased 72 per cent between the end of 1944 and mid-1947. Their revenue from circulation was no longer enough to support them. Some publishers, like Standard Magazines, Inc., and Better Publications, Inc., the publishers of the Thrilling Fiction Group, hired commercial research organizations to discover the reading habits and purchasing power of readers of pulp magazines and then aggressively sought national advertising. Other publishers, like Street & Smith, abandoned their pulps as unprofitable and turned to publications that could attract lucrative national advertising. Still others converted their pulps into slick publications eligible for national advertising and thus contributed to a postwar development in the magazine industry—the emergence of a new class of magazines, general magazines for men.

Even in the nineteenth century there had been magazines for men, of course, and many more sprang up in the first four decades of the twentieth century. Virtually all of them, however, carried specialized content. Many were edited for the hunter and fisher,

---

[12] *Time,* 26 (Sept. 16, 1935) 33.

as were *Field and Stream* and *Hunting and Fishing.* A number of them, like *Popular Mechanics* and *Mechanix Illustrated,* were for the home craftsman who puttered at his work bench. A few dealt with specific sports, as did the *Ring,* and fewer still with sports generally, as did *Sport.* Several fraternal magazines carried some general interest material besides their organizational material— *American Legion, Foreign Service* of the Veterans of Foreign Wars, and *Elks,* for instance. Perhaps the closest to a general magazine for men was *Esquire,* but even its appeal was somewhat specialized and to an upper-income audience. In short, the term "men's magazines" was a broad one covering such dissimilar publications as the *Police Gazette,* that hardy perennial which brought cigar-store loungers reports of crimes and sporting events and pictures of buxom beauties, and *Gentry,* which addressed itself to an elite hundred thousand in 1951 as a lavish quarterly with detachable inserts and with packets of herbs and swatches of textiles glued to its pages to illustrate the subjects of its articles.

The magazines in the new class were none of those. Although the trade called them "general magazines for men," the term was somewhat misleading; a more descriptive phrase might have been "true adventure magazines for men," for the factual account of adventure was their stock in trade. They first appeared during World War II.

The great increase in the number and in the circulation of men's magazines generally during and after the war was, as the editorial director of Fawcett Publications put it, "one of the biggest turns in the publishing business" in a long time. As a broad class, men's magazines increased their sales tremendously during and after the war. The men's magazines covered by the Audit Bureau of Circulations showed a circulation growth of 134 per cent between 1940 and 1949, according to tabulations in a publishing trade paper.[13] The study included four magazines either not in existence or not reporting to A.B.C. in 1940. However, even if one excluded them and compared only the magazines reporting in both years, the increase for men's magazines was 93 per cent, or roughly twice that of magazines generally.

As some publishers converted their pulps to slick publications for men, as sales of men's magazines generally increased, there developed a new and distinct genre of men's publications—the

---

[13] Carle Hodge, "For Men Only," *Magazine Industry,* 1 (Winter, 1950) 13.

general magazines for men. They were clearly the grandchildren of the pulps, these new slick magazines, and they dealt in the same basic commodity, escape; but whereas the pulps had provided fiction for escape, the new magazines provided fact. It was fact that sometimes bordered on fiction; indeed, some of the publications adapted the techniques of fiction to factual material as the true detective magazines had done. As one editor wrote a prospective author, "The style we're after is essentially that of the short story applied to the fact field—something that can be told mainly in chronological sequence, working up to a climax and a denouement." The publications also adapted a technique of the confession magazines, the first-person account, to their tales of adventure. However handled, their articles were based on conflict.

The standard formula of the magazines was a mixture of a few ingredients, usually crime, war, hunting, sports, speed, and sex. A few random titles illustrate the emphasis of the magazines on exploits of the individual and the excitement which crackled throughout their pages: "My Life as a Headhunter," "I Walked into a Bandit Death Trap," "The Toughest Fish in the Sea," "I Was Hitler's Master Spy," "Virginity Complex" ("are YOU afraid to love?"), "We Stalked a Man-Eater," "The Man Who Killed Convoys," "The Wonderful Legend of Colin Kelly," "I Sailed the Antarctic Killer Boats." Their photographs often showed a sadistic bent, as in pictures of men dying before a firing squad, a man burning to death in a motorcycle accident, the last moments in the life of a racing car driver ("This Is a Man Dying").

The true adventure magazine for men, as a distinct type of publication, had clearly emerged by the end of World War II; and in the years that followed, such titles as *Adventure, Man's Adventure, Cavalier, Action Caravan, Climax, Escape, Saga,* and *Real* showered upon the newsstands. Most were essentially imitators of *True,* a rotogravure monthly, and *Argosy,* a onetime pulp, which had been converted to slick-paper magazines during World War II.

The first magazine of the genre seems to have been *True.* In 1931 Ralph Daigh, who was then working for Fawcett Publications in Robbinsdale, Minnesota, came across a readership study that convinced him men were much more interested in factual material than in fiction. He prepared a rough dummy of a nonfiction men's magazine, blocked in a variety of appropriate titles, and drew up a list of possible names, among them *True, True Adventure, Male,* and *Man*. Roscoe Fawcett, the editorial director, rejected the idea. About a year later, when Daigh was working for Dell Publishing Company in New York, he tried the idea on his new employer, who also turned it down. In 1936 Daigh became editorial director of Fawcett Publications, which had since moved to New York. Again he tried his idea, and this time he persuaded the company officers to bring out not one men's nonfiction magazine but two— *For Men*, a pocket-sized monthly, and *True*, a sensational rotogravure monthly. *For Men* eventually ceased publication, although its title was revived by another publisher in the early fifties.

True underwent a gradual metamorphosis. As the company experimented with the magazine, it found that circulation grew as quality improved and sensationalism diminished. By late spring of 1943, Fawcett was ready to convert *True* into a slick general magazine for men, and for the job it picked Bill Williams, who had been editing the company's *Mechanix Illustrated*.

Williams had been a college football player, a guide at Yellowstone Park, and a detective before he left his job as city editor of the Minneapolis *Journal* to join Fawcett. He was a lusty man, a man who could down a full bottle of brandy after dinner to settle his stomach, an editor who transacted much of his business with authors after hours in a bar, and he conveyed much of his lustiness and ruggedness to *True*. He spent more than a year working out the idea that sent *True* on the way to becoming the best-selling men's magazine.

His editorial pattern was strong on adventure, sports, science, and personalities, all garnished with color illustrations. Williams sought well-known authors—Paul Gallico, Quentin Reynolds, Budd Schulberg, C. S. Forester, Robert Ruark, MacKinlay Kantor—and he paid up to $2,000 an article to get them. "For stories we really want, we'll outbid anybody, even the *Saturday Evening Post*," he remarked in 1948.[14] His formula was effective. When his overhaul was nearly completed in mid-1944, *True* had a circulation of about 440,000; when Williams died in 1948, it had become the first men's magazine to achieve a circulation of more than a million.

The magazine continued to grow in circulation and advertising volume under Williams' successor, Ken W. Purdy, who had edited *Victory* during World War II and *Parade* after that. Sales climbed

---

[14] *Time*, 51 (April 19, 1948) 62.

SAGA

SEPTEMBER 25¢

THE MAGAZINE OF TRUE ADVENTURE

MAROONED ON AN ICECAP Lt. Col. Beaudry's Epic Rescue

I KNOW MICKEY COHEN · THE REAL BABE RUTH · HERE COMES THE COMET!

THREE MEN IN A BALLOON · GREEN FIRE · THE MAN ELECTRICITY COULDN'T KILL

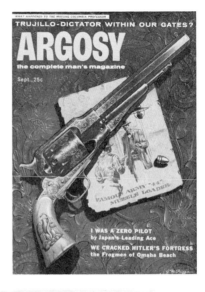

WHAT HAPPENED TO THE MISSING COLUMBIA PROFESSOR

TRUJILLO-DICTATOR WITHIN OUR GATES?

ARGOSY

the complete man's magazine

Sept., 25c

FAMOUS ARMY '44' MUZZLE LOADER

I WAS A ZERO PILOT
by Japan's Leading Ace

WE CRACKED HITLER'S FORTRESS
the Frogmen of Omaha Beach

THE MAN'S MAGAZINE

50 CENTS MAY 1964 A FAWCETT PUBLICATION

TRUE

STIRLING MOSS BUILDS | THE GREAT GUN GRAB
A BACHELOR DREAM PAD | AND HOW TO STOP IT
By Ken Purdy | By Robert Ruark

A Bonus Book Condensation By Tony Saulnier
WE FOUND THE LAST STONE-AGE HEADHUNTERS

to 1,821,000 and advertising revenues to $2,273,000 in 1954 when Purdy left to edit a competitor. Purdy has since recalled:

When I came to the magazine in 1949, it seemed to me that little needed to be done to the basic policy. Williams' notion had been to furnish his readers with a refuge from women; to offer vicarious adventure, humor, and good writing. . . . I did feel that the magazine should be improved in everything pertaining to quality; better writing, better layout, better art. I felt that the level of sophistication could be increased and that the magazine could and should be brought to serve a function more useful than mere entertainment: that it should expose, direct, and exhort like any other mature publication.[15]

Douglas Kennedy continued to steer the magazine in the editorial direction in which Williams and Purdy had pointed it. On its twenty-fifth anniversary in 1961, it was the most profitable of all Fawcett publications; it accounted for some 30 per cent of the company's revenues of $21,000,000. It brought in $3,327,000 in advertising that year, and its circulation had reached 2,400,000. One reason for its financial success, Daigh thought, was its carefully balanced ratio of 40 per cent single-copy sales to 60 per cent subscriptions. Several years earlier Ken Purdy had tried to explain its editorial popularity. One reason, he thought, was its escapist nature. "We run *True* like a portable twenty-five-cent private study or man's den," he said. "In *True*, the customer gets escapist material . . . no reminders of the sad state the world is in today . . . no whither-are-we-going stories, no doom-is-just-around-the-corner stuff. . . . Why should a reader . . . have to wonder if he can use a cure for cancer some time? The hell with it! I don't even like income tax stories." Another reason for its popularity, he suggested, was its ban on fiction. "The fact is that men don't read magazine fiction anymore," Purdy said. "They still want good reading, good stories, but they like them better when they know they're true." [16]

While Fawcett was changing *True* from roto to slick and establishing it as a general magazine for men, the publishers of *Argosy* were subjecting that venerable pulp to a series of alterations which culminated in 1945 with the emergence of *Argosy* as a competitor of *True*.

Frank Munsey founded *Argosy* in December, 1882, as a magazine for children, but he made it the first of the pulps in the nineties by printing it on coarse paper and filling it with adventure stories for

[15] Letter to the author, July 22, 1957.
[16] *Tide*, 26 (March 28, 1952) 56.

adults. After Munsey's death, *Argosy* was continued as a pulp by the Frank Munsey Company, which was taken over by William T. Dewart, general manager of the firm under Munsey; but the magazine in which Jack London, Edgar Rice Burroughs, and O. Henry had made early appearances sank into sad decline.

Early in 1942, in an effort to modernize the magazine, the publishers changed its name to *New Argosy;* dropped its familiar cover trademark, a galleon under full sail, in favor of a four-engined airplane; and began to devote half of each issue to factual material and to use photographs as well as the traditional drawings. The measures to enliven the magazine were so extreme that the Postmaster General in July, 1942, banned *Argosy* from the mails for "obscenity." Two months later, the Frank Munsey Company sold *Argosy* and some thirty other titles, only six of them then being published, to Popular Publications, Inc., a large publisher of pulps.

Under its new owner, *Argosy* appeared as a twenty-five-cent all-fiction slick in September, 1943. "We have stepped out of the pulp field entirely," said Rogers Terrill, its new editor. "We felt there was room in the country for an all-fiction slick, and we're it." [17] But apparently there was not room for such a magazine, for in 1944 and 1945, when *True* was selling well on the newsstands, Henry Steeger, president of Popular Publications, transformed *Argosy* into another general men's magazine similar to *True*. Steeger has explained the reasoning behind the change. The millions of men who had served in World War II had traveled all over the world, experienced a great deal, learned much more, and returned with a new awareness of themselves. The changed role of the American male held promise for men's magazines just as the changed role of women after World War I benefited women's magazines:

Women acquired the vote, they went into drinking places and smoked cigarettes in public, and there was quite an emphasis on the emergence of equality for the female. It is our thought that by contrast with this the American male "put on trousers again" at the end of World War II. Prior to that time, women had been catalogued as the operators of the family pursestrings and the purchasers of practically all commodities. After that time, new buying pursuits were adopted by the male and it began to be recognized by the advertising agencies all over that the male was an individual to be reckoned with in the purchase of all types of products. . . . [18]

---

[17] *Newsweek*, 22 (Aug. 23, 1943) 91.
[18] Letter to the author, Aug. 8, 1957.

Retaining some fiction, the new *Argosy* ran articles about adventure, sports, hunting and fishing, science, and crime. A feature that brought it a good deal of publicity in the nation's press was its "Court of Last Resort," in which it told the stories of persons believed to be unjustly imprisoned. The cases were investigated for *Argosy* by a team consisting of a private detective, a criminologist, a former prison warden, and Erle Stanley Gardner, the detective story writer. Several men serving prison terms were freed as a result of the series.

Ken Purdy moved from *True* to *Argosy* in 1954 but stayed for only about eight months, then left to do freelance writing. Under Steeger as editor and Alden H. Norton as executive editor, *Argosy* continued to rank with *True* as the best magazines of their kind. Circulation had been only 11,500 when Popular Publications acquired the magazine in 1942; twenty years later it was 1,265,000, advertising revenues, $1,926,000.

The success of *Argosy* and *True* in attracting readers and advertisers was no doubt responsible for the dozens of similar publications which began turning up on newsstands in the early fifties, and thus for the development of the general magazine for men. At one fork in an unprofitable road, then, the pulp magazine branched down a course that led to the general magazine for men. At another point, as we will see, it took a course that led to another new class of magazines, the comic books. The comic book was essentially the pulp magazine reincarnated; it was the pulp magazine simplified and summarized by vivid pictures.

Men who disliked the rugged outdoor life had their handbook in *Playboy*, a publishing phenomenon of the fifties that was as superior to its numerous imitators as *True* and *Argosy* were to theirs. It summarized its editorial pitch in its first anniversary issue: "*Playboy* is an entertainment magazine for the indoor man —a choice collection of stories, articles, pictures, cartoons, and humor selected from many sources, past and present, to form a pleasure-primer for the sophisticated, city-bred male. We never intended *Playboy* to be a big circulation magazine; we've never edited it to please the general public. We hoped it would be welcomed by that select group of urbane fellows who were less concerned with hunting, fishing, and climbing mountains than good food, drink, proper dress, and the pleasure of female company."

The young man who founded *Playboy* was Hugh Hefner, at the time only a few years out of the University of Illinois. For several years he had wanted to publish a magazine of his own similar to what *Esquire* had once been, and after leaving the university he found a job in the promotion department of *Esquire*. He wrote a friend at the time: "I'd like to produce an entertainment magazine for the city-bred guy—breezy and sophisticated. The girlie features would guarantee the initial sale but the magazine would have quality, too. Later with some money in the bank, we'd begin increasing the quality and reducing the girlie features. We'd go after advertising and really make it an *Esquire*-type magazine." [19] When *Esquire* wanted to transfer Hefner from Chicago to New York in 1952, he asked for a raise of $25 a month to offset the inconvenience and expense of moving. *Esquire* would go no higher than $20.

Hefner stayed in Chicago and began raising money for his own magazine. He persuaded a printer to give him forty-five-day credit. He borrowed $600 from a bank and from a finance company. From stock that he sold friends, he scraped together another $7,000. He ordered 70,000 copies of his first issue, which came out in December, 1953, although it bore no date because Hefner was not sure there would be a second issue.

A girlie feature that helped sell 70 per cent of the copies of that first issue was a much-discussed nude calendar photograph of actress Marilyn Monroe. Proceeds from the first issue enabled Hefner to get out a second and proceeds from that, a third, edited from a card table in his apartment. The first issues were notable more for their girlie features than for the quality Hefner had hoped for, and even after the magazine had changed, many persons tended to judge it by what it was then rather than by what it had become. Hefner did not solicit advertising until 1956 because he knew he could not attract the kinds that would be most profitable and in keeping with his ideas for the magazine. By the end of the first year, *Playboy* was selling 175,000 copies, and early in its second the circulation began to shoot up rapidly. By 1963 it had reached about 1,310,000.

From 1955 onward, *Playboy* improved its quality, toned down its content, and made its references to sex somewhat less predominant, although it was still not the magazine one would send to a maiden aunt. It published fiction and nonfiction by such writers as Evelyn Waugh, Carl Sandburg, Nelson Algren, Wolcott Gibbs,

[19] "World of Playboy," *Wall Street Journal*, March 28, 1962, p. 1.

Jack Kerouac, Herbert Gold, and Alberto Moravio, at first as reprints which it obtained inexpensively, later as originals for which it paid fairly high prices. Its articles dealt with fashions, travel, sports cars, food, jazz, and of course, sex. Surely one of its most popular features was its "playmate of the month"—a nude or near-nude model photographed in color and displayed in a gatefold insert. Although Jayne Mansfield got a movie contract after posing in *Playboy*, few of its "playmates" were the ubiquitous Hollywood starlets who turned up in more magazine pictures than in movies; most were supposedly working girls and the girl next door—airline hostesses, office managers, students, telephone operators, even members of the magazine's own staff. What all of the content conveyed was a somewhat undergraduate air of sophistication mingled with naivete.

As *Playboy* picked up a following, imitators began to spring up —*Escape, Nugget,* and *Rogue* in 1955, for instance, *Mr.* and *Dude* the following year. Most of the imitators remained what *Playboy* had been in its first year, and they were inexpensive to produce. Some scouted out sexy stories by well-known authors in obscure magazines and bought the reprint rights for little money. They depended heavily on single-copy sales, although they were doing well in the sixties if they had a quarter of *Playboy*'s circulation. Some publishers brought out bimonthlies with alternate months of publication—*Dude* one month, say, *Gent* the next.

In their drives to rid newsstands of objectionable magazines, religious and civic groups periodically singled them out for attack. Local bans, according to John H. Holmes of *Gent* and *Dude*, were "more of a nuisance than anything else." *Playboy* itself successfully fought one move to curtail its distribution. In 1955 the Post Office Department held that features in three of its issues were "unmailable" and refused to grant it the second-class mailing privileges for which it had applied. The court upheld the magazine's claim to the second-class mailing privileges.

Even so, *Playboy* had its detractors. A Minnesotan, in a typical complaint fired off to the editor of his newspaper, said that Hefner had "debased and prostituted sex and love and femininity to commercialize sex and sensualism." [20] A more sophisticated charge was that *Playboy* fed on a fear of sex. "Any theological critique of

[20] "Playboy Feature Is Criticized," Minneapolis *Sunday Tribune*, March 5, 1961, p. 3F.

Playboy that focuses on 'lewdness' will misfire completely," said a speaker at Andover Newton Theological School. "*Playboy* and its less successful imitators are not 'sex magazines' at all. They are basically anti-sexual. They dilute and dissipate authentic sexuality by reducing it to an accessory, by keeping it at a safe distance." [21] And in 1963, after Hefner had been explicating his philosophy in what seemed an interminable series, a critic in *Antioch Review* remarked: "Actually, *Playboy* is a relic of Victorianism. . . . For in spirit Hugh Hefner is a contemporary of Matthew Arnold and Ralph Waldo Emerson. And like the 'Matthew' and 'Waldo' in T. S. Eliot's poem, Mr. Hefner should be regarded as a guardian of the Victorian faith." [22]

In 1959, inspired by an article he had run in his magazine, Hefner began organizing a chain of Playboy Clubs in Chicago, New York, Miami, and other major cities. Membership keys cost from $25 to $100. In surroundings reflecting *Playboy*'s ideas of sophistication and the good life and decorated with blown-up reproductions of the magazine's artwork, members and their guests could dine, drink, dance, and listen to jazz. Waitresses and hatcheck girls were costumed as "bunnies" in adaptation of the magazine's trademark, a white rabbit. The clubs grossed $4,500,000 in 1961 and brought in a net profit of $1,500,000 before taxes. *Playboy*, too, was earning money. Its operating profit from circulation and sales amounted to $1,757,070 in 1961. That same year Hefner estimated the value of his enterprises at $20,000,000.

However, Hefner could lose money as well as make it. He hired Harvey Kurtzman, creator of *Mad*, and several staff members of that publication to bring out a new magazine of satire in the fall of 1956. *Trump* lasted until 1957, when its losses ended it as an unfortunate experiment. Hefner's next essay was *Show Business Illustrated*, a biweekly devoted to the world of entertainment. With a guaranteed circulation of 350,000, the magazine hopefully appeared in August, 1961. By the following March, Hefner had cut it back to monthly publication, and in February, 1962, after losing $1,500,000 on it in six months, he sold it to a new competitor, Huntington Hartford of *Show*, for $250,000.

The urban audience that Hefner chose for *Playboy* had been

---

[21] Quoted in *Current*, 2 (June, 1961) 56.
[22] J. A. Ward, "Hugh M. Hefner: Guardian of the Faith," *Antioch Review*, 23 (Summer, 1963) 214-15.

the market for another type of magazine in the prosperous twenties. In imitation of the successful *New Yorker*, local magazines addressed to the sophisticates of both sexes sprang up in major cities across the United States.

The local magazine of gossip and chitchat for socialites was nothing new. Colonel William Mann founded *Town Topics* for New York society before the turn of the century, for instance, and it lasted until 1932, when it collapsed after the attorney general of New York accused its publishers of forcing wealthy persons to buy stock in the company to keep out unsavory items about themselves and the court enjoined it from selling any more stock. The new local magazines that appeared in the twenties and thirties, while they owed something to such society organs as *American Sketch* and *Tatler*, were nevertheless of a different stamp. They much more obviously emulated the *New Yorker*, and even the names of some showed their debt: *Bostonian, Chicagoan, New Orleanian, Philadelphian, San Franciscan,* and *Washingtonian.* Cleveland had *Parade*, a "social, semi-humorous, and pictorial weekly," and Minneapolis and St. Paul had *Golfer and Sportsman.* Washington in 1939 got the *Senator*, a weekly published by Harry Newman of *Judge*, which sought a national readership but which concentrated on affairs within 150 miles of the capital in much the way that the *New Yorker* did for New York City.

The success of those imitators of the *New Yorker* was slight at best, and their mortality rate was high. Even granting that their goal was an upper-class audience, their circulations were low; the *Chicagoan* was selling only about 23,000 copies when it was enlarged and redesigned in the summer of 1931. Perhaps the magazines failed to hold readers because they tried too hard to transplant the *New Yorker* to their own localities instead of developing as indigenous products. The audiences they did attract were not large enough to be worth the attention of the big national advertisers whose accounts were essential if a publication were to become financially successful. The *New Yorker*, as its national circulation grew, may well have eliminated any economic justification for its local imitators, for through the *New Yorker*, a national advertiser could perhaps reach as large a discriminating audience in, say, Chicago as he could through a local Chicago magazine.

One of the most enduring of the derivations of the *New Yorker* was *Script*, which in its own fashion tried to do on the West Coast what the *New Yorker* was doing in the East. Rob Wagner founded *Script* in 1929, produced it at a small plant in Hollywood, and kept down editorial expenses by getting his friends who were celebrities to contribute to it without pay. Wagner built a following of a few thousand readers, but circulation began to fall off after his death in 1942 and had dwindled to about a thousand in 1947.

In 1947 Wagner's widow sold *Script* for $25,000 to Robert L. Smith, general manager of the Los Angeles *Daily News;* Ralph K. Davies, an independent oil operator; and Samuel B. Mosher, president of the Signal Oil Company. Smith said that they hoped within a few years to earn for *Script* a national position similar to that of the *New Yorker.*

The new owners changed *Script* from a biweekly to a monthly and appointed James Felton, a former city editor of the Los Angeles *Daily News,* as editor. Despite a low budget, Felton got the work of widely known authors and cartoonists, and put Salvador Dali under contract to produce a series of original paintings for the magazine. In about a year circulation rose to 53,000, although *Script* continued to lose between $15,000 to $20,000 an issue.

Ik Shuman, who had once been executive editor of the *New Yorker,* was brought in as publisher of *Script* in 1948. At the same time the magazine got additional financial backing from Samuel Goldwyn, the motion picture producer, and William Zeckendorf, a New York real estate operator.

Seven months later, however, all of the backers withdrew, and Ik Shuman bought title to the magazine for a dollar. He kept *Script* alive until March, 1949, when he finally suspended publication because of high production costs and low revenue.

Despite the bleak record of local magazines, publishers hopefully continued to try new ones. Chicagoans could read in an editorial in the first issue of *Chicago,* dated March, 1954, why Maurice English thought that his new monthly was justified: "No magazine has yet used the full resources of contemporary journalism—spot reporting, feature articles, fiction, the camera, the artist's pen and brush—to bring into focus one great city. Not an isolated section of it, not this class or that group, but all of its people, in their night-and-daily doings. . . ." *Chicago* bravely tried to live up to its prospectus, but it never attracted any appreciable amount of national advertising, and it ceased publication with its issue of October, 1956.

12

Expansion by Compression

In the late thirties, Gardner Cowles, Jr., remarked, "The most notable publication successes of the last decade have all been publications which condensed their content more than their predecessors: (1) the *Reader's Digest* substantially abbreviated, and, in the public opinion, improved, long-winded magazine articles; (2) *Time* magazine condensed the long-winded newspapers; (3) the New York *Daily News* further abbreviated the news and added many pictures." [1]

His observation was sound not just about the past decade but about the next one, too. Five of the new types of magazines to emerge in the twentieth century abbreviated the content of earlier media, and Cowles himself contributed to the development of two of them—the picture magazine and the miniature magazine, which had a short vogue in the early fifties.

First to appear were the news magazines and digest magazines, which condensed by text. They grew up side by side in the twenties when tabloid newspapers were rolling up huge circulations by giving news a more concise and lively treatment than newspapers previously had. Although the news magazines merely supplemented newspapers, they replaced the sober and prolix journals of commentary. They killed off the *Literary Digest*, which itself had risen

[1] Jackson Edwards, "One Every Minute," *Scribner's*, 103 (May, 1938) 23.

\

to popularity as a summarizer. The digests plucked articles from the hundreds of magazines which confronted the reader at the newsstand and boiled them down into short pieces with short words and short sentences.

About a decade later the picture magazine and the comic book grew up together, and they abbreviated not by text but visually by photographs and drawings. The picture magazine offered photographic condensations of the material carried by the news and feature magazines, and the comic book with drawings condensed the adventure and action stories of the pulps. Both appeared in the thirties, when Americans had been made picture-conscious by the movies and newspapers and when commercial television was but a few years away.

Perhaps inevitably publishers tried to combine the appeals of both the news and picture magazines in a publication that carried condensation to an extreme—the miniature magazine of news, features, and photographs which flashed brightly and briefly after Gardner Cowles, Jr., issued *Quick* in 1949. The miniature magazines appeared just as television, a medium requiring even less effort, was spreading across the country. Although they had some reader acceptance, they failed to get advertising support, and by the late fifties they had all but vanished.

Significantly perhaps, three of the five new types—the digests, picture magazines, and comic books—quickly won tremendous audiences; a digest and a picture magazine led all other magazines in circulation throughout the fifties. Yet each class of condensers, except for the comic book, was dominated by a sparse handful of readers. *Reader's Digest* was a giant after its imitators had come and gone, for instance, and *Life* and *Look* remained virtually alone despite many early attempts to challenge them.

As a class, news magazines became an important part of the magazine industry only after 1923, when *Time* first appeared. Although *Time* was indisputably the most successful and, in a sense, the most influential of all news magazines, it was not the first magazine which disseminated news as its primary function. Such publications had existed as early as the eighteenth century, but they had been so few and so separated from one another in time that they scarcely constituted a distinct category. Nor did even *Pathfinder,* the most immediate forerunner and a contemporary of *Time,* give the attention to news-gathering and timeliness that was to characterize the major news weeklies of the twentieth century.

The first two American magazines devoted exclusively to news appeared two months apart in 1786—the *New Haven Gazette, and the Connecticut Magazine* in February, the *Worcester Magazine* in April—and even before them, some magazines had run news as a part of their content. Sixteen years separated their appearance from that of the third news magazine, the *Balance and Columbian Repository*, which survived for almost seven years after its initial issue in January, 1802. The first American magazine of really long life and large circulation was also a news magazine, the fourth, *Niles' Weekly Register*, which published from September 7, 1811, until February 26, 1848, when it died as a result of competition from the growing number of newspapers and other magazines and from inefficient editing. Other nineteenth-century magazines, notably *Leslie's* and *Harper's Weekly*, covered the news in pictures and were more properly the forerunners of *Life* than of *Time*. The *Literary Digest* was close to being a news magazine, but it was also close to being a digest; actually, as one historian aptly described it, it was more "a clipping service for public opinion" than a true news magazine.[2]

The oldest of the news magazines still being published in 1954, when its name and editorial approach were changed, was *Pathfinder*, which had carried news, most of it rewritten from newspapers and the press services, to rural and small-town America for more than a half a century. George D. Mitchell, the Republican son of a Republican congressman from Pennsylvania, founded *Pathfinder* in Washington, D.C., on January 6, 1894. The weekly was filled with rewrites of news from other publications and with odds and ends chosen for their entertainment value. Late in covering events, *Pathfinder* favored news of social significance and rarely used material about crime and scandal. Although the advertising it attracted was largely for patent medicines and from mail-order firms, the magazine did a good job of supplying news and entertainment at a low price, a dollar a year, throughout World War I and into the peace. The circulation, which grew steadily during the twenties after a sharp climb during the war, was more than a million copies a week during the latter half of the thirties.

In the thirties, control of *Pathfinder* changed hands several times. Sevellon Brown of the Providence *Journal* and *Bulletin* owned the

---

[2] Calvin Ellsworth Chunn, "History of News Magazines" (unpublished doctoral dissertation, The University of Missouri, 1950), *passim*.

weekly from September, 1936, until August, 1938, when he sold it to James L. Bray, former business manager of the *U.S. News.* Bray sold the magazine eleven months later to Emil Hurja, a former executive director of the Democratic National Committee. Hurja had won himself a reputation as a political forecaster as a result of his pre-election statistical analyses, and he made public opinion polls on national issues a feature of the magazine. But Hurja had trouble in attracting advertising, probably because advertisers thought that they could reach a large share of *Pathfinder's* market through other media. To make *Pathfinder* an effective medium for reaching the rural and small-town market, Hurja in 1940 began to reduce its circulation in cities of more than a hundred thousand population, a policy which he said would mean sacrificing "some quarter of a million dollars in advertising due to the elimination of advertising now on the books." [3] The policy apparently did little to revive *Pathfinder*, for although the magazine guaranteed a circulation of 1,000,000 in 1940, its sales had fallen to 556,000 in the first half of 1941.

In August, 1943, Hurja sold operating control of *Pathfinder*, although he remained on its staff for another two years. The magazine was taken over by Graham C. Patterson backed by Joseph N. Pew, Jr., of the Sun Oil Company, the team which had bought and revived *Farm Journal* in 1935 and had acquired *Farmer's Wife* in 1939.

Patterson enlarged and redesigned *Pathfinder*, expanded its news-gathering staff, eliminated its patent medicine advertising, and sought national advertising. Converted from weekly to fortnightly publication in 1946, the magazine showed rapid gains in circulation after the war. At the start of 1947, its circulation had again reached 1,000,000, a gain of 600,000 in a year. In 1950 *Pathfinder* operated twenty-five departments, manned by a Washington staff of forty-one, and had bureaus in Chicago and New York and correspondents in various foreign cities. After its change to *Town Journal*, the magazine was strictly a general interest monthly for small-town America. As such, it failed to attract sufficient advertising to outpace rising production costs. It died with its issue of February, 1957.

Although *Pathfinder* antedated *Time* by almost thirty years, it had no discernible influence on the news magazines that sprang

[3] *Editor & Publisher,* 73 (March 23, 1940) 38.

up in the twenties and thirties. There was little about its treatment of the news to capture the imagination; indeed, because of its folksy appeal to a small-town and rural reading public, the vast majority of magazine readers probably never heard of it. Nor was it spectacularly successful. Its newsprint paper stock, its low subscription price, its patent medicine advertising, its audience all perhaps put *Pathfinder* in a class with the inexpensive farm papers and hence somewhat suspect as a reputable advertising medium. When Briton Hadden and Henry Luce drew up their prospectus for *Time*, the magazine with which they contrasted their proposed news weekly was not *Pathfinder*—there is no indication that they had ever heard of it—but the *Literary Digest*. However, it was not the *Literary Digest* that made the news magazine a distinct genre in the magazine field—it was *Time*.

As undergraduates at Yale and as second lieutenants of artillery at Camp Jackson, South Carolina, in World War I, Briton Hadden and Henry Luce often talked about a newspaper or magazine that would inform a poorly informed America. "People," Hadden said, "talk too much about what they don't know."

"This is not the fault of the newspapers," Hadden and Luce agreed in the prospectus which they drafted for *Time* in 1922; "they print all the news.

"It is not the fault of the weekly 'reviews'; they adequately develop and comment on news.

"To say with the facile cynic that it is the fault of the people themselves is to beg the question.

"People are uninformed because no publication has adapted itself to the time which busy men are able to spend simply keeping informed."

What was needed, Hadden and Luce agreed, was a publication that made sense of the chaotic torrent of news. After Luce had studied at Oxford and then gone to work for the Chicago *Daily News*, after Hadden had worked for the New York *World*, the two young men finished their plans for *Time* while working together for the Baltimore *News*. Their prospectus of eighteen pages had three major ideas:

1. News could be completely organized; each article would appear "in its logical place in the magazine." Each department would be broken into subcategories. Thus "Law" might be a sub-

category under "The Professions," although it actually took more than forty years to work its way into the magazine.

2. *Time* would show "what the news means." It would deal "*briefly* with every happening of importance" as news "rather than as comment." But, while giving both sides, it would "clearly indicate which side it believes to have the stronger position." It would run neither editorials nor articles to prove any special case. "But the editors recognize that complete neutrality on public questions and important news is probably as undesirable as it is impossible, and are therefore ready to acknowledge certain prejudices which may in varying measure predetermine their opinions of the news. . . . But this magazine is not founded to promulgate prejudices, liberal or conservative. . . . The magazine is one of news, not argument, and verges on the controversial only where it is necessary to point out what the news *means.*"

3. Individual persons, not governments and mysterious forces, make news. Influential men, the prospectus said, "are something more than stage-figures with a name. It is important to know what they drink. It is important to know to what gods they pray and what kinds of fights they love." Since "the personalities of politics make public affairs live," *Time* would describe the personalities and private opinions of public men. *Time* would even try to "make editors known to the public as Senators are known."[4]

Rejecting such titles as *Chance, Destiny,* and *Weekly News Budget,* Hadden and Luce settled on *Time* as a name because it was simple, yet dignified and catchy, was different from other titles, yet was a well-known word, and was adaptable to "many varied and catchy slogans."

The prospectus for *Time* impressed its authors far more than it did potential backers, many of whom warned them that their market was thoroughly covered by the *Literary Digest,* then one of the leaders in circulation and third among all magazines in advertising revenue. Hadden and Luce eventually raised enough money to begin publication. They hired a few staff members, none more than three years out of college, none paid more than $40 a week and some only $10. For practice, they published a specimen issue with departments, subdepartments, and a writing style that alternated between the brisk and the banal. Bernard Baruch looked from the cover, the top of his head inexplicably bracketed by huge

---

[4] Time Inc., "*Time*: The Weekly News-Magazine (A Prospectus)," 1922.

quotation marks, and the slogan "Time will tell" shared a line with the date, December 30, 1922.

Encouraged, they launched their magazine with a first issue of twenty-eight pages, a meager four of them advertising. Their source of copy was a bundle of newspapers left at their door each morning and evening. They could rewrite those newspapers without fear of legal retaliation. News could not be protected by copyright, and they had the opinion of Justice Holmes that their weekly probably would not infringe on the property rights of the original gatherers since news was so perishable a commodity.

When the first issue of *Time*, dated March 2, 1923, went to its 9,000 subscribers, the response was disconcertingly apathetic. Although circulation doubled in the first year, *Time* stumbled from one financial crisis to the next for its first five years. In 1928, however, it showed a net profit of $125,787. The next year its net jumped to $325,412; its advertising gross had more than doubled to reach $1,860,443, and circulation was more than a quarter-million. Thereafter *Time*—and Time Inc.—grew steadily.

As Hadden and Luce had recognized, there was a market for a news magazine. After World War I, colleges began turning out graduates at an accelerated rate—the number of regularly enrolled students in 1922 was almost double that of 1918—and *Time* appealed primarily to the person with a degree. The tempo of life was faster than before the war, and a person who wanted his news in a hurry had nowhere to get it. The radio newscast had not yet become commonplace; neither had the radio commentator who tried to clarify the news. *Time* more than filled the need; it filled it entertainingly. Its departmentalized stories were brief—at first never more than 400 words. Even its sentences were brief, an average of 19.96 words in 1923 as compared with the 30.15 of the *Literary Digest,* someone once painstakingly computed. Its tone, brash and irreverent, perhaps set well with a generation which was revolutionizing manners and morals.

As *Time* grew older, it developed practices that other news magazines copied. In the mid-twenties, it began to present all of its news in narrative form, a complete break with the traditional news-writing practice of daily newspapers. It evolved a research and checking system under which researchers supplied writers with pertinent details and word by word verified the statements in the writers' stories. In the thirties, perhaps because it could no longer count on other sources to furnish the sort of information it wanted for its treatment of the news, *Time* began building up its own network of bureaus and correspondents, and eventually its private news-gathering organization was below only the Associated Press and United Press International in size.

The manner in which *Time* reported events was distinctive, even though staff members denied that there was such a thing as a "*Time* style" after the early years. Parodists made sport of *Time's* inverted sentences, its piled-on adjectives ("shaggy-maned, beetle-browed John L. Lewis"), its coined words ("cinemaddict," "radiorator"), its hyperactive verbs, its footnotes of needless amplification. But the real significance of *Time's* experimentation with language lay in its attitude, of which style was but a symptom, according to Joseph J. Firebaugh in *American Speech* for October, 1941. "Postwar inconoclasm was the spirit which fostered *Time's* experimental attitude toward language," he wrote; and its significant linguistic achievement was adapting language to express "two great democratic ideals—disrespect for authority and reverence for success." It showed its disrespect for authority in such phrases as "weed-whiskered" and "bald-domed," he said, and its adulation of success in such words as "pundit" and "tycoon." Yet in the fifties and early sixties the most distinctive characteristic of *Time's* writing was its overall tone of omniscience which hinted that one person had studied all of the events of the week and was passing along the real story with its true significance.

In its fortieth anniversary issue of May 10, 1963, *Time* itself acknowledged that its basic formula had changed little over the years, although it had been modified and refined. Coverage of the news had been broadened and deepened, however, and other evolutions were fairly well summarized by the magazine: "Our covers have advanced to include a wide variety of treatments by the best portraitists in the world. Our illustration has broadened, with greater use of color pages to make editorial points and wider freedom in the size, shape and display of black-and-white pictures. And our style of operation—our timing—has accelerated to make us flexible to move fast and deep with the course of the news."

Imitators began to appear as *Time* became successful. Publishers in the Orient and in England borrowed ideas from *Time*. In Shanghai in October, 1933, Joseph Coughlin, who had once operated a newspaper at Carmel, California, established *East*, "Newsweekly of the Orient." In London in 1933, Francis Yeats-Brown edited *Everyman*, a "World News Weekly," with news condensations and pictures. The most frank imitation of *Time* abroad, however, was the British *News Review*, which first appeared in February, 1936. Openly acknowledging its debt to *Time* in its first issue, *News Review* continued at midcentury to ape the red-bordered cover, the format, and the style of *Time*.

In the United States as well, publishers saw a market for national, regional, and local news magazines. In 1929 McGraw-Hill took full-page advertisements in metropolitan dailies to announce that it was converting its *Magazine of Business* into a weekly news magazine, *Business Week*. "It will be preeminently the business-man's journal of business news, vital and vivacious, informative and dynamic, with something American in every characteristic," the advertisement said. "It will be keyed to the new tempo in business." *Business Week* resembled *Time* in some ways, although it restricted its coverage to news and analysis of developments in business and industry.

The two major national magazines of general news that followed *Time*—*Newsweek* and *U.S. News*—both appeared in 1933. By then *Time* had forcibly demonstrated the appeal of the news weekly. As the nation struggled out of the depression and then went along the road to war, the uncertainties and tensions, the complexities of the times perhaps made Americans more needful than ever of publications that tried to sift the news and to explain its significance.

Newsweek was founded by the first foreign news editor of *Time*, Thomas J. C. Martyn, an Englishman whom Hadden and Luce had imported on the mistaken notion that he was an experienced writer on world affairs.[5] After gaining his first professional writing experience on *Time*, Martyn had gone to the New York *Times*, which he quit to draw up a prospectus, raise backing, and establish a news magazine. With a staff of twenty-two, a bundle of news clippings, and two packing cases of books, he launched a magazine, *News-Week*, which guaranteed advertisers a circulation of 50,000. Martyn's original idea was for a news digest which on its cover would publish seven photographs depicting an important event for each day in the week. In June, 1934, Martyn discontinued such covers, which were confusing to newsstand customers.

---

[5] Noel F. Busch, *Briton Hadden: A Biography of the Co-Founder of Time* (New York, 1949), pp. 85-86.

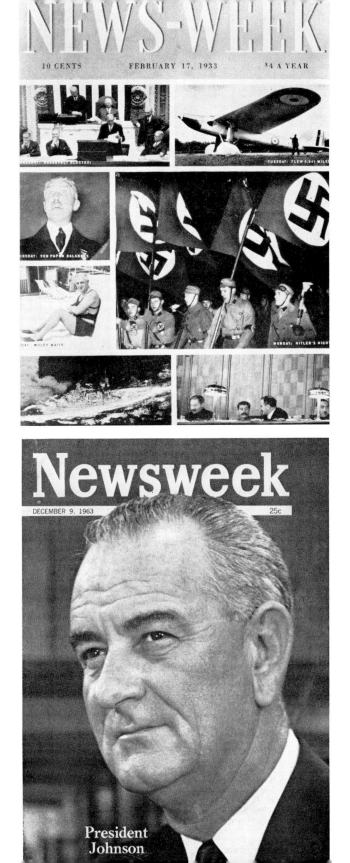

According to its rival *Time,* 120 individual investors furnished the $2,250,000 which *News-Week* went through in its first four years.[6] Although circulation had grown to a quarter of a million by early 1937, the magazine had encountered financial difficulties. Its difficulties were resolved in February, 1937, by a merger with *Today.* Raymond Moley had left Franklin D. Roosevelt's Brain Trust to edit *Today,* launched in November, 1933, with financial backing from Vincent Astor and W. Averell Harriman, to popularize the New Deal. *Today* was widely quoted, but it failed to achieve a circulation larger than 75,000. When it was merged with *News-Week,* officers of the new company included Vincent Astor, president; S. Winston Childs, Jr., vice president; DuSossoit Duke, vice president; Raymond Moley, editor; and Frank K. White, treasurer.

News-Week was given a revised name and a new editorial policy in October, 1937, when Malcolm Muir, who had been president of McGraw-Hill Publishing Company for ten years, became its president and publisher. Its name was changed to *Newsweek,* "The Magazine of News Significance." Departing from its simple digest of the news, the magazine announced a "three-dimensional editorial formula" consisting of the news itself, the background to the news, and interpretations of the significance of the news.

Unlike *Time, Newsweek* adopted signed columns—Raymond Moley had written the first of them—although the writers of its news columns remained anonymous. Like *Time, Newsweek* established a crew of researchers who aided writers in obtaining information for their stories. The magazine also set up its own news-gathering system of correspondents and bureaus to supplement the news coverage supplied it by the press associations. In the sixties, it had some 230 editorial employees and 200 correspondents. Like *Time, Newsweek* held to its basic editorial pattern, which, however, it modified and improved over the years. It added departments, and it increased the flexibility and speed of its news coverage. The day after the 1960 elections, for instance, it was able to distribute a sixteen-page "Election Blue Extra" across the country.

Newsweek shared in the big circulation gains of the news magazines generally in the fifties. Its distribution rose by about 80 per cent between 1950 and 1962, when its circulation was 1,531,000 and

---

[6] *Time,* 29 (Feb. 15, 1937) 50.

its advertising revenues $27,504,000. That same year its publisher reported that the magazine had earned a profit each year for the past twenty. Meanwhile, it had also undergone changes in top personnel. Muir turned the publisher's job over to Theodore F. Mueller in 1949. Gibson McCabe became publisher on Mueller's death in 1958 and president as well the next year when Muir advanced to board chairman.

Ownership of the magazine changed hands in March, 1961. Vincent Astor owned about 60 per cent of its stock when he died in 1959, Muir and Harriman together another 25 per cent. A management group headed by Muir tried to buy control from the Astor Foundation, and several other publishers negotiated for it. However, the foundation sold its shares to Philip L. Graham of the Washington Post Company for $8,985,000. In the next few months, the parent company added two other magazines, *Art News* and *Portfolio,* to its newspaper and broadcasting holdings. After Graham died in August, 1963, his wife Katharine succeeded him as head of the organization.

When David Lawrence established his *U.S. News* in Washington, D.C., in 1933, he was already well known as a political reporter. He had begun to earn his reputation while he was still an undergraduate at Princeton University. He had done so well there as a reporter for the Associated Press that he not only paid for his education but was graduated with $500 in the bank as well. His coverage also earned him the friendship of Woodrow Wilson. When Wilson moved into the White House, Lawrence was already a Washington correspondent, and his friendship with the President gave him special access to important news sources. The friendship lasted until Lawrence broke the news that Wilson had suffered a stroke impairing his capabilities.

In 1926 Lawrence started the *U.S. Daily,* which carried full texts of official government announcements, court decisions, documents, and similar material. After struggling with it for seven years, he dropped it for a news magazine. His *U.S. News* reported, analyzed, and forecast national news, but it trailed far behind *Time* and *Newsweek* in circulation. Because he thought there was a need for a magazine devoted entirely to world news, he brought out a sister publication, *World Report,* in May, 1946. It was similar to *U.S. News* in format, appearance, and style, but its content dealt only with international affairs. The two publications were joined into the single *U.S. News and World Report* in January, 1948, since Lawrence had decided it was impossible to tell where international affairs began and national affairs left off.

Unlike the other news magazines with departments of music, theater, press, and so on, the *U.S. News and World Report* kept its eye fixed only on national and international affairs, chiefly the economic and political, no doubt because Lawrence believed that economic factors were of prime importance and became interwoven with the political situation. Perhaps because of his earlier publishing experience, the magazine gave a good deal of space to what might be called primary sources—to full texts of statements, talks, interviews, documents—but it ran on-the-scene reports and analytical articles as well. Although the magazine reflected some of Lawrence's political conservatism, it also showed impartiality in much of its content and carried a good deal of material contrary to his views.

In the fifties and early sixties, the *U.S. News and World Report* was the fastest growing of all of the news weeklies. Its circulation increased by almost 244 per cent between 1950 and 1962, when it had reached 1,256,000. Lawrence and his family sold the magazine to its employees and the company that published it in the summer of 1962.

Among the faults that critics found with the news magazines were that they packaged news as entertainment, that they were politically conservative, and that they mingled their facts with judgments. After the 1956 Presidential election, one labor union, the United Automotive Workers, devoted an entire issue of its own magazine to analyzing the journalistic techniques in the pre-election coverage of *Time, Newsweek,* and *Life.* Dusting off the magazines as fiction factories, the union publication concluded: "Each was found to be loaded in favor of the GOP and against the Democrats. Loaded in every way: facts were sometimes suppressed, sometimes distorted, and Republicans almost always were given more space and friendlier treatment." [7] In twelve articles for the Providence *Journal-Bulletin* in 1958, Ben Bagdikian complained that the news magazines reconstructed the world to fit their own patterns: "The magazines look back at the end of the week, pick up the random blocks where they lie, rearrange them into an architecture, add their own backdrop, landscaping, climate and sound

[7] *Ammunition,* 14 (Dec., 1956) 2.

effects." He thought that the news magazine "presents a subtly loaded political story or a dramatically oversimplified one to an audience conditioned to having outright political argument labeled. The problem is compounded by the fact that the news magazines go largely to middle-class readers who probably do not have a high interest in literary analysis and political sophistication." [8]

In the thirties and forties, a number of regional and local news magazines appeared across the United States, and they, too, owed much to *Time*, although some showed the influence of *Life* and the *New Yorker* as well. One of the local news magazines to appear in the wake of *Time* was the *Pittsburgh Bulletin-Index*, which resulted from a merger of two old publications in the early thirties. Copying the typography of *Time*, it reported on activities in Pittsburgh and drew the bulk of its advertising from local concerns. The weekly, which had a peak circulation of 12,000, changed ownerships in 1942 and 1945 and was reportedly losing a thousand dollars a week before it ceased publication in February, 1949.

Among the regional publications which sprang up in the profusion after World War II were several news magazines. On the West Coast in 1946, for instance, O. D. Keep, a former promotion manager for *Time* and *Fortune*, launched *Fortnight*, "The Newsmagazine of California," which ran guides to entertainment in addition to its news and feature coverage of California affairs. In February, 1957, it shifted its emphasis from news to regional feature articles; a few months later its issues were appearing bimonthly, and it ceased publication in October, 1957. In Texas, also in 1946, Raymond Holbrook established *Texas Week*, which sought to present each week, "through text and pictures, a concise summary of the significant news in the nation's greatest state." The magazine, which was departmentalized like *Time* and *Newsweek*, and which had an initial press run of 20,000, suspended publication within a year.

The digest magazine found its reader audience about the time the news magazine did, but publishers had experimented with it, as with the news magazine, long before the twenties. Indeed, the first publication that called itself a magazine was a digest. Edward Cave of London started his *Gentleman's Magazine* in 1731 because he sensed a market for a publication that offered a selection of

---

[8] In reprint, Ben Bagdikian, *The Newsmagazines* (Providence, R.I., 1958), 2, 26.

essays and intelligence from other papers. Funk and Wagnalls started the *Literary Digest* in 1890 because they thought there was a need for a publication that would winnow instructive material from the periodicals of their day, and although the *Literary Digest* departed from its original purpose, it subsisted largely on the content of other publications until its death. Albert Shaw, Sr., founded his *Review of Reviews* in 1891 because he believed that readers would appreciate a publication which condensed informative material from the host of periodicals then available.

Frank Munsey had remarkable if brief success with a digest magazine shortly after the turn of the century. In March, 1906, he issued *Scrap Book*, a "granary for the gleanings of literature," as he called it, which consisted of reprinted stories and articles. *Scrap Book* sold a half-million copies in three days and did extremely well for a year. Then Munsey, deciding to expand it, issued the publication in two sections, one all pictures, the other all fiction. Sales of the magazine plunged. Within a year, one section had vanished into *Live Wire;* the other lasted until 1912.[9]

A decade later, in 1922, DeWitt Wallace issued the first number of the *Reader's Digest.* With its appearance, the modern digest as a distinct type of publication originated, for other publishers inevitably imitated the *Digest,* both in its pocket-sized format and in its practice of culling articles from other periodicals. There was a boom in both the pocket magazines and in the digests, especially in the thirties and forties. The two were not identical types. The term "pocket magazine" distinguished magazines by size, the term "digest" by content; most digests were pocket magazines, although some were not.

The imitators of the *Reader's Digest* began to spring up in the late twenties, despite Wallace's attempt to hide its success by keeping its circulation a secret. As the number grew, some of the newcomers limited their content to special areas instead of carrying the wide variety of articles that the *Digest* did. For instance, there appeared a *Science Digest* and a *Catholic Digest;* after World War II, there appeared a *Negro Digest* and a *Children's Digest.* And it was not just magazine articles that the digests condensed; they turned to the other media of books, newspapers, and radio. In 1938 *Book Digest* and *Omnibook* were established to provide readers

[9] George Britt, *Forty Years—Forty Millions: The Career of Frank A. Munsey* (New York, 1935), p. 100.

with abridgments of current books. A. Newton Plummer, Jr., in 1939 introduced *Cartoon Digest*, which proposed to reprint outstanding newspaper art each month. Two Chicago men in 1947 got out *Editorial Digest*, which reprinted leading editorial comment of the preceding month; *Column* set out in 1949 to interpret the American scene by a variety of reprinted newspaper columns. Still another magazine tried reprinting the best letters to editors of newspapers. Condé Nast in 1939 toyed with *Listener's Digest*, a summary of the best radio programs.

Compared with the *Reader's Digest*, most of the digest magazines were small operations with not especially impressive circulations. For instance, *Everybody's Digest*, which began publication in 1938 and which was one of the leaders for a few years, sold some 278,000 copies a month in 1949; but sales dropped to 138,000 in 1953, and the magazine had vanished by 1955. *The Woman*, which lived from 1938 until 1955, consistently reported a circulation of well under 150,000. Both of those magazines, like the *Reader's Digest*, ran original material as well as reprinted articles.

Most of the other digests, too, ran varying proportions of original material. One can easily guess why they did. In the thirties, the *Reader's Digest*, having the momentum of an early start, managed to obtain exclusive rights to reprint material from most of the available leading magazines of general interest, and after its first years it was always opulent enough to outbid competitors. There was certainly some limit to the amount of widely popular material which was available for reprinting, and widely popular material was a necessary ingredient of the digests, which were supported by circulation. As the number of digests grew, competition for material was keen; in the forties, it was not unusual for two magazines to carry different versions of the same reprinted article.

Rising costs pinched most of the digests and pocket magazines, especially after World War II. Traditionally, they had not carried advertising. But in 1947 and after, when the sale of copies alone did not produce enough revenue, a number of them went after it. *Magazine Digest*, *Reader's Scope*, the *Woman*, *Everybody's Digest*, *Success Today*, and *Coronet* all announced in 1947 that they would solicit advertising; and in 1950, after twelve years without advertisements, *Omnibook* sought its first accounts. The *Reader's Digest* kept its domestic edition closed to advertisers until April, 1955, when it, too, capitulated to economic pressure.

Digests came and went, the great majority with short lives, a few with long, but even some that survived for decades gave up in the fifties. *Magazine Digest*, which began publication in 1930, had a longer life than most. It was a grab bag of miscellany, much of it reworked from scientific and technical journals. Although for many years it was a Canadian magazine, published in Toronto and printed in Montreal, it drew most of its copy from periodicals in the United States, where it also had its largest circulation. It moved its offices to New York in 1948. It ceased publication in the fifties. For almost twenty years after 1938, *Omnibook* condensed several fiction and nonfiction books in each issue. Its publishers started a similar publication, *Book Reader*, in 1946, but suspended it in less than a year. In 1948 they set up two foreign editions of *Omnibook*, one in France, one in Australia. But high costs, low advertising volume, and static circulation killed the magazine in February, 1957.

Two general interest digests in the forties tried to break with the usual fare of the digest magazines. *Reader's Scope* hoped to capture the readership of liberals by giving them the sort of articles its editors thought they would like to find in the *Reader's Digest*. *This Month* was designed to promote international understanding without sacrificing entertainment. Neither had a long life.

Reader's Scope first appeared in the summer of 1944. Its editor was Leverett Gleason, a publisher of comic books, who said that he had worked out a new formula for digests as a result of a careful prepublication analysis of public taste. His plan was to run half reprinted material, half original material, and the articles would include about five biographical pieces an issue and a strong dose of humor. His articles were to be chosen for their timeliness, besides their liberal slant, instead of for the "lasting interest" of the *Reader's Digest* articles. Magazines which agreed to let him use material included the *New Yorker, Saturday Review of Literature, Mademoiselle*, and *Woman's Day*. His magazine had ceased publication within six years.

This Month began publication in February, 1945, on the wave of international goodwill which accompanied the establishment of UNESCO and which characterized the first years after the war. It was a nonprofit magazine backed by some fifteen members of the Association for Promotion of International Understanding, a Canadian organization formed to give North Americans a "liberal, democratic" view of the world. Edited in New York, printed in Canada, *This Month* also adopted a liberal slant and ran both original and reprinted material, the latter from publications in both Canada and the United States. After two years, it suspended publication.

Despite the high mortality, publishers in the fifties and sixties continued to bring out new digests which they thought might win at least moderate success. Jerome Ellison conceived the idea for his *Best Articles & Stories* while he was screening entries for the Benjamin Franklin Magazine Awards. Impressed by the large amount of excellent material which the busy reader might overlook, he planned a magazine that would consist entirely of reprints, mainly from magazines of small circulation and nominated by the editors themselves. His first issue came out in October, 1957, about a decade after he had founded his short-lived *'47*. His digest of quality reached its break-even point of 5,000 circulation by the following December, but it lasted only a few years when it was absorbed by *Atlas*.

Atlas itself was started in 1961 to give readers a rich sampling of the world's press. Its founder was Eleanor Davidson Worley, its editor Quincy Howe, network news broadcaster, writer, and one-time journalism professor at the University of Illinois. Each month its staff read more than 600 publications in twenty-five languages and, without abridging, translated a balance of the best criticism and reviews, poetry, short stories, travel pieces, and general articles dealing with political and economic affairs. The objective, according to Howe in a letter to the author in 1962, was to bring the widest assortment of complete material from the world press outside the United States to the American reader: "About every article, every item, we always ask one thing: 'is this something that could not be found elsewhere in the American press?' That is almost our guiding principle—to give American readers what they do not and indeed cannot get in any American publication. The role of *Atlas* is not to set forth any political, moral, religious, aesthetic, or any other kind of philosophy or point of view. It is a service of a unique kind." *Atlas* picked up more than 40,000 subscribers in its first eighteen months, but it was still running at a loss.

Current, which antedated *Atlas* by a year, had a similar but less global intent. It tried to help the concerned reader deal with the vast, varied outpouring of talks, interviews, broadcasts, articles, pamphlets, and interviews by abridging them and grouping them by topic.

The oldest follower of the *Reader's Digest* in 1963 was perhaps *Catholic Digest*, born in the cellar of the chancery of the Cathedral of St. Paul, Minnesota, in 1936. Its creators were two priests, the Rev. Paul C. Bussard and the Rev. Louis A. Gales, but the magazine was published privately and was not owned by the church. Its founders regarded the magazine as an extension of preaching the gospel. They set out to "select, condense, and publish articles from Catholic publications the world over," as they put it in the first issue. They originally called their magazine *Catholic Book and Magazine Digest*, and the first article they reprinted was from a Catholic student publication in St. Paul.

Early articles were almost all from Catholic publications, and contributors over the years included many prominent Catholics. However, the editors, who for several years went calling on subscribers to find out how they liked the magazine, soon learned that their readers wanted something other than sermons. They increasingly opened their pages to lay periodicals, and they included more and more general interest articles amidst their frankly religious material, which in the early sixties they held to 15 per cent of the total. Like the *Reader's Digest*, the magazine began to work up a good share of its own material; in the early sixties, it was originating about 75 per cent, much of which it planted in other Catholic periodicals for later reprinting. To find out what most interested their readers, the editors in 1952 began polling them regularly and using the results in planning content. The magazine began accepting advertising in 1955.

On the twenty-fifth anniversary of *Catholic Digest*, the firm publishing it was grossing about $5,000,000 a year from its many activities. It had begun launching editions of the digest abroad in 1946—in the United Kingdom, France, Belgium, Germany, Japan, Italy, the Philippines, India, South America—and although editions for Japan and South America were dropped, the others remained. The firm started to publish anthologies of articles and humor, culled from the back files of the magazine, in 1952. It founded *Catholic Market*, a business publication with a distribution of about 29,000, a decade later.

Besides inspiring the digests, the *Reader's Digest* also seems re-

LIFE

SPECIAL
DOUBLE
ISSUE

The SEA

65 color pages
articles by ROMAIN GARY
JAMES MICHENER
EUGENE BURDICK

TWO-IN-ONE ISSUE **35** CENTS

sponsible for the rise of a number of pocket magazines composed primarily of original material which imitated its short articles, its short sentences, its short words, sometimes its tone of chummy optimism, and its basic editorial formula. Most of them used some reprinted material, but the bulk of their copy was original.

Money from the defunct *Literary Digest* helped to finance a company that published several such pocket magazines. In 1937 Wilfred J. Funk, whose father had been a founder of the *Literary Digest*, used proceeds from the sale of the weekly to help form Kingsway Press, Inc. The first publication of the new company was *Your Life*, a "Popular Guide to Desirable Living," which capitalized on the popular desire for self-improvement that made best sellers of such books as Dale Carnegie's *How to Win Friends and Influence People* and Walter B. Pitkin's *Life Begins at Forty*. The magazine offered its readers help and inspiration in what its editor, Douglas Lurton, apparently regarded as life's major problem areas: health, charm, love, children, conversation, and fortune. *Your Life* found so hospitable a market that its publishers made a separate publication, *Your Personality*, out of the original department on charm in 1938. The following year they used the department on health as the basis for still another magazine, *Your Health*. Although the publishers kept circulations a secret, a trade paper reported in 1947 that their various magazines had shown a profit from the first issue.[10] However, Funk folded *Your Life, Your Health,* and *Your Personality* in January, 1961. They were based on a self-help formula that had been taken over by other magazines and even newspapers, he said, and their circulations gradually declined until they were in the red.

The pocket magazine ranking second in circulation to *Reader's Digest* was *Coronet*, which had sales of about 2,750,000 when it died in 1961. *Coronet* made its first appearance on newsstands in 1936 to test David A. Smart's contention that "beauty is still a very potent market." Smart's *Esquire* used two elegant black and gold pages in November to announce the newcomer, which would present "infinite riches in a little room" and seek "recognition as the most beautiful of magazines." For a time it perhaps achieved that distinction. The first number, with a five-color cover, carried drawings, etchings, and color reproductions of Raphael and Rembrandt

---

[10] *Tide*, 21 (Oct. 24, 1947) 38.

in addition to fiction, articles, and photographs. Its 250,000 copies were sold out in forty-eight hours, according to Smart. Subsequent issues in the late thirties were laden with classical and modern paintings, portfolios of photographs and individual studies, drawings and cartoons in color, satire, fiction, and articles.

But beauty was not the potent market that Smart had thought it was or that it was to become during the cultural boom after World War II. Sales declined from about 200,000 in 1936 to some 100,000 in early 1940.

In 1940 the cover yielded space once occupied by such paintings as Ghirlandaio's portrait of a lady of the Sassetti family and Corneille de Lyon's portrait of La Duchesse d'Estampes to photographs of models and Hollywood starlets, and the magazine settled down to a formula in keeping with those of the other digests and pocket magazines. Much of the change was the work of Oscar Dystel, who was moved from the circulation department into a top editorial position and who queried readers on their editorial preferences to develop a new editorial pitch. As *Coronet* did not accept advertising until 1947—it experimented briefly with advertising in 1937 but dropped it—its circulation figures were not made public during the boom war years, when several outsiders estimated its sales at as much as 5,000,000. However, when *Coronet* made its postwar bid for advertising, its circulation guarantee was but 2,000,000.

In the fifties *Coronet* became caught in the pressures on publishers to push circulations as high as they could. Its publisher, Arthur Stein, warned in 1959 that the course was leading to disaster: "The big mass books, the leaders in our field, have all pushed circulations up to artificial—and uneconomic—high levels, and if we don't watch out it will break us." [11] He conceded that he was as guilty as other publishers but contended that any general trend toward lower circulations would have to start with the giants in the industry. *Coronet's* losses were amounting to about $600,000 a year by 1961, according to trade estimates, and Esquire, Inc., negotiated with other publishers to take over the magazine.

Reader's Digest agreed to buy a ten-color press the company had installed for *Coronet* in 1958 at a cost of $1,300,000 and to divide the subscription list with Curtis Publishing Company. And then in July the publishers announced that the October issue would be the

---

[11] *Advertising Age,* 30 (June 1, 1959) 80.

final one. "The lesson for other publishers is to stop chasing numbers," said Lewis Gillenson, its last editor. "If the numbers game
continues, it will destroy many more magazines." [12]

Arnold Gingrich, its first editor, spoke its epitaph three years
later. In magazine publishing, he observed, it is as fatal to be too
early as too late:

> That lovely little art magazine, full of treasures of the world's great
> museums, was about twenty-five years ahead of the great art boom, on
> which it might have ridden like a surfboard. Instead of letting it die a
> natural death, we chose to make it into something that it wasn't born to
> be, with the result that it lived all the twenty-five years of its life on the
> crutch of family support. It became that anomaly, the world's largest
> midget, or the world's smallest giant, neither of which is a title with great
> natural box-office potentialities. In any event, it wound up in 1961 with
> insufficient riches in too little room. It lived to attend its twenty-fifth
> birthday party, reminding me of the League of Nations buildings in
> Geneva, which were finished just in time for World War II.[13]

Alex L. Hillman built Hillman Periodicals, Inc., into a profitable
company by publishing confession, factual detective, fan, and
comic magazines. In November, 1944, he added a pocket magazine
to his list. His experiences with *Pageant*, a slick-paper monthly
which at times resembled the offspring of a mating between
Reader's Digest and *Coronet*, provided a good study of the difficulties of publishing a magazine without advertising in a period of
shortages and rising production costs. The first editor of *Pageant*,
Eugene Lyons, left after about six months. In those six months,
Pageant had gone through about $300,000 of its original $500,000
budget, and Hillman had killed off his profitable detective and
comic magazines to provide it with paper. The second editor was
Vernon L. Pope, who had helped to develop the picture-sequence
technique used by *Look*. When Pope took over, he said he expected
to win *Pageant* a million readers within the next six or eight
months; but when he left a little more than two years later, in
August, 1947, *Pageant* had lost $400,000, and circulation had
dropped from an initial 500,000 to about 270,000. Neither Lyons
nor Pope had had sufficient paper supplies to justify promoting the
magazine, and increasing production costs had eaten away at their
budgets. When Pope left, Hillman said he would continue to pub-

---

[12] New York *Times*, July 12, 1961, p. 37; *Advertising Age*, 32 (July 17, 1961)
6, 52.
[13] Talk at Association for Education in Journalism, Lincoln, Neb., Aug. 28, 1963.

lish *Pageant* as a bimonthly until he had exhausted the features on hand.

In December, 1947, Hillman hired Harris Shevelson away from his job as managing editor of *Coronet* to make him editor of *Pageant*. When he took over, Shevelson remarked, "*Reader's Digest* is sort of the old senator with the long beard, *Coronet* the middle-aged prosperous businessman, and we the youngster. We'll have to be more electrifying, more shocking, and perhaps brasher." [14] Shevelson's *Pageant* was brighter and used more photographs than earlier versions. By 1949 circulation had pulled up to about 400,000 and the magazine was finally paying its way. Hillman sold the magazine and a line of paperback books to Macfadden in 1961, when its circulation was hovering around a half-million.

The digest and the news magazines, among the most successful publishing ideas of the twenties, brought the reader his news and features in capsule form. In the thirties, two of the most successful publishing ideas, the picture magazine and the comic book, carried summarization one step farther by using pictures instead of text to tell their stories.

One November day in 1936, after months of experimentation and promotion, Henry Luce's *Life* at last turned up on the newsstands, and the modern picture magazine was born. For their dimes, purchasers of that initial issue got ninety-six large pages full of photographs—the first, of an obstetrician slapping a baby to consciousness, captioned, "Life Begins." That issue of *Life* was sold out almost at once. Customers put their names on news dealers' waiting lists or bought secondhand copies for as much as a dollar.

Life was not the first of the modern picture magazines; Monte Bourjaily had completely revamped the twenty-two-year-old *Mid-Week Pictorial* and put it on sale the previous month. But *Life* was by all odds the most successful, and its success bred dozens of imitators. As it finally emerged, the picture magazine was the result of at least five influences. The illustrated weeklies at home, the illustrated magazines from abroad, the movies, the tabloid newspapers, and advertising photography all combined to produce the picture magazine. They were helped by technological advances in printing and photography.

From the middle of the nineteenth century onward, there were a number of illustrated magazines in the United States. *Leslie's*

---

[14] *Newsweek*, 30 (Dec. 29, 1947) 43.

Weekly, which began in 1855, built up a large circulation by running wood engravings of topical subjects; and *Harper's Weekly,* long a favorite with readers and advertisers, gave good pictorial coverage to the American scene after 1857. *Panorama* in 1928 and *Roto* in 1934 were unsuccessful experiments with the picture magazine.

In Europe, especially in Germany where the Berlin *Illustrirte Zeitung* was among the pioneers, periodicals used related photographs in sequence to tell a story several years before the modern picture magazine flourished in the United States. Some of the men who had worked on such publications came to the United States to escape the Nazis, and they influenced the development of the American picture magazine. Many of the publications themselves were available in this country. In libraries and on newsstands in large American cities, readers could get copies of perhaps a dozen illustrated periodicals from abroad, *L'Illustration,* for instance, and the *London Illustrated News.*

As the motion picture matured from a peepshow and vaudeville attraction and drew millions of persons to the box office each day, it no doubt made Americans picture conscious. In the thirties, Pare Lorentz and John Grierson, the men on the March of Time, and others were experimenting with the film as a form of journalism, and what they learned was important to the development of the picture magazine.

The tabloid newspapers of the twenties also helped to make photography a tool of journalism. Alongside their condensed, jazzed-up news stories, the tabloids ran more pictures than newspapers ever had before. Indeed, the first tabloid in New York, the *Daily News,* carried the word "Illustrated" in its title for part of its first year. In their contest in sensationalism, the tabloids used photography as a strong weapon. The *Daily News* smuggled a photograph of Ruth Snyder dying in the electric chair from the death chamber; the *Daily Graphic* invented "composographs," faked photographs depicting what was believed to have happened. Regular newspapers began to use more and more pictures, a trend aided by the establishment of such agencies as Acme Newspictures in 1924, the Associated Press Picture Service in 1928, and the Associated Press Wirephoto Service in 1935.

Advertising photography also has been credited with contributing to the development of the picture magazine. To catch the attention of the reader, advertisers used cartoons, drawings, and eventually photographs; and perhaps because they were better able to bear the cost, they seem to have used photography more lavishly than editors. One advertising agency man who pioneered in advertising photography was J. Stirling Getchell. Breaking away from the usual drawings in automotive advertising, he used photographs in his Plymouth account, and he dressed up advertisements for Goodrich Tires and Fleischmann's Yeast with news-style photos. As early as 1924 Getchell had toyed with the idea of publishing a picture magazine. In 1935 he prepared a sample but was unable to raise the $2,000,000 he thought necessary to launch it. He was interested in Luce's plans for *Life* and in 1938 started a magazine of his own, *Picture: The Photographic Digest.*

Magazines had used photographs editorially since the 1890's, both as covers and as illustrations of the text; and in the twenties, Bernarr Macfadden had hit upon the idea of photographic scenes posed by models to lend authenticity to his *True Story.* Condé Nast had attracted outstanding photographers to his magazines. Edward Steichen and Cecil Beaton had done their photographic studies for *Vanity Fair;* Remie Lohse, a master of the candid camera, began photographing for *Vogue* in 1933. *Vogue's* photographic trends were the candid, the exotic, and the surrealistic.[15] But magazine editors generally, like newspaper editors, had done little to develop photojournalism.

The most direct forerunner of the picture magazine of the thirties was *Mid-Week Pictorial,* first issued by the New York *Times* on September 9, 1914, as a "pictorial war extra." It was continued after the war as a rotogravure weekly with thirty-two pages of regular news pictures, not the picture stories later developed by *Life* and *Look.*

In September, 1936, when the idea for a picture magazine was in the air and, as one advertising trade paper later remarked, every advertising man carried a dummy for a picture magazine in his hip pocket, Monte Bourjaily, a former executive of United Feature Syndicate, bought *Mid-Week Pictorial* from the *Times* and converted it into a magazine somewhat along the lines of what *Life* was to become. Bourjaily increased the number of pages to sixty and improved the quality of the paper, but his major change was in approach, which was closer to the one that *Life* was working out

[15] John R. Whiting, *Photography Is a Language* (Chicago, 1946), 22-23.

than to that of the old *Mid-Week Pictorial.* His idea was to publish a news magazine that told its stories in pictures as well as text. Early in October, 1936, Bourjaily put his first issue on sale, and circulation shot from 30,000 under the *Times* to 117,750.

But the next month Time Inc. brought out its heavily promoted *Life,* which within a few weeks was selling a million copies. Bourjaily concluded that he had missed the market and with his issue of February 20, 1937, suspended publication until he could give *Mid-Week Pictorial* a new dress and format. That, as it turned out, was never.

As early as 1932, when *Time* was a success and *Fortune* was established, Henry Luce had had the idea of publishing a picture magazine. A staff at Time Inc. began experimenting in the fall of 1933 and produced a dummy called *Parade,* which borrowed ideas from *Vanity Fair, Time,* and *Fortune.* Luce and his staff were not satisfied with it, and further work on it was slowed up by the entry of Time Inc. into the motion picture field with the March of Time.

Yet the March of Time was one of several strong influences on the *Life* that appeared in November, 1936. March of Time was a serious attempt at photojournalism, one on which Time Inc. spent thousands of dollars, and it taught the editors how to get the sort of photographs they were looking for. Experiments on *Time* and *Fortune* also helped to develop the techniques of pictorial journalism that *Life* adopted.

For years *Time* had been doing some elementary, almost unpremeditated, experimentation in pictorial journalism. Its editors used a good many pictures, and they would shuffle through a score to find the one that best caught the mood of a story. They once ran a spread of color pictures to test reader response as indicated by requests for reprints. In *Time,* too, Daniel Longwell, an interested student of the new techniques in photographic presentation, tried arranging related photographs in sequence to tell a story, as comic-strip artists had long been doing.

Although it never used pictures to tell a story, *Fortune* contributed more to *Life* than *Time* did. Its editors introduced the candid camera to the United States and popularized the off-guard portrait in their efforts to make the faces of American businessmen interesting. In the *London Tatler* they spied some pictures by Dr. Erich Salomon, a German who in 1928 had become fascinated by the

Leica, a small camera which could take pictures indoors without flashbulbs, and who had set about catching shots of famous persons in unguarded moments. *Fortune* bought some of Salomon's pictures, but more important it brought him to the United States as one of its photographers. Salomon's work in *Fortune* inspired Thomas McAvoy, a pioneer *Life* photographer, to buy a Leica and learn to use it. *Fortune* also ran photographs by Margaret Bourke-White and Peter Stackpole, later associated with *Life*.

The immediate forerunner of *Life* was a promotion book, *Four Hours a Year*, which Daniel Longwell produced for the March of Time in 1936. Describing pictorial journalism, "a new language, difficult, as yet unmastered, but incredibly powerful and strangely universal," the book contained several examples of photographic experimentation. There was, for instance, an early example of a sequence of photographs to portray an event, a series of pictures showing the assassination of King Alexander of Yugoslavia and the French foreign minister in Marseilles in October, 1934. On facing pages were conventional portraits of well-scrubbed businessmen, all looking much alike, and candid shots of G. K. Chesterton, Herbert Hoover, and Benito Mussolini. In short, the book tried to apply what Longwell had learned about pictorial presentation.

By the time *Four Hours a Year* appeared, Longwell had a staff to develop a picture magazine, and he had a statement of purpose in the prospectus of what was to become of *Life:*

> To see life; to see the world; to witness great events; to watch the faces of the poor and the gestures of the proud; to see strange things—machines, armies, multitudes, shadows in the jungle and on the moon; to see man's work—his paintings, towers and discoveries; to see thousands of miles away, things hidden behind walls and within rooms, things dangerous to come to; the women that men love and many children; to see and take pleasure in seeing, to see and be amazed; to see and be instructed. . . .[16]

To the new magazine, Luce contributed, among other things, its "Speaking of Pictures," its "Life Goes to a Party," and its "Picture of the Week." Longwell contributed his technique of telling stories with pictures and was responsible for the typography, page size, and cover design.

The new magazine reached dummy stage, and advertising salesmen tried to sell space in it. While the men in advertising agencies recognized Luce's previous success, they were skeptical about his

---

[16] Time Inc., "A Prospectus for a New Magazine," n.d.

proposed picture magazine. One of them said that the prediction that the magazine would achieve a half-million circulation was "hysterical talk." In the Chicago *Journal of Commerce* in September, 1936, Phil S. Hanna warned that Luce was "sowing seeds for a fall." He granted that the new magazine might be successful but added: "we will wager that ten or fifteen years from now he will wish that he had confined his talents to his first-born and have returned some of his profits to his readers and advertisers so as to make the initial investment impregnable rather than have placed his profits in expansion."

Executives at Time Inc. counted on a circulation of no more than a half-million, for the new weekly was envisaged as a publication of limited appeal. Memoranda in the files of Time Inc. showed that the circulation department thought that it would sell about 200,000 copies by subscription, about 100,000 on the newsstand.

Until shortly before the first issue appeared, the new publication was nameless, although a number of names had been proposed— *Look, Parade, See, Focus, Picture,* and *Dime.* Someone had referred to it as "Uncle Harry's Show-Book," a name that so caught Luce's fancy that for a time he wanted to call it *Show-Book of the World.* In October, 1936, Time Inc. bought the name *Life* from the old humor magazine for $92,000.

Life told the news in pictures; but alongside its timely features, it ran material which its editors thought of permanent value. The magazine covered World War II with thoroughness and some artistry. Photographs by its staff members were hung by the Museum of Modern Art and later were the basis of a picture history book of the war. Memoirs of famous persons became a *Life* standby. It published those of the Duke of Windsor, Winston Churchill, Harry S Truman, General Douglas MacArthur. In 1943 the magazine ran the first of its occasional pieces of fiction, "The Silence of the Sea" by Vercors, which was followed by Ernest Hemingway's "The Old Man and the Sea" in 1952 and James Michener's "The Bridges at Tokori" in 1953. Nor did *Life* disdain culture, despite its mass audience. In 1953 it published a series of articles and pictures about "The World We Live In," and in 1955 it ran a series about the great religions of the world, both of which won Benjamin Franklin Magazine Awards. It ran articles by twelve prominent persons on "The National Purpose" in 1962.

Despite its excursions into culture, however, *Life* took pride in its exclusive and timely coverage of important events. In 1959, for $500,000, it signed up the first seven astronauts for their eyewitness stories, and four years later it bought all magazine rights to the personal stories of the sixteen men chosen to continue explorations into space. It issued a special souvenir supplement in January, 1961, to make use of the wealth of coverage of President Kennedy's inauguration and a special memorial edition after his assassination in 1963.

In a major redesign in 1961, *Life* regrouped its advertising and editorial material, adopted new layouts, and dropped the familiar red band on its cover. About the same time it proclaimed its intentions for its second quarter-century: to be a great magazine of events and politics, history, religion, science and nature, fine and lively arts, sport and adventure, and better living.

While Luce and his crew were planning *Life*, Gardner Cowles, Jr., was heading another group who developed *Look*, the second major picture magazine. *Look* was no imitator of *Life*. It evolved from the rotogravure section of the Des Moines *Register and Tribune*, a newspaper owned by the Cowles family since early in the century. In 1925 when Dr. George Gallup surveyed readers of the *Register and Tribune*, he found that they preferred pictures to text, and, in consequence, the staff began experimenting with the Sunday rotogravure section. Vernon Pope, who became the first editor of *Look*, tried running series of photographs instead of the single news or feature shots which other rotogravure editors were using. His picture series were so successful that in 1933 the *Register and Tribune* syndicated them to twenty-six other newspapers. From then on Gardner Cowles, Jr., in effect tested his idea for a picture magazine in his roto section.

As they planned *Look* and *Life*, Cowles and Luce traded ideas, for they never regarded their publications as competitors. There is a recurrent story that Luce for a time was even a minor investor in *Look*. Although Cowles and Luce agreed on the power of pictures, they differed on fundamentals. As a missionary, Luce favored pictures that transmitted news or information; as a merchant, Cowles thought that good pictures were inherently interesting. Luce visualized a limited audience, Cowles a mass audience. Their different concepts resulted in magazines of different characters, especially in their early years. *Life*, a weekly, was printed on slick stock and emphasized news, the arts, the cultural, the scientific, albeit with sex for seasoning. *Look*, first a monthly, then a biweekly, was printed by rotogravure on cheap paper and in its infancy dwelt on personalities and animals, food and fashions, photo quizzes and photo mysteries, the spectacular and thrilling.

The first issue of *Look*, drawing on the plant and personnel of Cowles newspapers, appeared in January, 1937. It gave readers a thousand eyes "to see round the world," it said, and promised to bring "current events, science, sports, beauty and education to both the Colonel's Lady and Mrs. O'Grady (and their respective husbands and children) to make them better informed on what's happening in the world." Word quickly spread that the innocent photograph on the cover could be converted into an obscenity by folding it in a certain way. Gardner Cowles, Jr., immediately sent wires to news dealers requesting that they destroy any copies remaining. Nonetheless, the first issue sold more than 700,000 copies.

The publishers kept *Look* a monthly for its first four issues, then switched to biweekly publication. Until they could estimate its future circulation, they accepted no advertising. In the first ten months, they increased their editorial budget tenfold and spent the $10,000 net profits from each issue on promotion. At the end of that time circulation had reached 1,700,000, and *Look* accepted its first advertising.

As *Look* matured, it forsook the shoddiness and sensationalism of its early issues. By the early fifties, it had worked out a pattern of articles dealing with national and world affairs, health and science, sports and entertainment, fashion and beauty, and foods and home living. Later in the decade it became serious without being dull. Although it dropped such gimmicks as its photo mystery, it spiced its pages with humor and cartoons. Although it retained its conception of photojournalism, under which both author and photographer kept text and visual presentation in mind, the magazine increased its load of full-length textual articles. Its authors included Adlai Stevenson, the Duchess of Windsor, Walter Lippmann, Bertrand Russell, and Ernest Hemingway, and the topics it dealt with had more social importance than those of its youth: civil liberties and the problems of minorities, current history, national and international affairs, problems of the mentally retarded, highway safety. In the fifties, it annually selected a number of All-American Cities, communities that had improved themselves

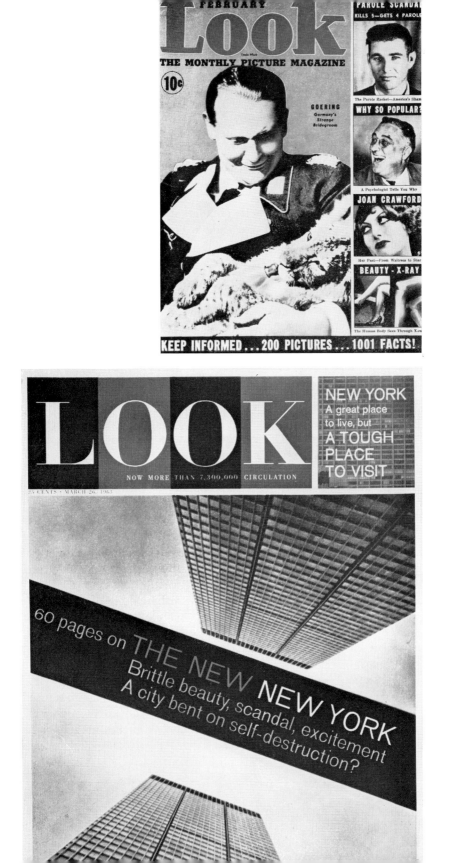

through citizen action, and in 1961 it joined with the U.S. Office of Education and a school administrators' group in honoring the teacher of the year.

In the fifties, *Look* joined other mass-circulation magazines in their race for large circulations and pushed its sales rapidly upward by aggressive promotion, by taking over the lists of fallen magazines, and by bargain rates. Its circulation of 7,000,000 in 1962 was more than double that of a decade earlier, and surveys indicated that about one in five American adults read the magazine. Advertising revenues also grew rapidly. They were but $1,150,000 in 1938, *Look*'s first year as an advertising medium, and had grown to $6,429,000 in 1946. They grew more than three and a half times in the decade after 1952 to reach $74,198,000 in 1963 and to give *Look* the second largest advertising income of any United States magazine.

In the wake of *Life* and *Look*, millions of copies of picture magazines poured onto the newsstands as other publishers introduced their entries. The mortality rate was high, but during 1937 and 1938 new ones hopefully appeared almost as fast as the failures disappeared. *Life* was virtually the only picture magazine to tell the news pictorially. The rest subsisted on feature pictures, and several capitalized on sex and sensation.

For his dime or quarter, the reader could buy such magazines as *Focus,* in which Leslie T. White sought "to bring the American scene into focus"; *Photo-History,* Richard Storr Childs's quarterly which devoted each issue to a single subject, such as the Spanish Civil War, China, and a history of the labor movement; *Peek,* "A Look at Life," which William Cotton filled with such features as "Peeking at Pictures" and "Peek-uliar Fishing"; *Now and Then,* in which former staff members of the *Pictorial Review* compared the present and past; and *Foto,* a rotogravure bimonthly of Dell Publishing Company which guaranteed a circulation of 400,000 but which died within a few months. J. Stirling Getchell, the advertising man who had pioneered in advertising photography, brought out his *Picture* in December, 1937, with a press run of 800,000. Shunning sex and sensation, the monthly was intended to edify its readers. After four or five issues it disappeared, perhaps because of competition, perhaps because Getchell's advertising clients feared he would neglect his agency for work on the magazine.

Life and *Look* emerged from the battle for circulation and advertising far in front, but a few other picture magazines had relatively long lives. One was *Click*, which the Annenberg interests began publishing in early 1938 and which became the third largest of the picture magazines. Its themes of sex and shock, and heavy promotion by Moe Annenberg, drove its circulation to 1,600,000 in two issues. Hunting for sensation to feed on, Annenberg instructed his editors to get a sequence of photographs showing a caesarean section, a project he abandoned only after Emile Gauvreau showed him a movie of what the operation was like. He found enough sensation, however, to get *Click* banned by the Canadian government, blacklisted by the Catholic church, and reviled by civic groups. Under such mounting pressure, the magazine was toned down, and thereafter its circulation ranged between 698,000 and 932,000. In 1942 the publishers reformed *Click* completely by making it a family magazine. They killed it off two years later, although its circulation was nearly a million, to get paper for their growing magazine for girls, *Seventeen*.

Pic, which Street & Smith launched in 1937, had a history similar to *Click*'s. Originally *Pic* was a rotogravure monthly heavily laden with photographs of young women not far removed from nudity. In 1945 its publishers redesigned it into a serious magazine for young men on the assumption that returning veterans would welcome a sober publication. *Pic* achieved a circulation of more than 600,000 under the new policy, but its publishers suspended it with the issue of December, 1948, to free paper and printing facilities for *Mademoiselle's Living*, a promising new publication.

As *Click* and *Pic* had done but at a swifter pace, a warborn picture magazine made the change from cheesecake to cheesecake-cum-culture. When Ned Pines first issued *See* in July, 1942, its sole emphasis was on pretty girls; but after its second issue, serious articles by well-known authors—Pearl Buck, Sumner Welles, and Harold Urey—shared its pages with the ubiquitous Hollywood starlets. As circulation climbed to more than a million, *See* replaced *Click* as third largest picture magazine, but in time it was changed into a general men's magazine.

The sensationalism that stirred some Americans to protest a few of the picture magazines also characterized a new class of magazines which paralleled the modern picture magazine in development—the comic books. They purveyed much the same inexpensive excitement that the pulps once had but in drawings and text that put a minimum strain on the partaker's literacy. Actually, the term comic book (or comic magazine—the trade used the names interchangeably) was a misnomer. The content of most comic books was anything but comic, stressing as it did crime, adventure, and romance. The name was a holdover from the days when publishers collected newspaper comic strips into booklet form.

One can argue plausibly that the comics were not magazines. Yet the typical comic appeared periodically under a continuing title, as magazines did, and some of the major publishers of comic books were also publishers of regular magazines, usually pulp, confession, romance, or movie fan magazines. Moreover, the advent of the comic book affected segments of the magazine industry. Therefore, the comic book deserves some attention in any history of the magazine industry after 1900.

It is hard to assign a date to the first comic book. Regular newspaper comic strips had been collected into book form early in the century, and in the 1930's a number of manufacturers of shoes, breakfast cereals, and the like gave away such books as premiums. Those publications were not periodicals, however, and they did not carry original material. The first regularly issued comic magazine was *Famous Funnies*, which Eastern Color Printing Company brought out in May, 1934, after a number of persons had rejected the idea as unsound. The magazine lost $4,150 on its first issue; and although it cleared $2,664 on its seventh issue, its publishers apparently saw no great future in comic magazines.[17]

In the next couple of years, a number of titles appeared as reprints of newspaper strips. After 1937, the comic magazine cut loose from the newspaper and soared on its own. The break began in January, 1937, when *Detective Comics* introduced a new editorial policy—all original material, and each issue devoted to one particular subject. Two years later, when Superman appeared, the pattern of production was established. Putting aside shears, pastepots, and stacks of old newspaper strips, publishers got teams of artists and writers to turn out stories exclusively for the comic magazines and gave them sixty-four pages instead of the dozen or so panels of a newspaper strip in which to develop their plots.

The comic magazine, which was primarily pictorial, boomed about the same time as the picture magazine. Its appeal, like that of many of the picture magazines, was to the emotions; neither its

[17] Colton Waugh, *The Comics* (New York, 1947), pp. 339-40.

text nor pictures taxed the intellect of its readers. Comic books grew phenomenally in numbers and in circulation just before and during World War II. The war, despite paper shortages, favored their development, for it provided them an opportunity to exploit conflict, horror, and sadism under the guise of patriotism, and it offered them a convenient market in the millions of troops seeking brief respite from the monotonies of garrison life. In military post exchanges they outsold *Life, Reader's Digest,* and the *Saturday Evening Post* by ten to one.

In 1955 comic magazines represented what *Barron's* estimated to be a $150,000,000 industry, and their aggregate circulation at times reached 90,000,000 copies a month. Although they circulated chiefly among children, they also were read by adults. A nationwide survey conducted for Fawcett Publications in 1943 revealed that comic magazines were read by 95 per cent of all boys and 91 per cent of all girls from the ages of six through eleven, and by 87 per cent of all boys and 80 per cent of all girls from the ages of twelve through seventeen. But they also were read by 41 per cent of all men and 28 per cent of all women from the ages of eighteen through thirty, and by 16 per cent of all men and 12 per cent of all women more than thirty. While those figures may have been promotional, there can be no denying that comic magazines, passed from hand to hand, reached a large section of the entire population.

As the popularity of comics grew, advertisers recognized their potentialities. When comics first appeared in the late thirties, publishers made their profits by producing the books for three cents and wholesaling them for six cents. Advertising was pure bonus, and publishers commonly sold it for twenty-five cents for each thousand readers. Sensing the reader appeal of comics, Casper Pinsker and Lester Wunderman, New York advertising men, in 1941 began buying up large blocks of space, as spacebrokers had in the nineteenth century, and reselling it in smaller units to clients. By 1943 a number of national advertisers, including Curtiss Candy Company, Republic Pictures, General Foods, Nehi Beverage Company, Bendix Aviation, and Westinghouse, were using comic magazines and the page rate had tripled.

Several of the publishers of pulps added comic books to their lists, and in them they played some of the themes that the pulps had dwelt on—crime, sex, war, adventure, science and pseudoscience, mystery, the West. The titles of just a few comics published in 1955 indicated their contents: *Gang Busters, Navy Action, Real Adventure, Journey into Mystery, Web of Mystery, Silver Kid Western, Hooded Horseman,* and *Strange Tales.* Romance, too, as it had come to the pulps, came to the comics. In 1949 comics with titles like *Sweethearts, Teen-Age Romances, Romantic Secrets, Life Story,* and *Young Love* were outselling even the comics of adventure, and the confession magazines felt the competition. Early leaders among the comics of love and romance were Fawcett's *Sweethearts,* which had a circulation of 1,000,000, and its *Life Story,* with a circulation of 700,000. Trade directories in 1955 listed about thirty-five love comics with titles such as *Boy Loves Girl, Love Experiences, Love at First Sight,* and *Lover's Lane;* but such listings were necessarily incomplete, and the actual number was probably at least twice that.

The comic book, because of its vivid pictorial treatment of themes which were often lurid and because of its accessibility to children, met strong opposition from parents, educators, psychiatrists and psychologists, government officials, and clergymen. Typical of the criticism that the comics engendered was that of Dr. Fredric Wertham, a psychiatrist: "The ingredients spelled out, pictured and glorified are violence, cruelty, sadism, crime, beating, promiscuity, sexual perversion, race hatred, contempt for human beings, descriptions of every conceivable crime, every method of concealing evidence, and every way to avoid detection." [18] Critics cited instances in which comic books had inspired youngsters to violence, even to murder. For example, two boys, aged fourteen and fifteen, were caught practicing the techniques of burglary they had read about in a comic; and a fourteen-year-old boy who had poisoned a woman told the sheriff of Los Angeles County that he had got the idea and the recipe for the poison from a comic book.

On the other hand, parents could find authorities who assured them that comics were harmless and even educational. J. Edgar Hoover, head of the Federal Bureau of Investigation, said: "It is doubtful . . . that an appreciable decrease in juvenile delinquency would result if crime books of all types were not readily available to children." [19] Dr. Laura Bender, psychiatrist at Bellevue Hospital, New York, said, "The comics may be said to offer the same type of

---

[18] Fredric Wertham, "It's Still Murder," *Saturday Review,* 38 (April 9, 1955) 12.
[19] *Tide,* 24 (Nov. 24, 1950) 56-57.

mental catharsis to their readers that Aristotle claimed was an attribute of drama." [20]

To protect themselves from criticism and restrictive legislation, fourteen major publishers of comic books formed the Association of Comics Magazine Publishers in July, 1948, as a self-policing body for the industry, and hired Henry Schultz, an attorney and member of the Board of Higher Education in New York, as executive director. The code of ethics adopted by the association urged members to abstain from publishing "sexy, wanton comics"; glorified or sympathetic treatments of crime; "details and methods of a crime committed by a youth"; vulgar and obscene language; and scenes of sadistic torture. However, the members belonging to the association produced only about 30 per cent of the comic magazine output. Some of the largest publishers, Dell, Fawcett, and National Comics Publications, refused to join the association because, they said, they saw no need to be regulated when their own publications were not offensive and because they did not wish to shelter the rest of the industry.

Criticism of comic books continued after the attempt at self-regulation. In September, 1954, the industry formed a new self-regulatory group, the Comic Magazines Association of America, and retained Charles F. Murphy, New York lawyer and magistrate, to head the association. Soon after taking office, Murphy banned "horror and terror" comic books and announced a new code of performance, similar to the earlier one. Again Dell refused to join the association, this time on the grounds that the group sought to "regulate rather than eliminate" crime and horror books, although the company offered to cooperate with Murphy.

More than fifty cities had sought action against the sale of comic magazines by 1948. Some had passed local ordinances regulating their sale; others had set up censorship committees. Thirty-two bills or resolutions to curb comic books were introduced in state legislatures in 1949, although none passed. Only one, in New York, passed both houses, and it was vetoed by the governor. However, in May, 1955, New York state did make it illegal to sell "obscene and objectionable comics" to minors and use such words as "crime sex, horror, terror" in titles of comic books. The Canadian Parliament outlawed crime comics in 1949 with a law providing up to two years' imprisonment for any person who "makes, prints, pub-

---

[20] *Time,* 46 (Oct. 22, 1945) 67-68.

lishes, distributes, sells" a comic which "exclusively or substantially comprises matter depicting pictorially the commission of crimes, real or fictitious."

As television became a universal medium and children literally spent more time in front of television sets than in the schoolroom, its programing took much of the criticism that earlier had been directed at comic books. However, television also probably cut into the demand for comics. Children used the two media for the same basic purpose—fantasy and escape—and studies showed that television typically reduced the amount of comic reading, although the heaviest readers of comic books were also likely to be the heaviest watchers of television.[21] Television, by providing even more effortless escape, did not make the comic books anachronistic; the major ones in the early sixties still had an aggregate distribution of about 35,000,000 copies an issue. But comics seemed less often the subject of public debate than in the forties and fifties; and, no doubt because of pressures on the industry, the most offensive types seemed to have pretty much disappeared.

In 1949 there appeared the first of several publications which carried the summarization of the conventional news and picture magazines to an extreme—the midget magazines of current events, personalities, and photographs. These super digests carried the conciseness of the news magazines almost to the point of absurdity, and they borrowed its brightness of style, its preoccupation with personalities. They exploited the appeal of the picture magazines. They packaged their contents in a publication so small that it scarcely covered a man's hand. Their fad as a type of magazine of any importance was correspondingly short; it lasted less than a decade.

First to show the popular appeal of the small magazine was Gardner Cowles, Jr., who thought that Americans needed news in handy capsules to read "on the bus or in the beauty parlor." He and the *Look* staff prepared trial issues of *Quick*, a pamphlet of four by six inches, and put it on sale in nine "test cities." The first issue of sixty-eight pages needed but a single sentence to cover most news items and just six sentences for its longest story. Sales were so encouraging that Cowles gave *Quick* national distribution. Circulation reached 200,000 by the seventh issue, 850,000 a year

[21] Wilbur Schramm, Jack Lyle, and Edwin Parker, *Television in the Lives of Our Children* (Stanford, Calif., 1961), *passim.*

later, and 1,300,000 in 1953 when Cowles disposed of the magazine.

At first Cowles intended to accept no advertising for *Quick* because its small page size required advertisers to prepare special printing plates. He soon discovered, however, that its low price did not cover production costs. His staff campaigned for advertising and showed advertisers how to adapt their copy and layouts to the small page size. But advertisers were reluctant to prepare special copy for the magazine, and production costs continued to bound upward. Although *Quick* grossed $936,961 in advertising in 1951 and had a total income of almost $4,000,000 in 1952, it lost heavily; and in April, 1953, Cowles announced that he would cease publishing *Quick* on June 1.

Walter Annenberg of Triangle Publications bought the name from Cowles for a reported $250,000 and tried to establish *Quick* as a larger sized biweekly without advertising. After nine months, in March, 1954, he abandoned the title, and three other publishers scrambled to claim it. Pocket Magazines, Inc., added the name to that of its miniature *Tempo,* which had first appeared about the time that Cowles disposed of *Quick.* Handicraft Publications brought out another *Quick,* and Macfadden Publications later issued a *Quick Digest.* While it initiated law suits against the other two publishers, Pocket Magazines, Inc., continued to publish *Tempo and Quick.*

Inevitably, *Quick* was imitated. The publishers of *Newsweek* in June, 1950, started *People Today,* a ten-cent magazine "to portray fortnightly in words and pictures people in all their facets—at work, asleep, and very much alive." After publishing the magazine for eight months, the owners sold it to Hillman Periodicals, Inc. The circulation of *People Today* began at 80,000, rose to more than 500,000, but had dropped to about 219,000 in 1957. Other publishers brought out magazines in the pattern of *Quick.* In July, 1951, Martin Goodman launched *Focus;* and in November, John Johnson, publisher of *Ebony,* began publishing *Jet,* "The Weekly Negro News Magazine," which promised complete coverage on happenings among Negroes all over the United States.

But advertisers did not become reconciled to the tiny magazines, and their production costs made them risky ventures for reader support alone. By the late fifties, virtually all of the titles of a few years before had vanished. As a magazine type of any consequence, the super compressors had failed to establish themselves.

Magazines for Everybody

The American of 1900 could probably have found at least one magazine devoted to his special interests no matter what they were. Magazines had begun to appear in profusion after the Civil War, and never before had they so completely represented the diverse tastes of the public. Politics, religion, science, fashions, society, music, drama, art, literature, sports, and recreation—by 1900 there were periodicals covering all of those fields and dozens of others.

If his tastes ran to politics, the American at the opening of the century could subscribe to such partisan periodicals as William Jennings Bryan's the *Commoner* or to journals like the *Nation*, which over the years stood above the battle of party politics. If he were devout, he had his choice of innumerable magazines published for Protestants, Catholics, and Jews and of such nonsectarian magazines as the *Guide to Holiness*. If he were interested in sports, recreation, and nature, he could, like 7,500 other readers, subscribe to *Shooting and Fishing*, send his dollar off to New York for a subscription to that new magazine, *American Golf*, or browse through publications like *American Angler*, *American Sportsman*, and *Bird-Lore*. If he were curious about photography, he could read *Snap-Shots;* if about drama, *Stage and Foyer Chat*. There were even several matrimonial periodicals like *Cupid*, edited in New York for 5,000 readers who were seeking mates.

The American of the early sixties had an even more diversified field to choose from, and the magazines he chose were likely to be superior in technical execution if not necessarily in content. Magazines of politics ranged from the extreme left to the extreme right. Religious magazines of many faiths abounded, and several denominations maintained sizable publishing companies; but freethinkers also had their organs. There were magazines for lovers of classical music, for lovers of jazz, for amateur magicians and amateur astronomers, for believers in astrology and students of the occult, for collectors of coins, stamps, and antique automobiles, for ex-servicemen, yachtsmen, women bowlers, campers, ham radio operators, folklorists, teen-agers, retired persons, and square dancers.

Some of those magazines dated back to the early years of the century. Others, however, were in their first volumes, for one of the striking developments in publishing in the fifties and early sixties was the proliferation of magazines of specialized appeal. Noting the scores of new magazines that were hopefully making a play for narrow audiences in 1961, Vernon C. Myers of *Look* offered an explanation: "As education, income, and leisure time have continued to rise, the interests of American people have ranged more broadly and more deeply into more subjects than ever before. Hence, it's not surprising that many new magazines are appearing to cater to specific needs and interests." [1] Appear they did, some briefly, since just being specialized was no guarantee of survival, some with good prospects for long-term success.

Among the new magazines were a good many that capitalized on the American's strenuous pursuit of his new leisure. In just a dozen years after 1950, more than a score of them appeared: *Archer's Magazine* and *Archery World; Golf Digest* and *Golf; Guns, Gun Report, Guns and Ammo, Gunsport, Gun World,* and *Precision Shooting; Popular Boating, Boatcraft, Inland Boating, One-Design Yachtsman; Skier* and *Ski-Faring; Better Camping.*

Indeed, by cashing in on the interest in the active life during the fifties, Robert Petersen of Los Angeles built up a publishing company with sales of $12,000,000 a year and tucked aside a personal fortune that the *Wall Street Journal* estimated at $3,500,000. After he had been laid off from his job as a movie publicity man, which paid him $35 a week, Petersen and a partner, Robert Lind-

---

[1] *Wall Street Journal,* Oct. 19, 1961, p. 1.

say, started *Hot Rod* in 1948 on $400 in cash and credit with a printer. It was a magazine for fans of stripped-down, souped-up automobiles, and the partners hung around race tracks to sell copies. "Sometimes we'd sell a hot-rodder a three-dollar yearly subscription on one side of a drive-in restaurant, then go around to the other side and use the money for something to eat," Petersen once recalled.[2] In a year, the magazine was earning money; in four years, Petersen bought out his partner for $225,000; in fifteen years, he turned down an offer of $5,000,000 for the business, which he valued at $7,500,000.

The company he headed was publishing ten specialized magazines dealing with sports on land and sea besides a line of books in 1963—*Car Craft, CARtoons, Guns and Ammo, Hot Rod, Motor Trend, Rod and Custom, Skin Diver, Sports Car Graphic, Surfing,* and *'Teen.* The company's first magazine, *Hot Rod,* with a circulation of 638,000, raced ahead of a trackful of other automotive magazines that had come along since its appearance and that included *Car and Driver, Cars and Speed, Car Life, Custom, Custom Craft, Custom Rodder, Popular Hot Rodding, Road and Track,* and *Speed Mechanics.*

Sports magazines had always been among the most specialized of the periodicals addressed to men. Despite the great interest in spectator sports which developed in the twentieth century, there were few magazines edited for the fan interested in more than one sport. The titles of magazines reflected their preoccupation with single sports—*American Lawn Tennis, Golf, Ring, Yachting.* Until the mid-thirties about the only periodical covering more than one athletic activity was *Sportsman,* and it was edited for the gentleman who could afford a shooting box, not for the fan in the bleachers.

From time to time, publishers tried general magazines covering all of the major spectator sports, but most of them were financial failures. *Sports Illustrated,* the name which Time Inc. took for its new general sports magazine in 1954, had been used as a magazine title almost twenty years earlier. In 1935 two *Time* writers, John Escher and Samuel H. McAloney, worked out plans for a periodical which would break with the traditional parochialism of sports magazines. They formed a company with Kurt Simon, a publisher who had fled Hitler's persecutions and who had once planned a similar magazine in his native Germany. Their *Sports Illustrated,*

---

[2] *Wall Street Journal,* July 22, 1960, p. 1.

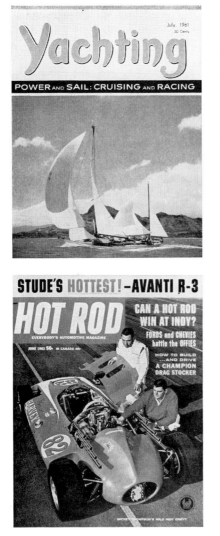

a monthly, first appeared in December, 1935. About half of its content was by staff members, the remainder by such name writers as Paul Gallico and John Tunis. The magazine absorbed Condé Nast's *American Golfer* in 1936, and the combined publication managed to pick up some 35,000 readers before it died in 1938. But the name *Sports Illustrated* continued to float about in the magazine world. Dell Publishing Company borrowed the title from its owner, Stuart Sheftel, for a slick general fan magazine which it introduced after World War II. That *Sports Illustrated* was killed off in June, 1949, after it had cost Dell about $250,000 in a year. Time Inc. bought the title from Sheftel.

A contemporary of the original *Sports Illustrated* was *Sports-Week,* which first came out in 1936, vanished after a few issues, reappeared during the war and eventually built up a circulation of 59,000, then disappeared again. *Sports Pictorial Review,* begun in 1943, survived into the peace with some 30,000 subscribers.

Macfadden's *Sport* was among the most durable of the magazines paying attention to all of the major sports. Early in the war, the idea for such a magazine seemed a good one to O. J. Elder, then president of Macfadden, but the war deferred its publication. The company brought out 350,000 copies of the first issue in August, 1946, as its first new magazine in eleven years. In its illustrated human interest stories, *Sport* gave athletes much the same worshipful treatment that Macfadden's fan magazines gave motion picture stars, and it supplemented the personality pieces with predictions by famous sports figures, sports quizzes, and analyses. In 1948, Macfadden charged Dell with unfair competition in bringing out *Sports Album,* which it alleged was deliberately designed to take advantage of *Sport's* popularity, but the matter was settled amicably after Dell redesigned the format of its magazine. After seventeen years of publication, a long life for such a periodical, *Sport* had built up a circulation of about 616,000, the largest of any general magazine for spectators until Time Inc. brought out its *Sports Illustrated.*

While those few magazines sat on the sidelines of the major sports, another small band of publications tramped the great out-of-doors. The band grew smaller as death or merger wiped out some of its members, and in the sixties three elderly survivors dominated the field—*Field and Stream, Outdoor Life,* and *Sports Afield.* Although outdoorsmen had their preferences among them, the magazines were cut from much the same pattern. They worried about such concerns of outdoorsmen as the depletion of wildlife, the pollution of streams and rivers, and as a class they were no doubt responsible for bringing about a number of conservation measures. Many of their authors were hunters or fishermen who seemed as interested in chatting about their adventures on bear hunting expeditions or canoe trips as in getting paid for their manuscripts, although the magazines also retained staff specialists who spoke authoritatively about the best in guns, dogs, lures, and camping equipment.

The oldest of the three leaders in 1964 was *Sports Afield*, which sportsmen had been reading since 1887 and which the Hearst organization acquired in the fifties, but it was pressed hard and often overtaken by *Field and Stream* and *Outdoor Life*.

In the nineties, John A. McGuire, a young Denver publisher who had learned the printing trade at thirteen, was bringing out a magazine called *Cycling West*. He dropped it in 1898 to try his luck with a monthly magazine for sportsmen, *Outdoor Life*. The new magazine was a natural choice for McGuire, who loved the out-of-doors; by the time he died in 1942, he had taken part in twenty-two expeditions to hunt big game or to collect scientific specimens. In the late twenties, he turned editorial direction of the magazine over to his son, who was studying at the Yale School of Fine Arts. Apart from an interval after ownership changed hands in 1931, Harry A. McGuire edited *Outdoor Life* until 1934, when the publishers of *Popular Science* acquired the magazine. During his tenure, he had kept *Outdoor Life* among the leading outdoor magazines, and it remained there in 1963.

The idea for *Field and Stream*, the third of the leaders, came to its founders, John P. Burkhard and Henry W. Wack, while they were talking in a duck blind in September, 1895. Deploring the wholesale slaughter of wildlife, they decided to publish a magazine which would arouse sportsmen to the cause of conservation. Seven months later they sent out the first copies of their *Western Field and Stream*. After a couple of years of trying to keep the magazine alive in St. Paul, their hometown, they moved it to New York, where they still had a difficult time breaking even. According to one story, Henry Ford offered them $1,200 worth of stock in his motor car company in 1905 in exchange for a full-page advertisement in each of twenty issues, but they turned him down because they were desperate for cash.[3] The years of financial hardship for *Field and Stream* ended soon after Eltinge Warner, a printing salesman and circulation manager, took over its business management in 1906. In 1908, after Burkhard's death, Warner bought control of the magazine, and while building up *Field and Stream* he expanded in other directions. He was publisher of *Smart Set* from 1914 to 1926, an executive in two motion picture companies from 1916 to 1924, and head of a magazine chain after 1933. Meanwhile *Field and Stream* crusaded for a number of conservation measures, built up a library of films of wildlife, and commissioned paintings of wildlife by well-known artists. As the magazine grew prosperous, Warner bought an island in the St. Lawrence River where his staff members could test new sports equipment and hold editorial conferences. The book-publishing house of Holt, Rinehart, and Winston bought the publication for its magazine division in 1951.

All three of those magazines greatly expanded their audiences during and after World War II. They rode the boom in men's magazines generally in the fifties, and they profited from the gaps created in their market when competitors died off. Their combined circulation in 1963—more than 3,700,000—was about four and a half times as great as it had been in 1940.

For Americans who forsook sedentary pleasures, magazine after magazine came along to indoctrinate them into the arcane matters of their active cult and to keep them informed of its esoterica. When the century was young and yachting was for only the wealthy few who could afford to hire a paid crew, brevet commodores kept in printed touch through such magazines as Hearst's *Motor Boating* and *Yachting*. The editor of *Yachting* from 1908, the year after its founding, until 1952, three years before his death at eighty-four, was Herbert L. Stone, who had seen yachting evolve from a pleasure of the rich to a pleasure of anyone who owned a craft larger than a rowboat. His magazine and such other old-timers as *Rudder* and *Sea and Pacific Motor Boat* were joined by a number of new publications when even land-locked sailors began to buy boats and the trailers to convey them to water—*Skipper* in 1947, *Boatcraft* in 1952, *Popular Boating* in 1960, *One-Design Yachtman* in 1961, *Inland Boating* in 1962. Magazines for water skiers and skin divers

---

[3] Amos Stote, "Born in a Duck Blind," *Magazine Industry*, 1 (Summer, 1949) 13.

Per $1.00 Year

Outdoor Life

A Magazine of the West.

Vol. I.   MARCH, 1898.   No. 3.

Table of Contents

Per 10c Copy

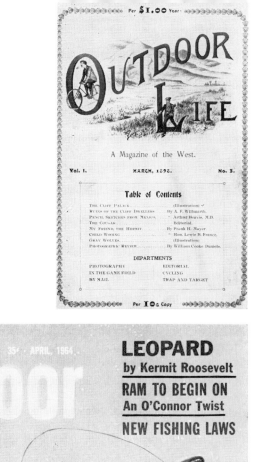

35c   APRIL, 1964

Outdoor Life

LEOPARD
by Kermit Roosevelt

RAM TO BEGIN ON
An O'Connor Twist

NEW FISHING LAWS

Wherever You Are

HOW TO CATCH TROUT ON OPENING DAY

RAMPAGING BEARS
Why 1963 Attacks?

6 TROUT KILLERS
Foolproof Flies

2 BASS STORIES
PLUS: Cougars, Antelope

began to appear for the first time in the early fifties, and from then on there was a burst of periodicals dealing with sports. New magazines for skiers turned up to compete with *Ski*, around since 1935, for instance, and a half-dozen new publications looked for an audience among gun collectors and marksmen.

While such magazines glorified the active life, other magazines were designed for man's reflective moments. The layman curious about science could satisfy his interest with several publications which reported progress in science and technology and which, at the same time, passed along plans for iceboats, cabinets, gliders, and bookcases that he could build at his workbench.

One of the oldest magazines in the United States in 1964 was a general magazine of science, *Scientific American*. It was established in 1845 by Rufus Porter, a muralist and portrait painter of recognized stature who was earning his living from his painting when he took over a journal of science and invention in 1841. A creative mechanic with more than a hundred successful inventions to his credit, Porter saw the need for a weekly to cover the news of science which played little part in the content of regular newspapers and popular magazines. He stayed with that first magazine for less than two years. After experimenting with the new art of electrotyping, he brought out *Scientific American*, which was not greatly different from its predecessor. Fire destroyed the publication offices after Porter had published eight of his weekly numbers, and although he managed to save his subscription list, he never quite recovered from the blow to his pocketbook. He sold his interest in the magazine to Orson D. Munn and Alfred E. Beach for $800 in the summer of 1846. For many years *Scientific American* took a paternal interest in inventors; it encouraged the dedicated ones, maintained a service for answering questions about patents, and exposed the cranks whose inventions seemed more fraudulent than original. Men such as Morse, Gatling, Howe, and Edison came to its editorial offices to confer with its line of brilliant editors.

In 1921, when the popular press had begun to give adequate coverage to scientific news, *Scientific American* became a monthly magazine stressing industrial research. From early in its existence, it had identified itself with applied research as distinguished from pure research. In 1943 it intensified its coverage of industrial research in electronics, engineering, chemistry, and similar areas. Yet senility seemed to have overtaken the publication, and its circulation fell to 40,000 from a onetime high of 94,000. In 1947, Orson D. Munn, whose family had owned the periodical for most of its existence, sold it for $40,000 to a group which proposed to give it a new life. The purchasers were Gerard Piel and Dennis Flanagan, former science editors of *Life*, and Donald H. Miller, Jr., a management consultant, who had $450,000 capital raised among several wealthy backers. Their plan was to make *Scientific American* a medium through which scientists of all kinds could tell one another of their work in language that each could understand. On the day they took over the magazine, they found a letter from an advertising agency canceling the space of their last advertiser, Bell Laboratories. The first issue of their new *Scientific American* appeared in May, 1948, and the magazine used up more than a million dollars in working capital before it went into the black in 1951. By seeking contributions from leading scientists in various fields, by requiring the authors to write in language understandable to the intelligent layman and helping them to do so when they could not, the new management made *Scientific American* an authoritative monthly with an elite readership. The magazine could boast in 1963 that thirty-two Nobel Prize winners from six nations had contributed forty-nine articles to it since its rebirth. The magazine grew with fantastic speed. Its circulation of 353,000 in 1963 was nearly nine times as great as it had been when the new group bought the magazine, and advertising revenues in the early sixties were almost $5,000,000 a year.

Scientific American was already a respectably aged magazine in 1872 when Edward L. Youmans talked the publishers of *Appleton's Journal* into bringing out *Popular Science* to help perform what he regarded as the important task of diffusing scientific knowledge. Youmans, a science editor, writer, and lecturer, was impatient to reach a larger audience than he had been able to. Years before he had established a business relationship with D. Appleton and Company when he had stopped into its store to borrow a book he could not locate in the libraries and could not afford to buy. He had become interested in the ideas of Herbert Spencer, and a friendship had grown between them. After he had written Spencer that he had decided to postpone starting his magazine, he received a series of articles that Spencer had promised to contribute to the new publication. With backing from the Appleton firm, Youmans brought out his first issue the following month. When churchmen first saw his *Popular Science,* they damned it and its publishers as atheistic. But the magazine found an audience of 12,000 men devoted to science—a large enough audience, according to Spencer, who wrote that he was inclined to shake his head when Youmans spoke of making the magazine more popular. More and more persons bought the magazine; and in Youmans' day and after, they read in it articles by the great minds of the time, Darwin, Huxley, Pasteur, William James, Edison, John Dewey.

After Youmans died in 1887, his brother edited the magazine until 1900. Ownership changed several times between then and 1915, when Henry J. Fisher, Robert Cade Wilson, and Oliver Capen bought the magazine and merged it with *World Advance.* Less recondite than in Youmans' time, *Popular Science* sought the home craftsman and hobbyist who wanted to know something about the world of science. The magazine capitalized on the sharpened interest in science and technology during World War II by increasing its coverage of science and industry through prose and pictures and by putting its how-to-do-it material in its back pages. Shortly after the end of the war, it was reaching more than a million readers each issue; in 1963 it had a circulation of 1,287,000 and took in some $3,171,000 in advertising revenues.

McGraw-Hill chose a science magazine for its first and only attempt at publishing a consumer magazine. In 1940 Dagobert Runes, publisher of the Philosophical Library, began a little pocket-size magazine, *Science Illustrated,* which set out to show how science affected everyday life. He disposed of it in 1944 to a publisher who sold it to McGraw-Hill in the fall of 1945. After five months of intensive work, McGraw-Hill introduced its version of *Science Illustrated,* an elaborately pictorial magazine of standard size which conducted sound but popular excursions into the land of science and which avoided the how-to-do-it features of magazines like *Popular Mechanics.* From the start, *Science Illustrated* operated at a heavy deficit, although it attracted a following of more than a half-million readers. The publishers gave insufficient advertising and high production costs as their reasons for dropping the magazine with its issue of July, 1949.

Servicemen and war veterans had their own magazines, some of them official publications under loose or strict control by the armed forces, some of them organs of veterans' organizations, and some of them purely commercial enterprises. The Marines had their *Leath-*

SCIENTIFIC AMERICAN

PROGRESSIVE ASSEMBLY IN THE AUTOMOBILE FACTORY

Vol. CXXII. No. 1
January 3, 1920

Published Weekly by
Scientific American Publishing Co.
Munn & Co., New York, N. Y.

Price 10 Cents
$5.00 a year

SCIENTIFIC AMERICAN

CLEANING SYMBIOSIS

FIFTY CENTS

August 1961

erneck from 1917 on, for instance; members of the national guard had their *National Guardsman;* and military fliers and their ground crews had their *Air Force,* begun as a newsletter in 1918, turned into a slick monthly in World War II, and discharged to civilian control in 1947. *Confederate Veteran* was an outgrowth of pamphlets circulated in the nineties to raise funds for a memorial to Jefferson Davis. Veterans of the Confederacy found the pamphlets so interesting that their author, Sumner A. Cunningham, started the monthly magazine to carry historical articles and reminiscences of the War Between the States. By the thirties, death had reduced the number of Confederate veterans to a few thousand, and the depression forced the United Daughters of the Confederacy to drop its support of the magazine. In December, 1932, at the age of forty, *Confederate Veteran* mailed its final 6,000 copies. From 1914, members of the Veterans of Foreign Wars received copies of *Foreign Service,* a slick-paper monthly of organizational news and general interest material which was redesignated *V. F. W. Magazine* in 1951. Membership in the American Legion carried with it a subscription to *American Legion,* which was born on July 4, 1919, as a weekly. For seven years, the publication remained a weekly, a tool in building and strengthening the Legion organization; then it was changed into a monthly magazine. After a brief period of uncertainty in its early years, the publication lured Harold Ross and five of his onetime *Stars and Stripes* writers to its staff. One of them, John T. Winterich, edited *American Legion* for fifteen years after Ross resigned in 1924. Reaching a heterogeneous audience of millions, the publication became a slick general interest magazine.

Commercial publishers tried to profit from the popularity of *Stars and Stripes* among troops in both world wars and of *Yank* in World War II, but their civilian counterparts of service publications lacked the sparkle of the originals and failed in their attempt to follow servicemen back into mufti. Butterick recruited Harold Ross and other former staff members of *Stars and Stripes* for its *Home Sector* after World War I. The weekly began hopefully in September, 1919, but failed to survive 1920. *Salute,* with Leverett Gleason as publisher, tried to capture the readership of veterans of World War II. When its first issue went on sale in the spring of 1946, each name on the masthead was one which had appeared in *Stars and Stripes* or *Yank,* and the magazine managed to catch some of the tone and flavor of *Yank.* The ownership of *Salute* changed hands three months after the first issue, at about the time that three top editors resigned, apparently in a disagreement over policy. The new publishers sought to make *Salute* interesting to nonveterans as well as to veterans, and they entirely dropped the appeal to ex-servicemen early in 1948. They stopped publication with the issue of August, 1948, after losing about $250,000 on the magazine. At its peak, *Salute* was bought by only 300,000 of the millions of veterans who were its potential market.

In the murky underworld of magazines for men, where dwelled such publications as *Gay Parisienne, Paris Nights, Pep, Snappy,* and *Titter,* the raffish patriarch was the *National Police Gazette,* which George Wilkes and Enoch Camp began issuing in 1845, as they said, "to assist the operations of the police department by publishing a minute description of felons' names, aliases, and persons" and by recording "horrid murders, outrageous robberies, bold forgeries, astounding burglaries, hideous rapes, vulgar seductions." The pink-covered weekly lived up to its founders' promise in giving minute accounts of criminals and their handiwork, if not in assisting police departments, and it thoroughly covered the sporting scene in the days before athletics had become a major industry. At the end of the nineteenth century, it had become as standard a fixture of barbershop and saloon as the decorated shaving mug and the Anheuser-Busch painting of Custer's Last Fight.

The *Police Gazette* determinedly purveyed its gaslight-era brand of sensationalism in the twentieth century; but after World War I, the tabloids covered crime with more diligence than the *Police Gazette* ever had, and a shady crew of magazine publishers had arisen to market sex in more alluring packages. At auction in 1932, the defunct *Gazette* brought only $545. Its new owners, who already had five magazines of dubious respectability on the stands, hoped to revive it with articles about sex, sports, and the underworld, and pictures of seminude nightclub chorines. The number of readers dropped to 20,000, about a tenth of what had once been an average circulation for the magazine, and they sold it in 1935 for less than a thousand dollars to Harold H. Roswell, a former newspaper man. Although the *Police Gazette* never again became the institution it once had been, Roswell pushed circulation to what it had been in the magazine's heyday by converting the publication into a slick-paper monthly and by periodically overhauling its editorial approach to its raw ingredients, which in essence were the same mixture as before. In the early sixties, the *Police Gazette* was still around with Roswell listed as editor and with a following of about 175,000.

Throughout the twentieth century, publishers in shabby offices on the fringe of the magazine industry loaded newsstands with periodicals which trafficked heavily in borderline obscenity, pornographic and quasi-pornographic fiction, and photographs of nude and seminude females. The magazines which presented sex photographically often were ostensibly for the artist or photographer, the art lover, and the serious devotee of nudism, although from the mid-thirties on they increasingly seemed to assume that nudity was its own excuse. A few of the prose magazines, too, insisted that they were edited for discriminating readers. *Casanova Jr.'s Tales* was shipped by express in 1926 to the cultured few able to pay its price of $5 a copy or $15 for a year's subscription. Most of the magazines of off-color jokes and erotic fiction, however, offered no justification other than public demand.

From time to time, government officials and private citizens protested the flood of salacious magazines and tried to clean up the newsstands. In 1925, for instance, officials in Chicago, Omaha, and the state of Washington took action to stop the distribution of such magazines as *La Vie Parisienne, So This Is Paris, Artists and Models,* and *Hot Dog.* The following year Kansans discovered a law which they thought they could invoke to prevent the sale of *Art Lover's Magazine, Hi-Jinks, Snappy Stories,* and similar publications. Authorities in scattered cities across the United States cracked down on news dealers selling such magazines in 1932, and the commissioner of licenses in New York warned them that their licenses might be revoked if they handled *Artists' Notebook, Brevities,* and *Paris Models.* In 1934 New York police were ordered to keep newsstands from displaying fifty-nine periodicals with such titles as *Cupid's Capers, Wild Cherries,* and *Hollywood Squawks.* Two publishers, apprehended by the Federal Bureau of Investigation, were fined $1,000 each and sentenced to three months in jail for engaging in interstate commerce in off-color magazines in 1936. The Post Office Department summoned a number of publishers of "girlie books," as the trade called them, to Washington in 1949 and warned that their second-class mailing privileges would be taken away if they did not cleanse their magazines. In 1952 the Gathings Committee of the House of Representatives conducted a lengthy investi-

FEBRUARY — 25 Cents

Popular Science

Founded MONTHLY 1872

YOU WON'T BE ABLE TO FLY WITHOUT LANDING FIELDS PAGE 74

WHY JAPAN WILL LOSE ON LAND PAGE 130

POPULAR SCIENCE

MAR. 25¢

gation of pornography in magazines, comic books, and paperbound books. New York police in November, 1962, conducted simultaneous raids on seven bookstores near Times Square, where along Forty-Second Street shops had shelves and bins full of domestic and imported magazines with titles such as *Black Nylons, Striparama, Boudoir,* and *Sizzle.*

But protests, investigations, and restrictions did little to slow the presses of publishers who wallowed in the muck at the bottom of the sea of magazines. There was always some demand for their products, and readers bought their magazines not so much by title as by content. If one title were banned, publishers could always bring out the same sort of editorial matter in a magazine of different name. Even if they were forced out of business, they could easily incorporate again under another name, for they had a low overhead, no enormous editorial expenses, and no dependence on advertising.

In the twenties and thirties, most of the low-caste magazines seemed to consist of uncomplicated sex and unsophisticated smut. There were no untoward psychological implications, for instance, in the nude photographs of the *Nudist,* in the smoking-car jokes of *Calgary Eye Opener,* or in the erotic prose of *Spicy Western.*

In the forties and fifties, however, many of the magazines looked as if their editors had pored over the works of Freud, Krafft-Ebing, and Wilhelm Stekel. Sadism, masochism, fetishism, perversions, all were implicit in the prose and pictures of a covey of magazines— *Night and Day, Wink, Brief, Paris Life, Keyhole, Eye, Pepper, Candid Whirl, Cover Girls Models, Scope, Picture Fun, Flirt, Eyeful, Beauty Parade.* The female with an enlarged bosom was one of their staples, as in the days of the nineteenth-century *Police Gazette;* but when she posed in the nude or its approximation, it was not always with simple seductiveness. She wore stilt heels or let her long hair drape her body; she was enmeshed in chains or covered with gilt and powdered glass which, the caption pointed out, could "cut into the skin." She wrestled lion cubs and vicious dogs. She was shown being flogged, being frozen in a cake of ice, being shot from a cannon. Alongside such photographs were articles and picture spreads of men who had died in racing accidents or prison breaks, who earned their living surviving dynamite blasts or wrestling matches with alligators, who exposed vice or profited from it. Some of the magazines exploited sex and sadism in alternate features as their editorial pattern. They represented a world of morbid desires and dark, seething repressions.

Ralph Ginzburg set out in early 1962 to pull the sex magazine out from under the counter and to put it on the living room coffee table with *Eros*, a quarterly "on the joy of love," which he sold for $15 a year. Just as *Time, Reader's Digest,* and the *New Yorker* were all children of circumstance, he said in his prospectus, so *Eros* was the child of a climate of sexual candor, an offspring of court decisions that "had realistically interpreted America's obscenity laws." Designed by a leading graphic artist, printed in black and white and lavish color on presses at home and abroad, bound between hard covers, *Eros* gave textual and pictorial treatment to such topics as Japanese love-making manuals, the contraceptive industry, and the proper interpretation of the sexual passages in *Lady Chatterley's Lover*. It reached into the past for drawings by Gillray, for DeMaupassant's "Madame Tellier's Brothel," and for Mark Twain's "1601." A government attorney called *Eros* "pornography for snobs," and in December, 1963, Ginzburg was sentenced to five years in prison and fined for sending it and other publications through the mails. He was freed on $10,000 bond pending an appeal. Meanwhile, *Eros* suspended publication.

For a time in the fifties, magazines that purported to give readers a peek into the sexual lives of celebrities and a tongueful of other gossip had a period of shabby glory. Their progenitor was *Confidential*, conceived during the Kefauver crime hearings of 1951 when Robert Harrison realized, as he later put it, that "finally the public had become educated to the fact that there was excitement and interest in the lives of people in the headlines." The excitement and interest that Harrison used to attract readers were sin and sex. Most of the articles supposedly revealed incriminating secrets in the lives of celebrities; others exposed "dangerous" medicines, graft and corruption in high places, and similar social evils. The articles were heavier on lurid innuendo than on hard fact, and they were illustrated with photographs which managed to convey the impression that they were sensational even when they were not.

When he started *Confidential* in 1952, Harrison was an alumnus of the motion picture trade press, for which he had worked for six years, and of Bernarr Macfadden's sensation-mongering New

York *Graphic*. In the early forties, he had started his own magazine, *Beauty Parade*, which he published from a two-room apartment. After *Beauty Parade* came *Eyeful*, then *Titter*.

Like its predecessors, *Confidential* was a relatively inexpensive magazine to produce. It was printed on cheap paper. Even at its peak, it had a fulltime staff of only seventeen persons; it drew the rest of its copy from perhaps thirty freelance writers, who generally wrote under pseudonyms. Selling for twenty-five cents, the bimonthly depended on single copy sales for most of its revenue. Nonetheless, in the first half of 1955, it was grossing about $92,000 an issue in advertising. At that time, outsiders estimated that the magazine was netting about $200,000 an issue.

By exploiting prurient curiosity, *Confidential* built up a large circulation, by far the greatest part of it in single copy sales, within a short time after its first appearance in 1952. In mid-1955 Harrison said that individual issues of the magazine had print orders of 4,000,000 each. In the first half of 1956, its audited circulation averaged 3,442,536 an issue.

Inevitably *Confidential* was widely imitated—by *Behind the Scenes, Dare, Exposed, Hush-Hush, Inside Story, Lowdown, Private Lives, Rave, Tip-Off, Secret, Uncensored*. Harrison himself brought out a sister publication, *Whisper*. He regarded the other imitators as harmless; he said they contributed to the demand for his own product.

Inevitably, too, *Confidential* encountered legal opposition. Many of the persons harmed by its stories were reluctant to sue; most of them, perhaps, did not want the further notoriety that a lawsuit would entail. But some did file damage suits, Doris Duke and Robert Mitchum among them. Lyle Stuart, editor of a rival exposé magazine, collected $9,000 in an out-of-court settlement of a libel suit he had filed.

Harrison publicly shrugged off the libel suits. More worrisome to him, no doubt, was a move by the Post Office Department in 1955 to review copies of *Confidential* before allowing it to use the mails. The attempts of postal authorities to bar the magazine from the mails, however, were unsuccessful.

In early 1957, three grand juries across the United States returned indictments against the magazine and its publisher. A federal grand jury in Chicago indicted it for "mailing obscene or crime-inciting matter," an indictment which was dismissed in a U.S. district court. A grand jury in Union County, New Jersey, indicted Harrison for

August 1924   10 Cents

Better Homes ᴬⁿᵈ Gardens

SPECIAL!
29¢

Better Homes and Gardens.

July 1963

HOW TO STAY YOUNG AND LOOK GREAT
Are You Better Off in Business for Yourself?
THE MOST SENSATIONAL SUMMER SALADS!
Remodel or Move Out? Here's How You Decide

100

IDEAS UNDER $100

Decorating, Building, and Landscaping Projects
for People Who Like To Do Wonderful Things!

conspiring to sell indecent literature. In Los Angeles a grand jury indicted *Confidential's* publisher, printer, distributor, and West Coast "research" affiliate—a major source of its Hollywood copy—on a criminal libel charge. After a two-month trial ended in a hung jury, the judge dismissed the charges of conspiring to commit criminal libel. However, a month later, in December, 1957, *Confidential* and *Whisper* were fined $5,000 each for conspiring to publish obscene matter.

Almost simultaneously with the dismissal of the criminal libel charges, the publishers announced a major change in policy. *Confidential* would adopt a new format with its issue of March, 1958, they said, and *Whisper* with that of April, 1958. No longer, they said, would the publications carry exposés of private lives. While the publishers had never felt such stories to be illegal, the announcement said, they were making the change in policy in cooperation with state and county authorities. Hy Steirman, a former editor of comic books and pulps, made additional changes after he bought the magazines from Harrison in May. He was still publishing both in 1964, although by then their heyday was long since past.

There was a wholesome world, too, of gleaming kitchens and sunlit living rooms, of shady patios and verdant lawns, of stability, comfort, and familial devotion; and that world, like the other, had its magazines.

In 1922 the presses of a publishing house in Des Moines rolled off the first fifty-two-page copies of a magazine which was to influence the editorial techniques of publications from the West Coast to the East. The magazine was *Fruit, Garden, and Home*, which its publisher renamed *Better Homes and Gardens* two years later.

Its success was built on a formula of service to the settled, middle-class American husband and wife whose big interest was their home and family. There had been home magazines before *Better Homes and Gardens;* both *House Beautiful* and *House and Garden* antedated it, for instance, but they were addressed to the well-to-do. There was nothing new in the idea of service to the reader. Since the days of Edward Bok, magazines had tried to help their readers, had tried to relate their content to the readers' lives and experiences. Such women's magazines as *Ladies' Home Journal* and *Woman's Home Companion* had made service an important ingredient in their editorial formulas. But *Better Homes and Gardens* adopted the policy of service so wholeheartedly that every possible article was measured by the test, "Is it possible to do something as a result of reading this article?" Every article helped the reader to do something: to remodel a house, to frame a picture, to teach a child to be a good sport, to decorate a room, to make a summer salad. The articles were not about things; they told readers how to do the thing itself. Further, the magazine sought a dual readership. Most service magazines were for women. *Better Homes and Gardens* won women readers with features about food, household equipment, decoration, and child care, but it also won their husbands with articles for the handyman and gardener.

Men trained on *Better Homes and Gardens* carried its concept of reader service to other publications. L. W. Lane, who had served on its advertising staff, bought *Sunset*, a magazine in San Francisco, and revamped it into a regional monthly that tried to make every article of some practical use to the reader. Robert P. Crossley, who had been on the *Better Homes and Gardens* editorial staff, made Capper's *Household* a sort of *Better Homes and Gardens* for the small-town family for a while before the magazine died in the fifties. Other *Better Homes and Gardens* alumni included Curtiss Anderson, who edited *Ladies' Home Journal* for a year in the early sixties; John Mack Carter of *American Home* and *McCall's;* and Robert Jones of *Everywoman's Family Circle.*

The man behind *Better Homes and Gardens* was E. T. Meredith, who got his first publishing experience helping out on the *Farmer's Tribune,* a Populist paper which his grandfather published in Des Moines. In 1895, when Meredith was nineteen, his grandfather gave him the *Tribune* for a wedding present. A note attached to its financial statement said simply, "Sink or swim." Meredith dropped partisan politics from the paper and in seven years built it into a modestly profitable business. He sold the paper to try out his idea of a larger publication, a magazine for farmers in the agricultural heart of the nation. In 1902 he sent the first issue of that magazine, *Successful Farming,* to the post office in a single mail bag. Money was scarce for a time, and Mrs. Meredith helped her husband to get out issues of the new magazine. When *Successful Farming* was a dozen years old and Eastern advertisers were worried about the prosperity of the Midwest, Meredith chartered a special train to bring them west for a tour of the agricultural region in which his magazine circulated. Advertising picked up as a result. *Successful Farming* gave its readers heavily practical instruction in profitable and labor-saving farming methods. By 1920, when Meredith became Secretary of Agriculture under Woodrow Wilson, it was already one of the major farm publications in the United States.

Meredith next conceived of a magazine which would be as useful to the average city dweller and suburbanite as *Successful Farming* was to the farmer. The result was *Better Homes and Gardens.* Meredith himself went East to sell advertising for the first issue, for which he guaranteed a circulation of 150,000. Although *Better Homes and Gardens* grew steadily from its first issue and had a circulation of a million by 1928, it shot ahead most rapidly in the fifties. In 1963, with a circulation of 6,228,000, it was one of the largest-selling magazines in the United States. Its advertising revenues, however, did not keep pace with its circulation; the $21,260,-000 that it carried in 1963 was less than it had carried a decade earlier.

If staff members of *Better Homes and Gardens* were good at giving readers assistance, one reason probably was that they were very much like their readers. There were no bachelors on the editorial staff and few unmarried women. Staff members were homeowners with families who liked to cook, sew, putter in the garden, and romp with their children in off-duty hours. In addition to empathy with their readers, they were guided by surveys which provided readership figures on nearly every feature which the magazine had run since the mid-thirties.

When Meredith died in 1928, he left his Meredith Publishing Company to his son-in-law Fred Bohen and his son E. T. Meredith, Jr., who were still active in its management in 1963.

In 1928, the year that Meredith died, L. W. Lane of the Meredith advertising staff paid $60,000 for *Sunset* to prove his conviction that homeowners on the West Coast would welcome a regional monthly magazine with a heavily practical emphasis. The Southern Pacific Railroad, taking the name of its crack train, the Sunset Limited, had started *Sunset* in 1898 to advertise the wonders of the West and to promote rail travel. The railroad had sold the magazine in 1914 to employees, who made it a literary monthly serving the Pacific Slope. When Lane bought the magazine, primarily because its name was well established, *Sunset* was a thin offering of fiction and travel articles.

Lane had definite plans for the sort of home magazine he intended to publish, and he stuck to them despite the counsel of acquaintances who suggested such alternatives as that he devote the publication entirely to Western fiction. First, Lane believed, a regional magazine could most surely succeed in a part of the country having distinct regional characteristics. He chose as his region the area west of the Continental Divide, which was set apart from the rest of the nation by its climate, its pattern of family life, and its system of marketing. Second, such a magazine should capitalize on the differences which distinguished its region from the rest of the country. Thus it could best serve its readers and at the same time remove itself from competition with the big national magazines. Lane chose the editorial areas of gardening, home building and remodeling, cooking, and travel as the ones in which *Sunset* might serve the differences which distinguished the West. Third, the magazine should never run an article just because it was interesting; every article should be useful to the reader.[4]

Lane had worked out that much of his plan before he took over *Sunset*. After he had been publishing it for a few years, he added two other elements to his strategy. In 1932 he began publishing three separate editions, each tailored to a specific locality within his territory; and in 1936 he made *Sunset* an entirely staff-written magazine because experimentation had convinced him that his own writers could cram more facts and ideas into a column of text than freelances could.[5]

Sunset lost Lane almost $72,000 in the year after his initial issue of February, 1929, and its next six years were hard ones; but it never failed to make a profit after 1937. *Sunset* had to hold its circulation down to about 200,000 during its first decade because no press on the West Coast was able to handle a larger press run. The lid on circulation was removed when the Coast Printing Company, organized to print *Sunset* and other magazines, installed $250,000 worth of rotary presses and other equipment in 1939.

In 1964, *Sunset* was by far the most successful regional magazine in the United States. It had a rambling, hacienda-like home covering seven acres of Menlo Park, to which it had moved from San Francisco in 1951. It was being read by more than 733,000 families,

---

[4] Proctor Mellquist, "Sunset Is Unique as a Magazine," *Quill*, 42 (Feb., 1954) 12-13.
[5] Mellquist, p. 13.

and its book-publishing adjunct, formed in 1949, was selling millions of copies of books on gardening and cookery.

Although the home service magazines prospered during the depression and recession, they were hard hit by the war. The curtailment of home construction shut down advertising from manufacturers of building supplies, and allocations of steel, lumber, and textiles reduced their advertising for home appliances, furniture, rugs, and draperies. Both *American Home* and *Better Homes and Gardens* carried about a million dollars less advertising in 1942 than in 1941, and their total advertising pages fell off almost a fourth. To offset their losses, the magazines tried to build up their linage in other areas. *Better Homes and Gardens,* for instance, expanded its editorial departments on meal preparation to attract more advertising for foodstuffs and promoted the business of drug firms.[6]

The end of the war gave the magazines a rich market, for the number of families owning or planning homes was the greatest in history and advertisers were competing for their business. The big jump in advertising came in the first half-dozen years after the war's end, when the combined advertising gross of *American Home, Better Homes and Gardens, House Beautiful,* and *House and Garden* more than doubled. Revenues grew at a slower rate thereafter —the combined revenues of the four magazines in 1963 were $47,-434,000, some $2,221,000 over a decade earlier—but circulation soared far beyond prewar levels.

Although the service magazines advised readers on everything from fixing a leaking faucet to refurbishing a living room, another type of publication dealt with just the garden. Gardening as a leisure-time activity was served by several magazines from the early years of the century onward and by new ones that blossomed in the fifties. Among the hardiest perennials was *Horticulture,* established in 1904 and published in Boston by the Massachusetts Horticultural Society. For several decades, *Flower Grower* was at the forefront in circulation, advertising linage, or both, and in stature among hobbyists. Established in 1914, it was merged in the fifties with *Home Garden* of the Doubleday company and as *Flower Grower, the Home Garden Magazine* had a circulation of 378,000 in the early sixties. Holt, Rinehart, and Winston published *Popular Gardening,* which found a following of 347,000 in the dozen years

[6] *Tide,* 22 (July 30, 1948) 17-18.

after its birth in 1950. Perhaps the fastest-growing magazine was *Flower and Garden*, which was started in Kansas City, Missouri, in 1957 and which had a circulation of 592,000 a half-dozen years later. To take account of variations in soil and climate, it published separate editions for the East, the West, and mid-America.

The central concern of one service magazine was what might be called family finances or personal economics. *Changing Times* ran articles about budgeting, borrowing, saving, investing, insurance, stocks, buying homes and automobiles, preparing for retirement, all chosen for their practical help to the reader.

Its founder was Willard M. Kiplinger, a newsman who had begun to interpret activities in Washington to businessmen in 1923 in a personal service, *Kiplinger's Washington Letter*, which in time was augmented by others dealing with agriculture, taxes, and foreign trade. In the early forties, he got the idea of bringing out a magazine for businessmen, but he deferred his plans because of the war. In 1946, with a staff of four working in two rooms over a typewriter repair shop in Washington, he put together a first issue. When press time came, he junked it because it was not good enough. Nor was the next issue, which he also scrapped.

The first issue that went to press, dated January, 1947, was a skimpy seven-by-nine pamphlet with perforated pages so that readers could easily tear out the articles and pass them on to friends. It was addressed mainly to businessmen: "But businessmen have broad interests and human interests, and so the scope of this publication will be both broad and human." Concentrating on the "broad and human" aspects of business, the magazine was pulled somewhat away from its original orientation by the interests of its readers. It later enlarged its page size and dropped the perforations as too costly. Its articles carried no bylines because they represented a staff effort of research and writing.

When the magazine appeared on the newsstands, sales were so bad that Kiplinger almost went broke. He had no advertising income to fall back on; he had refused to accept it, he said, lest it distract him from his editorial purpose of reader service. Sold only by subscription, largely as a result of direct mail campaigns and radio and television advertising, the magazine did far better than it had on the newsstand. It reached a circulation of a million by April, 1961, and was selling 1,154,000 copies a month in 1963.

A number of magazines gave Americans practical guidance in

yet another of their concerns—their role of parent. One of the pioneers in helping bewildered fathers and mothers rear their families was George J. Hecht, whose Parents' Institute, Inc., was a leading publisher of magazines for parents and their children. Looking back on a quarter of a century of publishing in 1951, Hecht estimated that his *Parents' Magazine* had given advice on child care and training to the parents of more than 25,000,000 children. His audience was ever changing, for new readers continuously replaced the ones who dropped away as their children reached maturity.

In 1925 Hecht, who had been doing social work in New York, noticed that one important interest was not being served by any magazine, and he brought out a publication for the neglected market in October of the following year. "There are magazines devoted exclusively to the raising of cattle, hogs, dogs, flowers, and what not," his first issue said, "but until now none on the most important work of the world—the rearing of children." Hecht called his new periodical *Children,* "The Magazine for Parents," a title so confusing that he changed it to *Parents' Magazine* with the issue of August, 1929.

Hecht's idea for the magazine appealed to the directors of the Laura Spelman Rockefeller Memorial Fund, which provided $325,-000 to establish the publication. Hecht, in exchange for the grant, assigned control of the publishing company to Columbia University, the State University of Iowa, the University of Minnesota, and Yale University. He bought control of the company in 1949.

The editor who established the direction of *Parents'* was Clara Savage Littledale, who held the position until shortly before her death in January, 1956. She joined *Parents'* after working as women's suffrage editor of Oswald Garrison Villard's New York *Evening Post* and as a correspondent for *Good Housekeeping* in World War I. In *Parents',* which described its contents as "on rearing children from crib to college," she ran articles by leading authorities on child care, a number of whom were listed on the masthead as advisory editors, and by parents themselves. She expanded the scope of the magazine to cover marriage problems and housing because she thought such things affected children, and the magazine adopted "Family Home Guide" as a subtitle. *Parents',* over the years, reflected the changing attitudes toward child-rearing. "Twenty-five years ago, we adhered to a very rigid schedule in feeding and raising children," she recalled in 1951. "John B.

Watson's theory of behaviorism was the thing at the time. It called for a very detached attitude. . . . Raising a child today calls for being warm and affectionate and expressing love for the child. . . . We thought they were little adults who were just being naughty; now we know they are children." [7]

Parents' was a commercial success from the start. Hecht had expected the magazine to attract perhaps a hundred thousand readers. He had that many by the end of the first five years, more than nineteen times that many by 1963. The increased birth rate and the increased interest in authoritative guidance in child-rearing provided him with an expanding market, and as his magazine grew, so did the business of feeding, clothing, and otherwise supplying the needs of babies and children. His advertising gross rose from $500,000 in the first year to more than $10,000,000 in 1963.

As *Parents'* prospered, Hecht originated other magazines, almost all of them for children, their parents, or their teachers. He suspended some of the new magazines when they failed to establish themselves, and he revamped others.

Two of Hecht's magazines dealing with child care were distributed free. *Metropolitan Mother's Guide*, edited by Mrs. Littledale, appeared in November, 1932. Hecht distributed it without charge to 50,000 mothers of pupils in more than 200 private and suburban schools in the New York area and sold advertising in it on the basis of its circulation among the well-to-do. In the fall of 1942, Hecht launched *So You're Going to Have a Baby*, a magazine of reprints from *Parents'*. He sold copies in bulk to department stores, which could have their own advertisements imprinted on the cover and which gave the publication to their customers. The magazine was renamed *Your New Baby* and made a quarterly in 1946.

In the dozen or so magazines for children and young people that he originated, Hecht apparently tried to furnish his readers good, interesting reading material as a substitute for the unwholesome fare of the lurid comics and to provide them with frank, realistic advice on the problems of growing up. Hecht began publishing periodicals for young people in 1935 when he brought out a seven-cent weekly *Boys' and Girls' Newspaper*, sixteen tabloid pages of news, entertainment, and comics. Subsequently, with varying degrees of success and for varying lengths of time, he published, among other titles, *Calling All Girls, Calling All Boys, Polly Pig-*

---

[7] *Time,* 58 (Sept. 24, 1951) 77-78.

tails, Senior Prom, Sweet Sixteen, Twenty-One, Compact, Varsity, Humpty Dumpty, and *Teen Digest.*

Parents' Magazine Enterprises branched out into other fields. In 1963, when it acquired 90 per cent of the stock in F. A. O. Schwarz of New York, one of the largest and oldest toy stores in the nation, it distributed magazines and books, owned a half-interest in two subscription sales agencies, published books for children and an encyclopedia for young people, and operated three children's book clubs.

As the number of patients in maternity wards increased and as supplying the needs of the young became an important industry, other publishers recognized young parents as an important market. The young mother changed in interests and outlook because of baby, as the publisher of *Baby Talk* observed in 1950; "she's vulnerable and sellable today as never before and as she never will be again." [8] His *Baby Talk* was born in 1935, and there were others that came and went: *American Baby, Baby Post, Congratulations, My Baby, Two to Six.* The majority of magazines devoted exclusively to child care were distributed free, often through diaper services and through department stores, which used them to promote business for their baby supply departments.

But it was not youth alone that magazines served; after the mid-thirties, the elderly also were served by at least one magazine. The first of the publications directed at persons over forty was *Journal of Living.* It was begun in 1935 as a house organ for the Serutan Company, but eventually it developed into a commercial magazine which sold some 225,000 copies an issue, most of them on the newsstand. In 1952 the publishers of *Christian Herald* noted that there were 53,000,000 Americans in the ages beyond forty "whom," as they said in their prospectus, "the publishing mores of our time either ignore entirely or force into a ridiculous imitation of youth." They introduced *Lifetime Living,* edited by Dr. Martin Gumpert, a gerontologist, for persons who feared old age—a magazine to help them plan their finances, decide where to retire, develop "second careers," enjoy life, keep well, get along with their children and grandchildren, draw on their inner resources during the period of readjustment. *Lifetime Living* and the *Journal of Living* were merged into the *Journal of Lifetime Living* early in 1955. Like many of its readers, the magazine moved from New

---

[8] *Tide,* 24 (June 23, 1950) 38.

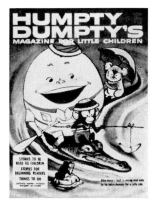

York to Florida a few years later, but by the early sixties it had disappeared from listings in the periodical directories.

A former editor of *Lifetime Living* once said he thought the magazine might have succeeded if it had depended on reader support alone rather than on advertising, since advertisers made a fetish of youth, and some of the publications that followed it eschewed advertising: *Senior Citizen* in 1954, *Modern Maturity* in 1958, *Harvest Years* in 1960.

Although their homes and families were the center of their existence, many Americans still wanted to know about other regions of their own vast country and about other lands, other peoples. Travel magazines took the armchair wanderer on vicarious trips to the huts of primitive African tribes, to the igloos of the Eskimo, to folk festivals in Scottish villages, to the wide boulevards of Paris, to the top of the world, and to the bottom of the sea. Some travel magazines pulled him from the armchair and set him packing.

The *National Geographic* with its old-fashioned yellow-bordered covers was a national institution even before the twenties. It was a safe bet that a considerable number of its copies from the twenties were still hoarded in attics and family libraries in the sixties, to be rediscovered and reread from time to time. There was a timelessness about most of the photographs and articles in the *National Geographic*, although a few of them were topical.

The National Geographic Society, which published *National Geographic,* was established in Washington, D.C., in 1888 for "the increase and diffusion of geographic knowledge." The society was made a tax-free educational institution by act of Congress, and all proceeds from *National Geographic,* apart from a considerable reserve, were plowed back into the magazine or used to promote the activities of the society. The society had sponsored almost 200 scientific expeditions by the early sixties. The *National Geographic* did not solicit subscriptions; it invited persons to membership in the society, which carried with it a subscription to the magazine.

For more than a half-century, the editor of *National Geographic* was Gilbert Grosvenor, whose life was dedicated to the interests of exploration and to acquainting Americans with the wonderful world they lived in. Throughout the globe were memorials to his devotion to his cause. A lake in Alaska, discovered in 1919, was named after him in recognition of the encouragement he had given Alaskan exploration. A glacier in Peru bore his name. A mountain in China was named for him by Joseph F. Rock, who headed an expedition of the society there in 1927. A range in Antarctica was named in his honor by Richard E. Byrd in 1929.

Grosvenor was born in Constantinople, Turkey, where his father taught history at Robert College. Soon after his graduation from Amherst, he fell in love with Elsie May Bell, the daughter of Alexander Graham Bell, who was then president of the National Geographic Society. When Bell offered him a job with the society, Grosvenor left his teaching position at Englewood Academy in New Jersey to take it so that he could be in Washington near Elsie. They were married in 1900, the year after he became director of the society and assistant editor of its magazine.

When Grosvenor took over, the society had 900 members and debts amounting to $2,000. Its magazine was an erudite journal without popular interest. Grosvenor became its managing editor in 1900, and its editor in 1903, but at first he did little to change it. Then one day in 1905 he became so intrigued by a batch of photographs of Tibet that he spread them over eleven pages. The reaction to the feature showed him that he had struck upon a way to build interest in the magazine.

The basic editorial pattern of *National Geographic* changed little over the next fifty years. The magazine was heavily photographic, and a large portion of its illustrations were in color; in 1910 it became the first magazine in the United States to use natural color photographs. It gave a loose interpretation to the word "geographic." Its articles—often quaintly florid and quietly enthusiastic—and its pictures dealt with such subjects as taming wild blueberries, America's national parks, traveling through England in a Canadian canoe, Ancient Ur, Burmese temples, the snow peaks of the Equator, work and war among the ants, parrots, kingfishers, flycatchers, the sculptured temples of India, and Ulster through mist and sunshine.

The formula was a popular one. Circulation grew from so few copies that Grosvenor himself could carry them to more than a million in the twenties, more than 2,500,000 in the sixties. As circulation grew, so did advertising. The magazine carried a million dollars worth of advertising for the first time in 1923, and the amount had grown to $6,651,000 in 1963.

Grosvenor resigned as editor of *National Geographic* in 1954. His place was taken by John O. LaGorce, who had ranked second to Grosvenor on the magazine for the previous forty-nine years. When LaGorce retired from the editorship in 1957, his place was taken by Grosvenor's son, Melville Grosvenor.

After the automobile had become a pleasure vehicle for millions instead of an expensive curiosity, the average reader no longer had to do his traveling at second hand, as he did when Grosvenor joined the staff of *National Geographic*. The automobile made every man his own explorer, and a number of magazines arose to tell him of places he could explore. *Motor News* was being published in Chicago as early as 1906, for instance, and *National Motorist* was founded in 1924. In 1930 the American Automobile Association brought out *Holiday*, a bright monthly full of general travel pieces, but it lasted only until the following year when it was merged with *Travel*, which dated back to 1902. In the early sixties, there were more than fifty periodicals devoted to motoring, most of them organs of automobile clubs but some of them commercial publications.

Travel magazines made up a large proportion of the hundreds of new magazines which decorated newsstands after World War II. Men and women in the armed forces had become accustomed to traveling, if involuntarily, during the war; presumably they would retain the habit under more pleasant circumstances. But more important, the war had severely restricted pleasure travel. Millions of persons had money to spend on trips of one sort or another, and even the middle class could afford a plane ticket to Europe or a cruise to the Bahamas.

From 1945 through 1947, one publisher after another made plans for travel magazines. *Smart Traveler* had a short life as a magazine for the middle-income traveler. *Travel and Camera* appeared briefly as the "first publication to recognize the relationship between travel and photography." *Pacific Pathways* turned up to promote the attractions of California, Oregon, Nevada, and Washington. Publishers worked on others—*Everywhere, Globe, Let's Go, Playtime, Trek, Traveltime*. Some of the magazines died before their first issues, and others withered on the newsstands. The interest in faraway places remained. The general magazines catered to it with occasional articles. House organs of the automobile manufacturers catered to it, and so did Sunday editions of metropolitan dailies, producers of short subjects for the movies, information offices of travel agencies, tourist bureaus of state and foreign governments, and professional travelers who wrote highly practical guidebooks.

Perhaps partly because they did, the only major survivor among the many travel magazines started after the mid-forties was Curtis' *Holiday*, although publishers still sought to capitalize on the restlessness of Americans in the early sixties with such entrants as *Happy Traveler* and *Europe, the Vacation You Can Afford*.

A camera was a standard piece of equipment for most travelers. Although photography magazines had been around since the turn of the century, the three leading ones in the early sixties were all born amidst the widespread popular interest in photography that surrounded the creation of the modern picture magazine in the thirties. All three came out within a year or two of *Life* and *Look* —*Popular Photography* and *Modern Photography* in 1937, *U.S. Camera* in 1938. There were others, including some for the home movie-maker, but those three were the largest in the early sixties. *Popular Photography* led with a circulation of about 400,000; the other two had about a quarter-million each.

From the time that printing came to America, the church used the press to propagate its faith, just as it had in Europe for centuries; and the querulous religious periodical, scrapping with its fellows and often subsisting on patent-medicine advertising, was a commonplace of nineteenth-century journalism. It had its champions, and it had its critics. The Reverend Robert E. Bisbee grumbled in 1898 that, although it claimed to broadcast the teachings of Jesus and to inspire love for truth, "the average American seeking to better earthly conditions would as soon search Alaska for orange groves, or hades for an ice crop, as turn to the religious press for help in a crisis like the present." [9]

Critics were delivering much the same sort of criticism nearly sixty years later. When the Methodists came out with a large-circulation, slick-paper monthly named *Together* in 1956, Dan Wakefield studied the first issues and gave a sigh of disappointment. "Too many religious leaders have sought to be *Together* with their era and become shabby followers and imitators rather than leaders. In the desperate effort to be up-to-date they have dressed Jesus Christ in a grey flannel suit and smothered his spirit in the folds of conformity. The new slick-paper Christianity cheerily rises in the midst of a world seeking answers to survival, and offers an All-Methodist football team." [10]

---

[9] Robert E. Bisbee, "The Religious Press and Social Reform," *Arena*, 20 (Aug., 1898) 212.
[10] Dan Wakefield, "Slick-Paper Christianity," *Nation*, 184 (Jan. 19, 1957) 59.

The All-American football team was not just an inconsequential bit of imitative journalism, editors of the large-circulation religious magazines would have responded, but a deliberate editorial technique to let readers know that many colleges and universities were related to the church and, more important, to preach a subtle lesson in racial tolerance. So it was with other features that seemed to stress human interest; each, like a parable, had some underlying religious message. The magazines themselves, by taking the word of the church into the homes of Americans, many of whom could be reached in no other way (the editors would have responded further), were the modern equivalents of the old-time circuit rider.

Together was an offshoot of the *Christian Advocate*, a Methodist organ since 1826. The church split the magazine into two parts in 1956—the *New Christian Advocate*, a professional journal for the clergy, and *Together*, a monthly intended to help and inspire lay families. In folksy prose and in a generous array of pictures, a good share of them in color, *Together* looked at education, church history, evangelism and world missions, family life and its problems, international affairs, successful Methodists, and other topics. It gave timely coverage to denominational news in special inserts for various geographical areas. It had a circulation of about 757,000 in 1963.

Even larger than *Together* was another Protestant denominational magazine, *Presbyterian Life*, which had a distribution of more than 1,136,000. Established in 1948, it evidently had a mission similar to that of *Together* and used church news and features of broad appeal to carry it out.

Those two magazines were at the forefront of more than a thousand Protestant periodicals of various types, most of them with some denominational affiliation. *Christian Herald* had none. It was an interdenominational monthly published by a nonprofit association that sponsored various charities. Eighty-five years old in 1963, it served its audience of 466,000 a balance of inspirational nonfiction and wholesome fiction. Nor was *Christian Life* bound to any denomination; indeed, it had never had an ordained minister on its staff.

Perhaps the most influential Protestant weekly was the *Christian Century*, which also was free from denominational ties, although it had begun life early in 1900 as an organ of the Disciples of Christ. The magazine itself accepted the date of its real beginning as 1908 when Charles Clayton Morrison purchased it—from an owner who had taken it over to satisfy a mortgage—and began a thirty-nine-year tenure as editor.[11] Under Morrison the *Christian Century* continued as a denominational paper for a time; but caught between its sectarian and ecumenical loyalties and bound to its objective of providing an outspoken, constructive viewpoint, it was forced to declare itself nondenominational after a few years. From the start Morrison was guided by his conviction that the church was responsible for the character of society and tried to apply Christian principles to a broad range of contemporary concerns. He made the magazine a vigorous, independent journal of intellectual stature and liberal outlook. It continued to be one under Paul Hutchinson, who assumed the editorship in 1947. Hutchinson likewise saw his task as "communicating and commending the Christian gospel to this age," and he forthrightly applied it to McCarthyism, loyalty oaths, segregation, and other issues of his time. When he retired in 1956, a few months before his death, Harold Fey took over editorial direction of the weekly, which maintained its social awareness and its hope for a union of the divided Protestant denominations and was one of the most frequently quoted religious periodicals.

The Catholic viewpoint was reflected in more than 375 magazines in the early sixties, some of them directed at specialized artistic, professional, and intellectual interests. They by no means spoke in unison; they represented a wide latitude of political outlook and several levels of sophistication. Many of the magazines were completely independent of church support; some of them were published by agencies and orders of the church to advance their specific causes.

Through *Extension*, established in 1906, the Catholic Church Extension Society reached some 383,000 families with articles and fiction of general appeal. The *Victorian*, started more than a decade earlier, was another family magazine of general interest. The Knights of Columbus used *Columbia* to carry its viewpoint to more than a million readers. To further its work, the Catholic Foreign Mission Society of America brought out *Maryknoll*, which first appeared in 1906.

Some of the publications were Catholic counterparts to the secular journals of opinion and comment. *Commonweal*, for instance, was begun by laymen in 1924 as a "weekly review of literature, the

---

[11] "The Century Personality," *Christian Century*, 75 (Jan. 1, 1958) 7-9.

arts, and public affairs" for Catholics, although it was widely read by persons outside the church. Liberal in orientation, it professed to be an open forum for writers of many religious faiths or of no faith at all. Like *Commonweal*, the quarterly *Crosscurrents* was published by laymen, but it gave greater attention to theological affairs, in which it represented the liberal outlook in American lay Catholicism. *America*, started in 1909, was another influential weekly of intellectual substance. *Thought*, a quarterly published by Fordham University, was a sober and distinguished "review of culture and idea."

More than 200 periodicals, some of them newspapers, appealed to Jewish interests. *American Judaism*, which dated back to 1873, was an official magazine of the Union of American Hebrew Congregations. A quarterly, it went into some 220,000 homes in the early sixties. The American Jewish Committee established *Commentary* in 1945 "to meet the need for a journal of significant thought and opinion on Jewish affairs and contemporary issues." It was a monthly of uncompromising intellectual standards, and it drew on a distinguished list of contributors for its explorations into economics, international affairs, popular culture, literature, American politics, and subjects of more parochial interest. Some of the magazines, like *Young Judean*, were addressed to young people. A few were in Yiddish; *Yiddishe Kultur*, for instance, was started in 1938 as a literary publication dealing with Jewish culture.

In the fifties, many publishers hoped to cash in on the cultural explosion that some observers saw reflected in the heavy sale of hi-fi sets, classical phonograph recordings, and books, and in the growing number of Americans who visited art galleries and attended concerts. The publishers perhaps saw promise for their ventures in the experiences of such magazines for the educated as *Atlantic*, *Harper's*, *New Yorker*, and *Saturday Review*, which all grew at a remarkable rate in the fifties when many magazines addressed to the least-educated segments of the population were losing ground. More of the new publications failed than succeeded, although a few managed to stay around for a while.

American Heritage grew out of a quarterly started on $2,000 in 1949 by Earle W. Newton, publisher of *Vermont Life*, who conceived of it as a means of dramatizing United States history and who found a backer for his idea in the American Association of State and Local History. Newton ran the quarterly in his spare time with the help of one paid employee, but he found 50,000

SHOW

THE
MAGAZINE
OF
THE
ARTS

75 CENTS
OCTOBER 1963

**KAYE AND
GARLAND:
IS TV
TUNING OUT
TALENT?**

A NEW
BRITISH
THRILLER
ABOUT
THE SPY WAR
IN BERLIN

THE
WAR BABIES
MATRICULATE—
CULTURAL
CHAOS
ON CAMPUS

readers in the first two years. The magazine was taken over in 1954 by James Parton, Oliver Jensen, and Joseph J. Thorndike, Jr., who raised $65,000 to give it a new dress and an expanded audience. They put the magazine between hard covers, devoted at least sixteen of its pages to four-color illustration, increased its frequency to six issues a year, and sought 55,000 persons willing to pay $2.95 a copy or $12 a year for their bright package, the number they needed to break even. Bruce Catton, historian of the Civil War and Pulitzer Prize winner, took over the editorship and set about coaxing authoritative but brightly written articles from his fellow historians. In 1958, when *American Heritage* was selling 300,000 copies an issue and earning a handsome profit, its publishers brought out *Horizon*, "a magazine of the arts." Like its companion publication, *Horizon* was a hardbound, heavily illustrated, expensive bimonthly, and it drew contributions from a long roster of distinguished critics, scholars, and authors. In 1964 it changed to quarterly publication and dropped its subscription price from $21 to $16 a year.

The final resting place of three other cultural magazines begun with high hopes was *Show*, which Huntington Hartford brought out in September, 1961, as "the magazine of the performing arts." Hartford was a millionaire heir to the A and P grocery fortune and a patron of the arts. His magazine, lavishly illustrated and handsomely designed, broadened its coverage after a few issues to cover all of the arts. Its mission, it said, was "to foster an awareness of the Golden Age" of American culture and "to counter what has been called the threat of leisure," and it gave attention to the theater, music, books, painting, dance, sculpture, movies, and television.

The first competitor swallowed was *Show Business Illustrated*, which Hugh Hefner of *Playboy* had started as a biweekly in August, 1961, to hold "a mirror up to the world of the entertainment arts— on stage, backstage, off stage." It was in its brief planning stage at the same time as *Show*, but Hefner foresaw no threat in the competition: "I don't think Hartford would be too worried if I decided to open up a chain of supermarkets." After about four months as a biweekly, *SBI*, as it was rechristened, went to monthly publication. In February, 1962, it was bought out by *Show*. Hefner said that he sold the magazine not because it failed to do well but because it failed to do well by his standards: "I didn't give the magazine close enough attention in the early stages." Frank Gibney, its editor, who moved to *Show*, thought that *SBI* had passed too rapidly from prospectus to newsstand; moreover, he and Hefner disagreed on its concept. "I wanted to intellectualize *SBI*," he said. "Hefner wanted to use his *Playboy* techniques and make everything breathless."[12]

Just seven months after *SBI* died, *USA-1* also disappeared quietly into *Show*. Rodney C. Campbell, a writer for *Time*, had raised $1,000,000 to bring out the elegant monthly that would put current events into the long perspective of history. He had hoped to find 125,000 subscribers willing to pay $15 a year for his magazine. His first issue came out in April, 1962, and he brought out three more before his 70,000 subscribers were added to *Show*'s list.

Third to vanish was *Bravo*, a quarterly for concertgoers, merged into *Show* in 1961. Hartford, tired of its losses, was trying to sell *Show* itself in mid-1964.

Despite their frightening mortality and their sometimes modest circulations, magazines that capitalized on circumscribed interests were an important part of the American communication network, and their significance was increased in the fifties and sixties by the pervasiveness and ubiquity of television and the mass-circulation magazines. Television and some of the large-circulation giants had to find a common ground on which to meet their mammoth audiences, and it was a ground with limited boundaries. They could not, or thought they could not, afford to play at length or in depth on the interests of a minority of the population. The specialized periodicals could, and they could do so with a continuity, timeliness, and flexibility denied the book, the other major vehicle for much of the content they carried. As readers turned to them for the particular kinds of information they provided, their circulation bounded. In the two decades before 1963, it grew from 13,000,000 to 41,000,000, according to Bernard Gallagher, and he apparently was counting just publications that were more restricted than some mentioned in this chapter.[13] Advertisers, too, paid them increasing attention in the late fifties and early sixties. The magazines that made the greatest advances in advertising page volume in the five years before 1963 were virtually all specialized. The magazines that prospered were, for the most part, those trafficking in information and practical guidance. Magazines specializing in ideas had a story all their own, and it is the subject of the next chapter.

---

[12] *Wall Street Journal*, March 22, 1961, pp. 1, 10.
[13] *The Gallagher Report*, 11 (Nov. 18, 1963) 2.

14

Magazines
for Cultural Minorities

Looking at the record of the ten-cent magazines in their first five years, Frank Munsey in 1898 attributed to them an extraordinary expansion of magazine reading. They had converted a half-million Americans to buying magazines and 3,000,000 to reading them, he estimated, but he still was not satisfied. He urged every family to make magazines a part of its home life for "more culture, broader information, better citizenship and happier lives."[1]

Such concern for large audiences horrified the editor of the *Independent*, who saw little good in talking to the masses. He feared that the proliferation of low-priced magazines would harm the quality magazines which wanted to maintain pure literary standards and to attract the best but not the most readers. "The fit audience in an educated country like ours is not few, but it is not yet unlimited; nevertheless, it is the only audience worth addressing, for it contains the thinking people. The rest may or may not be sturdy citizens, may count in the militia and the population and the lower schools; but they are not the ones who delight to seek the instruction they need most."[2]

Editors of staid magazines like the *Independent* could deplore the headlong pursuit of a mass audience that the popular monthlies

---

[1] "The Publisher's Desk," *Munsey's,* 20 (Oct., 1898) 158; (Jan., 1899) 662.
[2] *Independent,* 47 (June 27, 1895) 867.

and weeklies were engaging in, but there was nothing they could do to halt it. Yet a good many magazines refused to be tempted by the commercialization that overtook magazines in the late nineteenth century. Their editors and publishers were more interested in providing a public forum than in turning a private profit, and they made no attempt to satisfy mass tastes and interests. Oswald Garrison Villard spoke for many of their number in 1915: "It was not, and never has been, in the *Nation's* half-century of existence, a question of profits but of presenting certain definite literary, political, and social ideals and of urging them with all the power of righteous, patriotic purpose. . . ." [3]

In general, these magazines were of two broad types—the literary and the political. Yet that is a loose description, for art and politics were often entwined. Some of the magazines were literary with political overtones, others political with literary overtones. They included the so-called quality magazines that had survived from the nineteenth century into the twentieth; the little magazines of literary experimentation that sprang up after 1912, when *Poetry* was founded to make verse free; and the journals of opinion, reportage, and comment. Edited for a discriminating minority, they afforded writers a haven from the pressures of the marketplace. They opened their pages to authors whose ideas were too daring, too shocking, too recondite for the mass-circulation magazines. They provided an outlet for fiction, poetry, and criticism which was of literary value but of little popular appeal. They encouraged literary experimentation, and they pleaded for social reform. Their influence, as their editors saw it, lay not in the numbers of persons they reached but in the kind. By speaking to a few persons in positions of influence, their editors believed, the magazines would more surely affect the course of events than if they spoke to the multitude.

Whatever their type, magazines for cultural minorities had one thing in common—chronic financial difficulties. Editors of little magazines often had to postpone an issue while they raised money to pay off the printer. Even those depending on university support had to watch their costs, and they had no assurance that their subsidy would continue. Robert Penn Warren and Cleanth Brooks, Jr., learned in 1942 that Louisiana State University could no longer afford the $10,000 a year it had contributed to their *Southern Re-*

[3] Oswald Garrison Villard, "The 'Nation' and Its Ownership," *Nation,* 101 (July 8, 1915) 53.

view, although its admirers noted that the university subsidized the football team with $61,000.[4] So it was, too, with the journals of opinion. The editors of *Common Sense*, on the tenth anniversary of their publication in 1942, said that their deficit had averaged about $700 a month for a decade. William F. Buckley, Jr., reported the losses of his *National Review* at $136,000 in 1958, $132,000 in 1959, and about $100,000 in 1961.

Unable to make their own way, the magazines depended on the generosity of philanthropists and friends who believed in their causes. In the twenties, the *Freeman* was guaranteed its expenses for four years by Helen Swift Morris, a millionairess who had married one of its editors, Francis Neilson. When Max Ascoli launched his *Reporter* in 1949, he reportedly was prepared to finance it with $1,500,000 from his own fortune and that of his wife, a daughter of Julius Rosenwald. J. Patrick Lannan, who invested in *Collier's* in its last years, launched an aggressive campaign for funds to keep *Poetry* going when it appeared about to die for want of money in 1955. In the 1960's many cultural and literary magazines got help from universities, foundations, and charitable organizations. For instance, *Antioch Review*, *Colorado Quarterly*, and *Kenyon Review*, among others, found shelter on college campuses; *Partisan Review* got financial aid from the Congress for Cultural Freedom; and *Commentary* was sponsored by the American Jewish Committee. And in the 1960's some magazines—*Progressive*, for instance, and *New Leader*—still periodically appealed to friends and subscribers for contributions.

Drawing on his experiences with the *National Review*, William F. Buckley, Jr., in 1959 explained why magazines for cultural minorities could not earn their keep in the marketplace. Mass-circulation periodicals had conditioned readers to paying low prices for their magazines, he said. The reader could get a thick, advertising-fattened copy of *Life* for a quarter; he had to pay thirty cents for a slim copy of *National Review* and at that he was getting it for about half of what he should be paying. When costs rose, the publisher of a commercial magazine could turn to his advertisers for additional revenue. The publisher of a small magazine, with little or no advertising, had to pass the added expenses along to the reader or operate at a loss. Since he was competing with all other publications for the reader's subscription money, however, there

---

[4] *Time*, 34 (Feb. 2, 1942) 76.

was a limit to what he could charge. "And that point," Mr. Buckley ruefully observed, "is far this side of solvency." [5]

That gloomy outlook did not prevent new magazines from springing up, and their failure to make a profit did not necessarily mean that their life-spans were short. "The truth is that despite their deficits, and with due consideration to all their other troubles, the small magazines are tenacious," George Kirstein of the *Nation* has remarked. "Many are far longer-lived than their giant cousins, and several have survived through many vicissitudes to ripe old age." [6]

Two that survived were the *Atlantic and Harper's,* magazines of high standing in the nineteenth century and the revered patriarchs of publishing in the twentieth. Since their circulations were more than a hundred thousand in 1963, they did not qualify under Kirstein's definition of a small magazine; their problems, in fact, were not quite those of the little magazines or the journals of opinion. Yet they were magazines of the sort that the editor of the *Independent* feared for in the age of mass journalism, when they nevertheless managed to guard literary standards against the onslaught of commercialism and to survey the contemporary scene with perspicacity and authority.

The *Atlantic Monthly* entered the twentieth century with a tradition of literary excellence nurtured by a line of distinguished editors: James Russell Lowell, its first, James T. Fields, William Dean Howells, Thomas Bailey Aldrich, Horace E. Scudder, and Walter Hines Page. It seems to have enjoyed, as Frank Luther Mott has delightfully expressed it, "a perpetual state of literary grace, so that for a large section of the American public, whatever the *Atlantic* printed was literature." [7]

Ralph Waldo Emerson, Henry Wadsworth Longfellow, and Oliver Wendell Holmes were among the literary figures of New England who assisted at the birth of the *Atlantic,* and they helped to fill its pages for many years. In its first issue, Holmes resumed his *Autocrat of the Breakfast-Table,* suspended a quarter of a century earlier, with an, "As I was saying. . . ." Longfellow appeared often in it, and so did Emerson.

---

[5] William F. Buckley, Jr., "Can a Little Magazine Break Even?" *National Review,* 7 (Oct. 10, 1959) 393-94, 407.

[6] George G. Kirstein, "The Myths of the Small Magazine," *Progressive,* 27 (June, 1963) 25.

[7] Frank Luther Mott, *A History of American Magazines 1850-1865* (Cambridge, 1938), pp. 493-94.

Until the seventies, the *Atlantic* remained largely a New England journal, aloof to contributions from outlanders. But New England was then still the seat of American letters, and the *Atlantic* could count on its neighbors, John Greenleaf Whittier, Henry Thoreau, Harriet Beecher Stowe, and others, to provide all of the material it needed. Edward Everett Hale's classic "The Man Without a Country" first appeared in it, as did Julia Ward Howe's "The Battle Hymn of the Republic," for which the editors paid her $4. In the mid-seventies, the *Atlantic* lost some of its provincialism, and thereafter robust authors like Mark Twain and Bret Harte appeared alongside the sons of Harvard.

Yet the *Atlantic* seemed to shrink away from the profound changes which stirred American life after the Civil War. In the nineties, it continued its genteel way, parochial and academic, its circulation dwindling, its profits negligible. John Adams Thayer, a bustling young man who later made a success of *Everybody's*, proposed to take over management of the *Atlantic,* liven up its content and cover, and sell hundreds of thousands of copies. The conservative publishers were aghast at the suggestion. By 1897 circulation was down to a sad 7,000.

From that low point, the *Atlantic* climbed upward with a push from Walter Hines Page, editor for twelve months in 1898-99, and Bliss Perry, editor from 1899 to 1909. They acknowledged social problems with articles by Booker T. Washington and Jacob Riis, and they decorously engaged in the muckraking which characterized magazine journalism of their time with articles like Everett P. Wheeler's "The Unofficial Government of Cities" and Francis C. Lowell's "The American Boss." Yet a flavor of dilettantism, reflected by such titles as "February in England" and "Dante as Lyric Poet," clung to the magazine.

A fresh breeze began blowing through the musty pages of the *Atlantic* when Ellery Sedgwick became editor in August, 1909. Sedgwick had formed the Atlantic Monthly Publishing Company and purchased the magazine from Houghton Mifflin Company the previous year. He had worked for the popular magazines— *Leslie's Monthly*, the *American*, *McClure's*—and he had diagnosed the maladies which afflicted the quality magazines like the *Atlantic*. Their big trouble, he believed, was that they were too remote from life; they avoided the questions which really excited people. Frederick Lewis Allen, who served an editorial apprenticeship under Sedgwick and later went off to edit *Harper's,* has described Sedgwick's conception of the *Atlantic.* Sedgwick, he said, "resolved that the *Atlantic* should face the whole of life, its riddles, its adventures; the critical questions of the day, the problems of the human heart; and that no subject should be taboo if only it were discussed with urbanity." [8]

Sedgwick kept abreast of the news and cocked an ear to the subjects which active-minded people were discussing. He relied for manuscripts mainly on new writers and on authorities in various fields who were drawn to the *Atlantic* by its prestige, not by its rates of payment, which were low.

During his thirty years as editor, Sedgwick kept the *Atlantic* fresh and alert, yet high in literary quality. The magazine took up the subjects about which people were concerned—the direct-primary experiment; the government versus the corporation; the Sacco-Vanzetti case, which Felix Frankfurter discussed—and its articles were sometimes of genuine news value. In April, 1927, the *Atlantic* carried an article outlining the shortcomings of Alfred E. Smith as a Presidential candidate because of his religion. Governor Smith replied with a letter to the *Atlantic* in which he stated his creed as a Roman Catholic and as a public official. His letter was so newsworthy that two newspapers published a copy of it, stolen from the plant where the *Atlantic* was printed. The *Atlantic* was forced to rush its copies to the stands ahead of schedule and to release the letter to the press at large. The previous year the *Atlantic* had carried an article urging regulation of the stock market, which led to reforms in the New York Stock Exchange. But Sedgwick was as interested in works of literary merit as in articles of topical discussion. He published Ernest Hemingway's "Fifty Grand," which Ray Long of *Cosmopolitan* had rejected as too hardboiled, and Gertrude Stein's *The Autobiography of Alice B. Toklas.* Responding to his break with the parochialism of the past, sales climbed past the 100,000 mark by 1921.

Sedgwick traveled in Spain during the winter of 1938. He was sharply criticized by liberal writers for his public praise of the Franco regime. While he was abroad, his place on the *Atlantic* was filled by Edward A. Weeks, Jr., who officially took over the editorship in June, 1938. Sedgwick remained the majority owner

---

[8] Frederick Lewis Allen, "Sedgwick and the Atlantic," *Outlook and Independent,* 150 (Dec. 26, 1928) 1407.

of the *Atlantic* until December, 1939, when he sold his interest to Richard E. Danielson, former publisher of the *Sportsman.* After his death in 1956, the magazine continued in private hands, unaffiliated with other book or magazine interests.

Weeks, editing in the Sedgwick tradition, maintained the literary distinction of the *Atlantic* without letting the magazine sink into senile complacency. He still published the outstanding writers and thinkers, and even George Bernard Shaw submitted manuscripts to the *Atlantic* unsolicited. On the ninetieth birthday of the *Atlantic,* Weeks ran its first four-color pictorial cover and had its typography restyled by W. A. Dwiggins. He aggressively sought advertising. The *Atlantic* in 1951 tried to build up its institutional advertising by selling "advertorials," multiple-page advertisements resembling editorial text in which advertisers discussed subjects of public interest in rational, essay form. The next year it joined *Harper's* in forming Harper-Atlantic Sales, which sold advertising in both publications. In the next decade, the subsidiary increased the number of pages of advertising in *Atlantic* by 50 per cent, its revenues from $408,000 to $1,207,000.

To mark a century of publishing, the *Atlantic* brought out a 268-page anniversary issue in November, 1957. A new typographic design helped to reinforce the contention of its staff that the *Atlantic* was not a literary magazine but "a general magazine which has made substantial literary contributions." In 1964 it was still published in Boston, a home that Weeks thought gave the magazine a special independence; it had long since ceased to mirror just New England thought but spoke to the entire nation.

After World War II, sales of the *Atlantic,* like those of *Harper's,* grew at a faster rate than the population. Between 1949 and 1962, those of the *Atlantic* increased by nearly 80 per cent to 280,000; those of *Harper's* more than doubled to reach 291,000.

Harper's, 100 years old in 1950, enjoyed a stature no less than that of the *Atlantic.* The State Department ordered 10,000 copies of its centennial issue, sight unseen, for distribution to embassies and consulates. The 1,900 manuscripts a month which came unbidden to its book-crammed editorial offices in the late 1940's included many from persons highly respected in their fields of competence. Henry L. Stimson, former Secretary of War, called in person with his manuscript of "The Decision to Use the Atomic

Bomb," a historical document which the editors ran in February, 1947.

The four Harper brothers—James, John, Joseph, and Fletcher—had no grand notions for *Harper's New Monthly Magazine* when they got together the first issue of June, 1850. Years later Fletcher Harper confessed to one of his editors, "If we were asked why we first started a monthly magazine, we would have to say that it was as a tender to our business, though it has grown into something quite beyond that." [9] Their business was book publishing, and they had built up the largest publishing house in the world by printing cheap reprints of English fiction. A monthly magazine would help to keep their large printing plant busy in otherwise idle hours. They could fill it inexpensively with serializations of the best English novels, in which Americans were beginning to show an interest. Moreover, the magazine would be a good medium for advertising their books. For some thirty years the Harpers reserved their advertising pages for their own use and turned down offers from advertisers who wanted to buy space.

If the *Atlantic* looked to New England for its authors, *Harper's* looked to old England. Its chief contents for many years were English works unprotected by copyright in the United States. *Harper's,* following the custom of the times, at first simply reprinted whatever foreign stories it wished without paying the authors. In 1852, however, the firm paid Dickens for reprinting his *Bleak House,* and by the late fifties its custom was to pay for "advance sheets," proofs of the foreign work which by courtesy of the trade gave the purchaser a priority.

Harper's serialized novels by Dickens, Thackeray, Eliot, Bulwer, Trollope, the popular authors of the time, and readers showed their delight by subscribing to the magazine. Sales, which were but 7,500 when the magazine began, shot up to 50,000 in six months. Just before the Civil War, circulation was 200,000, remarkable for the period. The magazine ran more and more stories and articles by American authors alongside the English favorites. By the late nineteenth century, *Harper's* was at its peak as a general family monthly, rich in illustration, attractive in appearance, high in literary quality. Frederic Remington and Howard Pyle did its illustrations. Thomas Hardy and George du Maurier wrote for

---

[9] J. Henry Harper, *The House of Harper* (New York, 1912), p. 84.

it, and so did Mark Twain, Bret Harte, Richard Harding Davis, and Stephen Crane. Its coup of the nineties was the serialization of du Maurier's *Trilby*. People everywhere talked about it, merchandise was named after it, and a mother begged the concluding installments so that her desperately ill daughter could finish the story before she died.

Fletcher Harper was the chief editorial force behind the magazine in its first twenty years, although it had two editors during that period. Henry J. Raymond, a founder of the New York *Times*, was editor from 1850 to 1856, Alfred H. Guernsey from then until 1869. Henry Mills Alden became editor in 1869, shortly before Harper died. Alden edited *Harper's* for fifty years, a half-century in which it grew in diversity and distinction.

It was Alden who made *Harper's* give increasing attention after 1900 to contemporary problems. He explained his policy at the end of a decade: "The Magazine has a scope broad enough to meet the thoughtful readers at every point of essential and vital interest, without undertaking the function of daily or weekly journalism. But it must be timely. Its field is the living Present. What now, insistently, continuously, and as a part of the great living human movement concerns these thoughtful readers, must constitute for them the main interest of the *Harper* type of magazine." [10] The *Harper's* of Alden, still chiefly a magazine of fiction, nonetheless ran articles on archeology, exploration, sociology, science, surgery and medicine, history, and literary research. It published the narratives of the explorers Stefansson, Peary, Amundson, and Nansen; Woodrow Wilson's *The History of the American People;* William Dean Howells' "My Memories of Mark Twain." Its affinity for England was apparent in the authors of its articles on science, Sir William Ramsay, Sir Ernest Rutherford, Sir J. J. Thomson, Sir Oliver Lodge. *Harper's* remained a magazine for well-to-do readers of catholic tastes, despite Alden's concern with the contemporary. It is doubtful that the readers of *Munsey's* or the *Saturday Evening Post* would have found much to interest them in "The Question of the Atom," a treatise by a chemistry professor in 1910, or in "The Soil as a Battle-Ground" of the same year.

Thomas B. Wells, who edited *Harper's* from 1919 to 1931, pulled the magazine from the slump into which it had fallen after World

[10] Henry Mills Alden, "An Anniversary Retrospect, 1900-1910," *Harper's,* 121 (June, 1910) 39.

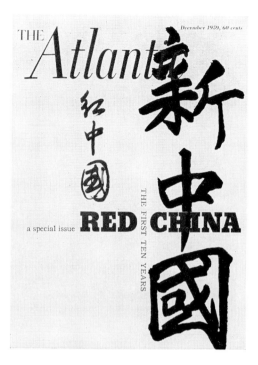

December 1959, 60 cents

THE *Atlant*新中國

红中國

a special issue **RED CHINA**

THE FIRST TEN YEARS

新中國

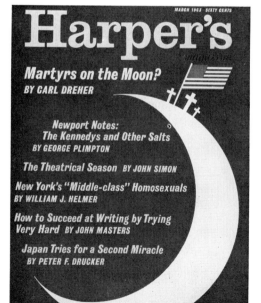

MARCH 1963 · SIXTY CENTS

Harper's

magazine

Martyrs on the Moon?
BY CARL DREHER

Newport Notes:
The Kennedys and Other Salts
BY GEORGE PLIMPTON

The Theatrical Season BY JOHN SIMON

New York's "Middle-class" Homosexuals
BY WILLIAM J. HELMER

How to Succeed at Writing by Trying
Very Hard BY JOHN MASTERS

Japan Tries for a Second Miracle
BY PETER F. DRUCKER

War I. The world had changed so fast that it had left *Harper's* behind, conservative, almost antiquarian, and only 75,000 readers remained faithful enough to buy their copies each month in the mid-twenties.

The audience of *Harper's* had not essentially changed, but the times had; and the new surroundings, as Frederick Lewis Allen has observed, called for new policies. When Fletcher Harper guided the magazine in the fifties and sixties, communication was slow between scattered communities, entertainment was not available at the click of a radio switch, and reading matter was hard to come by. *Harper's*, with its stories, aimed at a rather large proportion of American families. Henry Mills Alden, in the late nineteenth century and early twentieth, addressed his magazine to genteel, educated, well-to-do persons of wide tastes who recoiled from the vulgarities of a headlong industrialization. They had a greater choice of reading matter, but they found much of it crude and common; *Harper's* was a refuge of culture to which they could flee from the barbarities which they thought abounded. After World War I, when Thomas Wells became editor, the mass media flourished on the products of a mass education and an expanding economy. Opportunity was so widespread that, as Allen put it, "a taste for things of high quality had become less a matter of income status than a matter of personal temperament." It was no longer feasible to edit *Harper's* for a distinct social class. The magazine had to appeal to intellectually curious readers of any income who craved quality material which the mass media did not supply.[11]

Wells realized all that; he realized, too, that *Harper's*, once famed for its illustrations, could no longer compete in art work with the big slicks. His change in policy came with the issue of September, 1925, which signaled the event with a new orange cover. The illustrations were gone, except for a frontispiece, and the magazine had a new typography. But the important change was in editorial content. A shift in emphasis from fiction to articles was clearly discernible, and the articles were of more apparent pertinence to the reader than in the past. True, there were still historical articles; Philip Guedalla wrote about George Washington, for instance, and Jesse Grant reminisced about his father, the former President, in several issues. There was still good fiction. But increas-

---

[11] Frederick Lewis Allen, "One Hundred Years of Harper's," *Harper's*, 201 (Oct., 1950) 32-33.

ingly there were authoritative articles on the issues and subjects which stirred a thinking minority.

Lee Foster Hartman succeeded Wells as editor in 1931. When he died a decade later, Frederick Lewis Allen became editor. *Harper's* continued to change—in covers, in format, in editorial emphasis. The orange covers gave way in 1938 to covers in different colors, later to covers with illustrations. Line-cuts reappeared to illustrate the text. The page size was enlarged in 1948 when few presses remained which could handle the traditional size. The ratio of articles to fiction continued to increase. And as interests changed, so did the types of articles that *Harper's* ran. Looking back over two decades, Frederick Lewis Allen in 1941 recalled the subjects which had most interested *Harper's* readers:

> During the nineteen-twenties our most successful articles were on family questions, matters of personal conduct, sex and marriage, or personal belief. Business was booming too well, apparently, to offer burning issues; politics seemed dull, except for the always fascinating prohibition question; the great excitement of that decade . . . appeared to be over the changes in manners and morals and over the problem of personal religion brought about by the rising authority of science and the waning authority of the churches. But with the depression came a great change: suddenly the key questions seemed to be, not questions of individual conduct, but questions of corporate and government policy. Gradually *Harper's* became almost an organ of politics, economics, and sociology. Now the war has brought about still another change—but not back to the individual; rather it is a change to problems on a bigger and more impersonal scale. Now we are dealing with the affairs of nations and aggregations of nations.[12]

Harper's, still owned by the firm that had founded it, celebrated its hundredth anniversary in 1950 with a special issue of 300 pages. Allen retired in 1953 to devote full time to writing; he died the following year. His successor was John Fischer, a former Rhodes scholar who had worked for press associations in Europe and Washington before becoming general book editor for Harper and Brothers and contributing editor of the magazine.

Under Fischer, *Harper's* seemed as adaptable and full of editorial vitality as ever. It carried a heavy balance of articles about politics, international affairs, economics and finance, literary matters, science, and social issues against a light balance of good fiction. It seemed to give preference to comparatively unknown authors with something fresh and significant to say over well-known names.

---

[12] Frederick Lewis Allen in *American Magazines, 1741-1941* by Frederick Lewis Allen, William L. Chenery, and Fulton Oursler (New York, 1941), p. 7.

According to Fischer, the magazine had five major characteristics which represented the aspirations of its editors. It dealt mainly with ideas, especially those that would make important news sometime in the future. It gave a highly selective news coverage by analyzing the events and personalities that might have a lasting historical significance. It sought to make an independent evaluation of public issues. It welcomed controversy. And it provided a medium in which the literary artist—the short-story writer, essayist, critic—could perform uncramped by conventional forms and formulas.

Readers of the little magazines of literary experimentation and criticism, magazines like *Poetry*, the *Little Review* and *Story*, no doubt would have found the *Atlantic* and *Harper's* hopelessly middle class. The little magazines counted their readers in the low hundreds, and they proudly resisted the temptation to grow larger. In matters of art, the plain reader, even the educated one, was likely to be wrong; and as *transition* proclaimed in 1929, "The plain reader be damned."

The little magazine movement began a few years before World War I, and its story has been told in splendid detail by Frederick J. Hoffman, Charles Allen, and Carolyn Ulrich.[13] Harriet Monroe started her *Poetry* in 1912, and it was followed by others: by *Pagan*, an early outlet for the works of Malcolm Cowley, Kenneth Burke, Hart Crane, and e. e. cummings; by *Others*, a lonely runner ahead of even the avant garde poets and an early encourager of William Carlos Williams; by *Seven Arts*, an optimistic but powerful literary force that published the first of Sherwood Anderson's stories of Winesburg, Ohio, the first efforts of Eugene O'Neill, and early works by Van Wyck Brooks; by the *Little Review*, published in Chicago, New York, and Paris by Margaret Anderson and Jane Heap.

Just how many little magazines have come and gone, no one knows for sure. The University of Wisconsin had 716 titles in its Marvin Sukov Collection in the early sixties, and surely that did not include them all. Even the number being published in the sixties was in doubt. A correspondent for the *Wall Street Journal* estimated that 250 of them were being published in 1961 as compared with sixty in the 1920's. On the other hand, the editor of *Kenyon Review* in his issue for summer, 1960, put the number at

---

[13] Frederick J. Hoffman, Charles Allen, and Carolyn Ulrich, *The Little Magazine: A History and Bibliography* (Princeton, 1946).

about a hundred literary magazines and twenty-five poetry journals, ninety of them independently published and thirty-five under university or college auspices. Keeping track of the publications was difficult, for their lives were often precarious and short. "Five years for a little magazine is a ripe old age," the editors of *American Prefaces* observed on its fifth anniversary in 1940, and one can detect their awe at its own longevity. "The average influential little magazine flashes brightly for a year, like *Seven Arts*, then passes. For those who live the first winter, the fourth-year mortality is a fearful danger; Emerson's *Dial* fell victim to it."

Greenwich Village, where the rents were cheap and the companionship congenial, was a natural breeding ground for the little magazines, but it was not their only habitat. They appeared anywhere at home or abroad where young intellectuals could find a typewriter with which to issue a manifesto, a mailbox to receive contributions, and a printer to turn out a few copies.

The years before World War I were their period of birth and groping, the twenties their period of glory, but they continued to appear in greater numbers than ever in the sixties, although a change had come over them. Felix Pollak of the University of Wisconsin has summarized the phases they went through.[14] Before World War I, they most prized vitality, intensity, uninhibited expression of the ego. Among their strong philosophical influences were Nietzsche, Hegel, Darwin, Bergson, and Pavlov, and among their key phrases were symbolism, futurism, German expressionism, and French cubism. In the 1920's, their period *par excellence*, they reflected the fertility and ferment in literature and in all of the arts, and their titles symbolized their mood: *Exile, Fugitive, Broom, Experiment, Secession*. They were, as Pollak said, exultant messengers of new "ideas, theories, movements, trends, vogues, and fads adopting and adapting them, and engendering others; helping upcoming writers break into print, providing meeting places for kindred spirits, and also for vehemently and articulately unkindred ones, supplying the stimulation and high tension requisite for all artistic creation, furnishing elbowroom for serious as well as abstruse experimentation, scorning taboos and censorship of any kind."[15] In the 1930's, the little magazines were organs of idealistic

---

[14] Felix Pollak, "Landing in Little Magazines—Capturing (?) a Trend," *Arizona Quarterly*, 19 (Summer, 1963) 101-15.
[15] Pollak, p. 107.

radicalism that saw art as something to be harnessed to a cause. Waldo Frank, writing in one of them, championed the engagement of the literary artist with social reform in these terms: "We have not, as writers, given the full measure of our contribution in this hour of history in which . . . 'creation is revolution.' This deficiency of the writers, of the consciously revolutionary writers in great part, is at least one of the causes of the delay in the birth of the new world. . . ." [16] Although such titles as *Left, Left Front, Partisan Review,* and *Dialectics* bespoke their orientation, some of the magazines were unpolitical. *Southern Review* emerged as an early organ of the new criticism, for instance, and *Hinterland* sought to give expression to the Midwestern writer and his agrarian heritage. The 1940's were a decade of retreat from the cold realities of the world, of retreat from creativity to criticism, from iconoclasm to safety and respectability, from precarious independence to academic subsidy. The 1950's, which saw a proliferation of the little magazine, were hard to characterize; on the one hand, they were a time of protest organs published by the "beat" generation and on the other of conventional quarterlies, including a number with college or university sponsorship.

From the mid-forties onward, critic after critic complained that the little magazines had traded their fire and excitement for respectability and acceptance, that they had changed from a medium of creativity to a medium of criticism. Charles Angoff in 1946 was sorry that their "bubbling potency" had left them. Although they were sometimes cold and shabby, and cluttered with bizarre criticism, they had once provided a haven for the rebellious artist, he said, and the best of them were once edited with artistic integrity and dedicated to literary freshness.[17] More than a dozen years later Barry Spacks complained of much the same thing: "The little magazine is more conservative than it used to be, has less influence, and by and large generates less excitement in its readers and contributors." [18]

By 1962 the little magazines were so respectable that the editors of thirty-four of them could gather in New York for the second

---

[16] Waldo Frank, "The Writer's Part in Communism," *Partisan Review,* 3 (Feb., 1936) 15.
[17] Charles Angoff, "The Little Magazines," *American Mercury,* 63 (Sept., 1946) 370-74.
[18] Barry Spacks, "Circulation 'Bloody Low,'" *Nation,* 191 (Sept. 17, 1960) 167-68.

meeting of the Association of Literary Magazines of America, formed the year before "to increase the usefulness and prestige of the literary magazine." They heard reports on foundation support for their magazines and discussed ways of getting more. They talked about improved billing and distribution, considered plans for exhibits at booksellers' conventions, and set up the inevitable committees. The iconoclastic editors of the twenties, whose forte was manifestoes, would have found such talk a little bourgeois.

Yet the little magazines could claim a record of genuine accomplishment. They were originators or carriers of most of the modern movements—symbolism, imagism, expressionism, surrealism, cubism —and they were laboratories for talent. Indeed, someone has calculated that 80 per cent of the American writers who became famous after 1912 were first published in them, although that is not to suggest that those authors would have otherwise remained in obscurity.

Just as the little magazines represented a literary protest, so a good many magazines represented a political or social protest. Indeed, the history of the little magazines parallels that of the socio-political magazines, the journals of opinion, for many of the young writers were rebels in both art and politics.

Like the little magazines, the journals of opinion, comment, and controversy walked a lonely and precarious road in the twentieth century—lonely because their views were invariably the unpopular views of the minority, precarious because they were chronically in financial distress. The mass-produced magazines tended to be neutral or conservative in treating social issues, public affairs, and business once the era of muckraking had ended. Against the soothing chorus of the mass-circulation slicks, the journals of opinion raised their small voice. In large measure, they reflected the prevailing mood of the American intellectual, his optimism, his despair, his aspirations, his fears. They were often far ahead of their times in advocating social justice and political reform, yet they were an effective instrument for transmuting the ideas of an aggressive minority into those of an inert majority.

The *Nation*, born just after the Civil War ended, was the elder statesman among the journals of opinion in the twentieth century. Its founder was E. L. Godkin, a young journalist who had come to America from Ireland in 1856 to write about conditions in the South. He developed plans for an intellectual weekly paper, and

his idea interested James Miller McKim, a Philadelphia abolitionist who wanted to finance a periodical to aid freedmen. They found
forty stockholders who invested $100,000. Godkin was appointed
editor, with complete editorial independence. His associate editor
was Wendell Phillips Garrison, son of William Lloyd Garrison, the
abolitionist leader.

At the end of its first year, the *Nation* underwent the first of its
many changes in ownership. Its capital was all but gone, and there
were unwarranted insinuations that Godkin had mismanaged affairs.[19] Godkin then formed E. L. Godkin and Company, which
published the *Nation* for the next fifteen years. They were years
of financial insecurity, but the *Nation* grew in prestige and circulation. In 1881 Godkin sold the magazine to the New York *Evening
Post* and became associate editor of the *Post*. The *Post* was owned
by Henry Villard, the railroad builder and a brother-in-law of
Garrison, and he scrupulously refrained from interfering with the
editorial policies of his publications.

The *Nation* remained in the Villard family for more than half a
century. For thirty-three years it appeared as a weekly edition of
the *Post*. Its connection with the paper was completely severed in
1918 when Oswald Garrison Villard took over as owner and editor.
He served it without salary, spent substantial sums of his own
money on it, and raised funds for it among friends who recognized
its value as an organ of liberalism. To insure its independence, he
sold it in 1934, two years after he had resigned its editorship, to
the Civic Aid Foundation, a nonprofit organization established by
Maurice Wertheim, banker and philanthropist.

Wertheim at times took issue with the *Nation's* policies, which
were determined by its board of editors, but he made no effort to
control them. He disagreed so violently when the *Nation* endorsed
President Roosevelt's plan to reform the Supreme Court that he
took space in it to present his own stand. Wertheim sold the *Nation*
in June, 1937, to Freda Kirchwey, senior editor, who had been
actively associated with it for sixteen years. Group control and
absentee ownership were less likely to preserve the "independent
character and direction" of the magazine than centralized control
by an active editor, Wertheim explained in the issue of June 12.
The *Nation* paid its own way from 1937 through 1940, but it lost

---

[19] Villard, p. 53.

about $10,000 in each of the next two years because of increased operating expenses. In 1943 Freda Kirchwey transferred ownership from herself to a nonprofit organization, Nation Associates, Inc., in which she asked subscribers to enroll as members at from $10 to $100 a year. About 2,500 members joined in the first six months. In September, 1955, when Carey McWilliams succeeded Miss Kirchwey as editor, the *Nation* was still having financial difficulties. Among the other tasks taken on by its new publisher, George C. Kirstein, was assuring it of the funds it needed.

The mission of the *Nation,* as its founders saw it, was stated in its third issue. "This journal," they said, "will not be the organ of any party, sect, or body. It will, on the contrary, make an earnest effort to bring to the discussion of political and social questions a really critical spirit, and to wage war upon the vices of violence, exaggeration, and misrepresentation by which so much of the political writing of this day is marred." [20]

Subscribers received their first copies of the *Nation* in July, 1865, three months after General Lee had surrendered at Appomattox. Lincoln was dead, and the country bore wounds of hate as it faced the terrible problems of reconstruction. "The week has been singularly barren of exciting events . . ." the *Nation* reported in its opening sentence, and added, two paragraphs later, "The news from Europe is unimportant. . . ." [21]

The *Nation* found thousands of "exciting events" to record and comment on in the years after that first issue, and it saw an increasing importance in news from Europe and from other parts of the world. Godkin, with an aloofness which some of his contemporaries found exasperating, saw much to criticize, little to commend on the American scene. His *Nation* decried railroad barons, Tammany, currency inflation, and the Populists. It took capital's side against labor, attacked trade unionism, and opposed the eight-hour working day. It was a strong advocate of civil service reform. In its literary criticism, its standards were high, its reviews characterized by what Frank Luther Mott has called "casual brilliance."

After Oswald Garrison Villard became editor in 1918, the *Nation* at times adopted editorial policies which clashed with popular opinion. It was denounced as pro-German, pacifist, and "Bolshevik."

[20] *Nation,* 1 (July 20, 1865) 95.
[21] *Nation,* 1 (July 6, 1865) 1.

The Post Office Department held up its issue of September 13, 1918, as unmailable but released it five days later after President Wilson himself had intervened.

More than other journals of opinion, the *Nation* studied the significance of developments abroad. Its platform for the peace after World War I included such proposals as complete disarmament, free trade and an end to all tariffs, and creation of an international court and parliament. Even in the red-baiting twenties, the *Nation* tried to interpret the Russian Revolution, and it printed the texts of early Soviet laws and other documents. It denounced Mussolini at a time when he still had apologists in the United States. It foresaw the threat of Hitler long before the invasion of Poland.

As a part of its foreign affairs coverage, the *Nation* inaugurated an international relations section which carried interpretative articles, texts of documents of international importance along with explanations of them, summaries from the foreign press, book reviews, and similar material.

Villard developed the *Nation*'s domestic platform gradually. The magazine found little to admire in the Republican administrations of the twenties but was generally sympathetic to the New Deal. It took up the cause of Sacco and Vanzetti, helped to ferret out the Teapot Dome scandals, campaigned against lynching, favored collective bargaining, and approved of a liberal immigration policy.

A number of outstanding intellectuals worked for the *Nation* during Villard's regime. At one time or another the staff included Joseph Wood Krutch, Stuart Chase, Raymond Gram Swing, Norman Thomas, Lewis Gannett, Ludwig Lewisohn, and the four Van Dorens, Carl, Mark, Irita, and Dorothy.

As independent thinkers, they were bound to disagree with the editor and with each other from time to time. Several staff writers resigned from the magazine when their differences were too fundamental or too frequent for harmony. Heywood Broun, a regular contributor for a decade, left the *Nation* for the *New Republic* in 1937 because of his dissatisfaction with its policies. Oswald Garrison Villard continued to write for the *Nation* after he had relinquished the editorship, but he severed all connections with it in 1940. He did so, he said, because of "the editors' abandonment of the *Nation*'s steadfast opposition to all preparations for war, to universal military service, to a great navy, and to *all* war, for this in my judgment has been the chief glory of its great and honorable past." [22] Louis Fischer announced his resignation in the *Nation* of June 2, 1945, after an association of twenty-two years because he had noted a steady deterioration in its political matter and the emergence of a "line" which governed its inclusions and omissions. The "line" quite evidently, as the editors of the *Nation* guessed, was the weekly's benevolent attitude toward Soviet Russia. Fischer's was the first in a flurry of resignations at midcentury which apparently stemmed from the same reason.

The *Nation* promoted a number of causes after Carey Mc-Williams became editor in 1955: making racial equality an immediate reality, setting life imprisonment as the maximum punishment for any crime, achieving equal voting strength in state government for citizens in city and country, conserving natural resources, treating drug addiction as a medical rather than criminal problem. But its prime cause seems to have been disarmament and rule by international law, and it gave considerable space to the peace movement and to the dangers of nuclear war. It continued to give attention to foreign affairs, and it maintained its concern for civil liberties.

One of its regular reporters was Fred J. Cook, to whose exposés it devoted all or most of an issue from time to time—"The Shame of New York" in 1959, "The C. I. A." in 1961, "The Corrupt Society" in 1963, among others. Dan Wakefield and David Cort periodically contributed astringent pieces of reportage. Harold Clurman wrote about the theater, and Nelson Algren and Harvey Swados were among its book reviewers.

Some of the magazines of minority expression arose from the political ferment which made the years just before World War I a period of great expectations. America had examined herself, with help from the muckrakers, and her conscience was troubled. A legion of reformers stormed the bastions of the vested interests and battled to rout social injustice. There was no end of causes: an equitable redistribution of wealth, better conditions for the working man, women's suffrage, children's rights. But it was a time of protest and reform, not of revolution, for there remained a strong faith in American institutions. There was promise that evils and abuses in the system could be abolished by democratic means, and that promise contributed to the optimism of the day. The optimism infected the young intellectuals. Socialism, become respectable, had

---

[22] Oswald Garrison Villard, "Issues and Men," *Nation*, 150 (June 29, 1940) 782.

spread to the colleges. Some bright young minds flirted with it; others, in defiance or experimentation, explored the radical movements budding in such places as Greenwich Village.

The *Masses* was a child of those days of protest. It was edited by Greenwich Village socialists in a former plumbing shop, and it called itself "a monthly magazine devoted to the interests of the working people." The first issue was hawked on the streets of the Village in January, 1911. Piet Vlag, an immigrant restaurant manager, guided the *Masses* through its first issues with editorial assistance from Thomas Seltzer and Horatio Winslow and with financial assistance from a wealthy insurance man. By September, the *Masses* had foundered, however, and for three months its voice was silent against such enemies of the good life as war, child labor, and the high cost of living. During those three months a group of Greenwich Village writers and artists led by Art Young determined to rescue the magazine. They sent a wire to Max Eastman, who had taught philosophy at Columbia University, offering him the editorship without pay. Eastman became editor with the issue of December, 1912. He was later joined by Floyd Dell as managing editor.

John Reed, who was to be buried within the walls of the Kremlin, wrote the statement of purpose for the *Masses*: "To everlastingly attack old systems, old morals, old prejudices. . . ." The *Masses* well lived up to its aim. It took up the causes of feminism, Negro rights, sexual freedom, birth control, and pacifism, but its criticisms were often leavened with humor. Writers and artists of talent served the *Masses* without pay. Art Young, Jo Davidson, Walter Lippmann, Wilbur Daniel Steele, Carl Sandburg, Sherwood Anderson, John Reed, Mary Heaton Vorse, Louis Untermeyer, Amy Lowell—all of them donated their work to the magazine.

The *Masses* continued to espouse pacifism and socialism even after America entered World War I. It called upon President Wilson to repeal conscription, and it appealed for funds to defend agitators against the draft. Because of its editorial policies, it was banned from the newsstands of the New York elevated and subway systems after January, 1916. The Post Office Department barred it from the mails in August, 1917. Two hung juries failed to convict Eastman, Dell, Young, and the business manager, Merrill Rogers, for "conspiracy against the government" and for "interfering with enlistment."

But the *Masses* died soon after the government attempted to suppress it. It reappeared in March, 1918, as the *Liberator*. The *Liberator* embraced Marxist doctrines and in 1924 was given to American communists, who merged it with other of their publications. By then most of the staff of the old *Masses* had long since left the publication.

In 1926 Michael Gold and Joseph Freeman revived the old magazine as the *New Masses*. In the twenty-two years of its existence, the *New Masses* increasingly adhered to the line of the communist party, although Freeman denied in 1936 that the magazine was financed by the communists. Its editors included Granville Hicks, James Rorty, and Michael Gold. The magazine found many new subscribers during the thirties when the depression again brought a questioning of old institutions and when the rise of totalitarian governments in Europe solidified liberals against fascism. Its circulation rose from 25,000 in 1929 to 36,500 in 1933, and the magazine changed from monthly to weekly publication in 1934. After World War II, increased costs of production and a general hostility to communism in America helped to bring about the death of the magazine. *New Masses* ceased publication in January, 1948, after an unsuccessful effort to raise funds to cover its deficit. Later that year its name was combined with that of a literary quarterly, *Mainstream*. For a time the publication appeared as *Masses and Mainstream*, but in 1963 only *Mainstream*, which described itself as a cultural magazine, remained.

The *New Republic* was launched in the same atmosphere of prewar revolt and optimism which nourished the *Masses*. It stood alongside the *Nation* as an organ of liberalism, although it was younger by nearly half a century. For almost forty years the *New Republic* had fewer financial cares than the *Nation*, since its patrons unquestioningly made up its deficit.

The *New Republic* was subsidized by funds from Mr. and Mrs. Willard D. Straight, who allowed its staff complete editorial freedom. Straight had served as a diplomat in the Far East for several years, had represented American banking interests there, and in 1911 had married Dorothy Whitney, daughter of a Wall Street millionaire. He and his wife were impressed by their associations with Herbert Croly, who had been editor of the *Architectural Record*. In 1909 Croly had written a book which became the creed of many liberals, *The Promise of American Life*, and the Straights agreed to give Croly financial support for a magazine which would reflect his liberal viewpoint. Straight died in 1918, but Croly continued to draw whatever funds the *New Republic* needed from Mrs. Straight, who later married Leonard Elmhirst. When she became a British subject in 1935, she and her husband created a trust fund for the benefit of the four magazines in which she was interested, *New Republic, Asia, Antiques,* and *Theatre Arts.* However, on March 16, 1953, the magazine told its readers that the trust funds would no longer cover its losses. In response to an appeal for funds hundreds of friends sent contributions.

Early in 1914, however, Croly had enough money to guarantee publication of his proposed weekly for four years, and he had already chosen his first board of editors, which included Walter Lippmann and Walter Weyl. He had an idea of what his magazine would be—a progressive journal that would promote the reform thought of which Theodore Roosevelt was spokesman, although it would be independent of party and individual. Since Croly's first choice for a name—the *Nation*—was already taken, the staff settled on the *Republic* but added the "New" on discovering that their second choice, too, had a prior claimant.

The staff set to work on the magazine with optimism, for the period immediately preceding the war was one of bright promise. Lippmann himself had written in 1914 that the question was not whether or not progressivism would triumph but how to consolidate its victory. An editorial writer for *Collier's* had spoken for many Americans that same year when he said: "Fifty years from now, when some writer brings Woodrow Wilson's *History of the American People* up to date, we think he will say that the ten years ending about January 1, 1914, was the period of greatest ethical advance made by this nation in any decade." [23] Woodrow Wilson, that man of moral purpose, was in the White House. At first the *New Republic* regarded him warily, but by 1916 it saw him as the new advocate of reforms which progressives had sought since the 1890's. The good life was not won, of course, but the period was one of happy transition.

War cut short much of that bright promise, and it came to Europe on the very day that the *New Republic* opened its offices. The staff knew that America would be affected, if not actually involved, and that they would have to alter their ideas about domestic reform. They made a good many major changes in their

---

[23] "We Take Stock," *Collier's,* 52 (Jan. 24, 1914) 11.

plans for the first issue. When it appeared on November 7, 1914, the magazine carried the subtitle "A journal of opinion to meet the challenge of the new time," but it also carried an editorial, "The End of American Isolation."

Even with the war on its mind, the magazine found liberal causes to champion, although it broke with Roosevelt within its first month. It applauded the planned approach to almost any social, economic, or political question. Almost from the start, it crusaded for women's suffrage. At first it advocated America's neutrality in the war, chiefly so the nation could help plan for the peace, but in February, 1917, it called for intervention.

After the nation had entered the war, some persons regarded the *New Republic* as an organ of the Wilson administration. Oswald Garrison Villard, who found the competition of the *New Republic* stimulating, has recalled: "For a time during the war and immediately afterwards the *New Republic* was regarded by many as the mouthpiece of Woodrow Wilson; it was considered bad form in some official circles to be seen without it and its circulation climbed to about 45,000. It was believed that Walter Lippman and the *New Republic* had won the President to our participation in the war in order to shape the peace and that Lippmann had written the fourteen peace points." [24]

The *New Republic* had advocated American participation in a League of Nations, but it was disillusioned by the machinations at the Paris Peace Conference. It urged that this country stay out of the League of Nations, and it attacked the Treaty of Versailles as a betrayal of what the United States had fought for.

The twenties were a time of decline for the *New Republic*. Of the original founding board, Croly was almost the only one left. Many subscribers who had endorsed the Treaty and the League also had gone because of the magazine's position; Bruce Bliven once put their proportion at about 40 per cent. Then, too, the mood of the twenties was different from that of the prewar years. Croly's restatement of aims for his magazine in 1922 was far less optimistic than the original one. The *New Republic* in the twenties was walled off from the mainsprings of political power, Richard H. Gentry has noted in his analysis of the magazine, and its response was to give more space to philosophy and social issues than to

---

[24] Oswald Garrison Villard, *Fighting Years: Memoirs of a Liberal Editor* (New York, 1939), p. 361.

politics.[25] But Croly's earnest analysis in his stiff and labored prose was less suited to the times than the bright, brash words of such dissidents as H. L. Mencken. Circulation figures for the magazine during that period seemed highly approximate, but Ayer's directory shows a decline from 37,000 in 1919 to a mere 12,000 in 1929.

The *New Republic* recaptured much of its lost audience in the thirties, when the depression intensified concern over social, economic, and political problems. After Croly died in 1930, an editorial board continued to set policies, although Bruce Bliven and George Soule were the two most responsible for them. Many of the New Deal Braintrusters had originally set forth their ideas in the *New Republic*, but the magazine was initially lukewarm to the reforms of Franklin D. Roosevelt. In 1935 the magazine took such a sharp turn left that one writer said it had renounced Croly for Marx. It turned back again later in the decade, when it became disillusioned by the Russian experiment and when it found some New Deal policies of which it could approve. Aware of totalitarianism abroad, the *New Republic* nevertheless pursued a course of isolationism in the thirties on the grounds that the United States should put its own house in order before meddling in the affairs of Europe. It abruptly abandoned that policy in late 1940 and thereafter became increasingly interventionist.

While Croly and Bliven were editors, many writers of brilliance and perception wrote political analyses and literary criticism for the *New Republic*. Staff members and contributors from time to time included Charles Merz, Alvin Johnson, Randolph Bourne, Stark Young, Malcolm Cowley, Robert Morss Lovett, George Santayana, Edmund Wilson, and John Dewey.

When Michael Straight was discharged from the Air Force after World War II, he thought that the *New Republic* deserved a larger audience than the 41,000 subscribers it was then reaching. Straight was the son of the Willard Straights who had financed the magazine from its inception. He changed the format, restyled the cover, added political cartoons, set out to break what he regarded as the "sameness" of its editorial policies, and even hired an agency to conduct a campaign of radio advertising.

---

[25] Richard H. Gentry, "Liberalism and the New Republic: 1914-1960" (unpublished doctoral dissertation, University of Illinois, 1960). Most of the information about the editorial policies of the magazine in this chapter comes from Gentry's work.

Henry Wallace, former Secretary of Agriculture, Secretary of Commerce, and Vice President of the United States, was appointed editor in December, 1946, as part of the program to increase the audience and influence of the *New Republic*. Bliven and Straight remained on as senior editors. The wartime friendship of the United States and Soviet Russia had cooled by the time Wallace joined the *New Republic* "to help organize a progressive America." Wallace, however, believed that continued cooperation between America and Russia was possible. There could truly be One World, he said, only if there were jobs, freedom, and peace in all nations. "I prefer to accept the willingness of the Soviet leaders to think more and more in democratic terms," he wrote. "We cannot hide the weaknesses in our democracy. If we take steps to overcome these weaknesses, then I believe the Russians believing in the genuineness of our democracy will move toward greater political freedom." [26]

When Wallace announced his candidacy for the Presidency on a third-party ticket in January, 1948, he relinquished the editorship of the *New Republic*. He continued as contributing editor for another six months, but he and the editors were at odds on several issues. Wallace wrote his last article for the magazine in July, 1948. Two days later Michael Straight endorsed William O. Douglas, Supreme Court justice, as Presidential candidate.

Sales of the *New Republic* more than doubled in the thirteen months that Wallace was editor. At its peak, the magazine was selling about 96,000 copies a week. But it did not develop into the sort of magazine that Straight had envisioned. He had hoped to build circulation to more than 300,000 and to win a comfortable amount of advertising; instead he is said to have lost a half-million dollars.

The magazine settled down to a tone of moderate liberalism and to a circulation of about what it had had before the experiment. It moved its offices from New York to Washington in 1952, the year Bliven retired. Gilbert A. Harrison bought the magazine in 1953 and succeeded his friend Michael Straight as editor in 1956.

By the mid-fifties, the *New Republic* had come closer to the middle of the political spectrum than at any time in its history, and it still held that position in the early sixties. Richard Gentry has described its temper this way: "The editorials were still as critical

---

[26] Henry A. Wallace, "Jobs, Peace, Freedom," *New Republic,* 115 (Dec. 16, 1946) 789.

in tone as ever, and dangers to liberty were as quickly pounced upon, but the criticisms tended to be less about the basic structure of American institutions than about faulty details in their management. The institutions, including a controlled capitalism, were accepted as more or less permanent." [27] What had come over the magazine, he suggested, was a shift from political philosophy to political journalism. Just as the little magazines had turned from creativity to criticism, so the *New Republic* had turned from shaping events to commenting upon them.

The intellectual climate which had nurtured the *New Republic*, *Masses*, and similar periodicals before World War I had largely disappeared by the twenties. Prewar intellectuals had identified themselves with movements to fulfill the promise of American life. Intellectuals of the twenties often disassociated themselves from the shortcomings they found instead of working to eliminate or to change them. They were detached observers, not part of the society which they professed to despise.

Some of the spirit of protest and reform remained in the twenties, of course, and on it were built such magazines as the *Liberator* and the *New Leader*. The *New Leader*, for years a tabloid weekly, became a magazine in 1950. Founded in 1923 in the backwash of the prewar enthusiasm for socialism which had led to the establishment of the New York *Call*, it was the organ of the American socialist party for more than a decade but ended its affiliation in the mid-thirties when its editors thought that a segment of the party was showing antidemocratic tendencies. For thirty years the *New Leader* was run with fierce dedication by S. M. Levitas, who became its general manager in 1930 and took over its editorial direction as well a few years later. Born in Kiev, a socialist at fifteen, Levitas was active in the Russian Revolution. He edited the first *Labor Daily* in Moscow, where he served briefly as vice-mayor. He took refuge in the United States after the Bolsheviks came to power. When he died in 1961, the New York *Times* paid tribute to the "warm and vibrant man" who had made his magazine "a free forum for every variety of democratic opinion." It was a strongly anticommunist magazine that paid considerable attention to Russia and to communism throughout the world, but it opened its pages to writers of varying political complexions. From time to time, it issued special supplements carrying analyses too lengthy for

---

[27] Gentry, p. 394.

its regular format, and alongside its political articles it ran criticisms of the arts. Despite its inability to pay for articles, it regularly carried contributions by such authors as James T. Farrell, Daniel Bell, Sidney Hook, and Max Eastman. Herb Lubalin, the graphic artist who had redesigned *McCall's,* restyled the *New Leader* without fee in 1961. Its circulation then was about 28,500.

The early twenties also saw the birth and death of the *Freeman* of Francis Neilson and Albert Jay Nock. In a sense, the *Freeman,* too, had its roots in prewar rebellion and radicalism, for it shared Nock's devotion to the single-tax principles of Henry George. Nock was a strong individualist who abhorred powerful and aggressive government, so strong an individualist that he shunned even organized movements to promote the single tax, and there were traces of his personality in his weekly's statement of purpose: "The *Freeman* will be more interested in discovering sentiment than in creating it and will aim rather at enlightening and unifying public opinion than at controlling or instructing it." [28] The *Freeman* was a quiet magazine of excellent prose. It reached a small audience, about 10,000, and it died early in 1924, just short of its fourth birthday, when its funds ran out.

The *American Mercury* of Henry L. Mencken and George Jean Nathan was far more in harmony with the intellectual atmosphere of the twenties than the *Freeman,* the *Leader,* or even than the *New Republic* and *Nation.* The *American Mercury* was the voice of the skepticism and iconoclasm which in the twenties replaced the rebellious idealism and optimism of the days before the war. The *New Republic* may have had a hard time finding 20,000 readers in the twenties and the *Freeman* 10,000; the *American Mercury* had no trouble finding 77,000. Some of the magazines started before the war may have hoped to aid in remaking the world; not so the *Mercury.* It stood apart from the fumblings and follies of society, mocking and superior. Politics in the United States, its editors said, remained "mainly utopian—an inheritance from the gabby, gaudy days of the Revolution." The editors had heard "no Voice from the burning bush. They will not cry up and offer for sale any sovereign balm, whether political, economic, or aesthetic, for all the sorrows of the world. The fact is, indeed, that they doubt any such sovereign balm exists. . . ." Their aims were to tell the truth with novelty, "to keep common sense as fast as they can, to belabor

---

[28] *Freeman,* 1 (March 17, 1920) 24.

sham as agreeably as possible, to give a civilized entertainment." [29]

The *American Mercury* was not, strictly speaking, a bedfellow of the *Nation, New Republic,* and the other journals of opinion and comment, although it was an opinionated and caustic commentator. Nor was it a bedfellow of the quality magazines, *Harper's* and the *Atlantic,* although it was a magazine of literary quality. It was a unique monthly review which nimbly straddled those two broad types of publications.

The immediate predecessor of the *American Mercury* was *Smart Set,* of which Mencken and Nathan were coeditors from 1914 until the end of 1923. *Smart Set,* founded in 1890, was a magazine of many lives. Before Mencken and Nathan, it had been first a magazine for New York society; then an urbane literary journal edited by Charles Hanson Towne and Arthur Griscom for, as it said, "minds that are not primitive"; then a magazine of literary excellence edited by bearded, monocled Willard Huntington Wright, scholar and aesthete, who later reached a far wider audience as an author of detective fiction under the pseudonym S. S. Van Dine. After Mencken and Nathan, it was a magazine of romantic confession, then a magazine of commonplace light fiction.

Mencken and Nathan became coeditors of *Smart Set* entirely by chance. Aboard a ship homeward-bound from Europe, a stranger accosted Nathan to ask where he had got his tweed overcoat. The stranger was Eltinge F. Warner, who had just acquired the magazine. When he learned that Nathan was an author, he offered him the editorship. Nathan accepted on the condition that Mencken join him as coeditor. During their decade with *Smart Set,* they gave readers a faint taste of what the *Mercury* was to be like. Mencken wrote literary reviews, Nathan wrote dramatic criticism, and their pieces were flanked by novels, short stories, essays, satires, and burlesques by authors such as Theodore Dreiser, Aldous Huxley, Ruth Suckow, Ben Hecht, Michael Arlen, and Thomas Beer. The magazine cast an eye on American institutions in a long series, "The Higher Learning in America," for which various writers examined the universities they knew: John Peale Bishop, Princeton; Gilbert Seldes, Harvard; Donald Ogden Stewart, Yale; John Gunther, Chicago; and so on. *Smart Set* promoted itself in its subtitle from "The Magazine of Cleverness" to "The Aristocrat Among Magazines." But at the end of 1923 Mencken and Nathan were ready to

---

[29] "Editorial," *American Mercury,* 1 (Jan., 1924) 27.

move to a magazine which would afford a wider audience than the 22,000 readers of *Smart Set* and which would put less emphasis on fiction and greater emphasis on scrutinizing the American scene.

Alfred A. Knopf, a young man who had built up a successful business publishing books of high quality and beautiful design, offered to publish the magazine which Mencken and Nathan had in mind. The *American Mercury* in its bright green cover first turned up on newsstands in January, 1924. From its opening page, it debunked the idols and ridiculed the mores of middle-class America. The leading article of the first issue was Isaac R. Pennypacker's "The Lincoln Legend," which argued that Lincoln was descended from a wealthy family, was a doubtful judge of men, but was a canny politician. Ernest Boyd a few pages later in "Aesthete: Model 1924" traced the disillusionment of the young American intellectual who had gathered from the *Masses* before the war that the socialist revolution was imminent but who in his wartime service "bitterly regretted the collegiate patriotism responsible for his devotion to the lofty rhetoric of the *New Republic*." There was an article on "The Communist Hoax," another by a college professor on "The Drool Method of History," an assortment of readable stabs at convention.

Nathan left the *Mercury* after the first year, although he continued to write for it. Mencken stayed on for a decade, until 1933 when the detached derision of the *Mercury* was out of joint with the almost universal despair engendered by the depression. Mencken's years on *Smart Set* were his happiest, Nathan recalled with affection decades later. When he helped found the *Mercury*, a change came over him. "His relative sobriety took the alarming form of a consuming interest in editorial politics and a dismissal of his previous interest in *belles-lettres*, which had been so great a factor of our former periodical," Nathan said. "The newspaperman in Mencken superseded the literary man and he favored filling the *Mercury* with pieces written by assorted jailbirds, hobos, politicians and riff-raff of all species." [30]

But for a while the *Mercury* was the high priest of the cult against orthodoxy. It echoed the animadversions of some of its disciples, and it revealed to others just what they should not like

---

[30] George Jean Nathan, "Memoirs of Mencken and Fitzgerald," in Arnold Gingrich and L. Rust Hills, editors, *The Armchair Esquire* (New York, 1958), p. 345.

about American civilization. More than 77,000 readers bought the *Mercury* in 1927, when it had its greatest following, but they dropped away year by year. About one-third of its 62,000 subscribers in 1931 had gone by the following year, and Mencken was addressing an audience of but 33,000 when he resigned in 1933.

Mencken summed up the progress of the *Mercury* at the end of its first five years. The magazine had won over advertisers, he said, and had begun to make money. It had cast a cold eye on many persons and things for the edification of "the minority which stands clear of the prevailing national superstitions."

The chiropractors and the Socialists, the Holy Rollers and the homeopaths, the pacifists and spiritualists have all taken their turns on its operating table. It has exhibited, mainly in their own words, the dreams and imbecilities of the prophets of high-powered salesmanship, vocational guidance, osteopathy, comstockery, and pedagogy. It has brought to notice, in the chaste, dispassionate manner of the clinic, the hallucinations of Rotary, the Gideons, the D. A. R., the American Legion, the League of American Penwomen, the Methodist Board of Temperance, Prohibition, public morals, and a multitude of other such klans and sodalities. . . .[31]

Contributors to the *Mercury* during Mencken's regime included unknown writers with something fresh to say—a condemned prisoner who made notes on conversations in the death cells, a bank robber who explained how to rob a bank—in addition to authors who were or were to become well known: Sinclair Lewis, William Faulkner, Theodore Dreiser, Vachel Lindsay, F. Scott Fitzgerald, Charles Beard, Elmer Davis.

Some of the spirit of the *Mercury* vanished with Mencken and with the twenties of which his zestful impudence was so much a part. Henry Hazlitt of the *Nation*, who took Mencken's place, was the first of several later editors, and the emphasis of the magazine shifted as ownership of the magazine changed hands.

Paul Palmer bought the *Mercury* and its circulation of 30,000 in the mid-thirties. He cut the price in half, shortened the length of the articles, and trimmed the format to digest size. His stated policy was to furnish "a voice for the intelligent minority," as Mencken had. Declaring its complete independence, the *Mercury* said that it recognized "no enemies save fraud, hypocrisy, bigotry, dishonesty, and stupidity" and claimed no friends "save those who shared its view concerning the ultimate value of truth."[32] Circula-

---

[31] Henry L. Mencken, "Editorial," *American Mercury*, 15 (Dec., 1928) 407-10.
[32] "Editorial," *American Mercury*, 34 (Oct., 1936) 221-24.

tion had more than doubled before Palmer sold the *Mercury* and took a position with the *Reader's Digest.*

Lawrence E. Spivak, who had been its business manager since 1933, purchased the *Mercury* from Palmer in 1939. The targets and tactics of his *Mercury* were not those of Mencken's, but the magazine managed to regain some of its old vitality by giving early hearing to pleaders of causes and maintaining a literary tone with names like Thomas Wolfe and Walter de la Mare in its bylines. Jan Valtin, a repentant communist who made a cause of exposing communism, wrote for it; so did John Roy Carlson, a diligent foe of native fascism. Major Alexander de Seversky in August, 1940, began a series of highly publicized and highly influential articles crusading for military air power. At times Spivak's *Mercury* had more readers than Mencken's had. It never had fewer than 50,000 from 1940 until 1947, and it had more than 84,000 at its peak in 1945.

Yet the magazine was no money-maker. Indeed, it never had been except for a brief period under Mencken. Spivak gave the *Mercury* a measure of financial security by adding as sidelines a series of paperbound books, *Ellery Queen's Mystery Magazine,* and magazines of science fiction. Profits from those publications covered the *Mercury's* losses.

Spivak retained the *Mercury* for eleven years, despite its proclivity for losing money. In 1950 he sold the magazine to Clendenin J. Ryan, a millionaire investment banker. Ryan's editor was William Bradford Huie, a journalist with a taste for sensational exposés. They did not propose to recreate the *Mercury* in the image of Mencken, but they hoped to transfer some of its "delicious juices" into their magazine, which stated its intent as follows: "We will do battle to most of Mencken's old adversaries as well as to some new ones. . . . The boobs have become bureaucrats; the censors have become commissars; the yahoos have been marshaled into pressure groups. . . . Now, perhaps even more than in the Twenties, is the time for those who value the human personality to attack those who would sacrifice it to Order and Security." [33] Ryan and Huie soon dissolved their association, however, and the magazine under Huie's direction became a mixture of excitable inside-stories and revelations, conservative political commentary, and articles of durable interest somewhat like those in the *Reader's Digest.*

---

[33] "In the Mercury's Opinion," *American Mercury,* 71 (Dec., 1950) 665.

The *Mercury* was running up too large a deficit for Huie to cover, so he sold it in August, 1952, to J. Russell Maguire, but remained as editor. The new owner seemed bent on making the *Mercury* an organ of reaction. Two of the top editors resigned in protest soon after the new ownership became effective. They had understood that the magazine would represent a "dynamic and sophisticated conservatism," they said, but Maguire had shown little sympathy with that objective. Although Huie thought that he could control policy no matter who owned the magazine, he also resigned soon afterwards. The *Mercury* continued publication; but it resembled the *American Mercury* of Mencken neither in cover, in size, in caliber of authors, in quality, in style, nor in content, and it might just as well have borne some other title.

The *American Mercury* which had spoken for and to the young iconoclasts of the twenties was buried in 1933 when Mencken quit, and it had lost much of its following even before then. The miseries and uncertainties of the depression of the thirties put an end to mere iconoclasm and brought about a resurgence of protest and reform. As Merle Curti has observed, the intellectuals who had said in the twenties that business enterprise could not meet the needs of the spirit said in the thirties that it could not even provide men with food and clothing. They re-examined the economic system and questioned its ability to survive. Some of them believed that the salvation of America lay with communism; others looked hopefully to socialism; a few saw in fascism a plan for the new order.

The discontent of the thirties revived interest in the old liberal journals of opinion, *Nation* and *New Republic*, and turned an increasing number of readers to the *New Masses,* which switched from monthly to weekly publication. It also set publishers to issuing new magazines for small audiences of intelligent readers.

Selden Rodman and Alfred M. Bingham, two Yale intellectuals, began *Common Sense* as a semimonthly in December, 1932, and made it a monthly a half-year later. They promised to "stand on a platform of protest and to present a forward-looking program." *Common Sense* was progressive in politics and looked with skepticism on communism. Varian Fry became its editor after he resigned from the *New Republic* in 1945 over the magazine's policy toward Soviet Russia. The owners sold *Common Sense* to Lawrence Spivak of the *American Mercury* in 1946 when they were no longer able to foot its losses.

There were similar magazines begun in the thirties, some with short lives. Suzanne LaFollette, who had worked on the old *Free-man,* tried to revive the journal as a left-wing organ called the *New Freeman* in the thirties but quit when funds ran out. Sydney J. Harris, a Chicago newspaper man, started the *Beacon,* a liberal journal patterned after the *Nation,* in the late thirties on $30 cash and $1,000 credit with the printer. It also died after about a year for want of money.

Among the journals of opinion born after World War II were magazines to combat communism, to speak up for conservatism, and to foster world peace. Such magazines were to be expected in view of the climate of the times. If the great fear in the thirties was economic insecurity, the great fear after the late forties was communism. Prosperity made experiments with the economic system seem less pressing than they had in the thirties. On the other hand, the trend toward a more powerful federal government which had begun in the thirties continued and a number of citizens saw it as a threat to freedom of the individual. The war and its aftermath dramatized the terrors of the totalitarian state. Communism seemed no longer a noble experiment but a frightening and ruthless enemy. Many Americans who had once been sympathetic toward it fled in revulsion, some arriving at a philosophy of liberalism, others at one of extreme conservatism. Fear of communism was mingled with fear of war. With the advent of nuclear weapons, many persons believed that civilization could not withstand another war.

Plain Talk from its first issue in October, 1946, dedicated itself to exposing what its cover called "the dark forces at home and abroad plotting a world dictatorship." Much of its emphasis was on reports of purported Soviet intrigue in America. "There is no time to lose in forestalling another and greater Pearl Harbor," its editor, Isaac Don Levine, wrote in the first issue. "The elementary prerequisites of our national safety require the ruthless exposure and the elimination through democratic processes from our national life of the Soviet fifth column." [34] *Plain Talk* was almost unrelievedly anticommunist. Each month it carried such titles as "Stalin's Spy Ring in the U. S. A.," "Stalin's Hand in the Panama Canal," "Stalin's Hand in Our Ballot Box," "Stalin's Rogues Gallery," "Soviet-American Spy Prodigies," and "Europe's Secret Armies."

The staff of *Plain Talk* and its contributors included several men and women who had once served radical causes or who had written for the left-wing journals of opinion. Ralph de Toledano, the man-

---

[34] Isaac Don Levine, "Our Next Pearl Harbor," *Plain Talk,* 1 (Oct., 1946) 5.

aging editor, had been an associate editor of the *New Leader*. Suzanne LaFollette of the old *Freeman* and the *New Freeman* was a contributing editor. So was Eugene Lyons, a onetime correspondent in Russia for the United Press who described his disillusionment with communism in *Assignment in Utopia*. Contributors included Louis Fischer, who had been on the staff of the *Nation* for almost a quarter-century, and Howard Rushmore, a former movie reviewer for the *Daily Worker*.

Plain Talk, sold only by subscription, never had a circulation of more than a few thousand. It carried no advertising. It was helped over its financial rough spots by Alfred Kohlberg of New York, a wealthy importer who had helped found the American China Policy Association.

In 1950 Kohlberg withdrew his backing from *Plain Talk* to support a second revival of the *Freeman*, which made its debut in October as a fortnightly "journal of opinion devoted to the cause of traditional liberalism and individual freedom." The *Freeman* took over about 5,000 unexpired subscriptions to *Plain Talk*, which had died the previous June.

The suggestion for the *Freeman* came from Suzanne LaFollette; Henry Hazlitt, a onetime staff member of the *Nation* and *American Mercury* who had become a contributing editor of *Newsweek;* and John Chamberlain, an author who had largely forsaken his leftist views of the thirties. Chamberlain became editor and president of the new magazine; Miss LaFollette and Hazlitt were on its editorial board. Kohlberg, its treasurer, helped to raise $130,000, of which he contributed one tenth.

The *Freeman's* politics were those of the extreme right wing of the republican party. The magazine extolled individualism and opposed big government in all forms; it attacked communism, and it defended Senator Joseph R. McCarthy in his efforts to rout subversives from government. Its contributors included such conservatives as George Sokolsky, Raymond Moley, John T. Flynn, and Senator John Bricker.

Circulation gained by about a thousand a month until the *Freeman* was distributing 20,000 copies in March, 1952. However, the magazine needed a sale of at least 30,000 to break even, and it lost $97,000 in 1951.

The *Freeman* floundered in 1952 because of internal dissension over politics and editorial policies. The editors quarreled among themselves and with the board of directors. Hazlitt quit in October, 1952. Chamberlain and Miss LaFollette resigned early in 1953. Then Hazlitt returned as chief editor to find a new staff and to publish a *Freeman* more temperately conservative than the magazine had become. But the magazine had a hard time. In July, 1954, when it was on the verge of suspending, it was taken over by the Foundation for Economic Education, which described itself as "a nonpolitical, nonprofit educational champion of private property, the free market, the profit and loss system, and limited government." The foundation converted the magazine into a pocket-sized monthly, which was still being published in 1964 with Paul L. Poirot as editor.

Adding their voices to those speaking from the right were the *Independent American,* which appeared in newspaper format every four to six weeks after its founding in 1955; *American Opinion,* which was started as the monthly organ of the John Birch Society the following year; and an assortment of newsletters, student publications, and quarterlies.

Perhaps the best known and most widely circulated spokesman for conservatism in the late fifties and early sixties was the *National Review.* Announcing that he had raised $290,000 among 125 investors and had put up another $10,000 of his own, William F. Buckley, Jr., launched the publication in November, 1955, as one of the chief weapons in his warfare against, as he put it, the liberals who ran the United States and who muzzled their conservative opposition. As members of his brigade, he recruited some of the circle earlier associated with *Plain Talk* and the *Freeman—* John Chamberlain, Suzanne LaFollette, Ralph de Toledano, Eugene Lyons, Frank Chodorov—but he found other volunteers. His sister Priscilla Buckley returned from a position with a press association in Paris to become managing editor. His brother-in-law, L. Brent Bozell, with whom he was coauthor of *McCarthy and His Enemies,* was one of his regular contributors. So was Russell Kirk, a leading conservative. And to his banner came a number of writers who in times past had been identified with liberal or left-wing causes, among them Whittaker Chambers, who contributed his "Confessions of a Middle-Class Radical" to the *National Review;* James Burnham, who was an editor and frequent contributor; and Max Eastman, who had once edited the *Masses.*

Buckley was twenty-nine when he started his magazine. He had come into national prominence a few years earlier with publication of a controversial book, *God and Man at Yale*, an attack on the atheism and socialism he had found rampant on the campus he had left the year before and a criticism of American education generally. He had followed it with a book justifying the activities of Senator Joseph McCarthy of Wisconsin.

Almost from the time his *National Review* appeared, critics charged that while it may have been antiliberal, it was not truly conservative. Dwight Macdonald, for one, could find no conservative principles underlying its position; it made its appeals to the heart rather than to laws or even tradition.[35] And Dan Wakefield in 1961 summoned several witnesses on behalf of his contention that Buckley had become more a socially accepted symbol of the right wing than a genuine contributor to the national dialogue.[36]

Buckley himself believed that his *National Review* provided a rallying point for rightists who had lacked an adequate organ. As evidence he could perhaps cite its circulation, which more than doubled in a single year in the early sixties to reach some 68,000.

A half-dozen years before the *National Review* gave the right a new voice, Max Ascoli started his *Reporter* as a liberal fortnightly of "facts and ideas." Ascoli, born in Italy and jailed briefly for his opposition to Mussolini, came to the United States in 1931. He taught political philosophy at the New School for Social Research for several years and for a short time was dean of its graduate faculty.

For Ascoli, a liberal was one who perfected the skills that made freedom operational, and he saw his magazine as dedicated to freedom. His aim was to make the publication objective but not impartial; it was to correct for the oversupply of news by conscientiously studying the facts to find their causes and weight. It was, in short, to be a magazine of ideas about facts.[37]

The fortnightly first appeared in April, 1949, without advertising and with an initial circulation of about 15,000. In 1963 it carried $689,000 worth of advertising, and its circulation had risen to 174,000.

In the interim the magazine had earned a reputation for depth

[35] Dwight Macdonald, "Scrambled Eggheads on the Right," *Commentary*, 21 (April, 1956) 367-73.
[36] Dan Wakefield, "William F. Buckley, Jr.: Portrait of a Complainer," *Esquire*, 55 (Jan., 1961) 49-52.
[37] Max Ascoli, "This Liberal Magazine," *Reporter*, 12 (April 21, 1955) 12-13.

reporting. It had examined, among other things, the China lobby in the United States, wire-tapping by government and industry, the uses of lie detectors by government agencies, the case of a government employee wrongfully suspended as a security risk, the machinations of the trucking lobby, the activities of Texas millionaires in financing pressure groups, the work done for foreign governments by U.S. public relations firms, and the press as a fourth branch of government. It assessed foreign affairs as well as domestic, and it tempered its political orientation with fiction and critical reviews.

The war and cold war brought forth a number of magazines dedicated to the cause of peace. *Freedom and Union,* a monthly, began publication in the fall of 1946. Clarence Streit, its founder and editor, had been a crusader for world government since 1933; had written *Union Now,* a book outlining a plan for democratic world federation; and had set up Federal Union, Inc., a nonprofit association of persons sharing his ideas. *Freedom and Union* assumed that the United Nations had insufficient powers to be a truly effective force for peace and was intended to serve the cause of world federation as Tom Paine's *The Crisis* had served the American Revolution. It was reaching about 10,000 subscribers in 1963. As the peace movement grew in the late fifties and early sixties, a number of other publications provided forums for discussions of disarmament, the means of achieving it, and related issues, among them *Sanity,* a student quarterly; *Liberation,* a monthly; *International Conciliation;* and *International Friendship Guide,* a quarterly started in 1963.

The influence of the minority magazines could not be measured by their circulations. Men accustomed to reaching vast audiences sometimes found their power a little puzzling. Frank P. Walsh once called the *Nation* the greatest mystery in American journalism. He had written an article about railroads for it in the days when its circulation was about 27,000. He had done a series on the same subject which was syndicated by the Hearst newspapers, which then had a total circulation of about 10,000,000. Soon after the *Nation* appeared, he got phone calls from senators, lobbyists, persons of importance. But never, he later recalled, had he ever met a person who mentioned his articles syndicated by Hearst.

Probably one reason for the influence of the minority magazines was that they reached an audience in a position not only to influence the tastes and opinions of countless others but also to exert a strong hand in the shaping of public affairs. "Thus," as Richard H. Gentry has remarked on the influence of the *New Republic,* "Theodore Roosevelt borrowed parts of his New Nationalism from Croly, Wilson drew the official interpretation of his Fourteen Points (some say even the points themselves) from Lippmann, and Franklin Roosevelt's New Deal was indebted to a lot of economic writing in the *New Republic* during the early depression years." [38] The magazine counted President John F. Kennedy and several of his policy-makers among its readers in the sixties. *Foreign Affairs,* a quarterly with a circulation of about 46,000, in July, 1947, carried an article called "The Sources of Soviet Conduct" by an author who signed it simply "X" and who proposed a policy of containing Soviet Russia. The author was George Kennan, later ambassador to Moscow, and the containment he advised subsequently became government policy.

Probably another reason minority magazines were especially influential was that readers regarded them as personal spokesmen. Paul Lazarsfeld discovered that the organ of the Townsend movement changed as many votes in the 1940 Presidential campaign in Erie County, Ohio, as *Life* or the *Saturday Evening Post,* which had far larger circulations. In explanation, Joseph Klapper speculated that the reader saw a specialized publication as expressing his own values and interests, hence was especially disposed to accept advice from it.[39] The reader did choose such a magazine because its content attracted him; he may even have paid a premium for it, as magazine prices went. And in the magazine he found reflected his own beliefs and values, his own basic assumptions, quite often applied to unfamiliar issues and events. Therein, perhaps, lay its greatest strength.

---

[38] Gentry, p. 415.
[39] Joseph T. Klapper, *The Effects of Mass Communication* (Glencoe, Ill., 1960), pp. 103-04.

15
Magazines, 1900-64:
An Assessment

To speak of the part that magazines have played in American life
in the twentieth century is to speak in generalities and with a good
deal of subjectivity. The long-term social and economic effects of
the magazine cannot be described with any great precision or
documentation. There seems no good way of measuring the impact
of so universal a medium on several generations, no good way of
isolating magazines from the culture in which they were a force
and by which they were conditioned, no good way of separating
the effects of magazines from those of other forms of communication.

For the most part, the most important effects of magazines were
probably imperceptible and cumulative. Just reading a copy of a
magazine did not significantly alter an individual, even if he did
clip a coupon or a recipe. But being exposed to magazines all of
his life probably had a profound effect on the individual and on
the society of which he was a part.

The accomplishments of magazines resulted from their twofold
nature as an editorial medium and as an adjunct of the marketing
system. Whether or not all publishers took full advantage of them,
the magazine had certain characteristics that distinguished it from
other media. Because of them the magazine by nature was admir-
ably suited for a highly important role in a democratic society, that
of introducing new ideas, putting them up for critical examination,

and if they had merit, feeding them into the mainstream of thought.

Although the magazine lacked the immediacy of the broadcast media and the newspaper, it nevertheless was timely enough to deal with the flow of events. Its timeliness and continuity set it apart from the book. As a continuing publication, it could provide a forum of discussion by carrying responses from its audience, could sustain campaigns for indefinite periods, and could work for cumulative rather than single impact. Yet its available space and the reading habits of its audience enabled it to give fairly lengthy treatment to the subjects it covered. Like the other print media, it appealed more to the intellect than to the senses and emotions of its audience. It was not as transient as the broadcast media, nor did it require attention at a given time; it was not as soon discarded as the newspaper: its issues remained in readers' homes for weeks, for months, sometimes even for years. In short, the magazine by nature well met the requirements for a medium of instruction and interpretation for the leisurely, critical reader.

Indeed, with a good deal of justification, John Fischer in 1963 called the magazine article "the characteristic literary medium of our generation." Many of the best writers—Loren Eiseley, James Baldwin, Richard Rovere, Edmund Wilson—found it the most effective means of presenting what they had to say, he noted, and with good reason. The article had immediacy; it could be written, printed, and distributed in a matter of weeks, an important advantage in a time of swift social change. It had flexibility; it lent itself to a variety of lengths and approaches and to gradations in tone.[1]

Like the other media, magazines bestowed prestige upon persons, organizations, institutions, movements, and issues. They gave a certain importance to whatever they mentioned in their editorial and advertising columns. A businessman whose success story was told in the *Saturday Evening Post,* a manufacturer whose advertisements were parodied in *Ballyhoo,* a civic-improvement plan which was recorded in *Look* all gained prestige because they had been singled out for attention. After World War II, some advertisers even labeled their products "as advertised" in such-and-such a magazine to capitalize on this phenomenon.

As a major carrier of advertising, magazines certainly played a significant part in raising the material standard of living in the

---

[1] John Fischer, "Helping Hand for a Literary Upstart," *Harper's,* 277 (Sept., 1963) 20-24.

twentieth century. They served the system of mass production and mass distribution by bringing together the buyers and sellers of goods and services, and in doing so they no doubt helped to promote a dynamic, expanding economy.

Scholars have examined the effects of advertising on some aspects of American economic life.[2] Their claims are impressive even when one allows for the criticisms that advertising fostered waste, monopoly, and other evils. Among other things, according to economists, advertising encouraged entrepreneurs to invest in the plants, equipment, and technological improvements which raised the national income fourfold in a century. It helped to create the mental attitudes necessary for a level of consumption high above basic needs. It stimulated product variety and differentiation as manufacturers competed for the favor of consumers, for each producer sought to give his product some special quality or feature which he could exploit in his sales message. It helped to allocate the economic resources of the nation by diverting supplies according to the wants and needs of consumers, who expressed their preferences by the purchase of goods. By contributing to large-scale demand, it helped to make possible lower prices for goods and services. Magazines as a chief medium of national advertising were a party to such accomplishments.

Magazine advertising, while contributing to the betterment of the material conditions of life, tended to be a force for conservatism in the realm of ideas. Business and industry were understandably anxious to protect the system under which they flourished and to safeguard the large investment in the machinery of production and distribution which had raised the material welfare. Advertising tended to promote allegiance to the existing system in several ways. For one thing, its mere presence was conducive to faith in the system of free enterprise. For another thing, advertisers, even the public utilities and the near-monopolies, spoke in the symbols of free competition. For still another thing, advertising tempered editorial policies, since it gravitated toward the publications which did not offend the majority and which were not inimical to the conditions under which business operated.

By playing on existing drives and attitudes in its attempts to sell goods and services, magazine advertising certainly reinforced many

---

[2] See, for example, Neil H. Borden, *The Economic Effects of Advertising* (Chicago, 1942) and C. H. Sandage, "The Role of Advertising in Modern Society," *Journalism Quarterly*, 28 (Winter, 1951) 31-38.

of the values of American society. One was material success. In advertisements and in American life in the twentieth century, an individual's status in the community and even his happiness were equated with owning an automobile of latest model, a wardrobe of fashionable clothing, a refrigerator, a washing machine, and a home full of gadgets. Indeed, consumption became akin to patriotism, and the old Christian virtue of self-denial became largely outmoded. Magazine advertising was also no doubt in part responsible for converting man's natural gregariousness into the social conformity which characterized American life in the twentieth century. The American was driven by a compulsion to be accepted by others, to be "well liked." Magazine advertising emphasized social approval as a major goal in life, and the penalty for laxity in bathing or in brushing one's teeth or for neglecting to read the best sellers was to be alone, an outcast on the fringe of the happy crowd. What advertising really did, Martin Mayer once contended, was to give new meanings to lust, sloth, greed, and pride. Lust became the desire to be sexually attractive, every woman's birthright; sloth the desire for rest and recreation; greed the desire to share the world's bounty; and pride the desire for social status.[3]

Magazines as an advertising medium also affected manners and morals in the twentieth century. After that April day in 1927 when a model named Betty Honeyman was photographed actually smoking a Marlboro for an advertisement in *Vanity Fair,* magazine advertising did a great deal toward eradicating the notion that a female who smoked was surely fallen, and toward making a package of cigarettes as standard an item in a woman's purse as lipstick and compact. This is not to say that magazine advertising made smokers of women; what it probably did was to make an existing desire socially acceptable. The repeal of the Eighteenth Amendment and magazine advertising of the thirties and forties legitimatized what the speakeasy had started—social drinking between the sexes. The stigma vanished from drinking, and the cocktail party became a national institution. With its pictures of both men and women in scanty attire, magazine advertising no doubt helped to bring about the American's casual acceptance of bodily exposure. Two generations of magazine advertisements which had made such advertising catchwords as "halitosis" and "body odor" parts of the popular

---

[3] Martin Mayer, "The American Myth and the Myth of Advertising," in C. H. Sandage, editor, *The Promise of Advertising* (Homewood, Ill., 1961), pp. 128-29.

language probably aided in developing what many Europeans regarded as the American's fetish for cleanliness.

As an editorial medium, magazines also were inclined to perpetuate the ideological status quo. There were exceptions to that generality, of course. Magazines spoke to and for little publics within the population as a whole, and some of them mirrored the progressiveness of their readers. However, the commercial magazine, a magazine published to earn a profit, was essentially conservative for two reasons. On the one hand, the magazine was a business enterprise with a vested interest in the maintenance of the existing economic system, and it could be expected to share the fundamental views of the industries which filled its pages with advertising. On the other hand, the magazine had to earn its keep in the marketplace. To stay in business, a publisher needed readers, a very large number or a few with exceedingly high purchasing power. If his publication did not carry advertising, the publisher required many readers in order to keep down the unit cost of his periodical. If his publication did accept advertising, the publisher needed as many readers as he could attract from his chosen market both to hold down unit cost and to justify profitable advertising rates. In either event, the publisher was impelled to seek a large audience; and as his audience widened, it increasingly determined what he could and what he could not publish. For to attract and hold his audience, the publisher was inclined to give his readers what he thought the majority wanted and agreed with. He seemed generally disposed to accept the social and cultural standards of the majority, which rarely in history has been responsible for the introduction of new ideas or for experimentation. Minority views perforce found little expression in the commercial magazine. True, magazines did tackle controversial subjects. All too often, however, the controversy was essentially meaningless, since the answers to the questions of debate were either foreordained or inconsequential.

In fiction and in articles, commercial magazines were inclined to maintain the status quo. Their fiction, for the most part, tended to glorify the traditional values and goals and to sanction the conventional virtues.[4] But in that sentence, let us underscore the words "for the most part" and "tended," for any magazine reader during

---

[4] See, for example, Patricke Johns-Heine and Hans Gerth, "Values in Mass Periodical Fiction, 1921-1940," *Public Opinion Quarterly*, 13 (Spring, 1949) 105-13; and Joseph T. Klapper, "The Mass Media and the Engineering of Consent," *American Scholar*, 17 (Autumn, 1948) 419-29.

the twentieth century could summon scores of examples to qualify that generality. Yet for a high proportion of magazine short stories, as James T. Farrell once noted, "the ideal of life is success," and the fruits of that success were a mate and a home equipped with all the gadgets advertised on the surrounding pages.[5] While such magazine fiction overtly accepted the principles of racial and religious equality, Berelson and Salter found,[6] it actually perpetuated minority stereotypes, approved caste lines, and, in the words of Joseph T. Klapper, pictured "a world where the highest income is reserved for white, American-born gentiles who practice the Protestant ethic."

Even the articles of magazines edited for Negroes gave their chief emphasis to such themes as that Negroes received just treatment from individuals, organizations, and business firms and that they and other races lived, worked, and enjoyed equal rights together.[7] Biographical articles in popular magazines from the turn of the century onward dealt largely with individuals who embodied the popularly sanctioned values.[8]

Despite all their variety, moreover, magazines were highly imitative. They were inclined to run with the pack. Certain authors and certain subjects became momentarily fashionable. If an author showed his popularity, a number of magazines competed for his output, as they did for the writings of statesmen, generals, entertainers, and other public figures. If a topic seemed to catch the public's fancy, magazine after magazine took it up. The net result was that the mass-circulation magazines perhaps provided a narrower range of discussion than they should have, especially since in other content they simply played many basic themes in different ways.

Magazines must also share blame with the other mass media for

---

[5] James T. Farrell, "Preface," *The Short Stories of James T. Farrell* (New York, 1941), p. xl.

[6] Bernard Berelson and Patricia Salter, "Majority and Minority Americans: An Analysis of Magazine Fiction," *Public Opinion Quarterly*, 10 (Summer, 1946) 168-90.

[7] Hallie Beachem Brooks, "A Description of Negro Newsstand Magazines and an Analysis of the Contents of a Selected Number of Negro Magazines" (unpublished Master's thesis, University of Chicago, 1946).

[8] Leo Lowenthal, "Biographies in Popular Magazines," in Bernard Berelson and Morris Janowitz, editors, *A Reader in Public Opinion and Communication* (Glencoe, Ill., 1950), pp. 289-98.

creating a pseudoworld, a picture out of focus which readers sometimes confused with the real thing. The world was spun of both
articles and fiction. It was a world of optimism and good works in
which science worked only beneficent miracles, in which poverty
was at worst a nuisance, in which anyone could do anything if he
persevered, in which the most ill-matched couples would find
marital happiness if they really tried, in which evil was justly pun-
ished, in which virtue and talent were inevitably recognized and
reaped their due rewards, a world of golden light and few shadows.

This pseudoworld was a harmless creation so long as readers did
not confuse it with the world of reality, but there was always the
danger that they would. Margaret Mead, the anthropologist, has
mentioned that the American ideal of marriage is one of the most
difficult ever attempted by the human race because it embodies
choice by both partners, romantic love, equality of husband and
wife.[9] Fulfillment of the ideal must have been complicated for some
persons by the fiction in many popular magazines in which heroes
were uniformly poised, charming, well-groomed, financially secure,
and constantly romantic. There was certainly a frustratingly wide
chasm between what such stories led women readers to expect
from marriage and what they eventually got. The medical and
psychological articles in the mass-circulation magazines were often
a dangerous thing, a veteran author of them believed, for they
inspired false hopes with their optimistic titles and themes and
inspired false fears with their overemphasis on such diseases as
cancer and polio. When the author herself became mildly in-
capacitated by osteo-arthritis, she was emotionally shocked, for her
experience in medical writing had made it difficult for her to accept
some ills and disorders as an almost inevitable concomitant of
aging.[10]

The contributions of commercial magazines to serious literature
in the twentieth century were moderate at best. The large-circulation periodicals did bring good fiction inexpensively to millions of
persons who otherwise perhaps would have been denied it. Even
the magazines of huge circulation, *Life* and the *Saturday Evening
Post,* carried works by Nobel-Prize-winners William Faulkner and

[9] Margaret Mead, *Male and Female* (New York, 1949), pp. 342-66.
[10] Edith Stern, "Medical Journalism—With and Without Upbeat," in *Saturday
Review Reader No. 3* (New York, 1954), pp. 127-31.

Ernest Hemingway. Yet the commercial magazines appear to have been less the discoverers of talent than the exploiters of talent once it was recognized. Nor did they appear to contribute much to literary experimentation. In their fiction and articles, as the century progressed, magazines became increasingly concerned with formula rather than form, and experimentation was left largely to the little magazines, although some of the commercial magazines did encourage authors who departed from the conventional molds. While magazines prided themselves on the conscientiousness of their reporting, a reader sometimes had the feeling that they were not as good as they should have been. Their articles too often answered the "what" instead of the "why," too often assumed that any subject could be discussed in terms of personalities and anecdotes, too often ignored large areas of man's accomplishments and perplexities as dull or dangerous. The trend toward brevity in articles made it impossible for magazines to treat certain subjects at all and contributed to superficial treatment of some which were covered. When they did treat serious subjects, the large-circulation magazines, especially, tended to deck them out in all of the bright dress of entertainment.

Those shortcomings lay neither in a lack of integrity nor in a lack of capabilities on the part of editors and publishers. They lay rather in the commercial nature of the magazine. They were the perhaps inescapable result of a system which, among its benefits, made magazines an accessible, inexpensive source of entertainment, guidance, and instruction. And, despite their shortcomings, magazines as an editorial medium made many genuine contributions to American life and culture. They come out very well indeed when one weighs their faults against their achievements.

First, magazines certainly were responsible in some measure for the social and political reforms made during the century. While magazines were basically conservative, the large volume of advertising and the large circulations which helped to make them so did not come until after 1912, when the period of muckraking had ended. Then, too, the magazines which exposed the abuses and excesses on the American scene at the turn of the century expressed the sentiments of a large following, and the changes which resulted were within the framework of the existing order. The magazines which carried on where the muckrakers left off were chiefly, although not entirely, the journals of opinion and comment, publications made possible partly by the nature of the magazine industry, which remained open to the newcomer. The muckraking magazines have been credited with helping to bring about the Congressional investigation, a pure food law, a tariff commission, child labor laws, workmen's compensation, and other reforms. The journals of opinion, as Charles Beard has noted, worked for many of the measures adopted under the auspices of both Democratic and Republican administrations: women's suffrage, old age pensions, social insurance, state and federal housing, regulation of the issue of securities and exchanges, wages and hours laws, public ownership and the development of water sites, and so on.[11]

Second, magazines not only interpreted issues and events but also put them in national perspective. America was a vast land, a land of sectional interests and rivalries; and unlike some foreign countries, it had no national newspapers. Its closest approximations were the *Christian Science Monitor* and the New York *Times*, but they did not penetrate deep into the population. Magazines did, however, and they looked at happenings and public questions not with parochialism, not with local prejudice, but with their national and international implications in view. Magazines supplemented rather than competed with the other media in this connection. Newspapers were inclined to see much of what they reported from a local viewpoint. Moreover, like radio and television, they were generally concerned with reporting occurrences hour by hour, day by day, not with the leisurely examination and reflection which characterized the magazine. Magazines brought their national approach to a wide variety of topics, for periodicals were edited for many followings with specialized interests.

Third, the national viewpoint of magazines no doubt fostered what might be called a sense of national community. The reader was aware, however dimly, that other people across the nation read the same magazines as he did and they provided a cultural bond between them. Magazines furnished Americans with a common fund of subjects for discussion. They standardized certain externals of behavior. They helped to diffuse what had once been regional specialties—Southern cooking, for instance, and ranch-type houses.

Fourth, magazines provided millions of Americans with low-cost

---

[11] Charles Beard, "Looking Backward," *New Republic*, 101 (Nov. 8, 1939) 74, 76, 78, 80.

entertainment. In America the magazine occupied the place in reading habits that the book did in some other countries, and never before in history had a medium devoted primarily to subjects other than news reached so vast an audience. The night watchman with his copy of *True Detective*, the homemaker with her copy of *Good Housekeeping*, the school boy with his copy of *Boys' Life*, the sales girl with her copy of *True Confessions* picked them up not necessarily from any motive of self-edification but because the magazines fleetingly transported them beyond the confines and monotony of their everyday routine. As readers identified themselves with the successful characters in the stories and articles, they may have felt a sense of prestige and gratification, and the editorial material may have served, as Klapper has suggested, as a "safety valve for social tensions." [12] The quality of the entertainment the reader found depended on his tastes. He could have found it in execrably written pulps; but he also could have found it in the outstanding authors of the day—in Mann and Sandburg and Huxley and Hemingway. If most magazine fiction was published for the moment, some of it was of lasting literary value. It may have been but a small fraction of the total output of the magazine industry, but it amounted to a considerable number of novels and short stories, many of which were given greater permanence between the hard covers of books.

Fifth, for millions of Americans, the magazine was an inexpensive instructor in daily living. It counseled them on rearing children, on marital and financial problems, on getting along with one another. It told them how to furnish and decorate their homes, how to tend their gardens, how to prepare food nutritiously and inexpensively. It advised them on care of face and figure, on the latest fashions of coiffure and clothing, on matters of decorum. It instructed readers in making lamps and bookcases and chairs and tables and even the homes in which to put them.

Sixth, magazines were an educator in man's cultural heritage. With their historical articles, they explored the nation's past; with their biographical articles, they recalled the men who had shaped it. They acquainted Americans with the accomplishments of other peoples. They introduced them to the best in architecture, painting, sculpture, and thought. *Life* alone was perhaps the greatest disseminator of art that mankind had ever known. Between its incep-

---

[12] Joseph T. Klapper, *The Effects of Mass Media* (New York, 1949), Memorandum III, p. 16.

tion and the mid-fifties, it had spent an estimated $25,000,000 on its colored reproductions of great paintings and other works of art. In a sense, magazines were showcases of culture. Through their reviews, they surely made readers aware of books, plays, music, and movies they otherwise would not have known about. Even the sometimes superficial treatment of the significant in magazine articles may have done the same thing; by calling the subject to the reader's attention, by arousing his interest, such articles might well have sent the reader to explore other sources of information.

Finally, one of the most reassuring strengths of magazines was their variety in entertainment, information, and ideas. Their variety arose from their selectivity of audience. To be sure, some magazines built circulations in the millions by appealing to audiences of highly diversified tastes and interests. But the typical magazine was not edited for just "everybody"; it was edited for a following with some mutual activity or outlook. Because they sought out little publics within the population at large, magazines in the aggregate represented a wide range of tastes and opinions. So long as the nature of the magazine industry enabled new publications to arise as freely as they had in the first sixty-four years of the century, dangers to the free flow of ideas and information were diminished.

Index

Here is an enlarged, revised, and redesigned edition of a prize-winning book that has become recognized as the standard work on American magazines in the twentieth century — the period of their greatest development and greatest importance.

In bringing the story of the modern magazine down to 1964 in this new edition, the author has extensively reworked some of the original material, added accounts of new publications, given greater attention to religious magazines and the so-called little magazines of literature and criticism, and analyzed the many dramatic and important changes that have taken place in the magazine industry since the first edition of this book appeared in December 1956.

The few years between the two editions have seen the end of the Crowell-Collier magazines, the troubles of Curtis and the company's struggles to solve them, the race for multimillion circulations at any cost, the spread of regional editions, the virtual disappearance of the digest magazines (*Reader's Digest* excepted), the boom among special interest magazines, the dwindling profits and diversification, the swift climb of *Playboy* to affluence and a circulation of more than a million, the rise and decline of *Confidential,* the birth of *Together* and the death of *Coronet.*

In tracing the modern magazine from its beginnings in the late nineteenth century to the present time, the author reveals the major trends in the magazine industry and the social and economic forces which helped to shape them. He draws on a variety of sources — on the magazines themselves; on the annual reports of publishing companies and the statements that have appeared in Standard and Poor; on industry reports; on reminiscences and observations of publishers, editors, writers, and others; and on the advertising trade press.